Praise for *Exclusion and Embra*

"This book is a major contribution to political
ness to the God who forgives and does not rer.   ..., ...g a
new community out of enemies."

—Jürgen Moltmann, professor emeritus of systematic theology,
University of Tübingen, Hamburg, Germany

"Combining personal witness, moral passion, and theological erudition
with a refreshingly clear style, Volf demonstrates the multiple ways in
which the exclusion of the "other" perpetuates a desperate cycle of violence. He finds hope in the healing embrace of the suffering servant Jesus."

—Luke Timothy Johnson, Robert W. Woodruff Professor Emeritus
of New Testament and Christian Origins, Candler School of Theology,
Emory University, Atlanta, GA

"While serving a cross-racial pastoral appointment in the 1990s, *Exclusion and Embrace* rocked my world theologically speaking. Volf confronted my naive, simplistic approach to healing the racial realities and
divides I had known all my life. By telling his own story and narrating
his struggles with the pernicious evil of religious and ethnic 'cleansing,'
he offered me a framework and a vocabulary to live my life and assume
my vocation as both herald and practitioner of the gospel of reconciliation. This revised and updated version has given me a timely 'booster
shot' to press on."

—Gregory V. Palmer, bishop, Ohio West Episcopal Area, UMC

"Enormous problems happen, Volf says, when we exclude our enemy
from the community of humans and when we exclude ourselves from
the community of sinners—when we forget that our enemy is not a
subhuman monster but a human being, when we forget that we are
not the perfect good but also flawed persons. By remembering this, our
hatred doesn't kill us or absorb us, and we can actually go out and work
for justice."

—Tim Keller, Redeemer Presbyterian Church, from his sermon the
Sunday after September 11, 2001

"*Exclusion and Embrace* presents the idea of loving embrace as a theological response to the problems of alienation. This embrace is based on remembering events and actions truthfully and appreciating the position of people who have wronged you. And Miroslav Volf goes even a step further: he wants us to remember past wrongdoings as already forgiven."

—Mike Bird, academic dean and lecturer in theology, Ridley College, Melbourne, Australia

"One of the finest theological works of Christian theology. . . . Whether we are dealing with international relations or one-on-one personal ones, evil must be named and confronted. . . . When both evil and the evildoer have been identified as to what and who they are—this is what Volf means by 'exclusion'—there can be the second move toward 'embrace,' the embrace of the one who has deeply hurt and wounded us or me."

—N. T. Wright, author, *Evil and the Justice of God*

Miroslav Volf

REVISED AND UPDATED

EXCLUSION & EMBRACE

A Theological Exploration of Identity,
Otherness, and Reconciliation

🔴) Abingdon Press
Nashville

EXCLUSION AND EMBRACE, REVISED AND UPDATED:
A THEOLOGICAL EXPLORATION OF IDENTITY, OTHERNESS, AND RECONCILIATION

Copyright© 2019 by Abingdon Press

All rights reserved.

Library of Congress Cataloging-in-Publication Data has been requested.

ISBN: 9781501861079

Unless otherwise noted, all scripture quotations are from The New Revised Standard Version Bible, copyright© 1989 by the Division of Christian Education of the National Council of the Churches of Christ in the USA. Used by permission.

Scripture quotations noted CEB are taken from the Common English Bible, copyright 2011. Used by permission. All rights reserved.

Cover Photograph provided by: Eric Kilby

Sand Sculpture: "Imprinted" by Sue McGrew

19 20 21 22 23 24 25 26 27 28—10 9 8 7 6 5 4 3 2 1
MANUFACTURED IN THE UNITED STATES OF AMERICA

Contents

Contents

To Peter Kuzmič—
brother-in-law and friend—
who kindled my passion for theology,
guided my first theological steps,
and opened some doors whose handles I was too small to reach.

Preface to the Revised Edition

An acquaintance recently told me, "*Exclusion and Embrace* is more relevant today than it was twenty-five years ago when you first wrote it." He made the comment with an eye on "Make America Great Again!" and Brexit, and he was right. As I was writing the book in the early 1990s, the world was uniting and I was fighting dangerous rip currents of identity-centered conflicts, which were pulling nations and communities apart. Today, we are up against a powerful tide; the world is separating. "Identity talk has exploded"[1]—on university campuses, in electoral politics, on the global stage. Francis Fukuyama, a thinker who celebrated the end of history in the triumph of the liberal state linked to market economy, observed in his 2018 book *Identity*, "Demand for recognition of one's identity is a master concept that unifies much of what is going on in world politics today."[2] Authoritarianism and fascism, the most worrying forms of assertion of identity, are on the rise.[3] In the new introduction, I sketch the resurgence of identity and explore its relation to the main argument of the book.

When I set out to write *Exclusion and Embrace*, I had in mind a slim volume, an expansion of the lecture I gave in Berlin early in 1993 in which I first formulated the idea. The book ended up three times as long as I originally thought it would be. While writing it, I had no audience in mind. I wrote it for myself, to figure out how to manage the

1. Kwame Anthony Appiah, *The Lies That Bind: Rethinking Identity* (New York: Liveright, 2018), xiii.

2. Francis Fukuyama, *Identity: The Demand for Dignity and the Politics of Resentment* (New York: Farrar, Straus and Giroux, 2018), loc. 114.

3. See Rob Riemen, *To Fight Against This Age: On Fascism and Humanism* (New York: W. W. Norton, 2018); Timothy Snyder, *On Tyranny: Twenty Lessons from the Twentieth Century* (New York: Tim Duggan, 2017).

identity-centered conflict that was raging in my own soul, an internal echo of the war that was tearing apart the country in which I was born. But by writing to nobody, it turned out that I was writing for people in all parts of the world. The book has been translated into ten languages, and two more translations are planned. Academics have found it useful—not just constructive theologians but also biblical scholars, ethicists, pastoral theologians, missiologists; and not just scholars working in theological disciplines but also psychologists, sociologists, cultural anthropologists, and others. Some visual artists, too, have found inspiration in the book. Most gratifying, though, was its impact on ordinary people. Many have written or told me in person that the book changed their life. I resonated with their experiences with the book; it changed my life, too, and not just as I was writing it. Many times, after I had decided on a course of action, I saw the book raise its eyebrow in disapproval. No other of my books has been as unsparing with me, and I love it for that.

As I was considering the second edition, I decided to change almost nothing in the main body. As it is written, it bears the marks of intellectual and existential struggle, and I was afraid that in revising it extensively I would edit out the intensity of search and the drama of discovery. Instead, in addition to writing a new introduction, I decided to write an extensive epilogue—to indicate a set of integrated basic theological convictions that underpin the book, to explain myself a bit (about the stress on the *will* to embrace, for instance), to defend myself from criticism that touches the foundation of the argument (for instance, on the nature and place of the Trinity, which is also why I have reprinted in the appendix a subsequent text on that very topic), and to note what I wish I had not omitted (for instance, restitution as a key element of reconciliation). But I have made one major intervention in the original text: I have eliminated the chapter on gender. Since the publication of the book, the field of gender studies has exploded. Over the years I was not able to observe developments in the field closely enough to revise and update the text in light of both the amount and the weight of intellectual work accomplished. Responsible rewriting would have taken more time than I was able to give the project.

Preface to the First Edition

After I finished my lecture, Professor Jürgen Moltmann stood up and asked one of his typical questions, both concrete and penetrating: "But can you embrace a četnik?" It was the winter of 1993. For months now the notorious Serbian fighters called "četnik" had been sowing desolation in my native country, herding people into concentration camps, raping women, burning down churches, and destroying cities.

I had just argued that we ought to embrace our enemies as God has embraced us in Christ. Can I embrace a četnik—for me at the time the ultimate other, so to speak, the evil other? What would justify the embrace? Where would I draw the strength for it? What would it do to my identity as a human being and as a Croat? It took me a while to answer, though I immediately knew what I wanted to say. "No, I cannot—but as a follower of Christ, I think I should be able to." In a sense this book is the product of the struggle between the truth of my argument and the force of Moltmann's objection.

It was a difficult book to write. My thought was pulled in two different directions by the blood of the innocent crying out to God and by the blood of God's Lamb offered for the guilty. How does one remain loyal both to the demand of the oppressed for justice and to the gift of forgiveness that the Crucified offered to the perpetrators? I felt caught between two betrayals—the betrayal of the suffering, exploited, and excluded, and the betrayal of the very core of my faith. In a sense even more disturbingly, I felt that my very faith was at odds with itself, divided between the God who delivers the needy and the God who abandons the Crucified, between the demand to bring about justice for the victims and the call to embrace the perpetrator. I knew, of course, of easy ways to resolve this powerful tension. But I also knew that they were easy precisely because they were false. Goaded by the suffering of those caught in the vicious cycles of conflict, not only in my native Croatia but around the globe, I went on a journey, whose report I present in this book.

Almost inescapably, the report is intensely personal—even in its most abstract and exacting sections. I do not mean that I indulge here in a public display of mushy sentiments. The book is personal in the sense that I struggle intellectually with issues that cut close to the heart of my identity. No free-floating and unaffected mind is trying here to resolve an intriguing intellectual puzzle! I chose not even to try the impossible. I, a citizen of a world at war and a follower of Jesus Christ, could not hang up my commitments, desires, rebellions, resignations, and uncertainties like a coat on a coat rack before entering my study, to be taken up and put on when the work of the day was over. My people were being brutalized, and I needed to think through the response appropriate for me, a follower of the crucified Messiah. How could I abstract from my commitments, desires, rebellions, resignations, and uncertainties? I had to think through them, with as much rigor as I could muster. The tension between the message of the cross and the world of violence presented itself to me as a conflict between the desire to follow the Crucified and the disinclination either simply to watch others be crucified or let myself be nailed to the cross. As an account of an intellectual struggle, the book is also a record of a spiritual journey. I wrote it for myself—and for all those who in a world of injustice, deception, and violence have made the gospel story their own and therefore wish neither to assign the demands of the Crucified to the murky regions of unreason nor abandon the struggle for justice, truth, and peace.

The Resurgence of Identity

In the early 1990s, at the time I wrote *Exclusion and Embrace*, globalization processes were in full swing. The world was uniting. Europe, too, was uniting, even integrating, except at one of its edges, where the constituent parts of Yugoslavia, the country of my birth and my youth, were violently separating. Catholic Croatians, Muslim Bosniacs, and Orthodox Serbs were fighting each other in the name of their ethnic and religious identities. At the time, similar fires were flaring up elsewhere in the world, more than fifty of them, all centered on ethnic, religious, racial, and cultural identities. Some of these smoldered on at low intensity, while others, like the Rwandan genocide of 1994, were violent conflagrations of human cruelty and suffering. In the 1990s, Europeans and Americans were puzzled by these identity-centered conflicts, often dismissing them as residues of unenlightened barbarity. In 1992 Alain Finkielkraut, a conservative French Jewish philosopher, felt the need to explain people's continued strong investments in ethno-cultural identities and wrote a whole book about the matter, titled in the original *How Can One Be Croatian?*[1]

I wrote *Exclusion and Embrace* in the setting of identity-centered clashes in a rapidly globalizing world. My goal, however, was different from Finkielkraut's, though like him but in my own way, I pushed against the idea that people's investments in group identities are ballast from the past that needs to be discarded. Instead of explaining and defending identity struggles as he did, I sketched a Christianly-inspired alternative account of social identities and of their negotiation, and I proposed a

---

1. Alain Finkielkraut, *Comment peut-on être Croate?* (Paris: Gallimard, 1992); in English: *Dispatches from the Balkan War and Other Writings*, transl. Peter S. Rogers and Richard Golsan (Lincoln: University of Nebraska Press, 1999).

pathway toward reconciliation, in fact, a vision of reconciled and reconciling life together. To counter the practice of identity-based exclusion, I developed a theology of embrace.

Identity-centered conflicts within and among nations were mere rip currents in the tide of global integration processes and the spread of global monoculture—or so we thought at the end of the last millennium. But the world is no longer uniting; more precisely, resistance to globalization is no longer coming only from marginal groups and smaller nations. Major opposition parties and governments of the major world powers are now some of the most ardent anti-globalists. Why? Partly because the awareness of centuries-long oppression of some groups has increased dramatically (of women and black people, for instance). But also certainly because run-away globalization processes have left in their wake a trail of suffering and disorientation, exemplified most potently by extraordinary discrepancies of wealth and power among and within nations, progressive ecological devastation, and loss of a sense of cultural, religious, and national identity and control.[2] In reaction, anti-globalist, nationalist and regionalist sentiments have conquered the world, and struggles over identity and recognition are dividing societies.[3] The whole globe looks now more like Yugoslavia did on the eve of the outbreak of hostilities among its ethnic groups than like Europe when the Berlin Wall, that symbol of the bipolar world, came down and the European Union was expanding.

National, ethno-cultural, religious, racial, gender, and sexual identities are major drivers of politics everywhere. The "Make America Great Again!" election campaign that brought Donald Trump into the White House was above all about identity, a choice between a white "Judeo-Christian," nationalist America and a pluralist America of groups with distinct dominant identities coexisting under the same roof.[4] Much of

---

2. My point here is not that the consequences of globalization have *only* been negative, but that these processes have *also* had undeniable and significant negative consequences and that, in their current form, they are both unjust and unsustainable. The effects of globalization processes have been highly ambivalent. With regard to the three effects of globalization mentioned in the main body of the text, it is true to say that unconscionable disparities in wealth, environmental degradation, and loss of identities are generated simultaneously with unprecedented economic growth, partial environmental improvements, and revitalization of traditions. It is easy to identify other ambivalences of globalization processes: ease of communication combines with loss of privacy; life-saving and life-enhancing technological innovations combine with the threat of technological self-destruction, and so on.

3. On the rise of fascism in the 1920s and 1930s as a reaction to globalization, see Timothy Snyder, *On Tyranny: Twenty Lessons from the Twentieth Century* (New York: Tim Duggan, 2017), 11–12.

4. John Sides, Michael Tesler, Lynn Vavreck, *Identity Crisis: The 2016 Presidential Campaign and the Battle for the Meaning of America* (Princeton: Princeton University Press, 2018). See also Arlie Russel Hochschild, *Strangers in their Own Land: Anger and Mourning on the American Right* (New York: The New

the European far right is about identity.[5] Chinese, Indian, Myanmarian, and Russian nationalisms are about identity. Granted, none of these movements is *only* about identity, and none of them is about a single identity. They are mostly about multiple and intersecting identities, often bundled into a dominant one;[6] and, yes, they are about money, power, and territory. But the dynamic of assertion and contestation of social identity, of the attempts at reassertion of erstwhile dominance and anger over its loss, of the search for recognition and resentment over its refusal, is central to them all.

Not all identity struggles are equal. Some are aggressive, like the assertion of national or racial supremacy by the imposition of colonial rule upon conquered lands and peoples or like the struggle for the recognition of authoritarian patriarchal masculinity. Other identity struggles are defensive, like the striving of the colonized against the erasure of their indigenous cultures or like the reaffirmation of racial identity in the contestation of pervasive racism in many nations, both Western and non-Western. Some identity struggles, defensive and aggressive ones alike, are troublingly "innocent": like birds of prey, to use Nietzsche's metaphor, some groups engage in identity struggles by bracketing moral questions and exerting power as they feel they must in order to survive and thrive. Other identity struggles are morally hyper-charged and utterly devoid of self-criticism: with the zeal of fundamentalists, combatants inhabit different moral universes and struggle against each other in the name of their own nonnegotiable values. Still other identity struggles are culturally and morally self-aware. Combatants recognize that even a successful struggle both establishes and distorts their identities, that it reifies practices, excludes not-quite-fitting members, and leaves a seemingly indelible trace of evil suffered and committed on their souls. As I note in Chapter III, differences among identity struggles are often tied to ambivalence in the process of boundary maintenance, specifically to the blurry lines between

---

Press, 2016). For an argument about the insufficiency of identity liberalism and the need for "civic liberalism," see Mark Lilla, *The Once and Future Liberal: After Identity Politics* (New York: HarperCollins, 2017). For a critique of Lilla, see Sarah Churchwell, "America's Original Identity Politics," *New York Review Daily*, 2/17/2019.

5.   See, for instance, Martin Sellner, "Der Grosse Austausch in Deutschland und Österreich: Theorie und Praxis," in Renaud Camus, *Revolte gegen den Grossen Austausch*, transl. Martin Lichtmesz (Schnellroda: Verlag Antaios, 2017), 189–221.

6.   On intersectionality, see Kimberle W. Crenshaw, "Mapping the Margins: Intersectionality, Identity Politics, and Violence Against Women of Color," *Stanford Law Review* 43 no. 6 (July 1991): 1241–99.

boundary maintenance in the mode of other-rejecting exclusion and in the mode of identity-constituting differentiation.

Two and a half decades ago as the world was uniting, religions seemed the prime forces pulling it apart, as former Prime Minister Tony Blair, a cheery champion of global integrations, was fond of saying when he and I taught a class on "Faith and Globalization" at Yale University (2008–2010). He was only partly right. People's investment in other forms of identity as well as their economic and political interests were fueling resistance to the processes of globalization as well, and often rightly so.[7] The same is true today. But it is also true that religions are both an identity concern and force in their own right and that they often get attached to other identities and interests, legitimizing and reinforcing them. Whether as primary or supporting factors, religions are often in play in identity-centered clashes. Two varieties of Christianity, Catholicism and Orthodoxy, along with Islam, were motivating the war among ethnic groups in former Yugoslavia as I was writing *Exclusion and Embrace*. The same is true today of Buddhism in Myanmar, Hinduism in India, and varieties of Islam in the Middle East, for example.

In identity-centered struggles, religions tend to function as markers of group identities and tools in service of political forces acting as guardians of these identities. They transport the conflict into the realm of the sacred and heighten its stakes. That's bad for the world, above all for the people immediately affected. But that's also bad for these religions themselves. In their origins and in their best historic expressions, all world religions are *universal* religions, addressing every person as a human being, a member of the global *human* "tribe," rather than primarily as a member of any local cultural tribe.[8] When such religions become markers of group identities and weapons in political struggles, they push their universal character into the background and morph into particular *political* religions.[9] In monotheist versions of political religions, God becomes a servant of the group, identifying who are "us" and who are "them," whom we should befriend and whom we should colonize or destroy, whom we should exclude and

---

7. See Miroslav Volf, *Flourishing: Why We Need Religion in a Globalized World* (New Haven: Yale University Press, 2015), 28–58.

8. See ibid., 36–38.

9. See below, epilogue.

economy and contemporary individualism.[24] Still, individualism, the primacy of instrumental reason, the current form of market economy and globalization, and the slide into superficiality in post-industrial societies are debilitating maladies in need of serious treatment. For me, the practice of embrace and the theology that underpins it, is a dimension of the true life, a kind of life enacted by and made possible through Jesus Christ, the Word become flesh. Commitment to Christ as the true life stands in contrast to the disregard of what matters the most in contemporary, hyper-individualistic, market-driven societies, and to the obsession with improving and multiplying the means for life and indifference to its proper ends.[25] The identitarians—at least the European ones—and I agree that an alternative is needed. We also agree about the importance of particular cultures, languages, and modes of belonging, such as family, ethnic group, religious community, or nation. In a phrase, we agree on the *need* for "home." But a chasm yawns wide between us about the nature of group identities, their purity, their ways of overcoming identity-centered conflicts, and above all, their relation to common humanity. We disagree on the *nature* of "home."

When I was writing *Exclusion and Embrace*, the idea of common humanity was generally accepted; in the text I could simply assume it. Not anymore. And the identitarians of the New Right are not the only ones contesting it; some on the left are doing so as well[26]—hence the absence of a shared horizon and competing moral universes, and this right at the time when the New Climactic Regime is sweeping across all our boundaries with a vengeance.[27] What I could assume then needs defending now. No such defense is possible in this introduction, only the barest sketch of it. De Benoist is right: the belief in one God and the affirmation of common humanity and equal dignity belong together. De Benoist is also wrong: equality here is not sameness but presupposes differences; each

---

24. On this, see Charles Taylor, *The Ethics of Authenticity* (Cambridge: Harvard University Press, 1991), 95–96.

25. See Miroslav Volf and Matthew Croasmun, *For the Life of the World: Theology That Makes a Difference* (Grand Rapids: Brazos, 2019).

26. For African American contestation of common humanity see, for instance, Calvin L. Warren, *Ontological Terror: Blackness, Nihilism, and Emancipation* (Durham: Duke University Press, 2018). Sylvia Wynter's position, summed up under the rubric of "genres of being human," is more nuanced (see *Sylvia Wynter: On Being Human as Praxis*, ed. Katherine McKittrick [Durham, NC: Duke University Press, 2015]). For African American theological affirmation of the primacy of common humanity, see for instance, Howard Thurman, *Jesus and the Disinherited* (Boston: Beacon Press, 1976), 104–5.

27. The phrasing is adapted, with alterations, from Bruno Latour, *Down to Earth: Politics in the New Climactic Regime*, transl. Catherine Porter (Cambridge: Polity Press, 2018), 10.

human being shares equally in common humanity, but each is human in a unique way.[28] Uniqueness no less than equality are rooted in the one God. Simultaneous affirmation of human equality and differences is a feature of all monotheisms, but it is especially congruent with versions of trinitarian monotheism in which divine unity and differences are equi-primordial.[29]

Universalist anthropologies that tie common humanity to the possession of certain capacities, most notably to the possession of reason, tend to denigrate differences. Since these capacities are seen as dimensions of normative humanity, human beings who are thought not to possess them or to possess them in diminished form are deemed subhuman. Given that the capacities of humans differ, capacities-based universalist anthropologies end up always denying (equal) humanity of some human beings.[30] The same is even more true about those, mostly implicitly held, universalistic anthropologies that tie humanity to certain cultural practices. Theistic anthropologies can dispense with the appeal to shared capacities and instead ground common humanity and equality in *God's relation* to humans. God's unchangingly and unconditionally loving relation to everyone born of a human grounds their common humanity and equality.[31] The one triune God is the God of all humans, each a unique and dynamic creature of a given time, place, and culture, *and* each also fashioned equally as an image of the pleromatic God, each equally a brother or a sister of Christ.

In *Exclusion and Embrace* I assume some such account of the character and derivation of common humanity. The two intertwined strands of the main argument are entirely devoted to the nature of identity and to identity-centered conflicts. The strand about identity pushes *against* "pure"

---

28. On a position about God and individual natures influenced by Duns Scotus, see John Hare, *God's Call: Moral Realism, God's Commands, and Human Autonomy* (Grand Rapids: Eerdmans, 2001), 77–78; on Duns Scotus himself, see John Hare, *God and Morality: A Philosophical History* (Oxford: Blackwell Publishing, 2007), 111–15. For an application of this argument for the need for "home," see Natalia Marandiuc, *The Goodness of Home: Human and Divine Love and the Making of the Self* (New York: Oxford University Press, 2018).

29. See the appendix.

30. That holds true also for Immanuel Kant, though in a limited way. By the capacity for making rational choices, which for him grounds equal dignity, he meant the ability to make rational choices, not the quality of reasoning while making any concrete choice (see Allen Wood, *Kant's Ethical Thought* [Cambridge: Cambridge University Press, 1999], 132). Still, there are, arguably, human beings who have no capacity for making rational choices. Kant's capacities-based approach has no resources to affirm their humanity and their equal dignity.

31. For one version of this position, see Nicholas Wolterstorff, *Justice: Rights and Wrongs* (Princeton: Princeton University Press, 2010). For an evolutionary account of common humanity, see Nicholas Christakis, *Blueprint: Evolutionary Origins of a Good Society* (New York: Little, Brown Spark, 2019).

and "hard" identities, identities out of which alterity has been driven and into which alterity is not permitted to enter, and pushes *for* "soft" and "dialogically formed" identities. The strand about identity-centered conflicts rests on the conviction that the love of enemy, enacted in God's embrace of sinful humanity in Christ, is fundamental to Christian faith and life in the world: the unconditionality of divine love requires and makes possible the corresponding unconditionality of human love. The two strands come together in the claim that commitment to the God revealed in Jesus Christ and made present by the Spirit should regulate identity-constituting boundary maintenance and other kinds of relations among people with diverse identities.

The two strands of the book's argument seek to support claims that are almost the exact obverse of the two pillars of identitarianism. Its main thesis is this: "The will to give ourselves to others and 'welcome' them, to readjust our identities to make space for them, is prior to any judgment about others, except that of identifying them in their humanity." But *Exclusion and Embrace* is not an anti-identitarian tract. It is a sketch of a vision of how to negotiate major tensions constitutive of the modern world—among selves and among various communities, as well as between locality, ethnicity, particularity and globality, cosmopolitanism, and universality—that have flared up in a world that seems to be on a course toward self-diminishment, even self-destruction.[32] At the foundation of the vision is a shared universal horizon of God's project with the world unveiled in Jesus Christ, the Word and the Lamb, through whom the worlds were made and reconciled to God.[33] That project is to make the world into God's home and thereby also into the home of God's creatures—each creature unique and "locally rooted" and each, precisely in its delimited uniqueness and rootedness, constitutively open to all others, both indwelling them and being indwelled by them.

---

32. On tensions on the path of self-destruction, see Latour, *Down to Earth*.
33. On Christ and creation, see Rowan Williams, *Christ the Heart of Creation* (London: Bloomsbury Continuum, 2018).

CHAPTER I

The Cross, the Self, and the Other

Images of Three Cities

When Los Angeles exploded in the spring of 1992, a letter of invitation was lying on my desk in Pasadena. I was to come to the city of "Prussian greatness," Potsdam, and speak at a conference of the German "Gesellschaft für Evangelische Theologie." The theme was timely: "God's Spirit and God's People in the Social and Cultural Upheavals in Europe." On the flyer about the conference I read:

> The hope for emergence of a "new democracy" in Europe which has inspired so many people in East and West...has not been fulfilled. Instead, increasingly heated national conflict—to the point of armed confrontation—is being carried out in many countries and societies of the former East Bloc. In Yugoslavia, there is a war raging in which religions and Christian confessions are also involved. At the same time, in the West there is a spreading European listlessness from which neo-nationalist and neo-fascist groups profit. And in the reunited Germany dangers are springing up for democracy which until recently no one would have thought possible: a blatant and open Radical Right movement demonstrating militant hostility to foreigners.

By inviting me, a native of what used to be part of Yugoslavia and is now an independent state called Croatia, the organizers were looking for a voice from the part of the world that used to be Eastern Europe and that was still searching for a new identity.

When I accepted the invitation, I had no sense of mission, not even a clear idea of what to say. During the intervening eight months, images from three cities invaded my mind with a clear intention of leading there an erratic life of their own. For the most part I managed to control the intruders either by suppressing them or by occasionally reflecting on them. Stimulated by the visual impulses coming from TV screens and the cover pages of magazines and dailies, they would surface unexpectedly in the middle of a faculty meeting, in the lull during a dinner conversation, in the quiet of the night. Shells falling into a crowd patiently waiting for bread that was in short, very short supply. People running the "death alleys" to escape snipers: Sarajevo. Scenes of Rodney King being beaten by white policemen and of Reginald Denny being dragged out of his truck by black gang members, pictures of people running in all directions with looted goods like oversized ants, images of flames engulfing whole blocks: Los Angeles. And then Berlin: neonazi skinheads marching through the city, their hands lifted occasionally in a Hitler salute, shouting "Ausländer raus!" (Foreigners out!)

That the intrusive images came from Sarajevo, Los Angeles, and Berlin was no accident. The cities represented respectively the country of my origin, the location of my residence, and the place I was to speak on the cultural and social upheavals in Europe. What they had in common, however, was more than just accidents of my biography in the year 1992. They were connected by a history of vicious cultural, ethnic, and racial strife.

That was not the only history of these cities, of course. Did not Catholic Croats, Orthodox Serbs, Muslims, and Jews live peacefully next to each other for centuries in Sarajevo, just as their many churches, mosques, and synagogues did? Is there not *some* truth to the official myth of Los Angeles as a city in which each of its two hundred cultural and ethnic groups "brings its own ethos, arts, ideas, and skills to a community that welcomes and encourages diversity and grows stronger by taking the best from it," all of them comprising "a mosaic, with every color distinct, vibrant, and essential to the whole"?[1] Was not Berlin the city in which the wall separating East and West had fallen down?

---

1. "L. A. 2000: A City of the Future," Los Angeles 2000 Committee, commissioned by the Office of Los Angeles Mayor Tom Bradley, 1988, as quoted by Judith Tiersma, "Beauty for Ashes," *Theology, News and Notes* 38 no. 4 (1992): 17.

Such narratives of harmony notwithstanding, there is an ugly history to these cities too, as the images that hounded me insisted. And it did not start yesterday. Already in the 1920s the Croat Nobel laureate, Ivo Andric, thought it symbolic that the clocks on the churches and mosques in Sarajevo were at odds when striking on the hour. This "being-at-odds" spoke of difference; and difference in Bosnia, he wrote, was "always close to hate, and often identical with it."[2] In Los Angeles, before there was the upheaval of 1992 there was the Watts uprising of 1965, triggered by a California highway patrolman following a black man off the freeway, but caused by centuries of racial prejudice and oppression. Finally, it was in Berlin that the demons of the Third Reich engineered the "final solution" and went about executing it with Prussian vehemence, discipline, and dutifulness.

The images from the three cities almost forced upon me the theme of my talk in Potsdam: I would address conflicts between cultures. As the diverse origins of the images suggested, cultural conflicts are by no means simply a feature of societies that have not yet tasted the "blessings" of modernization. I knew better than to dismiss them as outbursts of receding barbarism at the fringes of an otherwise peaceful modernity. Subtler but nonetheless real wars between rivaling cultural groups are threatening to tear the fabric of social life in many Western nations.

Far from being aberrations, the three cities gradually emerged for me as symbols of today's world. When the ideological and military wall separating the East and the West crumbled, when the constraints of the mega-conflict called the "cold war" were lifted and the importance of long-established global spheres of influence diminished, hosts of suppressed mini-conflicts flared up into so many "hot wars." In a special edition of the *Los Angeles Times* of June 8, 1992, entitled "The New Tribalism," Robin Wright reported:

> In Georgia, little Abkhazia and South Ossetia both seek secession, while Kurds want to carve a state out of Turkey. French Quebec edges toward separation from Canada, as deaths in Kashmir's Muslim insurgency against Hindu-dominated India pass the 6,000-mark. Kazakhstan's tongue-twisting face off pits ethnic Kazakhs against Russian Cossacks, while Scots in Britain, Tutsis in Rwanda, Basques and Catalans in Spain and Tauregas in Mali and Niger all seek varying degrees of self-rule or

---

2. Rupert Neudeck, "Europa am Ende? Das gute Beispiel: Albanien," *Orientierung* 57, no. 10 (1993): 120.

statehood. The world's now dizzying array of ethnic hot spots...starkly illustrates how, of all features of the post-Cold War world, the most consistently troubling are turning out to be the tribal hatreds that divide humankind by race, faith and nationality. "The explosion of communal violence is the paramount issue facing the human rights movement today. And containing the abuses committed in the name of ethnic or religious groups will be our foremost challenge for the years to come," said Kenneth Ross, acting executive director of Human Rights Watch.[3]

The article went on to indicate over fifty spots around the globe—Western countries included—where violence had taken root between people who share the same terrain but differ in ethnicity, race, language, or religion.[4]

The end of the Cold War did not produce these conflicts, of course. They were there all along, playing a stable role in the bloody global drama of modern times. The conflicts may go through cycles of resurgence and remission, depending mainly on international conditions; large-scale upheavals "create a setting in which ethnic demands seem timely and realistic."[5] In the judgment of a careful student of ethnic and cultural conflicts, Donald L. Horowitz, at least over the past century these conflicts have been "ubiquitous."[6]

A look around the globe confirmed my decision to make cultural conflicts the topic of my talk at the conference in Potsdam. A more precise formulation of the problem occurred to me only after I spent some six weeks in war-torn Croatia in the fall of 1992—its territories occupied, its cities and villages destroyed, and its people killed and driven out. There it became clear to me what, in a sense, I knew all along: the problem of ethnic and cultural conflicts is part of a larger problem of identity and otherness. There the problem of identity and otherness fought and bled and burned its way into my consciousness.

A World without the Other

I was crossing the Croatian border for the first time since Croatia declared independence. State insignia and flags that were displayed

---

3. Robin Wright, "The New Tribalism," *Los Angeles Times*, June 8, 1992, H1.

4. Robert D. Kaplan, *The Ends of the Earth: A Journey at the Dawn of the 21st Century* (New York: Random House, 1996), 7f.

5. Donald L. Horowitz, *Ethnic Groups in Conflict* (Berkeley: University of California Press, 1985), 3ff.

6. Ibid., 5.

prominently at the "gate to Croatia" were merely visible signs of what I could sense like a charge in the air: I was leaving Hungary and entering Croatian space. I felt relief—something of what a Hispanic or Korean person must feel in the parts of South Central Los Angeles where they are surrounded by their own, something of what South African blacks must have felt after Apartheid was dismantled. In what used to be Yugoslavia one was almost expected to apologize for being a Croat. Now I was free to be who I am.

Yet the longer I was in the country, the more hemmed in I felt. At the time, I sensed an unexpressed expectation to explain why, as a Croat, I still had friends in Serbia and did not talk with disgust about the backwardness of their Byzantine-Orthodox culture. I am used to the colorful surrounding of multi-ethnicity. A child of a "mixed marriage," I have Czech, German, and Croatian "blood" in my veins; I grew up in a city that the old Hapsburg Empire had made into a meeting place of many ethnic groups; and I lived in the (tension-filled) multicultural city of Los Angeles. But the new Croatia, like some jealous goddess, wanted all my love and loyalty. I must be Croat through and through, or I was not a good Croat.

It was easy to explain this excessive demand of loyalty. After forced assimilation under communist rule, the sense of ethnic belonging and cultural distinctness was bound to reassert itself. Moreover, the need to stand firm against a powerful and destructive enemy who had captured one-third of Croatian territory, swept it clean of its Croatian population, and almost completely destroyed some of its cities, left little room for the luxury of divided loyalties. The explanations made sense and they gave reasons to believe that the disturbing preoccupation with the national self was a temporary phase, a defense mechanism whose services would no longer be needed once the danger was past. Yet the unsettling questions remained: Did I not discover in oppressed Croatia's face some features Croats despised in their occupiers? Might not the enemy have captured some of Croatia's soul along with a good deal of Croatia's soil?

During my stay in Croatia I read Jacques Derrida's reflection on Europe, *The Other Heading*. Commenting on his own European identity he writes in his familiar, convoluted style:

> I am European, I am no doubt a European intellectual, and I like to recall this, I like to recall this to myself, and why would I deny it? In the name of what? But I am not, nor do I feel, European in every part, that

is, European through and through.... Being a part, belonging as "fully a part," should be incompatible with belonging "in every part." My cultural identity, that in the name of which I speak, is not only European, it is not identical to itself, and I am not "cultural" through and through, "cultural" in every part.[7]

The identity of Europe with itself, Derrida went on to say, is totalitarian. Though I will later distance myself from postmodern musings on identity, is not Derrida's main point well taken? Europe's past is full of the worst of violence committed in the name of European identity (and with the goal of European prosperity!). Europe colonized and oppressed, destroyed cultures, and imposed its religion all in the name of its identity with itself—in the name of its own absolute religion and superior civilization. Think only of the discovery of America and its genocidal aftermath, so masterfully analyzed in Tzvetan Todorov's classic essay *The Conquest of America*—a sad story of dehumanization, depredation, and destruction of millions.[8] And it was not too long ago that Germany sought to conquer and exterminate in the name of its purity, its identity with itself. Today, I thought as I was reading Derrida in the Croatian city of Osijek whose many houses bore scars of Serbian shelling, today the Balkan region is aflame in the name of Serbia's identity with itself and its mirror image, Croatian identity with itself. Might not the will for identity be fueling a good deal of those fifty or so conflicts around the globe?

Various kinds of cultural "cleansings" demand of us to place identity and otherness at the center of theological reflection on social realities. This is what I called for in my address in Potsdam,[9] and this is what I intend to pursue in the present volume. But am I not making too much of identity? One could argue that some events in my native country and the city in which I lived—the Balkan war and the Los Angeles upheaval—afflicted me with myopia. One might even suggest that I am too fascinated with some cultural trends, designed in the workshops of Parisian intellectual fashion, in which everything seems to turn around "the other" and "the same." Would we not be better advised to keep problems of identity and otherness at the margins of our reflection, reserving the place at the center

7. Jacques Derrida, *The Other Heading: Reflections on Today's Europe*, transl. P. A. Brault and M. B. Naas (Bloomington: Indiana University Press, 1992), 82f.

8. Tzvetan Todorov, *The Conquest of America: The Question of the Other*, transl. Richard Howard (New York: HarperCollins, 1984).

9. Miroslav Volf, "Exclusion and Embrace. Theological Reflections in the Wake of 'Ethnic Cleansing,'" *Journal of Ecumenical Studies* 29, no. 2 (1992): 230–48.

for human rights, economic justice, and ecological well-being? After all, is not this what a long and honorable tradition of social thinking, both Christian and non-Christian, teaches?

Well, it all depends. It could also be that the accidents of my biography have cleared my vision. And it could be that Parisian intellectuals, though they might be dead wrong about some things, might nevertheless be onto something important with their talk about identity and otherness; indeed, it could be that with the help of these categories they are addressing the fundamental philosophical and social problem of the "one" and the "many" that has engaged thinkers from diverse cultures and over many centuries.[10] As to rights, justice, and ecology, the theme of identity and otherness need not—and indeed *must* not—suppress them. Their proper place is in the center of our interest (though what "rights," "justice," and "ecological well-being" mean and what it means for them to be in the center will always depend in part on the culture of a person reflecting on them). But along with these three, space should be made for a fourth—identity and otherness—and all four should be understood in relation to one another.

Before I give a sketch of the way I intend to approach the issue, let me briefly insert my autobiographical notes into the larger framework of some debates in political philosophy. They point to a shift in interest from universal to particular, from global to local, from equality to difference, a shift informed by the realization that "universality" is available only from within a given "particularity," that global concerns must be pursued locally, that stress on equality makes sense only as a way of attending to differences.

In an important essay entitled "The Politics of Recognition," Charles Taylor distinguishes between the typically modern "politics of equal dignity" and the recently discovered "politics of difference" (or identity). The politics of equal dignity seeks to establish what is "universally the same, an identical basket of rights and immunities."[11] Not so in the case of the politics of difference. "With the politics of difference," writes Taylor,

> what we are asked to recognize is the unique identity of this individual or group, their distinctiveness from everyone else. The idea is that it is precisely this distinctness that has been ignored, glossed over, assimilated

10. Anindita Niyogi Balslev, *Cultural Otherness: Correspondence with Richard Rorty* (Shimla: Indian Institute of Advanced Study, 1991), 3.

11. Charles Taylor, "The Politics of Recognition," *Multiculturalism: Examining the Politics of Recognition*, ed. Amy Gutmann (Princeton: Princeton University Press, 1994), 38.

to a dominant or majority identity. And this assimilation is the cardinal sin against the ideal of authenticity.[12]

The politics of difference rests on two basic persuasions. First, the identity of a person is inescapably marked by the particularities of the social setting in which he or she is born and develops. In identifying with parental figures, peer groups, teachers, religious authorities, and community leaders, one does not identify with them simply as human beings, but also with their investment in a particular language, religion, customs, their construction of gender and racial difference, and so on.[13] Second, since the identity is partly shaped by recognition we receive from the social setting in which we live, "nonrecognition or misrecognition can inflict harm, can be a form of oppression, imprisoning someone in a false, distorted, and reduced mode of being."[14]

---

12. Ibid.

13. Christian Bittner and Anne Ostermann, "Bruder, Gast oder Feind? Sozialpsychologische Aspekte der Fremdenbeziehung," in *Die Fremden*, ed. O. Fuchs (Düsseldorf: Patmos, 1988), 105ff. Vamik Volkan, *The Need to Have Enemies and Allies: From Clinical Practice to International Relationships* (Northvale: Jason Aronson, 1988), 49f., 90ff.

14. Taylor, "The Politics of Recognition," 25. Three brief comments are in order about the nature of particular cultures that provide a matrix for the emergence of the self. Following the lead of Michael Walzer (*Thick and Thin: Moral Arguments at Home and Abroad* [Notre Dame, IN: University of Notre Dame Press, 1994]), I will call these particular cultures here loosely "tribes." First, *complexity*: if tribal identities are forged in interaction with other tribes (A. L. Epstein, *Ethos and Identity: Three Studies in Ethnicity* [London: Travistock, 1978]), then there is no such thing as an "essence" of a tribe, no "pure identity" to which an appeal could be made. Just as the individual persons with whom I interact ("significant others") become a part of who I am, so also the groups with which my group interacts are part of who my group is.

Second is the strength of tribal identities: in situations of conflict a given group identity can become a terminal identity, subsuming under it and integrating a whole range of other identities; each member of the group must completely identify with the group. Under normal circumstances, however, a given group identity is for the most part one among a number of alternative and possibly competing identities. Especially in contemporary societies, the self is fragmented, divided not only among various group identities (such as gender, nation, ethnicity, religion) but also among various social roles, even among its various values (Zygmunt Bauman, *Life in Fragments: Essays in Postmodern Morality* [Oxford: Blackwell, 1995]). As a consequence, the (post)modern tribes are "constantly in *statu nascendi* rather than *essendi*, brought over again into being by repetitive symbolic rituals of the members but persisting no longer than these rituals' power of attraction" (Zygmunt Bauman, *Intimations of Postmodernity* [London: Routledge, 1992], 198). Any given tribal identity is therefore partly a matter of choice. It can be weak or strong, depending not only on whether the context is conflictual but also on choices made both by the concerned individual and his or her family. It can even be largely given up in favor of some other tribal identity (Michel Maffesoli, "Jeux De Masques: Postmodern Tribalism," *Design Issues* 4, nos. 1–2 [1988]: 141–51).

Third, the permanence of tribal identities: Does dynamic interpretation of cultural belonging suggest that at some point "tribal" loyalties could disappear completely? They could. The question is whether they will. The answer is that they will not. The psycho-social functions they perform are too important and viable alternative candidates to perform these functions too hard to come by (Walzer, *Thick and Thin*, 81). "Tribes" will continue to be generated and maintained. Hence even in modern societies the "selves" will continue to be situated, "tribal" selves.

The two above presuppositions of the politics of difference explain its inner logic. The growing awareness of cultural heterogeneity brought about by economic and technological developments of planetary proportions explains why "tribal" identity is today asserting itself as a powerful force, especially in cases where cultural heterogeneity is combined with extreme imbalances of power and wealth. It may not be too much to claim that the future of our world will depend on how we deal with identity and difference. The issue is urgent. The ghettos and battlefields throughout the world—in the living rooms, in inner cities, or on the mountain ranges—testify indisputably to its importance.

Social Arrangements, Social Agents

How should we approach the problems of identity and otherness and of the conflicts that rage around them? Solutions have been suggested along the following lines.

(1) *Universalist Option:* We should control the unchecked proliferation of differences, and support the spread of universal values—religious values or Enlightenment values—which alone can guarantee the peaceful coexistence of people; affirmation of differences without common values will lead to chaos and war rather than to rich and fruitful diversity.

(2) *Communitarian Option:* We should celebrate communal distinctives and promote heterogeneity, placing ourselves on the side of the smaller armies of indigenous cultures; the spread of universal values will lead to oppression and boredom rather than peace and prosperity.

(3) *Postmodern Option:* We should flee both universal values and particular identities and seek refuge from oppression in the radical indeterminacy of individuals and social formations; we should create spaces in which persons can keep creating "larger and freer selves" by acquiring new and losing old identities—wayward and erratic vagabonds, ambivalent and fragmented, always on the move and never doing much more than making moves.

Though in many respects radically different, these three "solutions" share a common concentration on *social arrangements.* They offer proposals on how a society (or all humanity) ought to be arranged in order to accommodate individuals and groups with diverse identities living together—a society that guards universal values, or that promotes the plurality of particular communal identities, or that offers a framework for

9

individual persons to go about freely making and unmaking their own identities. These proposals do entail important perspectives about persons who live in such societies, but their main interest is not social agents but social arrangements. In contrast, I will concentrate here on social agents.[15] Instead of reflecting on the kind of society we ought to create in order to accommodate individual or communal heterogeneity, I will explore *what kind of selves we need to be* in order to live in harmony with others. My assumption is that selves are situated; they are female or male, Jew or Greek, rich or poor—as a rule, more than one of these things at the same time ("rich Greek female"), often having hybrid identities ("Jew-Greek" and "male-female"), and sometimes migrating from one identity to another. The questions I will be pursuing about such situated selves are: How should they think of their identity? How should they relate to the other? How should they go about making peace with the other?

Why am I forgoing a discussion of social arrangements? Put very simply, though I have strong preferences, I have no distinct proposal to make. I am not sure even that theologians *qua* theologians are the best suited to have one. My point is not that Christian faith has no bearing on social arrangements. It manifestly does. Neither is my point that reflection on social arrangement is unimportant, a view sometimes advocated on the fallacious grounds that social arrangements will take care of themselves if we have the right kind of social agents. Attending to social arrangements is essential. But it is Christian economists, political scientists, social philosophers, and so on in cooperation with theologians, rather than theologians themselves, that ought to address this issue because they are best equipped to do so—an argument Nicholas Wolterstorff has persuasively made in his essay "Public Theology or Christian Learning."[16] When not acting as helpmates of economists, political scientists, social philosophers, and so on—and it is part of their responsibility to act in this way—theologians should concentrate less on social arrangements and more on *fostering the kind of social agents capable of envisioning and creating just, truthful, and peaceful societies, and on shaping a cultural climate in which such agents will thrive.*

Important features of contemporary societies, and not just the competencies of theologians, call for a sustained theological reflection on social agents. Zygmunt Bauman has argued that *modernity* is "prominent

---

15. See also epilogue.
16. Nicholas Wolterstorff, "Public Theology or Christian Learning," in *A Passion for God's Reign: Theology, Christian Learning, and the Christian Self,* ed. Miroslav Volf (Grand Rapids: Eerdmans, 1998), 65–88.

for the tendency to shift moral responsibilities away from the moral self either toward socially constructed and managed supra-individual agencies, or through floating responsibility inside a bureaucratic 'rule of nobody.' "[17] In its own way, *postmodernity* creates a climate in which evasion of moral responsibility is a way of life. By rendering relationships "fragmentary" and "discontinuous," it fosters "disengagement and commitment-avoidance."[18] If Bauman is right about modernity and postmodernity, then reflection on the character of social agents and of their mutual engagement is urgently needed. Again, this in no way entails slighting of social arrangements. Arguably, it is in part precisely the modern and postmodern social arrangements that create a context in which contemporary problems with the character of social agents and their engagements arise. Social arrangements condition social agents; and social agents fashion social arrangements.

But what should shape social agents so that they in turn can fashion healthy social arrangements instead of simply being molded by them? From what vantage point should we reflect on the character of the self in the engagement with the other?

The Cross at the Center

In *The Politics of Jesus,* John Howard Yoder argued against "the modern ethicists who have assumed that the only way to get from the gospel story to ethics, from Bethlehem to Rome or to Washington or Saigon, was to leave the story behind."[19] His case was a good one. More often than not, leaving the story behind issues in sterile parroting. If we decide, however, not to leave the gospel story behind, what in the story should provide "the substance of guidance in social ethics"?[20] Yoder's response is: "Only at one point, only on one subject—but then consistently, universally—is Jesus our example: in his cross."[21] Strangely enough, most of Yoder's seminal book is not about the cross. It consists of an insightful analysis of some key biblical texts, especially from Luke's Gospel. Yoder implies that other aspects of Jesus's life ought to serve as examples for Christians in addition to his passion, though the cross is the key for reading these other aspects

---

17. Bauman, *Life in Fragments*, 99.

18. Ibid., 156.

19. John Howard Yoder, *The Politics of Jesus. Vicit Agnus Noster* (Grand Rapids: Eerdmans, 1972).

20. Ibid., 115.

21. Ibid., 97.

of Jesus's life. But how should we understand the cross? More specifically, what does the cross tell about the character of the Christian self in relation to the other?[22]

The most significant contributions in recent years on the implications of the cross for the life in the world come from Jürgen Moltmann. Brief passages in *The Spirit of Life* (1991) contain his most mature thought on the issue, though they are no adequate substitute for the extended arguments in *The Crucified God* (1972), *The Trinity and the Kingdom* (1980), and *The Way of Jesus Christ* (1989). A major thrust of Moltmann's thinking about the cross can be summed up in the notion of *solidarity*. The sufferings of Christ on the cross are not just his sufferings; they are "the sufferings of the poor and weak, which Jesus shares in his own body and in his own soul, in solidarity with them."[23] And since God was in Christ, "through his passion Christ brings into the passion history of this world the eternal fellowship of God and divine justice and righteousness that creates life."[24] On the cross, Christ both "identifies God with the victims of violence" and identifies "the victims with God, so that they are put under God's protection and with him are given the rights of which they have been deprived."[25]

These Christological and trinitarian themes woven around the "passion of God" will be familiar to those acquainted with Moltmann's earlier works. In *The Spirit of Life,* however, he gives prominence to an aspect of the cross earlier left underdeveloped. The theme of solidarity with the victims[26] is supplemented by the theme of *atonement* for the perpetrators.[27] Just as the oppressed must be liberated from the suffering caused by oppression, so the oppressors must be liberated from the injustice committed through oppression. By seeking to retrieve some aspects of the traditional theological reading of the cross while remaining faithful to the liberationist thrust of his earlier work, Moltmann argues that the cross is "the divine atonement for sin, for injustice and violence on earth."[28] Like solidarity

---

22. As I pursue here the relation between the cross and the self in relation to the other, I am not implying that the cross has no other significance than to offer the *model* for the character of the Christian self. The cross will serve best as the model if it has first served as the *foundation*.

23. Jürgen Moltmann, *The Spirit of Life: A Universal Affirmation*, transl. Margaret Kohl (Minneapolis: Fortress, 1992), 130.

24. Ibid., 131.

25. Ibid.

26. Ibid., 129–31.

27. Ibid., 132–38.

28. Ibid., 136.

with the victims, the atonement for the perpetrators issues forth from the heart of the triune God, whose very being is love (1 John 4:8). Moltmann writes,

> On the cross of Christ this love [i.e., the love of God] is there for the others, for sinners—the recalcitrant—enemies. The reciprocal self-surrender to one another within the Trinity is manifested in Christ's self-surrender in a world which is in contradiction to God; and this self-giving draws all those who believe in him into the eternal life of the divine love.[29]

Without wanting to disregard (let alone discard) the theme of divine solidarity with victims, I will pick up and develop here the theme of divine self-donation for the enemies and their reception into the eternal communion of God. Moltmann himself has drawn the social implications of his theology of the cross and of the Trinity mainly from the theme of divine solidarity: As God suffers with victims, protects them, and gives them rights of which they have been deprived, he argued, so also should we. In contrast, I stress more the social significance of the theme of divine self-giving: as God does not abandon the godless to their evil but gives the divine self for them in order to receive them into divine communion through atonement, so also should we—whoever our enemies and whoever we may be.[30]

If the claim that Christ "died for the ungodly" (Rom 5:6) is "the New Testament's fundamental affirmation," as Jon Sobrino rightly states in *Jesus the Liberator*,[31] then the theme of solidarity, though indispensable and rightly rehabilitated from neglect by Moltmann and others, must be a sub-theme of the overarching theme of self-giving love. Especially when solidarity refers to "struggling on the side of," rather than simply to "suffering together with," solidarity may not be severed from self-donation. All *sufferers* can find comfort in the solidarity of the Crucified; but only those who struggle against evil by following the example of the Crucified will discover him at their side. To claim the comfort of the Crucified while rejecting his way is to advocate not only cheap grace but a deceitful

---

29. Ibid., 137.

30. In *The Gifting God: A Trinitarian Ethics of Excess* (New York: Oxford University Press, 1996), Stephen Webb develops the theme of giving modeled on the Trinity in the context of the discussion of the economies of "exchange" and "excess."

31. Jon Sobrino, *Jesus the Liberator: A Historical-Theological Reading of Jesus of Nazareth*, transl. P. Burns and F. McDonagh (Maryknoll, NY: Orbis, 1993), 231.

ideology. Within the overarching theme of self-donation, however, the theme of solidarity must be fully affirmed, for it underlines rightly the partiality of divine compassion toward the "harassed and helpless" (Matt 9:36).

How central is in fact the theme of divine self-donation for sinful humanity and human self-giving for one another? In *The Real Jesus,* Luke Timothy Johnson argued that the canonical Gospels "are remarkably consistent on one essential aspect of the identity and mission of Jesus." He continues,

> Their fundamental focus is not on Jesus' wondrous deeds nor on his wise words. Their shared focus is on the *character* of his life and death. They all reveal the same *patterns* of radical obedience to God and selfless love toward other people. All four Gospels also agree that discipleship is to follow the same *messianic pattern.* They do not emphasize the performance of certain deeds or the learning of certain doctrines. They insist on living according to the same pattern of life and death shown by Jesus. [32]

Johnson finds the same narrative of Christ's self-giving love at the center of the whole New Testament, not just the Gospels. The meaning of the ministry of Jesus lies in its ending, and the abbreviated story of the ending is the model Christians should imitate. In the New Testament as a whole, Johnson concludes, "Jesus is the suffering servant whose death is a radical act of obedience toward God and an expression of loving care for his followers." [33] And this is not just for followers only. As the Apostle Paul insists, Christ died for "sinners," "the ungodly," and "enemies" (Rom 5:6-10).

A good way to make the same point about the centrality of self-donation would be to look at the two fundamental rituals of the church as described in the New Testament: baptism, which marks the beginning of the Christian life and therefore determines the whole of it; and the Lord's Supper, whose reiterated celebration enacts ritually what lies at the very heart of Christian life. Baptism is an identification with the death of Christ (Rom 6:3); "crucified with Christ" through baptism, Christians live "by faith in the Son of God, who loved them and gave himself for

---

32. Luke Timothy Johnson, *The Real Jesus: The Misguided Quest for the Historical Jesus and the Truth of the Traditional Gospels* (San Francisco: HarperSanFrancisco, 1996), 157f.

33. Ibid., 165f.

them" (Gal 2:20). At the Lord's Supper Christians remember the One who gave his body "for them" so that they would be shaped in his image (1 Cor 11:21, 24).

There is no need to belabor the point. Indisputably, the self-giving love manifested on the cross and demanded by it lies at the core of the Christian faith. As Moltmann rightly emphasized, ultimately, the self-giving love of Christ is rooted in the self-giving love of the triune God.[34] The incarnation of that divine love in a world of sin leads to the cross;[35] inversely, the cross has no significance except as the outworking of divine love (no value in and of itself). The Orthodox theologian Dumitru Stăniloae speaks for the whole Christian tradition when he highlights the "two truths beside which there is no other truth"—"the holy Trinity as model of supreme love and interpersonal communion, and the Son of God who comes, becomes a man, and goes to sacrifice."[36]

A genuinely Christian reflection on social issues must be rooted in the self-giving love of the divine Trinity as manifested on the cross of Christ; all the central themes of such reflection will have to be thought through from the perspective of the self-giving love of God. This book seeks to explicate what divine self-donation may mean for the construction of identity and for the relationship with the other under the condition of enmity. A more general way of putting what I am after would be to say that the book is an attempt to reflect on social issues based on the same decision Paul made as he proclaimed the gospel to the Corinthians—"to know nothing among you except Jesus Christ, and him crucified" (1 Cor 2:2). Stated polemically with an echo of Nietzsche's last line in *Ecce Homo,* my program is: "The Crucified against Dyonisos"—the saint of postmodernity,[37] "The Crucified against Prometheus"—the saint of modernity.[38]

The Scandal and the Promise

The impulse to hold on to Prometheus, Dyonisos, or some other pagan god and reject the Crucified will be strong, though I would urge the reader not to give in to it before considering what I actually say about

34. Moltmann, *The Spirit of Life*, 137.

35. Sobrino, *Jesus the Liberator*, 239.

36. Dumitru Stăniloae, *7 Dimineti cu Parintele Staniloae*, ed. Soriu Dumitrescu (Bucureşti: Anastasi, 1992), 186.

37. Friedrich Nietzsche, *Ecce Homo: How One Becomes What One Is*, transl. R. J. Hollingdale (London: Penguin, 1979), 104.

38. Karl Marx, *Werke: Ergänzungsband*, vol. 1 (Berlin: Diez Verlag, 1968), 262.

self-donation (Chapter IV) and how I relate it to justice and truth (Chapters V and VI). Feminist thinkers will, for instance, have their own good reasons for suspicion. Giving was what women, as mothers and wives, were supposed to do so that men, as sons and husbands, could do most of the taking. Many women tend to give so much of themselves that they are in danger of being left almost without a self. In response to such suspicions, one could argue that the problem does not lie in "self-donation" but in that men conveniently exempt themselves from self-giving they expect from women. Would not a world of *reciprocal* self-donation, the response could continue, be "a world than which none better can be conceived" because it would be a world of perfect love? The response is good, provided the condition of reciprocity is fulfilled. But one of the reasons we can conceive of a much better world than the one we inhabit is that the condition of reciprocity is so rarely fulfilled. Self-giving is not met with self-giving but with exploitation and brutality. Perhaps what some feminist thinkers object to is not so much the *idea* of self-donation, but that in *a world of violence* self-donation would be held up as the Christian way. With this objection they are not alone. If we happen not to be on the receiving end of self-giving—if we are weak, exploited, or victimized—all *of us will object.* In a world of violence, the cross, that eminently countercultural symbol that lies at the heart of the Christian faith, is a scandal.

At its core, however, the scandal of the cross in a world of violence is not the *danger* associated with self-donation. Jesus's greatest agony was not that he suffered. Suffering can be endured, even embraced, if it brings desired fruit, as the experience of giving birth illustrates. What turned the pain of suffering into agony was the *abandonment*; Jesus was abandoned by the people who trusted in him and by the God in whom he trusted. "My God, my God, why have you forsaken me?" (Mark 15:34). My God, my God, why did my radical obedience to your way lead to the pain and disgrace of the cross? The ultimate scandal of the cross is the all too frequent failure of self-donation to bear positive fruit: you give yourself for the other—and violence does not stop but destroys you; you sacrifice your life—and bolster the power of the perpetrator. Though self-donation often issues in the joy of reciprocity, it must reckon with the pain of failure and violence. When violence strikes, the very act of self-donation becomes a cry before the dark face of God. This dark face confronting the act of self-donation is a scandal.

16

Is the scandal of the cross good enough reason to give up on it? There is no genuinely Christian way around the scandal. In the final analysis, the only available options are either to reject the cross and with it the core of the Christian faith or to take up one's cross, follow the Crucified—and be scandalized ever anew by the challenge. As Mark's Gospel reports, the first disciples followed, and were scandalized (14:26ff.). Yet they continued to tell the story of the cross, including the account of how they abandoned the Crucified. Why? Because *precisely in the scandal, they have discovered a promise.* In serving and giving themselves for others (Mark 10:45), in lamenting and protesting before the dark face of God (15:34), they found themselves in the company of the Crucified. In his empty tomb they saw the proof that the cry of desperation will turn into a song of joy and that the face of God will eventually "shine" upon a redeemed world.

Since the very beginning, *women* seemed most capable of discovering the promise in the scandal. Just before his arrest Jesus told his disciples in Mark's Gospel, "you will all become deserters" (14:27). He was talking to his *male* disciples. They "all" assured him that they would never deny him (14:31). They *all* did. The disciples who neither denied nor deserted him were the *women.* True, being women in a patriarchal culture, they did not matter much to Jesus's enemies and therefore had little to fear. But there is more to it. As Elisabeth Schüssler Fiorenza points out, right after Mark notes that "women were looking on from a distance" at the Crucified (15:40), he writes of women what we never read of Jesus's male disciples: as Jesus came into the world to serve and give his life (Mark 10:45), so *they* "followed" him and "served" him (15:41); standing by him at the cross they are portrayed as "the exemplary disciples of Jesus."[39] Building on this observation, Elisabeth Moltmann-Wendel rightly called for development of the theme of self-donation within a feminist theology of the cross.[40] All other theologies would do well to heed the call, fully aware that self-donation will not only bring joy and healing but will remain a source of danger even after we have set up all the necessary safeguards against misuse.

The pain and the frequent failure of the way of the cross are a scandal for all human beings, in every age. The cross is a peculiar scandal, however, in the *modern age* with its "vision of the human race, at last released from

---

39. Elisabeth Schüssler Fiorenza, "The Twelve," *Women Priests: A Catholic Commentary on the Vatican Declaration,* ed. Leonard Swidler and Ariene Swidler (New York: Paulist, 1977), 119.

40. Elisabeth Moltmann-Wendel, "Zur Kreuzestheologie heute: Gibt es eine feministische Kreuzestheologie?" *Evangelische Theologie* 50 no. 6 (1990): 554.

the empire of fate and from the enemies of progress, advancing with a firm and sure step along the path of truth, virtue, and happiness."[41] The inner logic of the cross demands acceptance of two interrelated beliefs that are deeply at odds with some basic sentiments of modernity. First, modernity is predicated on the belief that the fissures of the world can be repaired and that *the world can be healed.* It expects the creation of paradise at the end of history and denies the expulsion from it at the beginning of history.[42] Placed into the fissures of the world in order to bridge the gap that the fissures create, the cross underscores that evil is irremediable. Before the dawn of God's new world, we cannot remove evil so as to dispense with the cross. None of the grand recipes that promise to mend all the fissures can be trusted. Whatever progress actually does take place, it also "keeps piling wreckage and hurls it in front of the feet" of the angel of history, as Walter Benjamin wrote in his "Theses on the Philosophy of History."[43]

Second, modernity has set its high hopes in the twin strategies of *social control* and *rational thought.* "The right design and the final argument can be, must be, and will be found," is modernity's credo.[44] The "wisdom of the cross," to the contrary, teaches that ultimately salvation does not come either from the "miracle" of the right design or from the "wisdom" of the final argument (1 Cor 1:18-25). We cannot and ought not dispense with "design" and "argument." But if "design" and "argument" are not to create larger wounds than the ones they are seeking to heal, "design" and "argument" will themselves need to be healed by the "weakness" and "foolishness" of the self-giving love. This "weakness" is "stronger" than social control, and this "foolishness" is "wiser" than rational thought.

In his correspondence with the Indian philosopher Anindita Balslev, Richard Rorty has contrasted a "culture of endurance" and a "culture of social hope"; the one is nonmodern and the other typically modern. The culture of endurance assumes that "the conditions of human life are and always will be frustrating and difficult," whereas the culture of social hope "will center around suggestions for drastic change in the way things are done—will be a culture of permanent revolution."[45] Does the "wisdom of

---

41. Steven Lukes, *The Curious Enlightenment of Professor Caritat: A Comedy of Ideas* (London: Verso, 1995), 29f.

42. Bernard-Henri Lévy, *Gefährliche Reinheit*, transl. Maribel Königer (Wien: Passagen Verlag, 1995), 91ff, 199ff.

43. Walter Benjamin, *Illuminations: Essays and Reflections*, transl. Harry Zohn (New York: Schocken, 1968), 257.

44. Zygmunt Bauman, *Postmodern Ethics* (Oxford: Blackwell, 1993), 9.

45. Balslev, *Cultural Otherness*, 21.

18

the cross" that I here advocate suggest a "culture of endurance" because it has given up on the "utopian hope"? Unlike Rorty, I do believe that the "utopian hope" itself must be given up, not just its "philosophical guarantees," such as were attempted in Marxist philosophies of history. But when the hope that rests on "control" and "reason" and is blind to the "unbearable" and "irremediable" has died, then in the midst of an "unbearable" and "irremediable" world a new hope in self-giving love can be born. This hope is the promise of the cross, grounded in the resurrection of the Crucified.

Themes and Steps

Here are the contours of my attempt to spell out the promise of the cross in this volume. I present them here following the *inner logic* of my argument rather than tracing the path of its presentation. Chapter IV develops the basic argument, best summarized in the Apostle Paul's injunction to the Romans: "Welcome one another, therefore, just as Christ has welcomed you" (15:7). To describe the process of "welcoming," I employed the metaphor of "embrace." The metaphor seems well suited to bring together the three interrelated themes that are central to my proposal: (1) the mutuality of self-giving love in the Trinity (the doctrine of God), (2) the outstretched arms of Christ on the cross for the "godless" (the doctrine of Christ), (3) the open arms of the "father" receiving the "prodigal" (the doctrine of salvation). In some cultures the metaphor will not work (as I was made well aware when, at a conference in Sri Lanka where I spoke, an argument broke out between an African bishop, who defended the metaphor, and a North European theologian, who thought it was too intimate). Nothing of substance in the book would change, however, if the metaphor were dropped. For me, the metaphor is helpful (see the section entitled "The Drama of Embrace") but not essential; the most basic thought that it seeks to express is important: *the will to give ourselves to others and "welcome" them, to readjust our identities to make space for them, is prior to any judgment about others, except that of identifying them in their humanity.* The *will to embrace* precedes any "truth" about others and any construction of their "justice." This will is absolutely indiscriminate and strictly immutable; it transcends the moral mapping of the social world into "good" and "evil."

But what about truth and justice? In what way are they still relevant at all? This is the question I pursue in Part Two (Chapters V–VII). These chapters are devoted to the great triangle of themes that dominate not only social philosophy,[46] but also biblical prophetic and apostolic literature: truth, justice, and peace (see Zech 8:16 and Eph 6:14-16). As I stress the priority of the "will to embrace," *my assumption is that the struggle against deception, injustice, and violence is indispensable.* But how should the struggle take place? How should "truth" and "justice" be identified? Negatively, my argument is almost a Nietzschean one: there is far too much dishonesty in the singleminded search for truth, too much injustice in the uncompromising struggle for justice. The Nietzschean feel of the negative argument is, however, but the flip side of my positive argument, which rests squarely on the "wisdom of the cross": within social contexts, truth and justice are unavailable outside of the *will to embrace* the other. I immediately continue to argue, however, that *the embrace itself—full* reconciliation—cannot take place until the truth has been said and justice done. There is an asymmetrical dialectic between the "grace" of self-donation and the "demand" of truth and justice. Grace has primacy: even if the *will* to embrace—the opening of the arms to embrace the other—is indiscriminate, the *embrace* itself is conditional. In Chapter VII this asymmetrical dialectic (along with other reasons) leads me to insist on human nonviolence while "granting" God the prerogative of exercising violence against "false prophets" and "beasts" if they refuse to be redeemed by the wounds they inflicted on the Crucified.

The practice of "embrace," with its concomitant struggle against deception, injustice, and violence, is intelligible only against the backdrop of a powerful, contagious, and destructive evil I call "exclusion" (Chapter III) and is for Christians possible only if, in the name of God's crucified Messiah, we distance ourselves from ourselves and our cultures in order to create a space for the other (Chapter II).

As I move forward, note two formal features of the book. The first concerns my nontheological *dialogue partners.* Throughout the book I engage two sets of thinkers: those that are typically modern and those that are typically postmodern (though I am well aware how contested these designations are). Behind my choice of the primary dialogue partners lies the belief that contemporary societies are caught in an ambiguity, and

46. Michel Foucault, *Power/Knowledge: Selected Interviews and Other Writings 1972–1977*, transl. Colin Gordon et al. (New York: Pantheon Books, 1980), 93.

that this ambiguity stems above all from the fact that it is precisely modernity that keeps generating the most conspicuous features of the postmodern condition: "institutionalized pluralism, variety, contingency and ambivalence."[47] Contemporary societies are not quite "modern" (if they ever actually were), and they are not quite "postmodern" (if they ever will be). Yet these two forms of thought shape profoundly the present day cultural exchange, hence my decision to engage them.

The second feature concerns an aspect of my *method*, in particular the use of the biblical texts in relation to the theological theme of "the self-donation and reception of the other." Most chapters contain extended interpretation of some key biblical texts. This is my way of participating in the salutary revival of "biblical theology" within the field of systematic theology.[48] As I have argued following Luke Johnson, at the center of the New Testament lies the narrative of the death and resurrection of Jesus Christ understood as an act of obedience toward God and an expression of self-giving love for the ungodly as well as the model for the followers to imitate.[49] This narrative, in turn, is intelligible only as a part of the larger narrative of God's dealings with humanity recorded in the whole of Christian scripture. It is this overarching narrative that provides the proper context for the interpretation of the "unsystematic and polydox" contents of the biblical texts.[50] Without this overarching narrative (or some substitute for it) the texts would "fall apart," unable even to perform the "dance of clashing orientations"[51] let alone to normatively guide Christian faith and life. Hence, I combine reflection on a theme drawn from the overarching narrative ("embrace") and its various sub-themes ("exclusion," "repentance," "forgiveness," "justice," "truth," "peace," etc.) with detailed analyses of selected texts that address these themes. The result is a complex and unpredictable dynamic between the themes derived from the overarching narrative and the inner richness of the biblical texts, a richness that is reducible neither to the overarching narrative nor to a single theme, and certainly not to some closed system.

---

47. Bauman, *Intimations of Postmodernity*, 187.

48. Michael Welker, *God the Spirit*, transl. John F. Hoffmeyer (Minneapolis: Fortress, 1994); Michael Welker, *Schöpfung und Wirklichheit* (Neukirchen-Vluyn: Neukirchener Verlag, 1995); see also, Miroslav Volf, *Captive to the Word of God* (Grand Rapids: Eerdmans, 2010).

49. On imitation, see the epilogue.

50. Jon Levenson, "Why Jews Are Not Interested in Biblical Theology," *Judaic Perspectives on Ancient Israel*, ed. Jacob Neusner et al. (Philadelphia: Fortress, 1987), 296.

51. Burke O. Long, "Ambitions of Dissent: Biblical Theology in a Postmodern Future," *Journal of Religion* 76, no. 2 (1996): 288.

Part One

CHAPTER II

Distance and Belonging

Complicity

In the introduction to *Culture and Imperialism,* Edward W. Said writes that in the process of working on the book he came to a profoundly disturbing insight, namely "how very few of the British or French artists whom I admire took issue with the notion of 'subject' or 'inferior' races so prevalent among officials who practiced those ideas as a matter of course in ruling India or Algeria." "Estimable and admirable works of art and learning," he continues, were "manifestly and unconcealedly" implicated in the imperial process.[1] Writers who should have been a conscience of the culture were but a sophisticated echo of its base prejudices, their noble humanist ideals notwithstanding. It may well be that we should be surprised not at the writers, but at Said's surprise. Ought he not to have suspected at the outset that the veneer of artists' eloquent humanistic self-presentation might cover over a much coarser reality?[2] Friedrich Nietzsche noted in *The Genealogy of Morals,* that artists have all too often been "smooth sycophants either of vested interests or of forces newly come to power."[3] In any case, whether we are disappointed or cynical about artists' complicity in the imperial process, as Christians we should be slow to point the accusing finger. We have had our share of complicity in the imperial process. Though Frantz Fanon is not the most

---

1. Edward W. Said, *Culture and Imperialism* (New York: Alfred A. Knopf, 1993), xiv.

2. As one can read in his *Representations of the Intellectuals* (New York: Pantheon, 1994), Said is aware of the tendency of artists and intellectuals to echo regnant opinions. His point is that we should be justified in our expectations that the good ones will do better than that.

3. Friedrich Nietzsche, *The Birth of Tragedy and The Genealogy of Morals,* transl. Francis Golffing (Garden City: Doubleday, 1956), 236.

reliable guide on the matter, he is not entirely wrong when in *The Wretched of the Earth* he chides the church in the colonies for being "the foreigner's Church" and implanting "foreign influences in the core of the colonized people."[4] "She does not call the native to God's ways," he writes, "but to the ways of the white man, of the master, of the oppressor."[5] Of course, this is not all we must say about the impact of missionary endeavor on native populations, not even the most important thing. Lamin Sanneh has rightly pointed to the paradox that, by insisting on translation of the gospel into the vernacular, foreign missionaries established "the indigenous process by which foreign domination was questioned."[6] He suggested that Christian missions are "better seen as a translation movement, with consequences for vernacular revitalization, religious change and social transformation, than as a vehicle for Western cultural domination."[7] Yet, such subversions of the foreign domination notwithstanding, the complicity—witting or unwitting—of Christian churches with the imperial process remains an undeniable fact.

In one sense even more disquieting than the complicity itself is the pattern of behavior in which it is embedded. Our coziness with the surrounding culture has made us so blind to many of its evils that, instead of calling them into question, we offer our own versions of them—in God's name and with a good conscience. Those who refuse to be party to our mimicry we brand sectarians. Consider the following stinging indictment H. Richard Niebuhr makes in *The Social Sources of Denominationalism* (1929) on the issue of race:

> The color line has been drawn so incisively by the church itself that its proclamation of the gospel of the brotherhood of Jew and Greek, of bond and free, of white and black has sometimes the sad sound of irony, and sometimes falls upon the ear as unconscious hypocrisy—but sometimes there is in it the bitter cry of repentance.[8]

---

4. Frantz Fanon, *The Wretched of the Earth,* transl. Constance Farrington (New York: Grove Weidenfeld, 1963), 43.

5. Ibid., 42.

6. Lamin Sanneh, "Christian Missions and the Western Guilt Complex," *The Christian Century* (1987): 332.

7. Ibid., 334.

8. H. Richard Niebuhr, *The Social Sources of Denominationalism* (Hamden: The Shoe String Press, 1954), 263.

Still today, many black Baptists or Methodists feel closer to black Muslims than to their white fellow Christians.[9] Or think of the big schism in the church, finalized in 1054 and today gaping wide as ever. It simply redoubled and reinforced religiously the boundary line that ran between Greek and Latin culture, between East and West. As slaves to their cultures, the churches were foolish enough to think of themselves as masters.[10]

The overriding commitment to their culture serves churches worst in situations of conflict. Churches, the presumed agents of reconciliation, are at best impotent and at worst accomplices in the strife. The empirical research conducted by Ralph Premdas in a number of countries has shown "that the inter-communal antipathies present in the society at large are reflected in the attitudes of churches and their adherents."[11] Though the clergy are often invited to adjudicate, "the reconciling thrust quickly evaporates after the initial effort."[12] The most important reasons for failure are the "inter-locking relations of church and cultural section which spill into partisan politics marked by the mobilization of collective hate and cultivated bigotry."[13] Along with their parishioners the clergy are often "trapped within the claims of their own ethnic or cultural community" and thus serve as "legitimators of ethnic conflict," their genuine desire to take seriously the Gospel call to the ministry of reconciliation notwithstanding.[14]

At times even a genuine desire for reconciliation is absent. Cultural identity insinuates itself with religious force; Christian and cultural commitments merge.[15] Such sacralization of cultural identity is invaluable for

---

9. Cf. Teresa Berger, "Ecumenism: Postconfessional? Consciously Contextual?" *Theology Today* 53, no. 2 (1996): 213f.

10. The slide into complicity with what is evil in our culture would not be nearly as easy if the cultures did not so profoundly shape us. In a significant sense we are our cultures and we find it therefore difficult to distance ourselves from the culture we inhabit in order to evaluate its various elements. The difficulty, however, makes the distancing from our own culture in the name of the God of all cultures so much more urgent. The judgments we pass need not be always negative, of course. As I have argued elsewhere, there is no single correct Christian way to relate to a given culture we inhabit as a whole; there are only various ways of accepting, transforming, rejecting, or replacing various aspects of a given culture from within. Miroslav Volf, "Christliche Identität und Differenz: Zur Eigenart der christlichen Präsenz in den modernen Gesellschaften," *Zeitschrift für Theologie und Kirche* no. 3 (1995): 371ff.; Miroslav Volf, "Theology, Meaning, and Power," in *The Future of Theology: Essays in Honor of Jürgen Moltmann*, ed. Miroslav Volf et al. (Grand Rapids: Eerdmans, 1996), 101.

11. Ralph Premdas, "The Church and Ethnic Conflicts in the Third World," *The Ecumenist* 1, no. 4 (1996): 55.

12. Ibid., 55f.

13. Ibid., 56. See also epilogue.

14. Ibid.

15. Jan Assmann, *Das kulturelle Gedächtnis: Schrift, Erinnerung und politische Identität in frühen Hochkulturen* (München: C. H. Beck, 1992), 157ff.

the parties in conflict because it can transmute what is in fact a murder into an act of piety. Blind to the betrayal of Christian faith that both such sacralization of cultural identity and the atrocities it legitimizes represent, the "holy" murderers can even see themselves as the Christian faith's valiant defenders. Christian communities, which should be "the salt" of the culture, are too often as insipid as everything around them.

"If the salt has lost its saltiness, how can you season it?" asked Jesus rhetorically (Mark 9:50). The feel of doom hangs over the question. Since you cannot season it, tasteless salt "is no longer good for anything, but is thrown out and trampled under foot" (Matt 5:13). Yet the very warning about being thrown out calls for "the bitter cry of repentance," as Niebuhr put it, and invites a turnabout. What we should turn away *from* seems clear: it is captivity to our own culture, coupled so often with blind self-righteousness. But what should we turn *to*? How should we live as Christian communities today faced with the "new tribalism" that is fracturing our societies, separating peoples and cultural groups, and fomenting vicious conflicts? What should be the relation of the churches to the cultures they inhabit? The answer lies, I propose, in cultivating the proper relation between distance from the culture and belonging to it.

Yet what does distance mean? What does belonging mean? Distance in the name of what? Belonging to what extent? Many profound theological issues are involved in answering these questions. I will explore them by examining what kind of relation between religious and cultural identity is implied, first, in the original call of Abraham and, second, in its Christian appropriation. In the final section I will then discuss what kinds of stances toward "others" a Christian construction of cultural identity implies and what kind of community the church needs to be if it is to support these stances.

Departing…

At the very foundation of Christian faith stands the towering figure of Abraham.[16] He is "the ancestor of all those who…have faith in God" (Rom 4:11 CEB). What made Abraham deserve this title? "Faith" is the answer the Apostle Paul gave. Abraham was looking into the abyss of nonbeing as he contemplated his own body, "already as good as dead," and the "barrenness of Sarah's womb." There was nothing his hope could latch onto. Yet, "in the presence of God…who gives life to the dead and calls

---

16. See Karl-Josef Kuschel, *Abraham: Sign of Hope for Jews, Christians, and Muslims*, transl. John Bowden (New York: Continuum, 1995).

28

into existence the things which do not exist" (Rom 4:17, 19), Abraham "trusted the Lord" (Gen 15:6 CEB) that he would have an heir—and became "the father of all of us" (Rom 4:16 CEB).

Before we read that Abraham "trusted" (Gen 15:6), however, Genesis records that he "went forth" (12:4). God said to Abraham:

> Go from your country and your kindred and your father's house to the land that I will show you. I will make of you a great nation, and I will bless you, and make your name great, so that you will be a blessing. I will bless those who bless you, and the one who curses you I will curse; and in you all the families of the earth shall be blessed. (12:1-3)

Sarah being barren (Gen 11:30), the command to "go forth" placed Abraham before a difficult choice: he would either belong to his country, his culture, and his family and remain comfortably inconsequential or, risking everything, he would depart and become great—a blessing to "all the families of the earth."[17] If he is to be a blessing he cannot stay; he must depart, cutting the ties that so profoundly defined him. The only guarantee that the venture will not make him wither away like an uprooted plant was the word of God, the naked promise of the divine "I" that inserted itself into his life so relentlessly and uncomfortably. If he left, he would have to set out "not knowing where he was going" (Heb 11:8); only if the divine promise comes true will the land of his ancestors that he left emerge as the land of expulsion, a land to which Adam, Eve, Cain have been expelled from the presence of God. Abraham chose to leave. The courage to break his cultural and familial ties and abandon the gods of his ancestors (Josh 24:2) out of allegiance to a God of all families and all cultures was the original Abrahamic revolution. Departure from his native soil, no less than the trust that God will give him an heir, made Abraham the ancestor of us all.

The narrative of Abraham's call underlines that stepping out of enmeshment in the network of inherited cultural relations is a correlate of faith in the one God. As Jacob Neusner points out,

> the great monotheist traditions insist upon the triviality of culture and ethnicity, forming transnational, or transethnic transcendental communities...Judaism, Christianity, and Islam mean to overcome diversity in

---

17. Walter Brueggemann, *The Land: Place as Gift, Promise, and Challenge in Biblical Faith,* Overtures to Biblical Theology (Philadelphia: Fortress, 1977), 15ff.

the name of a single, commanding God, who bears a single message for a humanity that is one in Heaven's sight.[18]

As I will argue later, from my perspective the talk about the "triviality of culture" and about "overcoming diversity" is too strong when taken at its face value (and there are reasons to believe that Neusner does not mean what he says in a strong sense). His main point, however, is well taken: the ultimate allegiance of those whose father is Abraham can be only to the God of "all families of the earth," not to any particular country, culture, or family with their local deities. The oneness of God implies God's universality, and universality entails transcendence with respect to any given culture. Abraham is a progenitor of a people which, as Franz Rosenzweig puts it, "even when it has a home ... is not allowed full possession of that home. It is only 'a stranger and a sojourner.' God tells it: 'The land is mine.' "[19]

To be a child of Abraham and Sarah and to respond to the call of their God means to make an exodus, to start a voyage, to become a stranger (Gen 23:4; 24:1-9). It is a mistake, I believe, to complain too much about Christianity being "alien" in a given culture, as Choan-Seng Song has done, for instance, in the introduction to his *Third-Eye Theology* about the place of Christianity "in the world of Asia."[20] There are, of course, wrong ways of being a stranger, such as when an alien culture (say one of the Western cultures) is idolatrously proclaimed as the gospel in another culture (say one of the Asian cultures). But the solution for being a stranger in a wrong way is not full naturalization but being a stranger in the *right* way. Much like Jews and Muslims, Christians can never be first of all Asians or Americans, Croatians, Russians, or Tutsis, and then Christians. At the very core of Christian identity lies an all-encompassing change of loyalty, from a given culture with its gods to the God of all cultures. A response to a call from that God entails rearrangement of a whole network of allegiances. As the call of Jesus's first disciples illustrates, "the nets" (economy) and "the father" (community) must be left behind (Mark 1:16-20). Departure is part and parcel of Christian identity. Since Abraham is our ancestor, our

18. Jacob Neusner, "Christmas and Israel: How Secularism Turns Religion into Culture," in *Christianity and Culture in the Crossfire*, ed. David Hoekema et al. (Grand Rapids: Eerdmans, 1997), 51–52.

19. Franz Rosenzweig, *The Star of Redemption*, transl. William W. Hallo (New York: Holt, Rinehart, Winston, 1971), 300. I owe the reference to Rosenzweig to the Jewish scholar Michael S. Kogan. Referring to the Rosenzweig quote he wrote in a letter to me: "It makes the Jewish reader feel quite strange—at home nowhere but in the Divine embrace."

20. Choan-Seng Song, *Third-Eye Theology*, rev. ed. (Maryknoll, NY: Orbis, 1991), 9.

faith is always at least a bit "at odds with place," as Richard Sennett puts it in *The Conscience of the Eye*.[21]

In today's cultural climate Abraham's kind of departure might receive censure from two opposite, though in some important respects unified, fronts. On the one hand it might be challenged as too goal oriented, too linear, not radical enough; on the other, it might be dismissed as too detached, too aloof, in some sense too radical. The first challenge comes from postmodern thinkers, such as Gilles Deleuze. One way to describe his thought is to say that he made "departing" into a philosophical program; "nomadic" functions for him as a central philosophical category. "Nomads are always in the middle," writes Claire Parnet explicating Deleuze.[22] They have no fixed location, but roam from place to place, always departing and always arriving. "There is no starting point just as there is no goal to reach," underlines Deleuze;[23] every place of arrival is a point of departure.[24] Indeed, there is even no stable subject, either divine or human, who could give direction to the departures. One is always departing pure and simple, flowing like a stream, to use one of Deleuze's favorite images, merging with other streams and changing in the process, de-territorializing them as one is de-territorialized by them (57).[25]

Contrast the "nomadic" life of Abraham. Refusing to go with the flow, Abraham decided to *go forth* in response to a *call of God*. Both the call and the decision to obey it presuppose an acting agent, a relatively stable subject. Moreover, Abraham's departure had a starting point—his country, his kindred, and his father's house; and it had a definite goal—creation of a people ("a great nation") and possession of a territory ("the land that I will show you"). Departure is here a temporary state, not an end in itself; a departure from a particular place, not from all sites.[26] And this is the way it must be if the talk about departures is to be intelligible.

---

21. Richard Sennett, *The Conscience of the Eye: The Design and Social Life of Cities* (London: Faber and Faber, 1993), 6.

22. Gilles Deleuze and Claire Parnet, *Dialogue*, transl. Bernd Schwibs (Frankfurt A. M.: Suhrkamp Verlag, 1980), 37.

23. Ibid., 10.

24. The images of "vagabond" or "stroller" would probably express better the idea Deleuze wants to convey; the course nomads take is much more charted and predictable than Deleuze suggests. Zygmunt Bauman (*Life in Fragments: Essays in Postmodern Morality* [Oxford: Blackwell, 1995], 94ff.) has used images of "vagabond" and "stroller," alongside those of "tourist" and "player" to analyze the character of postmodern culture (ibid., 94ff.).

25. Deleuze and Parnet, *Dialogue*, 57.

26. Jill Robbins, *Prodigal Son/Elder Brother: Interpretation and Alterity in Augustine, Petrarch, Kafka, and Levinas* (Chicago: The University of Chicago Press, 1991), 107.

Departures without some sense of an origin and a goal are not departures; they are instead but incessant roaming, just as streams that flow in all directions at one and the same time are not streams but, in the end, a swamp in which all movement has come to a deadly rest. Of course, social intercourse happens not to follow the prescriptions of Deleuze's theory, at least not yet. Though Deleuze has difficulty thinking about human agency, people do act as agents; they have goals, *make* things happen, and often enough these are evil things. What can those who wish to depart without wanting to arrive do to resist the evildoer? Without subjectivity, intentionality, and goal-orientedness, they will be carried by the stream of life, blissfully taking in whatever ride life has in store for them, always saying and accepting everything, including every misdeed that those who have goals choose to commit.[27] Against his intention,[28] Deleuze would have to say "yes" without being able to say "no," somewhat like the Nietzschean "all-contented" ass who always says "yea."[29] No, father Abraham, better to stay with your family and in your country than to follow *Deleuze's* call to go forth!

"Stay within the network of your relations"—this is what the critics from the other side would advise Abraham. Such advice might come from those feminists who, unlike Simone de Beauvoir in *The Second Sex,* consider separation and independence ills to overcome rather than goods to strive for.[30] To them, Abraham could appear as a paradigmatic male, eager to separate himself ("go forth"), to secure his independence and glory ("great nation"), crush those who resist him ("curse"), be benevolent to those who praise him ("blessing"), and finally extend his power to the ends of the earth ("all the families"). Abraham is all transcendence and no immanence, the transcendence of a separated and conquering male "I" underwritten by the imposing transcendence of the divine "I." Such a transcendent self is "phallic" and destructive, the argument would go. Must not every son of Abraham count with the possibility that his father will be called to take him "to the land of Moriah and offer him there as a burnt offering" (Gen 22:2), with no guarantees that God will provide a

---

27. Manfred Frank, *Was ist Neostrukturalismus?* (Frankfurt: Suhrkamp, 1984), 404, 431.

28. Gilles Deleuze, *Nietzsche und die Philosophie,* transl. Bernd Schwibs (Hamburg: Europaische Verlagsanstalt, 1991), 195ff.

29. Friedrich Nietzsche, *Thus Spoke Zarathustra: A Book for Everyone and No One,* transl. R. J. Hollingdale (London: Penguin, 1969), 212.

30. Simone de Beauvoir, *The Second Sex,* transl. H. M. Parshley (New York: Vintage Books, 1952).

lamb as a substitute?[31] An "anti-phallic" revolution must bring down the detached and violent self, situate it in the web of relationships, and help it recover its immanence. "Immanence," writes Catherine Keller in *From a Broken Web,* "is the way relations are part of who I am."[32] The new, she suggests, comes not through the heroic history of separating selves that respond to a transcendent call ("restless masculine roving"), but is created "with and within the field of relations."[33]

Should Abraham have stayed "within the field of relations"?[34] Notice, first, that Abraham's departure does not stand for denial of relationality. He is not a lonely modern self, restlessly roving about. Modernity seeks "emancipation with no binding to the other";[35] Abraham is most radically *bound to God.* In marked contrast to the builders of the tower of Babel who wanted to make themselves great (Gen 11:4), Abraham will be *made great by God* whose call he has obeyed (12:2).[36] Related to God, Abraham is, moreover, not "a divinely winged animal that soars above life but does not alight on it," as Nietzsche writes of philosophers' ascetic ideal.[37] Rather, he is *surrounded by a wandering community.* Unlike Penelope of Homer's *The Odyssey,* Sarah is not at home waiting and weaving while Abraham is voyaging and fighting. Since Abraham left his native country "forever" without an intention of returning to "the point of departure,"[38] Sarah accompanied him, and his relationship to her, even if she was subordinate to him, helped define Abraham. Sarah is not simply the immanent other of Abraham's wandering transcendence; if she stands for immanence at all, then this is an immanence of *their common* transcendence. Finally, Abraham and Sarah must remove themselves from "within the field of their ancestral relations" if they are to stand *at the beginning of a history* of a pilgrim people, the body

---

31. Jean-François Lyotard and Eberhard Gruber, *Ein Bindestrich: Zwischen "Jüdischem" und "Christlichem"* (Düsseldorf: Parerga, 1995), 22.

32. Catherine Keller, *From a Broken Web: Separation, Sexism, and Self* (Boston: Beacon, 1986), 18.

33. Ibid.

34. In *From a Broken Web*, Catherine Keller does not comment on the story of Abraham, and I have no way of knowing what she would have said had she chosen to comment on it. What follows is *not* a defense of Abraham against Keller. Her own proposal, rooted as it is in process thought, is not to deny transcendence but to challenge "the epic polarization of our creative spontaneities into sedentary feminine spinning (immanence without transcendence) and restless masculine roving (transcendence without immanence)" (ibid., 45).

35. Lyotard and Gruber, *Ein Bindestrich*, 20.

36. Brueggemann, *The Land*, 18.

37. Nietzsche, *The Birth of Tragedy and The Genealogy of Morals*, 243.

38. Emmanuel Lévinas, "The Trace of the Other," in *Deconstruction in Context: Literature and Philosophy*, ed. Mark C. Taylor (Chicago: The University of Chicago Press, 1986), 348.

of Jewish people. Without a departure, no such *new* beginnings would have been possible. Novelty, resistance, and history all demand transcendence.

Even if we admit that the Abrahamic departure was necessary and salutary, we are still left with the question of how the people who trace their origin to Abraham's departure should relate to surrounding peoples and cultures. Since I will address this question as a Christian rather than simply as a fellow sharer in the Abrahamic faith, I will turn from the towering figure of Abraham, the common ancestor of Jews, Christians, and Muslims, to the Apostle Paul and his reflection on the fulfillment of God's promise to Abraham in Jesus Christ (Gal 3:16). The shift in interest from Abraham's story to its early Christian appropriation means that I will explore the relation of the Christian children of Abraham to culture by examining the transformation of the original Abrahamic departure.

...Without Leaving

In contrast to Abraham, the Apostle Paul was *not* "accompanied by a believing wife" (1 Cor 9:5), he was *not* a progenitor of a people, much less a people with a land. Instead, he insisted on the religious irrelevance of genealogical ties and on the sole sufficiency of faith. His horizon was the whole world, and he himself was a traveling missionary, proclaiming the gospel of Jesus Christ—the seed of Abraham who fulfilled God's promise that through Abraham "all the nations will be blessed" (Gal 3:8)—and laying the foundations for a multi-ethnic community.

Why the move away from the bodiliness of genealogy to the spirituality of faith, from the particularity of "peoplehood" to the universality of multiculturality,[39] from the locality of a land to the globality of the world? Here is how Jewish scholar Daniel Boyarin in *A Radical Jew* describes Paul's original predicament, one that was resolved through conversion:

---

39. Jacob Neusner (*Children of the Flesh, Children of the Promise: A Rabbi Talks with Paul* [Cleveland: Pilgrim, 1995]) has argued that, properly understood, Israel is a transcendental, supernatural entity and no more "a circumscribed and ethnic religion than is Christianity"; it is "formed by God's command and act, and whether its members have joined by birth or by choice, it is uniform and one" (xii). In the language of Judaism, he argues, *Israel* refers to "an entity of precisely the same type as *church* or *mystical body of Christ* in the language of Christianity" (5). The argument seems plausible, yet questions remain. Does the fact that a rabbi will say "we are Israel by reason of (bodily) birth into Israel" (41) whereas a Christian theologian could never say "we are Christians by reason of (bodily) birth into a Christian family" not indicate an important difference between Israel and the church that makes the church so much more unlike an "ethnic group" than is Israel? Neusner has offered no explanation as to how membership by birth, even if accompanied by membership by choice, will not result in a community that is in significant ways "ethnic" even though it may speak many languages and diverge in customs.

An enthusiastic first-century Greek-speaking Jew, one Saul of Tarsus, is walking down a road, with a very troubled mind. The Torah, in which he so firmly believes, claims to be the text of the One True God of all the world, who created heaven and earth and all humanity, and yet its primary content is the history of one particular People—almost one family—and the practices that it prescribes are many of them practices which mark off the particularity of that tribe, his tribe.[40]

Leaving aside the question of whether this is an adequate fictive narrative of Paul's conversion, Boyarin's description of a problem that Paul's own venerable religious tradition bequeathed to him, a bicultural citizen of a multicultural world, is correct. The belief in one God entails a belief in the unity of the human race as recipient of the blessings of this God,[41] yet in order to enjoy the full blessings of this God a person had to be a member of a particular "tribe."[42]

One way out of the dilemma, not available to a child of Abraham and Sarah, was to regard the different religions as only manifestations of the one deity, as was current among learned men and women in the Hellenistic period.[43] Particularity, then, would not need to be a scandal; each culture could find both the one God and the ground of a deeper unity with other cultures by plunging into the depths of its own cultural resources; the deeper it went, the closer to God and to one another it would get—a view not unlike the one John Hick proposed in *An Interpretation of Religion*.[44] As the example of Hick shows, however, if the solution is to work it must operate with an unknowable God, always behind each and every concrete cultural and religious manifestation of God.[45] The trouble is that an unknowable god is an idle god, exalted so high on a throne (or hidden so deep in the foundations of being) that the god must have the tribal deities do all the work that any self-respecting god must do. Believing

---

40. Daniel Boyarin, *A Radical Jew: Paul and the Politics of Identity* (Berkeley: University of California Press, 1994), 39.

41. Admittedly, the social implications of this theoretical human unity do not always "come to fruition," and monotheism is instead used to justify ethnic exclusion; nevertheless, monotheism should—and often does—lead to recognized human equality. Robert Gnuse, "Breakthrough or Tyranny: Monotheism's Contested Implications," *Horizons* 34, no. 1 (2007): 91.

42. N. T. Wright, *The Climax of the Covenant. Christ and the Law in Pauline Theology* (Minneapolis: Fortress, 1992), 170.

43. Martin Hengel, *Judaism and Hellenism: Studies in Their Encounter in Palestine During the Early Hellenistic Period*, transl. John Bowden (London: SCM, 1974), 261.

44. John Hick, *An Interpretation of Religion: Human Responses to the Transcendent* (New Haven: Yale University Press, 1989).

45. Ibid., 246–49.

in a god behind all concrete manifestations comes therefore close to not believing in one: each culture ends up worshipping its own tribal deities, which is to say that each ends up, as Paul puts it, "enslaved to beings that are by nature not gods" (Gal 4:8).

The solution to the tension created by God's universality and the cultural particularity of God's revelation had to be sought, therefore, in a God who is both *one* and who is *not hidden* behind concrete religions. The only god that Paul, the Jew, could consider was the God of Abraham and Sarah. And yet it was precisely the belief in this one and true God that created the original problem—this God was tied to the particularities of a concrete social entity, the Jews. At its core this concrete social entity is formed "by appeal to common origin with Abraham and Sarah" and entrusted with Torah as the revelation of God's will.[46]

As he worked it out in Galatians 3:1–4:11, Paul's solution to the problem that touched the very core of his religious belief contains three simple, yet momentous interrelated moves (which I have extrapolated from N. T. Wright's analysis in *The Climax of the Covenant*). First, *in the name of the one God, Paul relativizes Torah*: Torah, which is unable to produce a single united human family demanded by the belief in the one God,[47] cannot "be the final and permanent expression of the will of the One God."[48] Though still important, Torah is not necessary for membership in the covenant. Second, *for the sake of equality Paul discards genealogy*: the promise "had to be by faith, so that it could be according to grace: otherwise there would be some who would inherit not by grace but as of right, by race."[49] Third, *for*

---

46. Neusner, *Children of the Flesh, Children of the Promise*, xii.

47. For my purposes here it is not essential to go into the debate on precisely why, in Paul's view, Torah is unable to produce a single human family. In the chapter "The Seed and the Mediator" of *The Climax of the Covenant*, Wright has argued that this is because the Mosaic Torah was "given to Jews and Jews only" (173). Contrary to this view, Neusner has rightly underlined that Torah is "God's revealed will for humanity" (*Children of the Flesh, Children of the Promise*, 6). Correspondingly, from Jewish perspective "it is not God's people—which we comprise—that forms an exclusive channel of divine grace. It is God who takes up a presence where God's word lives. Israel is not elect because God chose Israel. Israel is elect because the Torah defines Israel, and the Torah is the medium of God's grace to humanity. Israel is Adam's counterpart, just as Christ, for Christianity, is Adam's counterpart" (62). Elsewhere in *The Climax of the Covenant*, Wright has argued that Torah cannot be "the means through which she [Israel] either retains her membership in the covenant of blessing *or* becomes ... the means of blessing the world in accordance with the promise of Abraham" because "Israel as a whole has failed to keep the perfect Torah" (146). Following the lead of a more traditional school of interpretation, Hans-Joachim Eckstein has argued that, in Paul's view, neither Israel nor the Gentiles could fulfill Torah, indeed that Torah was not given originally as a way of salvation at all (*Verheißung und Gesetz: Eine exegetische Untersuchung zu Galater 2,15–4,7* [Tübingen: J. C. B. Mohr (Paul Siebeck), 1996]). For either of the two Christian interpretations, Torah had to be relativized if the blessing of Abraham was to come to all nations.

48. Wright, *The Climax of the Covenant*, 170.

49. Ibid., 168.

the sake of all the families of the earth Paul embraces Christ: the crucified and resurrected Christ is the "seed" of Abraham in whom "there is no longer Jew or Greek, there is no longer slave or free, there is no longer male and female" (Gal 3:28). In Christ all the families of the earth are blessed on equal terms by being brought into "the promised single family of Abraham."[50]

Paul's solution to the tension between universality and particularity is ingenious. Its logic is simple: the oneness of God requires God's universality; God's universality entails human equality; human equality implies equal access by all to the blessings of the one God; equal access is incompatible with ascription of religious significance to genealogy; Christ, the seed of Abraham, is both the fulfillment of the genealogical promise to Abraham and the end of genealogy as a privileged locus of access to God;[51] faith in Christ replaces birth into a people. As a consequence, all peoples can have access to the one God of Abraham and Sarah on equal terms, none by right and all by grace. Put abstractly, the religious irrelevance of genealogical ties and the necessity of faith in the "seed of Abraham" are correlates of the belief in the one God of all the families of the earth, who called Abraham to depart.

Paul's solution might be ingenious, but what is the price of ingenuity? Does he not leave us with an abstract transcendence of a subject, detached much more than the father Abraham ever was from all communal and bodily ties and attached only to the one transcendent God? Does Paul not squander difference and particularity in order to gain equality and universality, thereby making equality empty and universality abstract? This is what Boyarin charges Paul of doing, though he recognizes at the same time the *necessity* of the kind of move Paul made. Instead of simply objecting that Paul did not push the egalitarian project to its end,[52] Boyarin, aware of the

---

50. Ibid., 166.

51. For Paul this does not imply that there is now no distinction whatsoever between Israel and the Gentiles. In Romans Paul argues both that "the grace of God is extended to Gentiles" *and* "that God has not broken covenant with Israel" (Richard Hays, *New Testament Ethics: Community, Cross, New Creation* [Harper: San Francisco, 1996], 582f.).

52. The standard objection leveled against Paul in recent decades is that he is still too particularistic, that even at his best—in Galatians 3:28—his egalitarianism stops at the boundary of Christian faith. He is unduly privileging the Christian way of salvation and thereby denying radical equality. The trouble with this objection is that so far no persuasive alternative to overcome particularism has been proposed. No one has shown how one can intelligently hold to a nonparticularist universalism. And this for a good reason. As it happens, every claim to universality must be made from a particular perspective. Hence it is understandable why for Christians as well as for the Jews "the implementation of the universal *agape* of God necessarily entails particularity. Particularity is always a 'scandal,' but it is also the only way of getting to the universal," as Douglas J. Hall has rightly stressed in polemic with Rosemary Radford Ruether (*God and the Nations* [Minneapolis: Fortress, 1995], 107).

significance of communal identities, censures Paul for affirming equality at the expense of difference.[53] Paul's solution, Boyarin argues, was predicated on "dualism of the flesh and the spirit, such that while the body is particular, marked through practice as Jew or Greek, and through anatomy as male or female, the spirit is universal."[54] Commenting on Galatians 3:26-28, the Magna Carta of Pauline egalitarianism and universalism, Boyarin writes, "In the process of baptism in the spirit the marks of ethnos, gender, and class are all erased in the ascension to a univocity and universality of human essence which is beyond and outside the body."[55] Never mind that Paul occasionally does affirm cultural particularities; the grounds on which he affirms them— the universality of the disembodied spirit—will ultimately lead to erasure of particularities, for these are all grounded in bodiliness. Although the Pauline solution offered a "possibility of breaking out of the tribal allegiances...it also contained the seeds of an imperialist and colonizing" practice;[56] Paul's "universalism even at its most liberal and benevolent has been a powerful force for coercive discourses of sameness, denying...the rights of Jews, women, and others to retain their difference."[57]

Boyarin, however, overplays the parallels between Paul and some platonic cultural themes, notably the belief that "the commitment to 'the One' implied a disdain for the body, and disdain for the body entailed an erasure of 'difference.'"[58] The "One" in whom Paul seeks to locate the unity of all humanity is *not disincarnate transcendence but the crucified and resurrected Jesus Christ*. The "principle" of unity has a *name,* and the name designates a person with a *body that has suffered on the cross*. In subsequent centuries Christian theologians have arguably made the particularity of Christ's body the foundation of the reinterpretation of platonic tradition. As Augustine puts it, he discovered in the Neoplatonists that "In the beginning was the Word, and the Word was with God, and the Word was God," but did *not* find there that "the Word became flesh and dwelt among us."[59] The grounding of unity and universality in the scandalous *particularity of*

---

53. Boyarin's critique of Paul should be located not so much within the American liberation movements of the 1960s, which were about equity, as within the "politics of identity" concerns of the 1990s, which are about respect for discrete cultures (Louis Menand, "The Culture Wars," *The New York Review of Books* 41 [1994]: 18). The subtitle of his book is telling: "Paul and the Politics of Identity."

54. Boyarin, *A Radical Jew*, 7.

55. Ibid., 24.

56. Ibid., 234.

57. Ibid., 233.

58. Ibid., 231.

59. Augustine, *Confessions*, VII, §9.

the suffering body of God's Messiah is what makes Paul's thought structurally so profoundly different from the kinds of beliefs in the all-importance of the undifferentiated universal spirit that would make one "ashamed of being in the body" and unable to "bear to talk about his race or his parents or his native country."[60]

Consider, first, the foundation of Christian community, the cross. Christ unites different "bodies" into one body, not simply in virtue of the singleness of his person ("one leader—one people") or of his vision ("one principle or law—one community"), but above all through his suffering. It is profoundly significant that, as Ellen Charry writes, "Jews and gentiles are made one body of God's children without regard to ethnicity, nationality, gender, race, or class" precisely in "the cross of Christ."[61] True, the Apostle Paul writes: "Since there is one loaf of bread, we who are many are one body, because we all share the one loaf of bread" (1 Cor 10:17 CEB). On the surface, the singleness of the bread seems to ground the unity of the body. And yet the one loaf of bread stands for the *crucified* body of Jesus Christ, the body that has refused to remain a self-enclosed singularity but has opened itself up so that others can freely partake of it. The single personal will and the single impersonal principle or law—two variations of the transcendent "One"—enforce unity by suppressing and subsuming the difference; the crucified Messiah creates unity by giving his own self. Far from being the assertion of the one against many, the cross is the *self-giving of the one for many*. Unity here is not the result of "sacred violence," which obliterates the particularity of "bodies," but a fruit of Christ's self-sacrifice, which breaks down the enmity between them. From a Pauline perspective, the wall that divides is not so much "the difference" as *enmity* (cf. Eph 2:14). Hence the solution cannot be "the One." Neither the imposition of a single will nor the rule of a single law removes enmity. Hostility can be "put to death" only through self-giving. Peace is achieved "through the cross" and "by the blood" (Eph 2:13-17).

Consider, second, a central designation for the community created by the self-giving of Christ, "the *body* of Christ":

> Christ is just like the human body—a body is a unit and has many parts; and all the parts of the body are one body, even though there are many. We were all baptized by one Spirit into one body, whether Jew or

---

60. Boyarin, *A Radical Jew*, 229.
61. Ellen T. Charry, "Christian Jews and the Law," *Modern Theology* 11, no. 2 (1995): 190.

Greek, or slave or free, and we all were given one Spirit to drink. (1 Cor 12:12-13 CEB)

The resurrected Christ, in whom Jews and Greeks are united through baptism, is not a spiritual refuge from pluralizing corporeality, a pure spiritual space into which only the undifferentiated sameness of a universal human essence is admitted. Rather, baptism into Christ creates a people as the differentiated body of Christ. Bodily inscribed differences are brought together, not removed. The body of Christ lives as a complex interplay of differentiated bodies—Jewish and Gentile, female and male, slave and free—of those who have partaken of Christ's self-sacrifice. The Pauline move is not from the particularity of the body to the universality of the spirit, but from separated bodies to the community of interrelated bodies—the one *body in the Spirit* with many *discrete members*.

The Spirit does not erase bodily inscribed differences but allows access into the one body of Christ to the people with such differences on the same terms. What the Spirit does erase (or at least loosen) is a stable and socially constructed correlation between differences and social roles. The gifts of the Spirit are given irrespective of such differences. Against the cultural expectation that women be silent and submit to men, in Pauline communities they speak and lead because the Spirit gives them gifts to speak and lead. The Spirit creates equality by disregarding differences when baptizing people into the body of Christ or imparting spiritual gifts. Differentiating the body matters, but not for access to salvation and agency in the community. Correspondingly, unlike Plotinus, Paul is not ashamed of his genealogy (see Rom 9:3); he is just unwilling to ascribe it religious significance.

The consequences of the Pauline move away from (differentiating but internally undifferentiated) bodies to the (unifying but internally differentiated) body of Christ for understanding of identities are immense. As I explore these consequences briefly here, I will take the discussion out of the specific context of Jewish-Christian relations.[62] In Christian theology, Judaism and the Jewish people have a unique place—gentile Christians are but a "wild olive branch" engrafted to "share the rich oil of the [Jewish] olive tree" (Rom 11:17 CEB)—and can therefore not be treated under the general rubric of the relation between Christian faith and group identities, which is my specific interest here.

---

62. Hays, *New Testament Ethics*.

What are the implications of the Pauline kind of universalism? Each culture can retain its own cultural specificity; Christians need not "loose their cultural identity as Jew or Gentile and become one new humanity which is neither."[63] At the same time, no culture can retain its own tribal deities; religion must be de-ethnicized so that ethnicity can be de-sacralized. Paul deprived each culture of ultimacy in order to give them all legitimacy in the wider family of cultures. Through faith one must "depart" from one's culture because the ultimate allegiance is given to God and God's Messiah who transcend every culture. And yet precisely because of the ultimate allegiance to God of *all* cultures and to Christ who offers his "body" as a home for all people, Christian children of Abraham can "depart" from their culture without having to leave it (in contrast to Abraham himself who had to leave his "country" and "kindred"). Departure is no longer a spatial category; it can take place *within the cultural space one inhabits*. And it involves neither a typically modern attempt to build a new heaven out of the worldly hell nor a typically postmodern restless movement that fears to arrive home. Never simply distance, a genuinely Christian departure is always also presence; never simply work and struggle, it is always already rest and joy.[64]

Is the result of this kind of departure some "third race," as the early Christian apologist, Aristides, suggested when he divided humanity into Gentiles, Jews, and now Christians? But then, as Justo L. González points out in *Out of Every Tribe and Nation*, we would be faced with "the paradoxical notion that, in the midst of a world divided by racism, God has created still another race."[65] No, the internality of departure *excludes* a cosmopolitan third race, equally close to and equally distant from every culture. The proper distance from a culture does not take Christians out of that culture. Christians are not the insiders who have taken flight to a new "Christian culture" and become outsiders to their own culture; rather when they have responded to the call of the gospel they have stepped, as it were, with one foot outside their own culture while with the other remaining firmly planted in it. They are distant, and yet they belong. *Their*

---

63. William S. Campbell, *Paul's Gospel in an Intercultural Context: Jew and Gentile in the Letter to the Romans,* Studies in the Intercultural History of Christianity, ed. Richard Friedli et al. (Frankfurt: Peter Lang, 1991), vi.

64. Lyotard and Gruber, *Ein Bindestrich*, 16.

65. Justo L. González, *Out of Every Tribe and Nation: Christian Theology at the Ethnic Roundtable* (Nashville: Abingdon, 1992), 110.

difference is internal to the culture.[66] Because of their internality—their immanence, their belonging—the particularities, inscribed in the body, are not erased; because of their difference—their transcendence, their distance—the universality can be affirmed.

Both distance and belonging are essential. Belonging without distance destroys: I affirm my exclusive identity as Croatian and want either to shape everyone in my own image or eliminate them from my world. But distance without belonging isolates: I deny my identity as a Croatian and draw back from my own culture. But more often than not, I become trapped in the snares of counter-dependence. I deny my Croatian identity only to affirm even more forcefully my identity as a member of this or that anti-Croatian sect. And so an isolationist "distance without belonging" slips into a destructive "belonging without distance." Distance from a culture must never degenerate into flight from that culture but must be a way of living in a culture.

This, then, was Paul's creative reappropriation of the original Abrahamic revolution. In the name of the one God of Abraham, Paul opened up a particular people to become the one universal multicultural family of peoples. An eloquent witness to this radical reinterpretation of the relationship between religion and cultural identity is Paul's seemingly insignificant replacement of a single word in a text from Genesis: the promise that Abraham will inherit the *land* (12:1) becomes in Paul the promise that he will inherit the *world* (Rom 4:13).[67] A new universe of meaning entailed in the switch from "land" to "world" made it possible, in Boyarin's words, "for Judaism to become a world religion."[68] The original Abrahamic call to depart from his country, kindred, and father's house remained; what Paul made possible was to depart without leaving. Hence whereas Abraham's original departure is lived out in the one body of Jewish people, Christian departure is lived out in the many bodies of different peoples situated in the one body of Christ.

Culture, Catholicity, and Ecumenicity

Let us assume that Christians can depart without leaving, that their distance always involves belonging and that their kind of belonging takes the form of distance. What positive services does distance provide? In

66. Miroslav Volf, "Soft Difference: Theological Reflections on the Relation Between Church and Culture in 1 Peter," *Ex Auditu* 10 (1994): 18f.
67. Wright, *The Climax of the Covenant*, 174.
68. Boyarin, *A Radical Jew*, 230.

response, let us consider the reasons for which Christians should distance themselves from their own culture. The answer suggested by the stories of Abraham and his seed, Jesus Christ, is this: in the name of God and God's promised new world. There is a reality that is more important than the culture to which we belong. It is God and the new world that God is creating, a world in which people from every nation and every tribe, with their cultural goods, will gather around the triune God, a world in which every tear will be wiped away and pain will be no more (Rev 21:4). Christians take a distance from their own culture because they give the ultimate allegiance to God and God's promised future.

The distance born out of allegiance to God and God's future—a distance that must appropriately be lived out as internal difference—does two important services. First, it *creates space in* us to receive the other. Consider what happens when a person becomes a Christian. Paul writes, "if anyone is in Christ, that person is part of the new creation" (2 Cor 5:17 CEB). When God comes, God brings a whole new world. The Spirit of God breaks through the self-enclosed worlds we inhabit; the Spirit recreates us and sets us on the road toward becoming what I like to call a "catholic personality," a personal microcosm of the eschatological new creation.[69] A catholic personality is a personality enriched by otherness, a personality that is what it is only because multiple others have been reflected in it in a particular way. The distance from my own culture that results from being born by the Spirit creates a fissure in me through which others can come in. The Spirit unlatches the doors of my heart saying: "You are not only you; others are part of you too."

A catholic personality requires a *catholic community.* As the gospel has been preached to many nations, the church has taken root in many cultures, changing them as well as being profoundly shaped by them. Yet the many churches in diverse cultures are one, just as the triune God is one. No church in a given culture may isolate itself from other churches in other cultures, declaring itself sufficient to itself and to its own culture. Every church must be open to all other churches. We often think of a local church as a part of the universal church. We would do well also to invert the claim. Every local church is a catholic community because, in a profound sense, all other churches are a part of that church, all of them shape—or ought to shape—its identity. As all churches together form a worldwide ecumenical

---

69. Miroslav Volf, "Catholicity of 'Two or Three': Free Church Reflections on the Catholicity of the Local Church," *The Jurist* 52, no. 1 (1992): 525–46.

community, so each church in a given culture is a catholic community. Each church must therefore say, "I am not only I; all other churches, rooted in diverse cultures, are part of me too." Each needs all to be properly itself.

Both catholic personality and the catholic community in which it is embedded suggest *catholic cultural identity*. One way to conceive cultural identity is to postulate a stable cultural "we" as opposed to an equally stable "them"; both are complete in and of themselves. They would interact with each other, but only as self-enclosed wholes, their mutual relations being external to the identity of each. Such an essentialist understanding of cultural identity, however, is not only oppressive—force must be used to keep everything foreign at bay—but is also untenable. As Edward Said points out, all cultures are "hybrid…and encumbered, or entangled and overlapping with what used to be regarded as extraneous elements."[70] The distance from our own culture, which is born of the Spirit of the new creation, should loosen the grip of our culture on us and enable us to live with its necessary fluidity and affirm its inescapable hybridity. Other cultures are not a threat to the pristine purity of our cultural identity but a potential source of its enrichment. Inhabited by people who are courageous enough not simply to belong, intersecting and overlapping cultures can mutually contribute to the dynamic vitality of each.

The second function of the distance forged by the Spirit of new creation is no less important: it *entails a judgment against evil in every culture*. A catholic personality, I said, is a personality enriched by the multiple others. But should a catholic personality integrate all otherness? Can one feel at home with everything in every culture? With murder, rape, and destruction? With nationalistic idolatry and "ethnic cleansing"? Any notion of catholic personality that was capable only of integrating, but not of discriminating, would be grotesque. There are incommensurable perspectives that stubbornly refuse to be dissolved in a peaceful synthesis;[71] there are evil deeds that cannot be tolerated. The practice of "judgment" cannot be given up (see Chapter III). There can be no new creation without judgment, without the expulsion of the devil and the beast and the false prophet (Rev 20:10), without the swallowing up of the night by the light and of death by life (Rev 21:4; 22:5).[72]

---

70. Said, *Culture and Imperialism*, 317.

71. Richard J. Mouw, "Christian Philosophy and Cultural Diversity," *Christian Scholar's Review* 17 (1987): 114f.

72. Miroslav Volf, *Work in the Spirit: Toward a Theology of Work* (New York: Oxford University Press, 1991), 120f.

The judgment must begin, however, "with the household of God" (1 Pet 4:17)—with the self and its own culture. In the course of his discussion of the ascetic ideal, Nietzsche pointed out that those who wish to make a new departure have "first of all to subdue tradition and the gods in themselves."[73] Similarly, those who seek to overcome evil must fight it first of all in their own selves. Distance created by the Spirit opens the eyes to self-deception, injustice, and the destructiveness of the self. It also makes us aware that, as Richard Sennett pointed out, group identities "do not and cannot make for coherent and complete selves; they arise from fissures in the larger social fabric; they contain its contradictions and its injustices."[74] A truly catholic personality must be an *evangelical personality*—a personality brought to repentance and shaped by the gospel and engaged in the transformation of the world.

The struggle against falsehood, injustice, and violence both in the self and the other is impossible without distance. "How can one avoid sinking into the mire of common sense, if not by becoming a stranger to one's own country, language, sex and identity?" asks Julia Kristeva rhetorically.[75] Of course, being a stranger pure and simple is a rather pathetic posture, verging on insanity. If I cut all the ties that bind me to any moral and linguistic tradition, I become an indeterminate "self," open to any arbitrary content. As a consequence, I simply float, unable to resist anything because I do not stand anywhere.[76] The children of Abraham are not strangers pure and simple, however. Their "strangeness" results not primarily from the negative act of cutting all ties but from the positive act of giving allegiance to God and God's promised future. When stepping out of their culture, they do not float in some indeterminate space, looking at the world from everywhere and anywhere. Rather with one foot planted in their own culture and the other in God's future—internal difference—they have a vantage point from which to perceive and judge the self and the other not simply on their own terms but also in the light of God's new world—a world in which a great

---

73. Nietzsche, *The Birth of Tragedy and The Genealogy of Morals*, 251.

74. Richard Sennett, "Christian Cosmopolitanism," *Boston Review* 19, no. 5 (1994): 13.

75. Julia Kristeva, "A New Type of Intellectual: The Dissident," in *The Kristeva Reader*, ed. Toril Moi (Oxford: Blackwell, 1986), 298.

76. Tzvetan Todorov has rightly pointed out that being an exile is fruitful only "if one belongs to both cultures at once, without identifying oneself with either." If a whole society consists of exiles, the dialogue of cultures ceases: it is replaced by eclecticism and comparatism, by the capacity to love everything a little, of flaccidly sympathizing with each option without ever embracing any. "Heterology," he concludes, "which makes the difference of voices heard, is necessary; polylogy is insipid." *The Conquest of America: The Question of the Other*, transl. Richard Howard (New York: HarperCollins, 1984), 251.

multitude "from every nation, from all tribes and peoples and languages" is gathered "before the throne and before the Lamb" (Rev 7:9; 5:9).

In the battle against evil, especially against the evil in one's own culture, evangelical personality needs *ecumenical community*. In the struggle against the Nazi regime, the Barmen Declaration called the churches to reject all "other lords"—the racist state and its ideology—and give allegiance to Jesus Christ alone "who is the one Word of God which we have to hear and which we have to trust and obey in life and death." The call is as important today as it was then. Yet it is too abstract. It underestimates our ability to twist the "one Word of God" to serve our own communal ideologies and national strategies. The images of communal survival and flourishing our culture feeds us all too easily blur our vision of God's new creation—America is a Christian nation, we then think, for instance, and democracy the only truly Christian political arrangement. Unaware that our culture has subverted our faith, we lose a place from which to judge our own culture. In order to keep our allegiance to Jesus Christ pure, we need to nurture commitment to the multicultural community of Christian churches. We need to see ourselves and our own understanding of God's future with the eyes of Christians from other cultures, listen to voices of Christians from other cultures so as to make sure that the voice of our culture has not drowned out the voice of Jesus Christ, "the one Word of God." Barmen's commitment to the Lordship of Christ must be supplemented with the commitment to the ecumenical community of Christ. The two are not the same, but both are necessary.

Let me suggest a text that confesses the need for ecumenical community in the struggle against "new tribalism." I will follow the format of the Barmen Declaration:

> "You were slain, and by your blood you purchased for God persons from every tribe, language, people, and nation" (Rev 5:9 CEB). "There is no longer Jew or Greek, there is no longer slave or free, there is no longer male and female; for all of you are one in Christ Jesus" (Gal 3:28).

> All the churches of Jesus Christ, scattered in diverse cultures, have been redeemed for God by the blood of the Lamb to form one multicultural community of faith. The "blood" that binds them as brothers and sisters is more precious than the "blood," the language, the customs, political allegiances, or economic interests that may separate them.

We reject the false doctrine, as though a church should place allegiance to the culture it inhabits and the nation to which it belongs above the commitment to brothers and sisters from other cultures and nations, servants of the one Jesus Christ, their common Lord, and members of God's new community.

In situations of conflict Christians often find themselves accomplices in war, rather than agents of peace. We find it difficult to distance ourselves from our selves and our own culture, and so we echo its reigning opinions and mimic its practices. As we keep the vision of God's future alive, we need to reach out across the firing lines and join hands with our brothers and sisters on the other side. We need to let them pull us out of the enclosure of our own culture and its own peculiar set of prejudices so that we can read afresh the "one Word of God." In this way we might become once again the salt to the world ridden by strife.

The two positive functions of distance from one's own culture that I have highlighted invite two objections. The first concerns the notion of "hybrid identity." Do we not reach a point at which we must close the doors not simply to what is evil but also to what is foreign because if we keep the doors open, our home will soon no longer be our own and we will no longer be able to distinguish home from a street? Put more abstractly, does not identity—even hybrid identity—presuppose boundary maintenance? A second objection goes in the opposite direction and concerns the struggle against evil: while the first objection insisted that I am too loose with cultural identity, the second insisted that I am too rigid with moral responsibility. What right do I have to insist that one can distinguish between darkness and light, and that one must struggle against darkness in the name of light? If we operate with such stark distinctions are we not in danger of demonizing and destroying whatever we happen not to like? I would not dispute the concern behind the first objection and would argue against the second that it is both impossible and undesirable not to distinguish between darkness and light. In the following chapter, I will elaborate on these claims.

CHAPTER III
Exclusion

The war in former Yugoslavia (1991–1995) increased the already oversized vocabulary of evil with the phrase "ethnic cleansing." Ethnic otherness is filth that must be washed away from the ethnic body, pollution that threatens the ecology of the ethnic space. The others will be rounded up in concentration camps, killed and shoved into mass graves, or driven out; monuments of their cultural and religious identity will be destroyed, inscriptions of their collective memories erased; the places of their habitation will be plundered and then burned and bulldozed. For those driven out, no return will be possible. The land will belong exclusively to those who have driven the others out—out of their collective construction of themselves as well as out of the land. People of pure "blood" and pure "culture" will live in a land that has been cleansed of the others. A company of political, military, and academic "janitors of the ethnic household" will employ their communicational, martial, and intellectual mops, hoses, and scrapers to re-sanitize "the ethnic self" and rearrange its proper space. The result: a world without the other. The price: rivers of blood and tears. The gain: except for the bulging pocketbooks of warlords and war profiteers, only losses, on all sides.

In this chapter I will examine the practice of "exclusion," for which "ethnic cleansing" has become the most powerful current metaphor. The chapter, however, is not so much about "them out there" as about "us right here" wherever we may be, not so much about the other as about the self. This chapter is also not only about exclusion from "ethnic" and other kinds of communities, but also about suppression of the situatedness of the *self,* without which exclusions from communities would not

49

nearly be as troublesome. My first step will be to point to a momentous inner tension in the typically modern narrative of inclusion, a narrative that serves as a backdrop for much of the contemporary critique of exclusion.

The Dubious Triumph of Inclusion

Consider the typical reactions in the West to ethnic cleansing. As Michael Ignatieff notes, Western discourse has tended to "redescribe all the combatants as nonEuropean savages."[1] The sanctimoniousness with which the term "savages" is often uttered is profoundly disturbing, but given the intensity and destructiveness of the Balkan will to exclusion, the usage of the epithet may be understandable. Clearly, the moral outrage that it expresses is appropriate. Yet there is something insidious about the epithet—"savages." For it describes not simply how "they" and "we" ought not to behave, but also it implicitly portrays "them" as the kind of people "we" are not. The adjective "nonEuropean" (in the sense of "nonWestern") underlines the distancing of "them" from "us" already contained in the noun "savages": we are moral and civilized; they are the wicked barbarians. Rightful moral outrage has mutated into self-deceiving moral smugness.

The desire to distance "Europe"—"the West" and "modernity"—from the practice of ethnic cleansing is, however, driven by more than just the simple displacement mechanism by which we locate evil and barbarity with others so as to ascribe goodness and civilization to ourselves. It has as much to do with certain aspects of our philosophy of history as with our moral perception of ourselves. What makes ethnic cleansing seem so "nonmodern" and "nonWestern" is that it is starkly at odds with a major public story we like to tell about the modern democratic West—a story of progressive "inclusion." Here is a version of such a narrative of modern liberal democracies as described by Alan Wolfe:

> Once upon a time, it is said, such societies were ruled by privileged elites. Governing circles were restricted to those of the correct gender, breeding, education, and social exclusiveness. All this changes as a result of those multiple forces usually identified by the term democracy. First the middle classes, then working men, then women, then racial minori-

---

1. Michael Ignatieff, "Homage to Bosnia," *The New York Review* 41, no. 8 (1994): 5.

ties all won not only economic rights but political and social rights as well.[2]

To put it slightly differently, once "hierarchically segmented" societies gave way to what sociologists call "functionally differentiated" societies, inclusion became the general norm: every person must have access to all functions and therefore all persons must have equal access to education, to all available jobs, to political decision-making, and the like.[3] The history of modern democracies is about progressive and ever-expanding inclusion, about "taking in rather than . . . keeping out."[4] By contrast, stories of ethnic cleansing are about the most brutal forms of exclusion, about driving out rather than taking in. Hence they strike us as "nonmodern," "non-European," "non-Western."

But how adequate is the modern story of the inclusion's triumph? I pose this question as an insider who wants to help build and improve rather than as an outsider who wants to destroy and completely replace. To a person, such as myself, who experienced "all the blessings" of communist rule, the suggestion that there is no truth to the liberal narrative of inclusion, and the claim that its consequences are mainly unfortunate, sounds not only unpersuasive but also dangerous. Similarly, most women and minorities would not want to give up the rights they now have; and most critics of liberal democracies would rather live in a democracy than in any of the available alternatives. The progress of "inclusion" is one important thing to celebrate about modernity.

Yet, though the narrative of inclusion is in an important sense true, like some magic mirror that gives the beholder's image an instant face-lift, it was also crafted in part to "make us feel that history has a purpose that in some way corresponds with a more positive understanding of human potential," as Alan Wolfe rightly underlines.[5] But how would the face look if the mirror were to lose its magic? How would the face look in a mirror that was not made by us in order to court our vanity? In the mirrors made in the sweatshops of "submodernity"[6] and held by the exploited and emaciated hand of "the other" a mean streak appears on the face of

2. Alan Wolfe, "Democracy versus Sociology: Boundaries and Their Political Consequences," in *Cultivating Differences: Symbolic Boundaries and the Making of Inequality,* ed. Michele Lamont and Marcel Fournier (Chicago: The University of Chicago Press, 1992), 309.

3. See Niklas Luhmann, *Funktion der Religion* (Frankfurt: Suhrkamp, 1977), 234ff.

4. Wolfe, "Democracy versus Sociology," 309.

5. Ibid.

6. Jürgen Moltmann, *Public Theology and the Future of the Modern World* (Pittsburgh: ATS, 1995).

modernity, acquired through the protracted practice of evil. Those who are conveniently left out of the modern narrative of inclusion, because they disturb the integrity of its "happy ending" plot, demand a long and gruesome counter-narrative of exclusion.

In *The Invention of the Americas,* Enrique Dussel argued that the very birth of modernity entailed an exclusion of colossal proportions. While undoubtedly a European epochal shift, modernity is unthinkable without Europe's long and shameful history with non-Europe that started in the year 1492.[7] There is no need to retell that history here; it suffices to consider briefly its most brutalized victims, African slaves. Dussel writes,

> In the famed *triangle of death,* ships left London, Lisbon, The Hague, or Amsterdam with European products, such as arms and iron tools, and exchanged these goods on the western coasts of Africa for slaves. They then bartered these slaves in Bahia, Hispanic Cartagena, Havana, Port-au-Prince, and in the ports of the colonies south of New England for gold, silver, and tropical products. The entrepreneurs eventually deposited all that value, or coagulated human blood in Marx's metaphor, in the banks of London and the pantries of the Low Countries. Thus modernity pursued its civilizing, modernizing, humanizing, Christianizing course.[8]

Barbaric conquest, colonization, and enslavement of the non-European other, legitimized by the myth of spreading the light of civilization—this is a non-European counter-narrative of exclusion suppressed by the modern narrative of inclusion. And that counter-narrative is no unfortunate side-plot that, were it excised, would leave the pace and the shape of the narrative of inclusion intact. The undeniable progress of inclusion fed on the persistent practice of exclusion.[9]

---

7. Enrique Dussel, *The Invention of the Americas: Eclipse of "the Other" and the Myth of Modernity,* transl. M. D. Barber (New York: Continuum, 1995).

8. Ibid., 122–23.

9. My point is not that there is something distinctly modern about the narrative of exclusion, say, something in the "logic" of modernity that made the modern history of exclusion qualitatively different from many premodern histories of exclusion. In *The Discourse of Race in Modern China,* Frank Dikötter gives abundant evidence of "a mentality that integrated the concept of civilization with the idea of humanity, picturing the alien groups living outside the pale of Chinese society as distant savages hovering on the edge of bestiality. The names of the outgroups were written in characters with an animal radical, a habit that persisted until the 1930s: the Di, a northern tribe, were thus assimilated with the dog, whereas the Man and the Min, people from the south, shared the attributes of reptiles" (Frank Dikötter, *The Discourse of Race in Modern China* [Stanford: Stanford University Press, 1992], 4). My point is simply that there is something profoundly misleading if the account of modernity is given as a progress of inclusion without paying attention to the shadow narrative of exclusion.

We should resist the temptation to try to redeem the modern narrative of inclusion by pointing to exclusionary practices elsewhere, such as the age-old Indian caste system, the modern practice of eugenics in China,[10] or "cultural cleansing" in Sudan where Muslims round up and relocate children from Christian and animist regions, to name but three rather disparate examples. And we cannot redeem the narrative of inclusion by noting that conquest, colonization, and enslavement all belong to a distant past of the West. "Segregation," "holocaust," "apartheid" are Western equivalents of the Balkan "ethnic cleansing" from a more recent past that match in inhumanity anything we encounter outside the boundaries of the West. There is far too much "cleansing" in the history of the West for the horror about ethnic cleansing in the Balkans to express legitimately anything but moral outrage about *ourselves*. The exclusion signified in "ethnic cleansing" as a metaphor is not about barbarity "then" as opposed to civilization "now," not about evil "out there" as opposed to goodness "here." Exclusion is barbarity *within* civilization, evil *among* the good, crime against the other *right within the walls of the self.*

One could argue that the barbarity within civilization and evil among the good arises from inconsistency. We simply need to press on with the program of inclusion, the argument could continue, until the last pocket of exclusion has been conquered. Exclusion would then be a sickness and inclusion undiluted medicine. Could it be, however, that the medicine itself is making the patient sick with a new form of the very illness it seeks to cure? I think this is the case. A long look at a good mirror—a mirror that refuses to reflect what the vain eye desires to see—would reveal not simply a mean streak in an innocent face but also a certain aura of meanness that exudes from its very innocence. As Friedrich Nietzsche and neo-Nietzscheans (such as Michel Foucault) have pointed out, exclusion is often the evil perpetrated by *"the good"* and barbarity produced by *civilization.*

In a profound reading of the Gospels in *Thus Spoke Zarathustra*, Nietzsche underscored the connection between the self-perceived "goodness" of Jesus's enemies and their pursuit of his death; crucifixion was a deed of "the good and just," not of the wicked, as we might have thought. "The good and just" could not understand Jesus because their spirit was "imprisoned in their good conscience" and they crucified him because

---

10. Frank Dikötter, "Throw-Away Babies," *Times Literary Supplement* (January 12, 1996): 4–5.

53

they construed as evil his rejection of their notions of good.[11] "The good and just," insists Nietzsche, *have* to crucify the one who devises an alternative virtue because they already possess the knowledge of the good; they *have* to be hypocrites because, seeing themselves as good, they must impersonate the absence of evil. Like poisonous flies, "they sting" and they do so "in all innocence."[12] Exclusion can be as much a sin of "a good conscience" as it is of "an evil heart." And Nietzsche's warning that "whatever harm the world-calumniators may do, *the harm the good do is the most harmful harm*" may not be entirely out of place.[13]

How about "the rational" and "the civilized"? Are they any better than "the good and just"? Much of Michel Foucault's work consists in an attempt to explicate the exclusionary shadow that stubbornly trails modernity's history of inclusion. *Madness and Civilization*, his first book, traces the history of nonreason in the age of reason.[14] As Foucault tells it, it is a story of "reason's subjugation of nonreason, wresting from it its truth as madness, crime, or disease,"[15] a narrative of assigning the nonreasonable— "poor vagabonds, criminals, and 'deranged minds'"[16]—to the regions of the excluded nonhuman whose symbolic inhabitant is the leper.

Later in *Discipline and Punish* he sums up his point like this: the mechanism of exclusion functions through a double repressive strategy of "binary division" (mad/sane; abnormal/normal) and "coercive assignment" (out/in).[17] In the same book, whose focus is "the birth of the prison" but whose theme is a more general social "power of normalization," he underscored, however, that exclusion is not simply a matter of repressive ejection but of productive formation. "Unlike the soul represented by Christian theology," writes Foucault, the modern individual "is not born in sin and subject to punishment, but is born rather out of methods of punishment, supervision and constraint."[18] A series of "carceral mechanisms"

11. Friedrich Nietzsche, *Thus Spoke Zarathustra: A Book for Everyone and No One,* transl. R. J. Hollingdale (London: Penguin, 1969), 229. Merold Westphal, *Suspicion and Faith: The Religious Uses of Modern Atheism* (Grand Rapids: Eerdmans, 1993), 262f.

12. Nietzsche, *Thus Spoke Zarathustra,* 204.

13. Friedrich Nietzsche, *Ecce Homo: How One Becomes What One Is,* transl. R. J. Hollingdale (London: Penguin, 1979), 100.

14. Michel Foucault, *Madness and Civilization: A History of Insanity in the Age of Reason,* transl. Richard Howard (New York: Random House, 1988).

15. Ibid., ix–x.

16. Ibid., 7.

17. Michel Foucault, *Discipline and Punish: The Birth of the Prison,* transl. Alan Sheridan (New York: Vintage Books, 1979), 199.

18. Ibid., 29.

that function throughout the society exercise "a power of normalization"[19] and render people docile and productive, obedient and useful. As a power of normalization, exclusion reigns through all those institutions that we may associate with inclusionary civilization—through the state apparatus, educational institutions, media, sciences. They all shape "normal" citizens with "normal" knowledge, values, and practices, and thereby either assimilate or eject the "abnormal" other. The modern self, claims Foucault summarizing his own work, is indirectly constituted through the exclusion of the other.[20] It was, of course, no different with the premodern self; it too was constituted by a series of exclusions.

If for Nietzsche "the good and just" are the hypocritical murderers of their rivals, for Foucault "civilization" is a smooth destroyer of those things inside and outside itself that it constructs as barbarity. Even if one is not fully persuaded by Nietzsche and Foucault—as I am certainly not—they rightly draw attention to the fact that the "moral" and "civilized" self all too often rests on the exclusion of what it construes as the "immoral" and "barbarous" other. The other side of the history of inclusion is a history of exclusion. The very space in which inclusion celebrates its triumph echoes with the mocking laughter of victorious exclusion. Moral outrage at brutal exclusion going on in such places as former Yugoslavia or Rwanda is appropriate; moral censure of manifold forms of exclusion everywhere—also in the best practices of the West—is appropriate too.

The logic of the modern story of inclusion suggests that "keeping out" is bad and "taking in" is good. But is this always right? Consider Foucault's critique of modernity from another angle. It can be plausibly argued that Foucault is not first of all a critic of the modern project of inclusion but its consistent advocate. The pathos of his critique of the shadow narrative of exclusion is the obverse of a deep longing for inclusion—his own, radical kind of inclusion. The unmasking of "binary divisions," "coercive assignments," and of "the power of normalization" all seek to broaden the space of the "inside" by storming the walls that protect it. Foucault shares a distaste for boundaries with other postmodern thinkers, such as Jacques Derrida or Gilles Deleuze. When commenting on the nature of postmodernism, Alan Wolfe rightly notes that

19. Ibid., 308.
20. Michel Foucault, "The Political Technology of Individuals," *Technologies of the Self*, ed. Luther H. Martin et al. (Amherst: University of Massachusetts Press, 1988), 146.

the essence of the approach is to question the presumed boundaries between groups: of signifiers, people, species, or texts. What appears at
first glance to be a difference is reinterpreted, discovered to be little more
than a distinction rooted in power or a move in a rhetorical game. Differences, in other words, never have a fixed status in and of themselves;
there are no *either/ors* (nor are there no *not either/ors*).[21]

A consistent drive toward inclusion seeks to level all the boundaries that
divide and to neutralize all outside powers that form and shape the self.
Correspondingly, the social "program" that informs Foucault's theoretical
work consists strictly speaking in an *absence of a program* expressed as the
goal of showing "people that they are much freer than they feel."[22] Radical indeterminacy of negative freedom is a stable correlate of a consistent
drive toward inclusion that levels all boundaries.

Does not such radical indeterminacy undermine from within the idea
of inclusion, however? I believe it does. Without boundaries we will be
able to know only what we are fighting against but not what we are fighting for. Intelligent struggle against exclusion demands categories and normative criteria that enable us to distinguish between repressive identities
and practices that should be subverted and nonrepressive ones that should
be affirmed.[23] Second, "no boundaries" means not only "no intelligent
agency" but also in the end "no life" itself. Aiming at Foucault, Manfred
Frank writes in *Neostrukturalismus*,

> It is impossible (and unappealing even for pure fantasy) to fight
> against all order and advocate a pure, abstract non-order. For, much
> like the mythical *tohuwabohu,* a non-order would be a "creature" with
> no attributes, a place where one could distinguish nothing and where
> neither happiness nor pleasure, neither freedom nor justice, could be
> identified.[24]

The absence of boundaries creates nonorder, and nonorder is not the end
of exclusion but the end of life.

21. Wolfe, "Democracy versus Sociology," 310.
22. Rex Martin, "Truth, Power, Self: An Interview with Michel Foucault," in *Technologies of the Self,*
ed. Luther H. Martin et al. (Amherst: University of Massachusetts Press, 1988), 10.
23. Allison Weir, *Sacrificial Logics: Feminist Theory and the Critique of Identity* (New York: Routledge,
1996).
24. Manfred Frank, *Was ist Neostrukturalismus?* (Frankfurt: Suhrkamp, 1984), 237.

Foucault could, of course, stop short of letting the waters of chaos rush in; he could refuse to level *all* boundaries. But if all boundaries are arbitrary and if they necessarily entail oppression, as Foucault seems to suggest, this move would amount to weaving domination into the very fabric of social life and a tragic acquiescence to the permanence of oppression. *A consistent pursuit of inclusion places one before the impossible choice between a chaos without boundaries and oppression with them.* This is one of the major lessons of Foucault's thought.[25]

If plausible, my account of the inner contradictions in the pursuit of inclusion suggests that the struggle against exclusion is beset with two major dangers. The first is that of generating new forms of exclusion by the very opposition to exclusionary practices: our "moral" and "civilizing" zeal causes us to erect new and oppressive boundaries as well as blinds us to the fact that we are doing so. The second danger arises from the attempt to escape the first. It consists in falling into the abyss of nonorder in which the struggle against exclusion implodes on itself because, in the absence of all boundaries, we are unable to name what is excluded or why it ought not to be excluded. For the sake of the victims of exclusion, we must seek to avoid both dangers. Adequate reflection on exclusion must satisfy two conditions: (1) it must help to name exclusion as evil with confidence because it enables us to imagine nonexclusionary boundaries that map nonexclusionary identities; at the same time (2) it must not dull our ability to detect the exclusionary tendencies in our own judgments and practices.

The present chapter is a contribution to such an understanding of exclusion. In the main body I will explore the anatomy, the dynamics, the pervasiveness, and the power of exclusion. In conclusion I will analyze the first and paradigmatic act of exclusion recorded in the Bible, Cain's murder of his brother Abel. But first I need to make some important

---

25. To evade the alternative, one could construe Foucault's deconstruction of boundaries as a social strategy rather than a principled philosophical position. In a world in which "the judges of normality are present everywhere" (Foucault, *Discipline and Punish*, 304) and "the power of normalization" has been normalized (296), Foucault is fighting boundaries, nothing more; he is not fighting all boundaries but these specific boundaries—unnecessary and oppressive boundaries. The immediate response could be to ask whether a problem more fundamental in contemporary societies than too much judging is the incapacity for the *right kind* of judging. Might we not be entering "inside a curious, sentimental reversal of Kafka's *Trial*, where the *court* is always found to be stacked and guilty," as Michael Wood puts it in *America in the Movies* ([New York: Columbia University Press, 1989], 145)? Has not a disturbing gulf opened up between the glaring visibility of evil and our frustrating inability to name it, as Andrew Delbanco has argued in *The Death of Satan* (New York: Farrar, Straus and Giroux, 1995)? Are we not witnesses to a paradoxical normalization of the *bizarre*, so much so that "normal" has become a dirty word (185)?

distinctions without which our outrage at exclusion would rest on nothing firmer than the arbitrariness and fickleness of our own displeasure.

Differentiation, Exclusion, Judgment

Vilify all boundaries, pronounce every discrete identity oppressive, put the tag "exclusion" on every stable difference—and you will have aimless drifting instead of clear-sighted agency, haphazard activity instead of moral engagement and accountability and, in the long run, a torpor of death instead of a dance of freedom. This is what I argued earlier. What I did not do is indicate how to engage in the struggle against exclusion without selling our souls to the demons of chaos. I want to address this question now by making a distinction between *differentiation* and *exclusion*, which in turn will lead to a distinction between *exclusion* and *judgment*, and then suggesting a profile of a self capable of making nonexclusionary judgments. Such nonexclusionary judgments passed by persons willing to embrace the other are what is needed to fight exclusion successfully.

First, *differentiation*. At the beginning of his "breviary of sin" entitled *Not the Way It's Supposed to Be*, Cornelius Plantinga draws attention to the way Genesis 1 portrays God's creative activity as a pattern of "separating" and "binding together."[26] At first there is a "formless void" (Gen 1:2); "everything in the universe is all jumbled together," writes Plantinga, and then continues:

> So God begins to do some creative separating: he separates light from darkness, day from night, water from land, the sea creatures from the land cruiser.... At the same time God binds things together: he binds humans to the rest of creation as stewards and caretakers of it, to himself as bearers of his image, and to each other as perfect complements.[27]

Though there is more "separating" and "binding" going on in Genesis 1 than Plantinga mentions, and they are undertaken not only by God but also by God's creatures, Plantinga has made his point. The point is a good one: as described in Genesis, creation exists as an intricate pattern of "separate-and-bound-together" entities. Put more abstractly but precisely, creation means, in the words of Michael Welker, "formation and

---

26. Cornelius Plantinga, *Not the Way It's Supposed to Be: A Breviary of Sin* (Grand Rapids: Eerdmans, 1995), 29.

27. Ibid.

maintenance of a network of the relations of interdependence."[28] In the following discussion, which will focus on human beings, I will use the term *differentiation* to describe the creative activity of "separating-and-binding" that results in patterns of interdependence.

Notice that *differentiation*, as I have defined it, differs from *separation* pure and simple. Differentiation consists in "separating-*and*-binding." By itself, separation would result in self-enclosed, isolated, and self-identical beings. Feminist thinkers rightly rejected separation as an ideal. Relational feminists, such as Nancy Chodorow, argued that separation always entails repression of existing relationships (especially to the mother) and therefore results in the domination of others.[29] Postmodern feminists, such as Judith Butler and Luce Irigaray, underscored that separation results in a "unitary" and "self-identical" self, which can be formed only by driving out of the self all that is nonunitary and nonidentical.[30] In their own way, both of these rather diverse strands of feminist thought reject "identity" because it rests on separation. If Allison Weir's analysis in *Sacrificial Logics* is correct, what also unites these two strands of feminist thought is an inability to conceive of "identity" in a way that does not repress either relationships to others or the differences within the self.[31] Is a more complex notion of identity possible, a notion of identity that is not "pure" but includes the other?

The account of creation as "separating-and-binding" rather than simply "separating" suggests that "identity" includes connection, difference, and heterogeneity. The human self is formed not through a simple rejection of the other—through a binary logic of opposition and negation—but through a complex process of "taking in" *and* "keeping out." We are who we are not because we are separate from the others who are next to us but because we are *both* separate *and* connected, *both* distinct *and* related; the boundaries that mark our identities are both barriers and bridges. I, Miroslav Volf, am who I am *both* because I am distinct from my sister Vlasta, *and* because over the past sixty-two years I have been shaped by a relationship with her. Similarly, to be "black" in the United States means

28. Michael Welker, *Schöpfung und Wirklichkeit* (Neukirchen-Vluyn: Neukirchener Verlag, 1995), 24. My translation.

29. Nancy Chodorow, *The Reproduction of Mothering: Psychoanalysis and the Sociology of Gender* (Berkeley: University of California Press, 1978).

30. Judith Butler, *Gender Trouble: Feminism and the Subversion of Identity* (New York: Routledge, 1990); Luce Irigaray, *This Sex Which Is Not One,* transl. Catherine Porter with Carolyn Burke (Ithaca, NY: Cornell University Press, 1985).

31. Weir, *Sacrificial Logics.*

to be in a certain relationship—all too often an unpleasant relationship—to "whites."[32] Identity is a result of the distinction from the other *and* the internalization of the relationship to the other; it arises out of the complex history of "differentiation" in which both the self and the other take part by negotiating their identities in interaction with one another. Hence, as Paul Ricoeur has argued in *Oneself as Another*, "the selfhood of oneself implies otherness to such an intimate degree that one cannot be thought of without the other."[33]

Second, *exclusion*. If the process of creation takes place through the activity of "separating-and-binding," should not then sin be described as some "devastating twister" that "both explodes and implodes creation, pushing it back toward the 'formless void' from which it came," as Plantinga suggests?[34] "Formless void" may be the ultimate result of sin if left unchecked, but sin's more immediate goal is not so much to undo the creation but violently to reconfigure the pattern of its interdependence, to "put asunder what God has joined and join what God has put asunder," as Plantinga states more correctly.[35] I will give the name "exclusion" to this sinful activity of reconfiguring the creation, in order to distinguish it from the creative activity of "differentiation."

What then is exclusion? In a preliminary and rather schematic way, one can point to two interrelated aspects of exclusion, the one that transgresses against "binding" and the other that transgresses against "separating." First, exclusion can entail cutting of the bonds that connect, taking oneself out of the pattern of interdependence and placing oneself in a position of sovereign independence. The other then emerges either as an enemy that must be pushed away from the self and driven out of its space or as a nonentity—a superfluous being—that can be disregarded and abandoned. Second, exclusion can entail erasure of separation, not recognizing the other as someone who in his or her otherness belongs to the pattern of interdependence. The other then emerges as an inferior being who must either be assimilated by being made like the self or be subjugated to the self. Exclusion takes place when the violence of expulsion, assimilation, or subjugation and the

---

32. K. Anthony Appiah, "Identity, Authenticity, Survival: Multicultural Societies and Social Reproduction," in *Multiculturalism: Examining the Politics of Recognition*, ed. Amy Gutmann (Princeton: Princeton University Press, 1994), 154ff.

33. Paul Ricoeur, *Oneself as Another* (Chicago: The University of Chicago Press, 1992), 3.

34. Plantinga, *Not the Way It's Supposed to Be*, 30.

35. Ibid.

indifference of abandonment replace the dynamics of taking in and keeping out as well as the mutuality of giving and receiving.

This is a bare-bones sketch of exclusion. Later on I will put flesh on the skeleton. Here I need only to note briefly how exclusion is different from drawing and maintaining boundaries. As I suggested earlier, boundaries are part of the creative process of differentiation. For without boundaries there would be no discrete identities, and without discrete identities there could be no relation to the other. As Elie Wiesel puts it in *From the Kingdom of Memory*, the encounter with a stranger can be creative only if you "know when to step back."[36] A stranger, he writes, "can be of help only as a stranger—lest you are ready to become his caricature. And your own."[37] To avoid becoming caricatures of one another and, caught in the vortex of de-differentiation, finally ending in a "formless void," we must refuse to consider boundaries as exclusionary. Instead, what is exclusionary are the impenetrable barriers that prevent a creative encounter with the other.

Third, *judgment*. In popular culture, passing a judgment is often deemed an act of exclusion. Strong disagreement with a lifestyle, religious belief-system, or a course of action—a disagreement that employs adjectives like *wrong*, *mistaken*, or *erroneous*, and understands these to be more than expressions of personal or communal preference—is felt to be exclusionary. Giving a sophisticated expression to such popular attitudes, Richard Rorty suggests that an "attitude of irony" ought to replace the "rule of judgment." Instead of naively believing that one can know what is right and what is wrong, a person should, as he puts it in *Contingency, Irony, and Solidarity*, face up "to the contingency of his or her own most central beliefs and desires," to the fact that they do not "refer back to something beyond the reach of time and chance."[38]

From my perspective, the distinction between *differentiation* and *exclusion* is meant to underscore that contingency does not, as he puts it, go "all the way down," that there are values that "time and change" cannot alter because "time and change" did not bring them about. I do not reject exclusion because of a contingent preference for a certain kind of society, say the one in which people are "able to work out their private salvations, create their private self-images, reweave their webs of belief and desire in

---

36. Elie Wiesel, *From the Kingdom of Memory: Reminiscences* (New York: Summit Books, 1990), 73.
37. Ibid., 65.
38. Richard Rorty, *Contingency, Irony, and Solidarity* (Cambridge: Cambridge University Press, 1989), xv.

the light of whatever new people and books they happen to encounter."[39] I reject exclusion because the prophets, evangelists, and apostles tell me that this is a wrong way to treat human beings, any human being, anywhere, and I am persuaded to have good reasons to believe them. An ironic stance may be all that people desire who are spoiled by affluence, because it legitimizes their obsession with "creating their private self-images" and "reweaving their webs of belief and desire." But an ironic stance is clearly not what people suffering hunger, persecution, and oppression can afford.[40] For they know that they can survive only if judgment is passed against those who exploit, persecute, and oppress them. In my vocabulary, in any case, *exclusion* does not express a preference; it names an objective evil.

A judgment that names exclusion as an evil and differentiation as a positive good, then, is itself not an act of exclusion. To the contrary, such judgment is the beginning of the struggle against exclusion. Of course, we do make exclusionary judgments, and we make them far too often. European settlers want more land and then judge indigenous populations as "barbarians" in order to justify their slaughter and expulsion;[41] men seek justification for their rule over women and therefore judge them "irrational" and "unstable." Here judgment leads to exclusion and is itself an act of exclusion. But the remedy for exclusionary judgments are certainly not "ironic stances." Instead, we need more adequate judgments based on a distinction between legitimate "differentiation" and illegitimate "exclusion" and made with humility that counts with our proclivity to misperceive and misjudge because we desire to exclude.

The Self and Its Center

But how do we make such nonexclusionary judgments? What kind of a person will be capable of making them? What kind of a person will be capable of struggling against exclusion without perpetuating exclusion by the very struggle against it?

Rorty's argument for "irony" has many important strands, one of which concerns the nature of the self. He writes, "If there is no center to the self, then there are only different ways of weaving new candidates for

39. Ibid., 85.

40. Cornel West, "The New Cultural Politics of Difference," *The Identity in Question,* ed. John Rajchman (New York: Routledge, 1995), 163f.

41. Ronald Takaki, *A Different Mirror: A History of Multicultural America* (Boston: Little, Brown and Company, 1993), 39.

belief and desire into antecedently existing webs of belief and desire."[42] The ironic stance is a posture of a centerless self. It would be tempting to argue for "judgment" and against "irony" by insisting that there is a center to the self and that therefore there are *right* and *wrong* beliefs and desires, not only *antecedent* and *subsequent* beliefs and desires, and that there are *right* and *wrong* ways of weaving beliefs and desires, not only *different* ways of weaving beliefs and desires. From my perspective, this would be a good argument, though it is fraught with danger. It directs all the attention to the question of whether the self has a center, while disregarding the much more important question of the *kind* of center the self ought to have. I will concentrate on this latter question by examining a key statement of the Apostle Paul about the character of the Christian life: "I have been crucified with Christ; and it is no longer I who live, but it is Christ who lives in me. And the life I now live in the flesh I live by faith in the Son of God who loved me and gave himself for me" (Gal 2:19-20).

Paul presumes a centered self, more precisely a *wrongly* centered self that needs to be decentered by being nailed to the cross: "I have been crucified with Christ." Though the self may lack an "objective" and "immovable" center, *the self* is *never without a center*; it is always engaged in the production of its own center. "Weaving" would be a rather innocent way to describe this production, possibly a fitting image for how Rorty's books are written but not for how human selves are shaped. "Struggle" and "violence" come closer to being an adequate description.[43] Psychologists tell us that humans produce and reconfigure themselves by a process of identifying with others and rejecting them, by repressing drives and desires, by interjecting and projecting images of the self and the other, by externalizing fears, by fabricating enemies and suffering animosities, by forming allegiances and breaking them up, by loving and hating, by seeking to dominate and letting themselves be dominated—and all this not neatly divided but all mixed up, with "virtues" often riding on hidden "vices," and "vices" seeking compensatory redemption in contrived "virtues." Through this convoluted process the center of the self is always reproducing itself, sometimes by asserting itself over against the other (a stereotypically male self), at other times by cleaving too closely to the other (a stereotypically female

---

42. Richard Rorty, *Contingency, Irony, and Solidarity,* 83f.

43. Vamik Volkan, *The Need to Have Enemies and Allies: From Clinical Practice to International Relationships* (Northvale: Jason Aronson, 1988).

self), sometimes pulled by the lure of throbbing and restless pleasures, at other times pushed by the rule of a rigid and implacable law.

Whichever way the "centering" takes place and whatever its result, the self should be decentered, claims Paul. The word he uses to describe the act is *crucified*, a word that tells a story whose high points are Good Friday and Easter. *Destroying* is the word Reinhold Niebuhr used in *The Nature and Destiny of Man* to render Paul's *crucifying*.[44] This term, however, is too all-encompassing, for Paul clearly has in view a continued life of that same self after its "crucifixion." Radical "decentering" might be better, for then a recentering of that same self can take place.

"It is Christ who lives in me," writes the Apostle Paul after giving the report of his own crucifixion. This suggests that the decentering was only the flip side of recentering. The self is both "decentered" and "re-centered" by one and the same process, by participating in the death and resurrection of Christ through faith and baptism. "For if we have been united with him in a death like his, we will certainly be united with him in a resurrection like his" (Rom 6:5). By being "crucified with Christ" the self has received a new center—the Christ who lives in it and with whom it lives. Notice that the new center of the self is not a timeless "essence," hidden deep within a human being, underneath the sediments of culture and history and untouched by "time and change," an essence that waits only to be discovered, unearthed, and set free. Neither is the center an inner narrative that the reverberating echo of the community's "final vocabulary" and "master story" has scripted in the book of the self and whose integrity must be guarded from editorial intrusions by rival "vocabularies" and competing "stories." The center of the self—a center that is both inside and outside—is the story of Jesus Christ, which has become the story of the self. More precisely, the center is Jesus Christ crucified and resurrected who has become part and parcel of the very structure of the self.

What happened to the self in the process of recentering? Has the self been simply erased? Has its own proper center been simply replaced by an alien center—Jesus Christ the crucified and resurrected? Not exactly. For if Christ "lives *in* me," as Paul says, then *I* must have a center that is distinct from "Christ, the center." And so Paul continues, "And the life *I* now live in the flesh I live...." By the process of decentering the self did not lose a center of its own, but received a new center that both transformed

---

44. Reinhold Niebuhr, *The Nature and Destiny of Man* (New York: Scribner's, 1964), 2:108.

and reinforced the old one. Recentering entails no self-obliterating denial of the self that dissolves the self in Christ and therefore possibly legitimizes other such dissolutions in the "father," the "husband," the "nation," the "church," and the like. To the contrary, recentering establishes the most proper and unassailable center that allows the self to stand over against persons and institutions which may threaten to smother it.

Significantly enough, however, the new center is a *decentered center*. Through faith and baptism the self has been remade in the image of "the Son of God who loved me and gave himself for me," Paul writes. At the center of the self lies self-giving love. No "hegemonic centrality" closes the self off, guarding its self-same identity and driving out and away whatever threatens its purity. To the contrary, the new center opens the self up, makes it capable and willing to give itself for others and to receive others in itself. In the previous chapter, I argued that Paul locates the unity of the church not in the disincarnate transcendence of a pure and universal spirit but in the scandalous particularity of the suffering body of God's Messiah. Correspondingly, Paul locates the center of the self not in some single and unchangeable—because it is self-enclosed— "essence" but in self-giving love made possible by and patterned on the suffering Messiah.

For Christians, this "decentered center" of self-giving love—most firmly centered and most radically open—is the doorkeeper deciding about the fate of otherness at the doorstep of the self.[45] From this center, judgments about exclusion must be made and battles against exclusion fought. And with this kind of self, the opposition to exclusion is nothing but the flip side of the practice of embrace. But before I proceed to analyze embrace (Chapter IV), I will take a closer look at exclusion. What is exclusion? What forms does it take? What drives it? Why is it so pervasive? Why so irresistible?

---

45. The metaphor of the door is helpful insofar as it implies a necessary demarcation, but it is also misleading insofar it suggests a sharp and static boundary. In analyzing the category "Christian," missiologist Paul Hiebert suggests that we make use of the mathematical categories of "bounded," "fuzzy," and "centered sets." Bounded sets function on the principle "either/or": an apple is either an apple or it is not; it cannot be partly apple and partly a pear. Fuzzy sets, on the other hand, have no sharp boundaries; things are fluid with no stable point of reference and with various degrees of inclusion—as when a mountain merges into the plains. A centered set is defined by a center and the relationship of things to that center, by a movement toward it or away from it. The category of "Christian," Hiebert suggests, should be understood as a centered set. A demarcation line exists, but the focus is not on "maintaining the boundary" but "on reaffirming the center." Paul Hiebert, "The Category 'Christian' in the Mission Task," *International Review of Mission* 72 (July 1983): 424.

The Anatomy and Dynamics of Exclusion

In Christian theology, there is a long tradition of tracing all sins to one basic form of sin; some prominent candidates being "sensuality,"[46] "pride,"[47] and more recently, "violence."[48] Each of these proposals can be criticized for failure to explain all concrete sins of all human beings. "Pride," for instance, does not seem to capture with precision the experience of most women[49]—and the whole effort of tracing sins to their common root suffers from being too abstract.[50] Keeping in mind the dangers of false universality and abstraction, I will not pursue here the search for the most basic sin. "Exclusion" names what permeates a good many of sins we commit against our neighbors, not what lies at the bottom of all sins.[51]

An advantage of conceiving sin as the practice of exclusion is that it names as sin what often passes as virtue, especially in religious circles. In the Palestine of Jesus's day, "sinners" were not simply "the wicked" who were therefore religiously bankrupt[52] but also social outcasts, people who practiced despised trades, Gentiles and Samaritans, and those who failed to keep the Law as interpreted by a particular sect.[53] A "righteous" person had to separate himself or herself from the latter; the latter's presence defiled the "righteous" person because the latter was defiled. Jesus's table fellowship with "tax collectors and sinners" (Mark 2:15-17), a fellowship that indisputably belonged to the central features of his ministry, offset this conception of sin. Since he who was innocent, sinless, and fully within God's camp transgressed social boundaries that excluded the outcasts, these boundaries themselves were evil, sinful, and outside God's

46. Gregory of Nyssa, *On the Making of Man*, in *Nicene and Post-Nicene Fathers*, vol. 5, ed. Philip Schaff, transl. H. A. Wilson (Buffalo: Christian Literature Publishing House, 1893), §18.

47. Niebuhr, *The Nature and Destiny of Man*, 1:178ff.

48. Marjorie Hewitt Suchocki, *The Fall to Violence: Original Sin in Relational Theology* (New York: Continuum, 1995).

49. Daphne Hampson, "Reinhold Niebuhr on Sin: A Critique," *Reinhold Niebuhr and the Issues of Our Time*, ed. R. Harries (Grand Rapids: Eerdmans, 1986); Judith Plaskow, *Sex, Sin and Grace: Women's Experience and the Theologies of Reinhold Niebuhr and Paul Tillich* (Washington: University Press of America, 1980).

50. Jürgen Moltmann, *The Spirit of Life: A Universal Affirmation*, transl. Margaret Kohl (Minneapolis: Fortress, 1992), 127.

51. For those interested in exploring the connection between "exclusion" and "pride"—that frequent candidate for the most basic sin—one could point out that exclusion could be considered, in Reinhold Niebuhr's words, as "the reverse side of pride and its necessary concomitant in a world in which self-esteem is constantly challenged by the achievements of others." *The Nature and Destiny of Man*, 2:211.

52. E. P. Sanders, *Jesus and Judaism* (Philadelphia: Fortress, 1985).

53. James D. G. Dunn, "Pharisees, Sinners, and Jesus," *The Social World of Formative Christianity: In Tribute to Howard Clark Kee*, ed. Jacob Neusner et al. (Philadelphia: Fortress, 1988), 276–80.

will.[54] By embracing the "outcast," Jesus underscored the "sinfulness" of the persons and systems that cast them out.

It would be a mistake, however, to conclude from Jesus's compassion toward those who transgressed social boundaries that his mission was merely to demask the mechanisms that created "sinners" by falsely ascribing sinfulness to those who were considered socially unacceptable.[55] He was no prophet of "inclusion,"[56] for whom the chief virtue was acceptance and the cardinal vice intolerance. Instead, he was the bringer of "grace," who not only scandalously included "anyone" in the fellowship of "open commensality"[57] but also made the "intolerant" demand of repentance and the "condescending" offer of forgiveness (Mark 1:15; 2:15-17). The mission of Jesus consisted not simply in *renaming* the behavior that was falsely labeled "sinful" but also in *remaking* the people who have actually sinned or have suffered misfortune. The double strategy of renaming and remaking, rooted in the commitment to both the outcast *and* the sinner, to the victim *and* the perpetrator, is the proper background against which an adequate notion of sin as exclusion can emerge.

First, *renaming*. No food, Jesus said, was unclean (Mark 7:14-23); division into clean and unclean foods creates false boundaries that unnecessarily separate people. The flow of blood from a woman's body is not unclean (Mark 5:25-34, implicitly); the laws of purity for women are false boundaries that marginalize them.[58] Put more abstractly, by the simple act of renaming, Jesus offset the stark binary logic that regulates so much of social life: society is divided into X (superior in-group) and non-X (inferior out-group), and then whatever is not X (say, people who eat different foods or have different bodies) is made into "non-X" and thereby assigned to the inferior out-group. The mission of renaming what was falsely labeled "unclean" aimed at abolishing the warped system of exclusion—what people "call clean"—in the name of an order of things that God, the creator and sustainer of life, has "made clean" (cf. Acts 10:5).

---

54. Jerome Neyrey, "Unclean, Common, Polluted, and Taboo: A Short Reading Guide," *Foundations and Facets Forum* 45, no. 4 (1988): 79.

55. *Pace* Marcus J. Borg, *Meeting Jesus Again for the First Time: The Historical Jesus and the Heart of Contemporary Faith* (San Francisco: HarperSanFrancisco, 1994), 46–61.

56. Luke Timothy Johnson, *The Real Jesus: The Misguided Quest for the Historical Jesus and the Truth of the Traditional Gospels* (San Francisco: HarperSanFrancisco, 1996), 43f.

57. John Dominic Crossan, *The Historical Jesus: The Life of a Mediterranean Jewish Peasant* (San Francisco: HarperSanFrancisco, 1991), 261–64; and *Jesus: A Revolutionary Biography* (San Francisco: HarperSanFrancisco, 1994), 66–70.

58. Judith Romney Wegner, *Chattel or Person? The Status of Women in the Mishnah* (New York: Oxford University Press, 1988), 162–67.

Second, *remaking*. In addition to removing the label *unclean* placed on the things that were clean, Jesus made clean things out of truly unclean things. People indwelled by unclean spirits—spirits that cut off persons from community, made them deeply at odds with themselves, and drove them to seek the company of the dead—such people were delivered from oppression and reintegrated into community (Mark 5:1-20). People caught in the snares of wrongdoing—people who, like tax-collectors, harm others in order to benefit themselves or people who, like prostitutes, debase themselves in order to survive, or people who, like most of us, are bent on losing their own souls in order to gain a bit of the world—such people were forgiven and transformed (Mark 2:15-17). The mission of remaking impure people into pure people aimed at tearing down the barriers created by wrongdoing in the name of God, the redeemer and restorer of life, whose love knows no boundaries. By the double strategy of renaming and remaking, Jesus condemned the world of exclusion—a world in which the innocent are labeled evil and driven out and a world in which the guilty are not sought out and brought into the communion.

Central to both strategies for fighting exclusion is the belief that the source of evil does not lie outside of a person, in impure things, but inside a person, in the impure heart (Mark 7:15). Against the background of the two strategies, the *pursuit of false purity* emerges as a central aspect of sin—the enforced purity of a person or a community that sets itself apart from the defiled world in a hypocritical sinlessness and excludes the boundary breaking other from its heart and its world. Sin is here the kind of purity that wants the world cleansed of the other rather than the heart cleansed of the evil that drives people out by calling those who are clean "unclean" and refusing to help make clean those who are unclean. Put more formally, sin is "the will to purity" turned away from the "spiritual" life of the self to the cultural world of the other, transmuted from spirituality into "politics" broadly conceived, as Bernhard-Henri Lévy puts it.[59]

Consider the deadly logic of the "politics of purity." The blood must be pure: German blood alone should run through German veins, free from all non-Aryan contamination. The territory must be pure: Serbian soil must belong to Serbs alone, cleansed of all non-Serbian intruders. The origins must be pure: we must go back to the pristine purity of our linguistic, religious, or cultural past, shake away the dirt of otherness collected

---

59. Bernhard-Henri Lévy, *Gefährliche Reinheit*, transl. Maribel Königer (Wien: Passagen, 1995), 77.

on our march through history.[60] The goal must be pure: we must let the
light of reason shine into every dark corner or we must create a world of
total virtue so as to render all moral effort unnecessary. The origin and the
goal, the inside and the outside, everything must be pure: plurality and
heterogeneity must give way to homogeneity and unity. One people, one
culture, one language, one book, one goal; what does not fall under this
all-encompassing "one" is ambivalent, polluting, and dangerous.[61] It must
be removed. We want a pure world and to push others out of our world;
we want to be pure ourselves and eject "otherness" from within ourselves.
The "will to purity" contains a whole program for arranging our social
worlds—from the inner worlds of our selves to the outer worlds of our
families, neighborhoods, and nations.[62] It is a dangerous program because
it is a totalitarian program, governed by a logic that reduces, ejects, and
segregates.

In extreme cases we kill and drive out. To ensure that the vengeance
of the dead will not be visited upon us in their progeny, we destroy their
habitations and their cultural monuments. Like the robbers in the story of
the Good Samaritan, we strip, beat, and dump people somewhere outside
our own proper space half-dead (Luke 10:30). This is exclusion as *elimination* at work with such shameless brutality in places like Bosnia, Rwanda,
Sudan, and Myanmar. The more benign side of exclusion by elimination
is exclusion by *assimilation*. You can survive, even thrive, among us, if you
become like us; you can keep your life, if you give up your identity. Using
the terminology employed by Claude Lévi-Strauss in *Tristes Tropiques,* we
can say that exclusion by assimilation rests on a deal: we will refrain from
vomiting you out (anthropoemic strategy) if you let us swallow you up
(anthropophagic strategy).[63]

Alternatively, we are satisfied to assign "others" the status of inferior
beings. We make sure that they cannot live in our neighborhoods, get
certain kinds of jobs, receive equal pay or honor; they must stay in their
proper place, which is to say the place we have assigned for them; as Lu-
cas Beauchamp's neighbors put it in William Faulkner's *Intruder in the
Dust*, they must be "niggers" first, and then we may be prepared to treat

60. Donald L. Horowitz, *Ethnic Groups in Conflict* (Berkeley: University of California Press, 1985),
72.

61. Julia Kristeva, *Powers of Horror: An Essay on Abjection,* transl. Leon S. Roudiez (New York: Columbia University Press, 1982), 76.

62. Lévy, *Gefährliche Reinheit.*

63. Claude Lévi-Strauss, *Tristes Tropiques* (Paris: Libraire Plon, 1955), 417ff.

them as human beings.[64] We subjugate them so we can exploit them in order to increase our wealth or simply inflate our egos. This is exclusion as *domination*, spread all over the globe in more or less diffuse forms, but most glaring in the caste system in India and former Apartheid policies in South Africa.[65]

A third form of exclusion is becoming increasingly prevalent not only in the way the rich of the West and North relate to the poor of the rest of the world,[66] but also in the manner in which suburbs relate to inner cities, or the jet-setting "creators of high value" relate to the rabble beneath them. It is exclusion as *abandonment*. Like the priest and the Levite in the story of the Good Samaritan, we simply cross to the other side and pass by, minding our own business (Luke 10:31). If others neither have goods we want nor can perform services we need, we make sure that they are at a safe distance and close ourselves off from them so that their emaciated and tortured bodies can make no inordinate claims on us.

Most of the exclusionary practices would either not work at all or would work much less smoothly if it were not for the fact that they are supported by exclusionary language and cognition. Before excluding others from our social world we drive them out, as it were, from our symbolic world. Commenting in *The Conquest of America* on the Spaniards' genocide against Native Americans, Tzvetan Todorov writes:

> The desire for wealth and the impulse to master—certainly these two forms of aspiration to power motivate the Spaniards' conduct; but this conduct is also conditioned by their notion of the Indians as inferior beings, halfway between men and beasts. Without this essential premise, the destruction could not have taken place.[67]

With somewhat more nuance than on the shores of the New World in the sixteenth century, the pattern of debasement is being repeated today all around the globe.

---

64. William Faulkner, *Intruder in the Dust* (New York: Random House, 1948), 18, 22.

65. Even where explicit and public exclusion is forbidden by formal rules, implicit and private exclusion still continues, often in the form of unconscious but nonetheless effectual aversion. Iris Marion Young, *Justice and the Politics of Difference* (Princeton: Princeton University Press, 1990), 130ff.

66. Elsa Tamez, *The Amnesty of Grace: Justification by Faith from a Latin American Perspective*, transl. Sharon H. Ringe (Nashville: Abingdon, 1993), 37ff.

67. Tzvetan Todorov, *The Conquest of America: The Question of the Other*, transl. Richard Howard (New York: HarperCollins, 1984), 146.

With a flood of "dysphemisms,"[68] others are dehumanized in order that they can be discriminated against, dominated, driven out, or destroyed. If they are outsiders, they are "dirty," "lazy," and "morally unreliable"; if women, they are "sluts" and "bitches"; if minorities, they are "parasites," "vermin," and "pernicious bacilli."[69] In a sense, the danger of "dysphemisms" is underplayed when one claims, as Zygmunt Bauman does, that these labels take the other outside "the class of objects of potential moral responsibility."[70] More insidiously, they insert the other into the universe of moral obligations in such a way that not only does exclusion become justified but also mandatory because not to exclude appears morally culpable. The rhetoric of the other's inhumanity *obliges* the self to practice inhumanity. Tutsis are *agents corrupteurs* and therefore they *ought* to be destroyed; women are "irrational" and therefore they *ought* to be controlled.

If indeed exclusionary language and cognition—we may call this "symbolic exclusion"—serve morally to underwrite the practice of exclusion, we should be warned against tracing them back to "ignorance," against seeing in it "a failure of knowledge," "obtuseness," or "a poverty of imagination."[71] Evil as ignorance presupposes too much false innocence and generates too many vain hopes. It implies that the corruption of the evildoers is, at the bottom, a noetic stance that needs only proper enlightenment to be overcome. Both the Christian tradition and experience tell us that this is rarely the case. Symbolic exclusion is often a distortion of the other, not simply ignorance about the other; it is a willful misconstruction, not mere failure of knowledge. We demonize and bestialize not because we do not know better but because we *refuse* to know what is manifest and *choose* to know what serves our interests. That we nevertheless believe our distortions to be plain verities is no counterargument; it only underlines that evil is capable of generating an ideational environment in which it can thrive unrecognized.

The "practice of exclusion" and the "language of exclusion" go hand in hand with a whole array of *emotional* responses to the other, ranging from hatred to indifference; these exclusions both call forth emotional

68. Dwight Bollinger, *Language—The Loaded Weapon* (White Plains: Longman, 1980).

69. Herbert Hirsch, *Genocide and the Politics of Memory: Studying Death to Preserve Life* (Chapel Hill: The University of North Carolina Press, 1995), 97–108.

70. Zygmunt Bauman, *Postmodern Ethics* (Oxford: Blackwell, 1993), 167.

71. Andrew Delbanco, *The Death of Satan: How Americans Have Lost the Sense of Evil* (New York: Farrar, Straus and Giroux, 1995), 232.

responses and are sustained by them. Before Itzaak Rabin was murdered in 1995, right-wing Israeli demonstrators carried large posters on which he was portrayed like Yasser Arafat, with a *kefijeh* on his head and blood dripping from his hands. The image was generated in hate and designed to generate *hate*, that revulsion for the other that feeds on the sense of harm or wrong suffered and is fueled by the humiliation of not having been able to prevent it.[72] Some of the most brutal acts of exclusion depend on hatred, and if the common history of persons and communities does not contain enough reasons to hate, masters of exclusion will rewrite the histories and fabricate injuries in order to manufacture hatreds.

Strangely enough, the havoc wreaked by *indifference* may be even "greater than that brought by felt, lived, practiced hatred."[73] In *Modernity and the Holocaust*, Zygmunt Bauman notes that mass destruction of Jews "was accompanied not by the uproar of emotions, but the dead silence of unconcern."[74] Especially within a large-scale setting, where the other lives at a distance, indifference can be deadlier than hate. Whereas the fire of hatred flares up in the proximity of the other and then dies down, cold indifference can be sustained over time, especially in contemporary societies. A "system"—a political, economic, or cultural system—insinuates itself between myself and the other. If the other is excluded, it is the system that is doing the excluding, a system in which I participate because I must survive and against which I do not rebel because it cannot be changed. I turn my eyes away (or I zoom in with a camera at some exotic exemplar of suffering, which amounts to turning the eyes away because it both satisfies my perverse desire to see suffering and appeases my conscience for having turned the heart away from the sufferer). I go about my own business. Numbed by the apparent ineluctability of exclusion taking place outside of my will though with my collaboration, I start to view horror and my implication in it as normalcy. I reason: the road from Jerusalem to Jericho will always be littered by people beaten and left half-dead; I can pass—I *must* pass—by each without much concern. The indifference that made the prophecy, takes care also of its fulfillment.

Why do we hate others or turn our eyes from them? Why do we assault them with the rhetoric of inhumanity? Why do we seek to eliminate, dominate, or simply abandon them to their own fate? Sometimes the

---

72. Arne Johan Vetlesen, *Perception, Empathy, and Judgment: An Inquiry into the Preconditions of Moral Performance* (University Park: The Pennsylvania State University Press, 1994), 252ff.

73. Ibid., 252.

74. Zygmunt Bauman, *Modernity and the Holocaust* (Ithaca, NY: Cornell University Press, 1989), 74.

dehumanization and consequent mistreatment of others are a projection of our own individual or collective hatred of ourselves; we persecute others because we are uncomfortable with strangeness within ourselves.[75] Others become scapegoats, concocted from our own shadows as repositories for our sins and weaknesses so we can relish the illusion of our purity and strength.[76]

We exclude also because we are uncomfortable with anything that blurs accepted boundaries, disturbs our identities, and disarranges our symbolic cultural maps.[77] Others strike us like objects that are "out of place," like "dirt" that needs to be removed in order to restore the sense of propriety to our world. In Bauman's words, others then become

> the gathering point for the risks and fears which accompany cognitive spacing. They epitomize the chaos which all social spacing aims staunchly yet vainly to replace with order, and the unreliability of the rules in which the hopes of replacement have been invested.[78]

We assimilate or eject strangers in order to ward off the perceived threat of chaotic waters rushing in.

Both of these accounts of exclusion are important because they help explain why blacks could be lynched just because they were blacks, and Jews persecuted just because they were Jews. Yet neither account will suffice. We exclude not simply because we like the way *things are* (stable identities outside) or because we hate the way *we are* (shadows of our own identity), but because we desire *what others have*. More often than not, we exclude because in a world of scarce resources and contested power we want to secure possessions and wrest the power from others. In *A Different Mirror*, Ronald Takaki points out that the demonization and deportation of the indigenous population in North America "occurred within the economic context of competition over land."[79]

The fate of the indigenous population at the hands of the colonizers is not unique; it is the extreme example of a stable pattern. Centuries ago, the prophet Isaiah announced judgment against those who dispossess and drive out others so that they alone can be the masters of the land (5:8):

---

75. Julia Kristeva, *Fremde sind wir uns selbst,* transl. Xenia Rajewsky (Frankfurt: Suhrkamp, 1990).

76. Volkan, *The Need to Have Enemies and Allies.*

77. Mary Douglas, *Purity and Danger: An Analysis of the Concepts of Pollution and Taboo* (London: Routledge, 1966).

78. Bauman, *Postmodern Ethics*, 162.

79. Ronald Takaki, *A Different Mirror: A History of Multicultural America* (Boston: Little, Brown, 1993), 39.

Ah, you who join house to house,
    who add field to field,
until there is room for no one but you,
    and you are left alone in the midst of the land!

We exclude because we want to be at the center and be there alone, single-handedly controlling "the land." To achieve such "hegemonic centrality," we add conquest to conquest and possession to possession. We colonize the life-space of others and drive them out. We penetrate in order to exclude, and we exclude in order to control—if possible everything, alone.

The need to control and the discomfort with internal and external "dirt" go a long way in explaining the practice of exclusion. Yet even after the explanations are given, the "why" question keeps stubbornly resurfacing. Why do we want to control everything alone instead of sharing our possessions and power, and making space for others in a common household? Why do others strike us as "dirt" rather than "ornament"? Why cannot we accept our shadows so as to be able to embrace others instead of projecting our own unwanted evil onto them? Ultimately, no answer to these questions is available, just as no answer is available to the question about the origin of evil. From the outset, the answer was lost in the intractable labyrinth of "the heart's desire that stiffens the will against all competing considerations."[80]

Contrived Innocence

A descent into the conflict-ridden underworld of evil reveals a strange but persistent anomaly. If we listen to what its inhabitants tell us about their enemies, we are overwhelmed by the ugliness and magnitude of wickedness. If we let these same enemies talk about themselves, however, the ugliness mutates into beauty and the wickedness into innocence; the magnitude remains the same. The clashing perspectives give rise to a glaring incongruity: in a world so manifestly drenched with evil, everybody is innocent in their own eyes. Those who do accept the blame hasten to mount equal or greater blame on the shoulders of others. And since in the twisted arithmetic of sin, blame on the one side and blame on the other do not add up but cancel each other out, acceptance of blame morphs

---

80. Plantinga, *Not the Way It's Supposed to Be*, 62.

into a clandestine proclamation of innocence. Yet all know and all agree that somebody must be guilty; somebody's eyes must be deceiving them badly. But whose eyes? The eyes of the perpetrators? Of the victims? Of both, I want to argue, and in addition declare a "third party" complicit in the generation of contrived innocence, that chimerical goodness of the self that is largely the flip side of the evil it projects onto others.

"It is well established that perpetrators rarely take responsibility for their acts; they deny their offenses," writes Sharon Lamb in *The Trouble with Blame*.[81] When confronted with the wrongdoing committed, perpetrators either respond with outright denial ("I didn't do it!") or offer excuses, such as insisting on the impossibility of having done otherwise ("I couldn't help it!"), or explaining away the evil of what they have done ("She asked for it!"). At times apologies even transmute perpetrators into victims: it is *the perpetrator* who is defending himself and protecting his vital interests against the clever, cruel, and malicious aggressor ("He's a wolf in sheep's clothing"; "I am a sheep in wolf's clothing").[82] Confirming over and again the age-old theological wisdom that at the heart of sin lies "the persistent refusal to *tolerate* a sense of sin,"[83] perpetrators tirelessly generate their own innocence, and do so by the double strategy of denying the wrongdoing and reinterpreting the moral significance of their actions. This double strategy is a fertile ground for ideologies by which systems and nations seek to mask the violence and oppression they perpetrate. And this same double denial is the stuff out of which the peculiar blend of fraud and self-deception is concocted, by which individuals seek to evade being held responsible for evildoing.

No one will dispute that the perpetrators are guilty; they are guilty by definition. But what about the victims? Are not *they* innocent? No doubt, many a person has been violated at no fault of his or her own. Yet even if they are not to be blamed for the violation suffered, should we call them innocent? Let us assume that they *were* innocent before they were violated. Will they remain innocent after the act? Will they stay innocent as they are drawn into a conflict and as the conflict gathers in momentum? Some heroic souls might, but will the rest? Moreover, rather than entering conflicts at their inception, people often find themselves sucked into a long history of wrongdoing in which yesterday's victims are today's perpetrators

---

81. Sharon Lamb, *The Trouble with Blame: Victims, Perpetrators, and Responsibility* (Cambridge: Harvard University Press, 1996), 57.

82. Vetlesen, *Perception, Empathy, and Judgment*, 256.

83. Plantinga, *Not the Way It's Supposed to Be*, 99.

and today's perpetrators tomorrow's victims. Is there innocence within such a history? With the horns of small and large social groups locked, will not the "innocent" be cast aside and proclaimed "guilty" precisely because they seek to be "innocent"? The fiercer the battle gets the more it is governed by the rule: "Whoever is not fighting with you is struggling against you." Can victims sustain innocence in a world of violence?

In *The Fall to Violence*, Marjorie Suchocki argues that there is "an intertwining of victim and violator through the very nature of violation."[84] The violence ensnares the psyche of the victim, propels its action in the form of defensive reaction, and—robs it of innocence. She writes, "To break the world cleanly into victims and violators ignores the depths of each person's participation in cultural sin. There simply are no innocents."[85] By denying the reality of absolute innocence, Suchocki is clearly not suggesting that we should blame the victim for being victimized. Instead, she is drawing attention to one of the most insidious aspects of the practice of evil. In addition to inflicting harm, the practice of evil keeps recreating a world without innocence. Evil generates new evil as evildoers fashion victims in their own ugly image.

We are uneasy about denying innocence to victims. If nothing else, it offends our sense of propriety: the burden of guilt should not be added to the heavy load of suffering. Nietzsche's portrayals of the seamy side of the "weak" and "underprivileged" strike us as heartless and insulting. Consider what he wrote about "failures" and "victims" in *The Genealogy of Morals*:

> In the marshy soil of such self-contempt every poisonous plant will grow, yet all of it so paltry, so stealthy, so dishonest, so sickly-sweet! Here the worms of vindictiveness and *arriere-pensee* teem, the air stinks of secretiveness and pent-up emotion; here a perennial net of malicious conspiracy is wove....And what dissimulation, in order not to betray that this is hatred! What display of grand attitudes and grandiose words![86]

Itself an outgrowth of self-contempt, Nietzsche's disdain for the "weak" is deeply un-Christian, as un-Christian as anything that the great "Anti-Christ" ever wrote. Yet is there not a strange honesty in his insulting

---

84. Suchocki, *The Fall to Violence*, 147.
85. Ibid., 149.
86. Friedrich Nietzsche, *The Birth of Tragedy and The Genealogy of Morals*, transl. Francis Golffing (Garden City: Doubleday, 1956), 259.

caricatures of the "weak"—of most of us when victimized or systematically denied our rights? Nothing suggests the innocence of the victims
except our deep desire for the wronged person not to be in the wrong, and
the victims' own tenuous sense of innocence sustained by the erroneous
supposition that the sin from which they suffer is a peculiar vice of their
oppressors.[87]

From a distance, the world may appear neatly divided into guilty perpetrators and innocent victims. The closer we get, however, the more the
line between the guilty and the innocent blurs and we see an intractable
maze of small and large hatreds, dishonesties, manipulations, and brutalities, each reinforcing the other. The more attentive we are, the more accu-
rate the portrait the Apostle Paul paints of humanity—of "all" from which
"no one" is exempt (Rom 3:9, 20)—strikes us. Echoing the words of the
psalmist, Paul strips down the pretenses of innocence and discloses people
whose throats are "open graves" and whose tongues "deceive," whose lips
hide "the venom of vipers" and whose mouths are "full of cunning and
bitterness," whose feet are "swift to shed blood" and in whose path is "ruin
and misery" (Rom 3:9ff.). Intertwined through the wrongdoing committed and suffered, the victim and violator are bound in the tragic and self-
perpetuating solidarity of sin. "All have sinned and fall short of the glory
of God," concludes the Apostle Paul after he has given the inventory of
sins (Rom 3:21). The "Rite of Reconciliation" (1996) of the South African Council of Churches has boldly made the doctrine of solidarity in sin
its own. After quoting 1 John 1:8, "If we say we have no sin, we deceive
ourselves, and the truth is not in us," the Rite goes on to name and confess
concrete sins of both the white perpetrators and the black victims.[88]

"Solidarity in sin" is disturbing because it seems to erase distinctions
and unite precisely where the differences and disjunctions matter the
most—where dignity is denied, justice is trampled underfoot, and blood
is spilled. Solidarity in sin seems to imply *equality of sins*, and the equality
of sins lets the perpetrators off the hook. The world of equal sins is a world
designed by the perpetrators. The logic is simple: if all sins are equal, then

87. Niebuhr, *The Nature and Destiny of Man*, 1:226. To the two above explanations of the tendency
to consider victims as innocent, one can add the temptation to commit what Merold Westphal (*Suspicion
and Faith: The Religious Uses of Modern Atheism* [Grand Rapids: Eerdmans, 1993], 230) calls "the Fonda
Fallacy," to entertain the expectation that "if one side was evil, the other side must be good" (so named
in honor of Jane Fonda's famous trip to Hanoi, undertaken with the persuasion that the manifest evils of
the American and South Vietnamese governments are good enough reason to canonize Ho Chi Minh).

88. Brigalia Hlophe Bam, ed., *Rite of Reconciliation* (Johannesburg: South African Council of
Churches, 1996), 2f.

the action of the perpetrator is no worse than the reaction of the victim; all are perpetrators and all are victims, all are equally evil—and perpetrators can walk away from the crime scene free to repeat the deed with impunity. But does solidarity in sin imply *equality of sins*?

Reinhold Niebuhr, who in the twentieth century contributed the most to a reaffirmation of the doctrine of sin, thought so; all distinctions between sins "should disappear at the ultimate religious level of judgment," he argued in *The Nature and Destiny of Man*.[89] He sought, however, to balance the equality of sins with the inequality of guilt.[90] If one affirms the equality of sins, then such a balancing-act is necessary. But why assert equality of sins in the first place? From "All are sinners" *it does not follow* that "All sins are equal";[91] from "Neither is innocent" one cannot conclude "The sins of both are equal." The aggressors' destruction of a village and the refugees' looting of a truck (and thereby hurting their fellow refugees) are equally sin, but they are *not* equal sins; the rapist's violation and the woman's hatred are equally sin, but they are manifestly *not* equal sins. The equality of sins dissolves all concrete sins in an ocean of undifferentiated sinfulness. This is precisely what the prophets and Jesus did not do. Their judgments were not general but specific. They did not condemn everyone and anyone but the mighty and the ruthless who oppress the weak and crush the needy. The sin of driving a person from his or her possession, from his or her work, from his or her means of livelihood, or the sin of pushing him or her to the margins of society and beyond, weighs high on their scales. How could there be general solidarity in *this* sin? The perpetrators are the sinners and the victims are the sinned against, their noninnocence notwithstanding.

Neither perpetrators nor victims are innocent, I have argued; in his or her own way, each is a transgressor. Could not the "third party"—either as onlookers or activists—be the best candidate for innocence? Possibly. But *are* they innocent? Do they stand on some neutral territory, suspended above the agonistic world of noninnocence, surveying the struggle and then getting involved as appropriate? Are they not, rather, immersed in that same larger world inhabited by the parties in conflict? They themselves are perpetrators and victims, often both at the same time, and they

---

89. Niebuhr, *The Nature and Destiny of Man*, 1:220.
90. Ibid., 221ff.
91. William John Wolf, "Reinhold Niebuhr's Doctrine of Man," *Reinhold Niebuhr: His Religious, Social, and Political Thought*, ed. C. W. Kegley and R. W. Bretall (New York: Macmillan, 1956), 240.

project their own struggles, interests, and expectations onto the conflict they either observe or try to resolve.

The tendency of the parties in conflict to see themselves as innocent and the others as guilty matches the tendency of the third party to see the one party as good and the other as evil. As Sharon Lamb puts it, those standing on the sidelines want to "see victims as absolutely pure and perpetrators as absolutely evil."[92] Or they may invert the roles: the victim is ultimately responsible and the perpetrator is in fact a victim. The tendency to set the morally pure over against the morally corrupt is understandable. We need morally clear narratives to underwrite morally responsible engagement. Yet the very act of mapping the world of noninnocence into the exclusive categories of "pure" versus "corrupt" entails corruption; "pure" and "corrupt" are constructs that often misconstrue the other. The reason is not simply the lack of adequate information about the parties in conflict. The deeper reason is that every construction of innocence and guilt partakes in the corruption of the one undertaking the construction because every attempt to escape noninnocence is already ensnared by noninnocence. Just as there is no absolute standpoint from which relative human beings can make absolute judgments, so also there is no "pure" space from which corrupt human beings can make pure judgments about purity and corruption.

Occasionally, the protagonists refuse to let themselves be inserted into the moral world constructed around the stark polarity of "corruption" and "purity." The "third party" tends then to withdraw in disgust; it locks up both protagonists into the murky world of noninnocence and abandons them to the consequence of their own irredeemable evil. This abandonment too is an expression of noninnocence. For one, it tends to rest on a misconstruction of the others who were not "accommodating" enough to fit preconceived moral polarities. More important, the abandonment flows from disdain for those whom we feel justified in excluding from our concern on account of their immoral behavior. Such "pious" disdain for the evildoers in the name of "goodness" is every bit as un-Christian as Nietzsche's "godless" disdain for the weak in the name of "strength." Withdrawal of concern from *any* human being is culpable. Both the moral mapping of the world into exclusive categories of "pure" and "corrupt," and disdain for what we have deemed as corrupt grow out of noninnocence.

---

92. Lamb, *The Trouble with Blame*, 88f.

There is no escape from noninnocence, either for perpetrators or for victims or for a "third party." Pristine purity is irretrievable; it can be regained neither by going back to the beginnings, nor by plunging into the depths, nor by leaping forward into the future. Every person's heart is blemished with sin; every ideal and project is infected with corruption; every ascription of guilt and innocence is saddled with noninnocence. This, I think, is what the doctrine of original sin teaches. In the wake of modernity's belief in progress, the doctrine was progressively dismantled. As Bernhard-Henri Lévy rightly argued,[93] the stubborn shadows of modernity, produced in part precisely by modernity's blind optimism, call for a judicious retrieval of the doctrine of original sin.

Where does the "no innocence" perspective leave us? Gazing paralyzed at a world in which "fair is foul and foul is fair"? Listlessly withdrawn from a world in which no improvement is possible, because every action is a shot in the dark? What gain does recognition of solidarity in sin bring? In addition to freeing us "from delusions about the perfectibility of ourselves and our institutions,"[94] it pricks the balloons of the self-righteousness of perpetrator and victim alike and protects all from perpetuating evil in the name of presumed goodness. Solidarity in sin underscores that no salvation can be expected from an approach that rests fundamentally on the moral assignment of blame and innocence.[95] The question cannot be how to locate "innocence" either on the intellectual or social map and work our way toward it. Rather, the question is how to live with integrity and bring healing to a world of inescapable noninnocence that often parades as its opposite. The answer: in the name of the one truly innocent victim and what he stood for, the crucified Messiah of God, we should demask as inescapably sinful the world constructed around exclusive moral polarities—here, on our side, "the just," "the pure," "the innocent," "the true," "the good," and there, on the other side, "the unjust," "the corrupt," "the guilty," "the liars," "the evil"—and then seek to transform the world in which justice and injustice, goodness and evil, innocence and guilt, purity and corruption, truth and deception crisscross and intersect, guided by the recognition that *the economy of undeserved grace has primacy over the*

---

93. Lévy, *Gefährliche Reinheit*, 91f., 199ff.

94. Walter Wink, *Engaging the Powers* (Minneapolis: Fortress, 1992), 71.

95. In his *Systematic Theology* (transl. Geoffrey W. Bromiley [Grand Rapids: Eerdmans, 1991], 2:238), Wolfhart Pannenberg rightly underscored the anti-moralistic function of the doctrine of the universality of sin.

economy of moral deserts.[96] Under the conditions of pervasive noninnocence, the work of reconciliation should proceed under the assumption that, though the behavior of a person may be judged as deplorable, even demonic, *no one should ever be excluded from the will to embrace* because, at the deepest level, the relationship to others does not rest on their moral performance and therefore cannot be undone by the lack of it.

Elaine Pagels concluded *The Origin of Satan* with the claim that "within Christian tradition" there is the struggle "between the profoundly human view that 'otherness' is evil and the words of Jesus that reconciliation is divine."[97] I do not wish to dispute this claim, at least not with respect to the Christian tradition as a whole. I want to suggest, however, that instead of locating a fault line between the claim that some people are "children of hell" (Matt 23:15) and the demand to "love your enemies" (Matt 5:44) as Pagels does,[98] it is more fruitful to ask why the claim and the demand surface together in one and the same gospel and why similar statements coexist throughout the New Testament. The answer, I hope, would be that at the core of the Christian faith lies the persuasion that the "others" need not be perceived as innocent in order to be loved, but ought to be embraced *even when they are perceived as wrongdoers*. As I read it, the story of the cross is about God who desires to embrace precisely the "sons and daughters of hell." "Since all have sinned," argued Apostle Paul, "they are now justified by his [God's] grace as a gift through the redemption that is in Jesus Christ" (Rom 3:23-24). Reflection on social issues rooted in the cross of Christ will have to explore what this interdependence of the "universality of sin" and the "primacy of grace" may mean when taken out of the realm of "salvation" into the realm where we—many of us "children of hell"—fight and wage wars against each other (see Chapters IV–VII).

The Power of Exclusion

In *The Killing of Sarajevo*, a soldier in the Serbian army says to his best friend living in Sarajevo, the city which was, even as they spoke, being pounded with Serbian shells: "There is no choice. There are no innocents."[99]

---

96. In *God the Spirit* (transl. John F. Hoffmeyer [Minneapolis: Fortress, 1994], 48), Michael Welker has rightly critiqued the social moralism "that confuses God's reality with the constitution of a moral market."

97. Elaine Pagels, *The Origin of Satan* (New York: Random House, 1995), 184.

98. Ibid., xvii, 182f.

99. Željko Vuković, *Ubijanje Sarajeva (The Killing of Sarajevo)* (Beograd: Kron, 1993), 41.

The two claims seem inseparable: since there is "no choice"—since, as the same friend will later say, it is "either us or them"—there can be "no innocents," and since there are "no innocents" there must have been "no choice." Though it has a ring of truth, the logic is faulty. Within the vast expanse of noninnocence whose frontiers recede with the horizon, there *are* choices to be made, important choices about justice and oppression, truth and deception, violence and nonviolence, about the will to embrace or to exclude, ultimately choices about life and death. The "no choice" world in which people's behavior is *determined* by social environments and past victimizations is *not* the world we inhabit; it is a world the *perpetrators would like* us to inhabit because it grants an advance absolution for any wrongdoing they desire to commit. Suspicion is called for when, from behind a smoking howitzer, we hear the words, "There is no choice."

As it is undeniable that "there *is* choice," so it is also undeniable that our choices are made under inner and outer constraints, pressures, and captivities. We choose evil; but evil also "chooses" us and exerts its terrible power over us. Consider an admittedly extreme example—the war in former Yugoslavia. (Massacres in Rwanda [1994] and even the Los Angeles riots [1992] could illustrate my point as well.) *Eruption* seems the right word to describe it. I am referring less to the suddenness by which it broke out than to its insuppressible power. Nobody seemed in control. Granted, the big and strategic moves that started the war and kept it going were all carefully calculated and made in the centers of intellectual, political, and military power. But apart from all this, there seemed to be an insatiable appetite for brutality among ordinary people. Once the war started and the right conditions were maintained, an uncontrollable chain reaction was underway.[100] These were mostly decent people, as decent as most of us tend to be. Many did not, strictly speaking, *choose* to plunder and burn, rape and torture, or secretly enjoy these. A dormant beast in them was awakened from its uneasy slumber. And not only in them. The motives of those who set to fight against the brutal aggressors were self-defense and justice. The beast in others, however, enraged the beast in them. The moral barriers holding it in check broke down and it went after revenge. In resisting evil, they were trapped by evil. In "After the Catastrophe," written right after World War II, Carl Gustav Jung wrote, "It is a fact that cannot

---

100. On the eve of World War II, Carl Gustav Jung wrote: "The impressive thing about the German phenomenon is that one man, who is obviously 'possessed,' has infected a whole nation to such an extent that everything is set in motion and has started rolling on its course towards perdition." "Wotan," *Collected Works of C. G. Jung*, ed. H. Read et al. (New York: Pantheon Books, 1964), 185.

be denied: the wickedness of others becomes our own wickedness because it kindles something evil in our own hearts."[101] Evil engenders evil, and like pyroclastic debris from the mouth of a volcano, it erupts out of aggressor and victim alike.

In *Engaging the Powers*, Walter Wink accesses the problem of the power of evil by looking at what he calls the "Powers" and their perversion into the "Domination System."[102] The Powers, he claims, are neither simply human institutions and structures nor an order of angelic (or demonic) beings. They are both institutional and spiritual; they "possess an outer, physical manifestation...and an inner spirituality or corporate culture."[103] The Powers are essentially good, but when they become "hell-bent on control," Wink claims, they degenerate into the Domination System. This system itself is neither only institutional nor spiritual; rather the "forces of this present darkness" (Eph 6:2) are the interiority of warped institutions, structures, and systems that oppress people.

Leaving aside here whether Wink correctly interprets the biblical language of "the Powers," he rightly points to a complex transpersonal and systemic reality of evil that dominates, ensnares, and lures persons to dominate others. I will modify his terminology and substitute "Exclusion" for his "Domination," for as a rule the purpose of domination is to exclude others from scarce goods, whether they are economic, social, or psychological. I will keep, however, his key idea: the power of evil imposes itself so irresistibly through the operation of a transpersonal "system" that is both "institutional" and "spiritual." Caught in the system of exclusion as if in some invisible snare, people behave according to its perverted logic.

How does the system work? Consider first what might be called the "background cacophony of evil." It permeates institutions, communities, nations, whole epochs, and it is sustained, as Marjorie Suchocki puts it, by "a multiply nuanced and mirrored and repeated intentionality of purpose that exercises its corporate influence."[104] This is the low-intensity evil of the way "things work" or the way "things simply are," the exclusionary vapors of institutional or communal cultures under which many suffer but for which no one is responsible and about which all complain but no one can target. This all-pervasive low-intensity evil rejuvenates itself by

---

101. Carl Gustav Jung, "After the Catastrophe," *Collected Works of C. G. Jung*, ed. H. Read et al. (New York: Pantheon Books, 1964), 198.

102. Wink, *Engaging the Powers*, 33–104.

103. Walter Wink, "All Will Be Redeemed," *The Other Side* 28 (Nov–Dec 1992): 17.

104. Suchocki, *The Fall to Violence*, 122.

engendering belief in its own immortality and imposes itself by generating a sense of its own ineluctability.

In extraordinary situations and under extraordinary directors, certain themes from the "background cacophony" are picked up, orchestrated into a bellicose musical, and played up. "Historians"—national, communal, or personal interpreters of the past—trumpet the double theme of the former glory and past victimization; "economists" join in with the accounts of present exploitation and great economic potentials; "political scientists" add the theme of the growing imbalance of power, of steadily giving ground, of losing control over what is rightfully ours; "cultural anthropologists" bring in the dangers of the loss of identity and extol the singular value of our personal or cultural gifts, capable of genuinely enriching the outside world; "politicians" pick up all four themes and weave them into a high-pitched aria about the threats to vital interests posed by the other who is therefore the very incarnation of evil; finally the "priests" enter in a solemn procession and accompany all this with a soothing background chant that offers to any whose consciences may have been bothered the assurance that God is on our side and that our enemy is the enemy of God and therefore an adversary of everything that is true, good, and beautiful.

As this bellicose musical with reinforcing themes is broadcast through the media, resonances are created with the background cacophony of evil that permeates the culture of a community, and the community finds itself singing the music and marching to its tune. To refuse to sing and march, to protest the madness of the spectacle, appears irrational and irresponsible, naïve and cowardly, treacherous toward one's own and dangerously sentimental toward the evil enemy. The stage for "ethnic cleansing" and similar "eruptions" of evil—personal as well as communal—is set. The first shot only needs to be fired, and the chain reaction will start.

Now rewind the film of the events that led to the setting of the stage and cut if off early, well before the eruption has taken place. Forget that you know the end, leave the place from which you can observe sinister directors at work, and—walk into the segment at its beginning. What do you see? Faith in oneself is generated by the tales of historical glory and plausible explanations of past failures; hope in the future is born, a future in which we will no longer suffer injustice and discrimination, a future underwritten by the unfailing promises of our god. "Faith" and "hope" mobilize energies and we start performing economic miracles and doing major cultural

84

accomplishments. A sense of belonging and of being somebody in the world replaces aimless drifting and self-denigration. Undeniably, a veritable renaissance—national, communal, or personal—is underway! Yet all this indisputable good is created by and channeled toward an inhumane and godless project! In the bosom of this manifest well-being there is an unrecognized corruption!

It has been often pointed out that the power of evil rests on the power of "imperial speaking," the power by which evildoers seek to create an illusion that "all is well"[105] when in fact all is anything but well; ruin is about to take place (cf. Jer 6:13-15; Ezek 13:8-16). But why do people believe the evildoers, we may wonder? Why do they believe "the mendacious spirit of a community, of a people, which determines public opinion," to quote Michael Welker?[106] Because they have been blinded by an "evil spirit"? This is part of the answer. The other, more important part is that evil is capable not only of creating an illusion of well-being but also of *shaping reality* in such a way that the lie about "well-being" appears as plain verity. Much of the power of evil lies in *the perverse truth it tells about the warped well-being it creates.* To such a real sense of well-being of nonetheless deeply sick persons Jesus was referring when he said, "those who are well have no need of a physician" (Mark 2:17). The *truth* about their *sense* of well-being holds them captive to the lie about their illness.[107]

Why this discrepancy between feeling well and being sick? Why are we such docile, even enthusiastic captives to the system of exclusion? Why is there so little need for surveillance and force? Why are the subtle disciplinary mechanisms so effective, to use a phrase of Michel Foucault?[108] Because our very selves have been shaped by the climate of evil in which we live. Evil has insinuated itself into our very souls and rules over us from the very citadel erected to guard us against it.

In Romans 7:14-20 Paul speaks of the inability of human beings to do the good they want, and of their slavery to doing the evil they do not want. The self is split into the weaker self that knows and wants the good, and the stronger self dominated by sin, which does the evil. A person is then capable of willing but not of doing what is right. Our deepest tragedy

---

105. Dale Aukerman, *Reckoning with Apocalypse: Terminal Politics and Christian Hope* (New York: Crossroad, 1993), 53.

106. Welker, *God the Spirit*, 85.

107. Ibid., 112ff.

108. Maurice Blanchot, *Michel Foucault*, transl. Barbara Wahlster (Tübingen: Edition Diskord, 1987), 38; Michel Foucault, *Discipline and Punish.*

in the face of evil is, however, that too often, contrary to the fictive Seneca of Steven Lukes's *The Curious Enlightenment of Professor Caritat*, we "want to want what we want" precisely when what we want is evil.[109] A particular evil not only "inhabits" us so that we do what we hate (Rom 7:15); it has colonized us to such a thoroughgoing extent that there seems to be no moral space left within the self in which it could occur to us to hate what we want because it is evil.[110] We are ensnared by evil not only with full consent but also without a thought of dissent and without a sigh for deliverance. With the inner workings of our will in its hold, evil can dispense with force and rule by lure. And so, paradoxically, we feel free only in the prison house of unrecognized evil.

Why have we not offered a more spirited resistance to the colonizer? Why do we let him capture the citadel of our wills? If we refused and resisted, we would subvert the power of evil enshrined in the system of exclusion. Even if evil vapors of cultures can enter the self and even if the structures—institutions, communities, nations—are more sinful than the individuals that comprise them,[111] the system needs persons to make it "breathe" with the spirit of evil. If people acquiesce, it is not because they are *forced* to acquiesce but because there is something in the texture of their selves that resonates with the logic of exclusion.

One reason proposed for such resonances is anxiety about our mortality.[112] But as Suchocki has pointed out, young people are capable of the most brutal acts of violence without a thought of mortality.[113] Instead, she proposes that anxiety stems from the more fundamental propensity toward violence.[114] But why violence? She explains it by calling attention to the innate aggressiveness (or assertiveness) necessary in the struggle for survival. But the question is why assertiveness mutates into violence. In his *Systematic Theology*, Wolfhart Pannenberg has suggested looking

109. Steven Lukes, *The Curious Enlightenment of Professor Caritat: A Comedy of Ideas* (London: Verso, 1995), 238.

110. In the present section I am not offering a description of a general phenomenon of sin and its power (as Paul does in Romans 7), rather, reflecting on the power of the concrete manifestations of evil. Hence, I am not suggesting that the particular evil that has come to inhabit the self cannot be diagnosed at all, except from the perspective of faith (say through the opening of the eyes by the Holy Spirit), but rather that it often cannot be perceived by those whose self is shaped by that particular evil. A third party may perceive this evil for what it is.

111. Reinhold Niebuhr, *Moral Man and Immoral Society: A Study in Ethics and Politics* (New York: Scribner's, 1960).

112. Jürgen Moltmann, *The Coming of God: Christian Eschatology*, transl. Margaret Kohl (Minneapolis: Fortress, 1996), 112f.

113. Suchocki, *The Fall to Violence*, 83f.

114. Ibid., 82–99.

for the root of sin in the desire for identity—the instinctive will to be oneself—that is written into the very structure of our selves.[115] Though essentially healthy, the will to be oneself carries within it the germ of its own illness. Pannenberg describes the germ as the tendency of the self "in fact [to] become the infinite basis and reference point for all objects, thus usurping the place of God."[116] He is right about the desire for identity, though I think the problem sets in long before the self starts entertaining thoughts of "infinity" and "totality" (unless one mistakenly sees in *every* transgression of a boundary an implicit reaching for infinity).

The formation and negotiation of identity always entails the drawing of boundaries, the setting of the self as distinct from the other. As Gillian Rose puts it in *Love's Work*, "a soul that is unbound is as mad as one with cemented borders."[117] The slippage into sinful exclusion takes place already in the process of "putting boundaries around the soul" without which a self is unthinkable, and not only at the point where the self insists on being "the whole of reality" and on using "everything" only as a means of asserting itself, as Pannenberg claims in *Anthropology*.[118] For exclusion to happen, it suffices for the self simply to strive to guard the integrity of its territory, while granting the others—especially the distant others—the full right to do whatever they please with the rest of the universe. The drawing and maintaining of boundaries requires assertiveness. In an environment of scarce goods inhabited by a plurality of actors whose lives are intertwined, the assertiveness of one confronts the assertiveness of the other, and therefore the one becomes a perceived or real threat to the other. Mostly, the threat is not so much to the life of the other as to his or her boundaries and therefore also to his or her inner organization of the self.[119] This is the point at which the healthy assertiveness of the self often slides into violence toward the other.

The tendency toward violence is, moreover, reinforced by an inescapable ambiguity of the self. The self is dialogically constructed. The other is already from the outset part of the self. I am who I am in relation to the other; to be Croat is, among other things, to have Serbs as neighbors; to be white in the United States is to enter a whole history of relation to African Americans (even if you are a recent immigrant). Hence the will to

---

115. Pannenberg, *Systematic Theology*, 2:260f.

116. Ibid., 261.

117. Gillian Rose, *Love's Work: A Reckoning with Life* (New York: Schocken, 1996), 105.

118. Pannenberg, *Systematic Theology*, 85.

119. Wilfried Härle, *Dogmatik* (Berlin: Walter de Gruyter, 1995), 469f.

be oneself, if it is to be healthy, must entail the will to let the other inhabit the self; the other must be part of who I am as I will to be myself. As a result, a tension between the self and the other is built into the very desire for identity: the other over against whom I must assert myself is the same other who must remain part of myself if I am to be myself. But the other is often not the way I want him or her to be (say, he or she is aggressive or simply more gifted) and is pushing me to become the self that I do not want to be (suffering his or her incursions or my own inferiority). And yet I must integrate the other into my own will to be myself. Hence I slip into violence: instead of reconfiguring myself to make space for the other, I seek to reshape the other into who I want him or her to be in order that in relation to the other I may be who I want to be.

Threats to the organization of the self by the other as well as the antipodal nature of the will to be oneself explain why slippage into exclusion is so easy, even if it is *not* given with the very nature of our humanity.[120] The separation necessary to constitute and maintain a dynamic identity of the self in relation to the other slides into exclusion that seeks to affirm identity at the expense of the other. The power of sin from without—the system of exclusion—thrives on both the power and the powerlessness from within, the irresistible power of the will to be oneself, and the powerlessness to resist the slippage into exclusion of the other. The desire for identity could also explain why so many people let themselves be sinned against so passively—why they let themselves be excluded. It is not simply because they may lack a sufficiently strong will to be themselves, but because one can satisfy the will to be oneself *by surrendering to the other*. Their problem is not so much exclusion of the other from their will to be oneself, but a paradoxical exclusion of their *own* self from the will to be oneself—what feminist theologians call "diffusion of the self."[121] As a rule, exclusion of the self from the will to be oneself comes about as a result of acts of exclusion that we suffer. Hence it is not so much sin as it is an evil that cries for remedy. The exclusion of the self from the will to be oneself not only damages the self but also makes the slippage into exclusion on the part of the other and therefore further damaging of the self so much easier.

120. Christoph Gestrich, *Die Wiederkehr des Glanzes in der Welt: Die christliche Lehre von der Sünde und ihrer Vergebung in gegenwärtiger Verantwortung* (Tübingen: J. C. B. Mohr [Paul Siebeck], 1989), 74f.
121. Valerie Saiving, "The Human Situation: A Feminine View," *Womanspirit Rising: A Feminist Reader in Religion*, ed. Carol A. Christ and Judith Plaskow (San Francisco: Harper, 1979), 37f.

Sandwiched between the system of exclusion and the exclusionary tendencies of the self, are we doomed to despair? How can the exodus from the "house of slavery" into the promised land take place when Pharaoh's horses and chariots are on *both sides* of the Red Sea? Indeed, how can it take place when we ourselves *are* Pharaohs ruling in the land of exclusion, from which we should be liberated? Ultimately, the hope for a new exodus lies exactly where the hope of the first exodus was: in the "strong wind" of God (Exod 14:21). Central to the Christian faith is the belief that the Spirit of the crucified Messiah is capable of creating the promised land out of the very territory the Pharaoh has beleaguered. The Spirit enters the citadel of the self, decenters the self by fashioning it in the image of the self-giving Christ, and frees its will so it can resist the power of exclusion in the power of the Spirit of embrace. It is in the citadel of the fragile self that the new world of embrace is first created (2 Cor 5:17). It is by this seemingly powerless power of the Spirit—the Spirit who blows even outside the walls of the church—that selves are freed from powerlessness in order to fight the system of exclusion everywhere—in the structures, in the culture, and in the self.

Cain's Assault

No other biblical text describes better the anatomy, dynamics, and power of exclusion than the story of Cain and Abel (Gen 4:1-16). On the surface it is a narrative about one brother killing the other. But Cain can be taken to allude to the Kenites, the descendants of Cain and Israel's southern neighbors. The story of Cain and Abel is then not only an example of rivalry between two brothers, but it narrates the structure of encounter between "them" and "us"—the Kenites who were unwilling to accept a special grace that the Israelites have received from God, as manifest in the blessings of King David's rule.[122]

If, as seems likely, "Cain" alludes to the Kenites, the story could easily function as a self-congratulating narrative of proud neighbors at the height of their glory seeking to incriminate others: the difficult nomadic life of the Kenites in the arid southern plain is a sign of God's judgment for wrongs they have committed against innocent Israel. Yet, as Walter Dietrich has argued, the point of the story is precisely to undermine

---

122. Thomas Willi, "Der Ort von Genesis 4:1-16 innerhalb der althebräischen Geschichtschreibung," *Isaac Leo Seeligmann Volume: Essays on the Bible and the Ancient World*, ed. Alexander Rofé and Yair Zakovitch (Jerusalem: E. Rubenstein's, 1983).

self-congratulation.[123] This is not a free-floating parable that "we" can tell about our relationship to "them" and thereby portray ourselves as "Abel" and cast them into the image of "Cain." The story is located within primal history. As Claus Westermann has argued, the intention of primeval history is to underscore that *every human being* is potentially Cain and Abel, just as every human being is Adam and Eve.[124] Cain's envy and murder do not prefigure how "they" (the Kenites or, in classical Christian interpretation, the Jews) behave in distinction to "us" (Israel or the church), but how *all human beings* tend to behave toward others.

In *Things Hidden Since the Foundation of the World*, René Girard suggested that the full significance of the story emerges when we recognize that, unlike the typical mythological texts, which take the perspective of the perpetrators in order to legitimize their deeds, the story of Cain and Abel takes the perspective of the victim and condemns the perpetrator.[125] Girard is right, though his way of putting things misses one of the most important dimensions of the story. For within primeval history, the story about a murderous "them" is a story about a murderous "us." Cain is "them," *and* Cain is "us"; "Cain" is all the sons and daughters of Adam and Eve in relation to their brothers and sisters. The story takes the perspective of the victim not only to condemn the perpetrator, as Girard claims, but at the same time to contravene the tendency of the victim to turn into perpetrator. Its greatness lies precisely in that it *combines* a clear judgment against the perpetrator with the commitment to protect him from the rage of the "innocent" victim. God both relentlessly questions and condemns Cain (4:6-12) and graciously places a protective mark upon him (4:15).

Formally, Cain and Abel are equals. They are two brothers, born of the same parents; they engage in two equally respectable occupations, the complementary vocations of a keeper of sheep and a tiller of the ground; they offer two equally appropriate sacrifices to God, animal offering and fruit offering. The equality of the brothers is underscored even by a literary

---

123. Walter Dietrich, "'Wo ist dein Bruder?' Zu Tradition und Intention von Genesis 4," *Beiträge zur Alttestamentlichen Theologie: Festschrift für Walter Zimmerli zum 70. Geburtstag,* ed. Herbert Donner et al. (Göttingen: Vandenhoeck & Ruprecht, 1977).

124. Claus Westermann, *Genesis 1–11: A Commentary,* transl. John J. Scullion (Minneapolis: Augsburg, 1984), 318.

125. René Girard, *Things Hidden Since the Foundation of the World,* transl. S. Bann and M. Metteer (Stanford: Stanford University Press, 1987), 146f.

device: in 4:2-5 the names of the two alternate four times: Abel, Cain, Cain, Abel, Abel, Cain. The effect is that neither takes center stage.[126]

Yet the formal equality of the two hides as well as heightens an inequality that defines their relation from the outset. The mother greeted the birth of the first son with a proud and joyous exclamation, "I have produced a man with the help of the Lord" (4:1) and inscribed her exuberance in the name of her firstborn: Cain, the name of honor, which means "to produce," "to bring forth." The birth of the second was a matter of course and he received a name whose meaning marked him as inferior: Abel, "breath," "vapor," "sheer transience," "worthlessness," "nothingness." The occupations of both were equally respectable, but Cain was a rich farmer, a big landowner, whereas Abel was a poor man with just enough infertile land to keep a small flock.[127] Each brought an equally acceptable form of offering to God, but the "great" Cain offered simply "the fruit of the ground" (4:3) whereas the poor Abel (keenly aware of his dependence on God?) brought the best parts ("fat portions") of the best animals ("oldest offspring" CEB) (4:4).[128] Appropriately, God noted the difference, and had regard for Abel's offering but not for Cain's (vv. 4-5). Before God both could have easily been equal (divine regard for the one in no way excludes regard for the other). Yet precisely there the most profound inequality between them emerged. God's recognition of *this* inequality inverted the "order of inequalities" between Cain and Abel that Eve and Cain have established: *Abel* (not just his offering) was regarded by God, Cain was not (4:4-5). Cain's reaction to this divine inversion makes up the heart of the story.

The initial problem of the story is the formal equality and common belonging (brothers with complementary vocations) in relation to the

126. Ellen van Wolde, "The Story of Cain and Abel: A Narrative Study," *Journal for the Study of the Old Testament* 52 (1991): 29.

127. So suggests Professor Hartmut Gese of the University of Tübingen in an unpublished transcript of his lectures on Genesis.

128. Together with many contemporary scholars (Pinchas Lapide, *Von Kain bis Judas: Ungewohnte Einsichten zu Sünde und Schuld* [Gütersloh: Gütersloher Verlagshaus], 1994), 12; Gordan J. Wenham, *Genesis 1–15.* Word Biblical Commentary, Vol. 1. [Waco: Word Books, 1987], 103; Willi, "Der Ort von Genesis 4:1-16 ," 101), I follow the older commentators, both Jewish and Christian (see Heb 11:4; 1 John 3:12), who consider the mention of "firstlings" and "fat portions" in Abel's offering significant (V. Aptowitzer, *Kain und Abel in der Agada, den Apokryphen, der hellenistischen, christlichen und muhammedanischen Literatur* [Wien: R. Löwit, 1922], 37ff.). The difference in the kind of relation to God suggested by Abel's offering of the best of his flock explains the otherwise inexplicable behavior of God, who, as the righteous judge, cannot simply capriciously have regard for Abel and his offering but not for Cain and his offering (Gen 4:4-5). To trace the inequality between Cain and Abel in the "inexplicable" action of God toward them (Westermann, *Genesis 1-11,* 297) rightly underscores the "inexplicability" of inequality—this is the way life simply is—but locates the inexplicability wrongly in the choice of God.

inescapable difference of being first and second, rich and poor, honored and despised, regarded and disregarded. From the outset, all human relations are fraught with the tension between equality and difference in the context of which the relation between the self and the other has to be negotiated. Outside God's Garden, rivalry sets in that drives the protagonists even farther "east of Eden" (3:24; 4:16). Since human work is threatened with failure, since value tags are inescapably placed on differences, and since recognition can be given or withheld by the ultimate judge, the self will engage in a struggle as it seeks to maintain its identity and attempts to assert itself at the expense of the other. This tendency opens the gate to the land of exclusion, a place in which exclusions are perpetrated and the excluding ones themselves live excluded—"banished"[129]—"from the presence," though never from the continued care of God (v. 16).

First came envy that Abel, who was clearly "nobody," should be regarded, and he, Cain, who is clearly "somebody," should be disregarded—and that by God whose judgment is incontrovertible. Then came anger, that "passionate againstness,"[130] directed both at God and Abel. It is directed against God not because God dealt unfairly with Cain,[131] but because it was precisely *justice* that slighted Cain's greatness. It is directed against Abel not because Abel was to be faulted—though there is a non-innocent way of being innocent, as Joaquin Monegro of Miguel de Unamuno's "Abel Sanchez" points out[132]—but because Abel's offering *was* truly acceptable, whereas Cain's was not. Cain was confronted with God's measure of what truly matters and what is truly great. Since he could not change the measure and refused to change himself, he excluded both God and Abel from his life. Anger was the first link in a chain of exclusions. Instead of looking up toward God, his countenance "fell" in a breach of communion with God (4:5); instead of listening to God, he turned a deaf ear to God's warning (4:6-7); by proposing to "go out to the field" he banished the community from exercising judgment over his act (4:8); finally, he performed the ultimate act of exclusion by "rising up against his brother Abel" and murdering him (4:8).

129. J. J. Rabinowitz, "The Susa Tablets, the Bible, and the Aramaic Papyri," *Vetus Testamentum* 11 (1961): 56.

130. Plantinga, *Not the Way It's Supposed to Be*, 165.

131. Westermann, *Genesis 1–11*, 297.

132. Miguel de Unamuno, *Abel Sanchez and Other Stories*, transl. Anthony Kerrigan (Chicago: Henry Regnery Company, 1956), 58f.

Cain's act of murder has been described as "meaningless."[133] It was not; murders rarely are. It was governed by a faultless logic, provided Cain's premises were right. Premise 1: "If Abel is who God declared him to be, then I am not who I understand myself to be." Premise 2: "I am who I understand myself to be." Premise 3: "I cannot change God's declaration about Abel." Conclusion: "Therefore Abel cannot continue to be." Cain's identity was constructed from the start in relation to Abel; he was great in relation to Abel's "nothingness." When God pronounced Abel "better," Cain either had to readjust radically his identity, or eliminate Abel. The act of exclusion has its own "good reasons." The power of sin rests less on the insuppressible urge of an affect than on the persuasiveness of the good reasons, generated by a perverted self in order to maintain its own false identity. Of course, these reasons are persuasive only to the self. God would not have been convinced, which is why Cain keeps silent when God asks, "Why are you angry?" (v. 6). To God Cain would have had to give the answer that contained no reasons, the same answer that the much more evil protagonist of Thomas Harris's *The Silence of the Lambs* tried to persuade Officer Starling to accept as the explanation of his own horrible crimes: I am angry "because I am evil."[134]

Cain is impervious to God's warning against giving in to anger. The logic of sin proves stronger than the injunction to do good. This is exactly what we should expect, for the logic of sin was originally designed for the very purpose of overcoming the obligation to do good. The knowledge of sin is impotent in the face of sin. Like a dangerous animal, sin is "lurking," "prowling," "desiring" to attack and destroy;[135] to protect oneself, one must not simply know of the animal, but set out to "master" it (v. 7), as Cain's failure to do so suggests. Hence even the knowledge that the knowledge of sin cannot overcome sin does not suffice. As a lawgiver and counselor only, God was impotent. Sin is not so much a failure of knowledge as a misdirection of will, which generates its own counter-knowledge. In an important sense, Cain alone was capable of overcoming sin. And yet it would be a mistake to think that he "freely chose" to sin, unconstrained by anything but the freedom of

---

133. Erich Zenger, "'Das Blut deines Bruders schreit zu mir' (Gen 4:10): Gestalt und Aussageabsicht der Erzählung von Kain und Abel," *Kain und Abel-Rivalität und Brudermord in der Geschichte des Menschen*, ed. Dietmar Bader (München: Schnell & Steiner, 1983), 17.

134. Thomas Harris, *The Silence of the Lambs* (New York: St. Martin's, 1988), 21.

135. Victor P. Hamilton, *The Book of Genesis: Chapters 1–17*, NICOT (Grand Rapids: Eerdmans, 1990), 227.

his own will. To commit sin is not simply to make a wrong choice but to succumb to an evil power. Before the crime, Cain was both a potential prey and a potential master of a predator called "sin"; Cain murdered, because he fell prey to what he refused to master.

The will to sin provides not only "good reasons" for the act, but also creates the conditions under which the act would remain undetected and, if detected, the blame could be evaded. First, there is the *geography* of sin. The crime scene is "the field" outside the public sphere (4:8), where no help can be procured, no witnesses are available, and no communal judgment can be passed. It may be that "the face facing a face" is "shot through with a moment of commitment," as Arne Vetlesen argues, echoing Emmanuel Levinas.[136] But a face facing the face that has wronged it in a deserted place, is shot through with the ultimate temptation; "now is your chance" eclipses "thou shalt not kill," written on the face of the other.[137] The preferred geography of sin is "the outside," where the wrongdoing can happen unnoticed and unhindered.

Second, there is the *ideology* of sin. Cain responds to the divine question, "Where is your brother Abel?" with a lie, "I do not know" (4:9). He implicitly denies the crime. Then he adds that, not being his "brother's keeper" (v. 9), he is not responsible for knowing where his brother is. To top it off, the comment about not being his "brother's keeper" is a subtle attempt to ridicule the question in order to deflect its challenge: "Does the keeper (of sheep) need a keeper?"[138] The ideology of sin functions to deny both the act and the responsibility for it, preferably with a touch of humor. Yet the "ideology of sin" is rarely simply an instrument of evasion, designed to silence the outside voice that accuses; perpetrators employ it also as an instrument of self-deception to hush the conscience inside.

In a way, the consequences of the murder correspond to the murder itself. By his crime, Cain has robbed himself not only of a brother but also of the possibility of belonging.[139] The land soaked with fraternal blood is inhospitable and no longer yields fruit (4:12); he has killed, and now he may be killed (4:14); he refused to look up to God (4:6), and now he is hidden from God's face (4:14). By his own act of exclusion he excluded himself from all relationships—from the land below, from God

---

136. Vetlesen, *Perception, Empathy, and Judgment*, 202.

137. Emmanuel Lévinas, *Ethics and Infinity*, transl. Richard A. Cohen (Pittsburg: Duquesne University Press, 1985), 87, 89.

138. Wenham, *Genesis 1–15*, 106.

139. Zenger, "'Das Blut deines Bruders schreit zu mir,'" 19.

above, from the people around. No belonging is possible, only distance. The distance here does not mark a lifestyle of an ordinary nomad, but denotes sheer transcendence ("wanderer") and anxious fugitation ("fugitive"). Why this rabbity vagrancy, we may ask? Why banishment into the land of unpredictability and fear, governed by the practice of exclusion that verges on chaos? Because belonging is home, and home is brother, who is no more.

To have a brother one must *be* a brother and "*keep*" a brother. Is there hope for Cain who had a brother but was not a brother[140] and who killed the brother he should have been "keeping"? In the story, the hope lies in God and God's insertion into Cain's affairs. God's insertion before the wrongdoing—"Why are you angry?" (4:6)—was ineffective; Cain turned away from God. The insertion did, however, underscore that though Cain may have had "good reasons" he had *no right* to be angry. After the wrongdoing, God's second insertion—"Where is your brother Abel?" (4:9)—did not seem to achieve much either; it elicited only self-justifying denial. But again, God's question made clear that life in community means sharing a common social space and taking responsibility for the other. God's third insertion was an angry word of judgment—"What have you done?" (4:10). Here we learn why God kept asking Cain questions. Yahweh, the God who hears the groans of the oppressed, saw the murder coming and warned against it; God, who attends to the harassed and brutalized, heard the innocent blood crying out and judged the perpetrator.

Divine judgment accomplished what divine questions did not; it elicited Cain's response. Commentators are divided on whether Cain complained about the weight of the sentence ("my punishment is greater than I can bear") or admitted the greatness of his transgression ("my iniquity is too great to be forgiven"), or did both. In any case, in addition to noting the danger of the chaotic land of exclusion to which he was consigned on account of his wrongdoing, Cain acknowledged his responsibility before God. God's fourth and final insertion was a response both to the acknowledgment of responsibility and to the weight of his punishment. In the land of exclusion, the "Lord put a mark on Cain," not to brand him as a perpetrator but to protect him as a potential victim.[141] The "mark" may symbolize a system of differentiation that protects from "mimetic

---

140. As Ellen van Wolde has pointed out, Abel is regularly called Cain's brother, whereas Cain is never called Abel's brother. Cain has a brother but is not a brother, whereas Abel is a brother but does not have a brother (van Wolde, "The Story of Cain and Abel," 33, 36).

141. Lapide, *Von Kain bis Judas*, 14.

violence" of all against all, as Girard has suggested.[142] But more important than differentiation is the *grace* that undergirds it. The same God who did not regard Cain's scanty offering, bestowed kindness upon the murderer whose life was in danger. God did not abandon Cain to the cycle of exclusions he himself has set in motion. Labeled by the mark of God, Cain belonged to God and was protected by God even as he settled away "from the presence of the Lord" (4:16).

We leave Cain protected in primeval history; on Good Friday we will find him redeemed. Cain, the one who acted out the exact opposite of an embrace, whose body went "forth totally against the other body in an intention to...kill it,"[143] will be drawn near and embraced by the Crucified. Will the embrace of the Crucified heal Cain of envy, hatred, and the desire to kill? In de Unamuno's "Abel Sanchez," Joaquín Monegro tells his wife Antonia, a saint, that she could not cure him because he did not love her (de Unamuno 1956, 175). In a sense, the same can be said of every Cain: the embrace of the Crucified will not heal him if he does not learn to love the one who embraced him. Cain, the anti-type who "murdered his brother," will be healed by Christ, the type "who laid down his life for us," only if he sets out to walk in Christ's footsteps (cf. 1 John 3:11-17).

---

142. Girard, *Things Hidden Since the Foundation of the World*, 146.
143. Z. D., Gurevitch, "The Embrace: On the Element of Non-Distance in Human Relations," *The Sociological Quarterly* 31, no. 2 (1990): 199.

CHAPTER IV
Embrace

A man who left Sarajevo before the war in 1992 and joined the Serbian army that was shelling the city said in the course of a phone conversation to his best friend, who had remained and whose apartment was destroyed by a shell: "There is no choice. Either us or them."[1] He meant, "Either we will inhabit this place or they will; either we will destroy them or they will destroy us; no other option is available."

In all wars, whether large or small, whether carried out on battlefields, city streets, living rooms, or faculty lounges, we come across the same basic exclusionary polarity: "us against them," "their gain—our loss," "either us or them." The stronger the conflict, the more the rich texture of the social world disappears and the stark exclusionary polarity emerges around which all thought and practice aligns itself. No other choice seems available, no neutrality possible, and therefore no innocence sustainable. If one does not exit that whole social world, one gets sucked into its horrid polarity. Tragically enough, over time the polarity has a macabre way of mutating into its very opposite—into "both us and them" that unites the divided parties in a perverse communion of mutual hate and mourning over the dead.

"There is no choice," says the man from Sarajevo echoing the inner logic of exclusionary polarities. But is he right? Is the inner logic of exclusionary polarities irresistible? There may indeed be situations in which "there is no choice," though we should not forget that to destroy the other rather than to be destroyed oneself *is itself a choice*. In most cases, however, the choice is not constrained by an inescapable "either

---

1. Željko Vuković, *Ubijanje Sarajeva* (Beograd: Kron, 1993), 42.

us or them." If there is will, courage, and imagination, the stark polarity can be overcome. Those caught in the vortex of mutual exclusion can resist its pull, rediscover their common belonging, and even fall into each other's arms. People with conflicting interests, clashing perspectives, and differing cultures *can* avoid sliding into the cycle of escalating violence and instead maintain bonds, even make their life together flourish. In the present chapter I will explore what it takes to overcome the polarity of "either us or them" and live as a community. I will examine the inter-related issues of how to make and sustain peace between the self and the other in a world threatened by enmity. In slightly different terms, I will seek to map a way of life under the threat of enmity, and use the meta-phor "embrace" to designate it.

The central thesis of the chapter is that God's reception of hostile hu-manity into divine communion is a model for how human beings should relate to the other. In four central sections I will explicate this thesis by analyzing "repentance," "forgiveness," "making space in oneself for the other," and "healing of memory" as essential moments in the movement from exclusion to embrace. Then I will describe the key structural ele-ments of a successful embrace. Finally, after elaborating on the political significance of embrace, I will end the chapter with a theological reflec-tion on the story of the Prodigal Son, a story of embrace (Luke 15:11-32). Before I introduce my subject by explaining why I think the typically modern and postmodern ways of construing social life around "freedom" are one-sided and therefore inadequate, I need to make one explanatory comment about the angle from which I approach the subject.

As I read Christian scripture, a good deal of its message is written from below, from the perspective of those who in some sense suffer at the hand of the mighty. The Hebrew prophets make the injustice endured by the "little people" into the primary lens through which they view the mighty, and in God's name they demand that the mighty mend their ways. The evangelists and the apostles instruct their marginalized fellow Christians how to relate to one another and to the inhospitable and hostile world as followers of the Crucified. I will try to follow this tradition, partly because I think this is what a Christian theologian ought to do and partly because I set out to work on this project in order to give an account to myself about how I, as a member of a people who has suffered brutal aggression, ought to react. Building primarily on the thought of the evangelists and apostles, in the present chapter I will speak mainly to those of us who see ourselves as "victims" about why it makes sense to imitate the self-giving love of the triune God in a world of enmity. Then in Chapters V and VI, I will have primarily the "perpetrators" in view: I will turn to the prophetic tradition calling for truth and justice, whose claims against deceivers and oppressors cannot be neglected if a lasting peace is to be won. In an important sense, however, my text is predicated on the belief that we do better not to make too much of the polarity between "victim" and "perpetrator." This undeniable and undeniably horrid polarity—the polarity that makes us wonder whether there can be a worse hell than the hell the perpetrators create for their victims—is best dealt with by practicing the self-giving modeled on the life of the triune God and engaging in the struggle for truth and justice in the context of that kind of love.

The Ambiguities of Liberation

In recent decades the dominant categories in theological reflection on social realities have been the correlative notions of "oppression" and "liberation." Those familiar with the theological scene associate them immediately with the various theologies of liberation. But also theologians who work with different methodologies and prefer to support more conservative social agendas operate at least tacitly with the same categories, though in a somewhat different manner. The categories were designed to ensure that human dignity is respected and justice for all upheld. For both dignity and justice are interpreted today in terms of freedom, that most potent social idea of the last three centuries.[2]

With the American and French Revolutions, the idea of freedom emerged as the pillar of modern liberal democracies. All people are equal and all are free to pursue their interests and develop their personalities in their own way, provided they respect the same freedom in others. Such freedom is inalienable; it is not conferred by others and cannot be taken away by them. Rather, if the exercise of freedom does not interfere with the freedom of other citizens, freedom must be respected, even if society at large finds the pursuits of its individual members repugnant. Freedom is the most sacred good. When this inalienable freedom is either denied by a totalitarian state or suppressed by a dominant culture we speak of

---

2. Charles Taylor, *Philosophy and the Human Sciences*, Philosophical Papers, vol. 2 (Cambridge: Cambridge University Press, 1985), 318ff.

oppression; when the cage that holds people back from doing and being what they prefer is dismantled, we speak of liberation.[3]

That is at least a rough sketch of how many Westerners (and an increasing number of non-Westerners) think of oppression and liberation.

There is another, presently more marginal, tradition of Western thinking about freedom. Initiated by socialist thinkers, it is particularly appealing today in the non-Western world. What can freedom to be my own master and pursue my interests mean, asks this tradition, if I can find no job to keep me and my family from starvation? What can freedom to develop my personality mean, if I have to work from dawn to dusk until the last drop of strength is squeezed out of me? The freedom either to be exploited or left alone to die of starvation? Hence socialist thinkers declared the liberal notion of freedom empty. They insisted that the concentration on the negative notion of freedom creates the kind of social dynamics that empties freedom of meaning. Freedom can therefore never mean simply the absence of external interference with the individual's will to do or not to do what she or he wants, as the Hobbesian tradition claims; freedom is actual power to live life with dignity, to be the artisan of one's own destiny. When people are kept in abject poverty and illiteracy while others grow rich and "develop their personalities" at the former's expense we speak of oppression; when structures and persons that perpetuate powerlessness are replaced by structures that allow people to stand on their own feet and have their own voice, we speak of liberation.[4]

Both liberal and socialist projects—the two major visions for organizing social life under the conditions of modernity—center on the idea of freedom. As Zygmunt Bauman observed in *Postmodern Ethics*,

> the Grand Idea at the heart of modern restlessness, [the] guiding lantern perched on the prow of modernity's ship, was the idea of emancipation: an idea which draws its meaning from what it negates and against which it rebels—from the shackles it wants to fracture, the wounds it wants to heal—and owes its allure to the promise of negation.[5]

---

3. In the essay "What Is Wrong with Negative Liberty," Charles Taylor has persuasively argued against the theory that "the modern notion of negative freedom which gives weight to the securing of each person's right to realize him/herself in his/her own way" cannot make do with the notion of freedom as the "absence of external obstacles" (ibid., 211ff.).

4. The two notions of freedom sketched here correspond roughly to the "negative" and "positive" freedoms as analyzed in Isaiah Berlin's famous essay, "Two Concepts of Liberty" (*Four Essays on Liberty* [London: Oxford University Press, 1969], 118–72).

5. Zygmunt Bauman, *Postmodern Ethics* (Oxford: Blackwell, 1993), 225.

The iron gates of social dungeons must be shattered; slaves must become their own masters. Every social project built around the notion of freedom tends therefore to operate with the stable pair of "oppression" and "liberation." Oppression is the negativity, liberation its negation, freedom the resulting positivity.

Try, however, to apply the categories of oppression and liberation to many concrete situations of conflict, such as in multiethnic states like former Yugoslavia or in multicultural metropolises like Los Angeles. In a way they fit all too well. They seem almost tailor-made for Croats, Muslims, and Serbs, for African Americans, Koreans, Latinos, and Anglos. If the plot is written around the schema of "oppressed" ("victims") and "oppressors" ("perpetrators"), each party will find good reasons for claiming the higher moral ground of a victim; each will perceive itself as oppressed by the other and all will see themselves as engaged in the struggle for liberation. The categories of oppression and liberation provide combat gear, not a pinstriped suit or a dinner dress; they are good for fighting, but not for negotiating or celebrating—at least not until the oppressors have been conquered and the prisoners set free.

One could object that if we placed ourselves above the immediate interests of the parties in conflict we would be able to tell who are the oppressed victims and who the oppressive victimizers. Would it not be perverse to argue that "oppressor" is but only the incriminating label that a self-styled victim likes to place on his or her enemy, or that "victim" is just the name a person who is as oppressive as anybody else likes to use in order to gain social advantage? Would not blurring the categories of "oppressed" and "oppressor" be a mockery of the millions who have suffered at the hands of the violent—battered women, exploited and dehumanized slaves, tortured dissidents, persecuted minorities? It certainly would. The categories cannot be given up. And yet the *schema* "oppression/liberation" remains beset with unresolved and deeply disturbing problems.

Leaving aside the paradoxical tendency of the language of victimization to undermine the operation of human agency and disempower victims,[6] and to imprison them within the narratives of their own victimization,[7] I want to underline two additional problems with the schema of "oppression/liberation." First, more often than not, conflicts are messy. Indeed, they are

---

6. Roberta C. Bondi, *To Pray and to Love* (Minneapolis: Fortress, 1991), 82; Jean Bethke Elshtain, *Democracy on Trial* (New York: BasicBooks, 1995), 50f.

7. Ellen Charry, "Literature as Scripture: Privileged Reading in Current Religious Reflection," *Soundings* 74, nos. 1–2 (1991): 65–99.

very messy. It is simply not the case that one can construe narratives of the encounter between parties in conflict as stories of manifest evil on the one side and indisputable good on the other. Is not too often Ephraim jealous of Judah and Judah hostile to Ephraim (Isa 11:13)? Do not people often "oppress each other, each one against the other, neighbor against neighbor" (Isa 3:5 CEB)? How will we disentangle those who are innocent from those who are blameworthy in the knotted histories of individuals, let alone the narratives of whole cultures and nations? The longer the conflict continues, the more both parties find themselves sucked into the vortex of mutually re-inforcing victimization, in which the one party appears more virtuous only because, being weaker, it has fewer opportunities to be cruel. If we organize our moral engagement around the categories of "oppression/liberation" we will need clear narratives of blame and innocence.[8] Failing to find a blame-less victim, however, we will be left with two equally unattractive choices: ei-ther to withdraw from engagement in moral disgust (and thereby give tacit support to the stronger party), or to impose clear-cut moral narratives with moral partisanship (and therefore share in the ideological self-deception of the one party).

But what about cases in which rights and wrongs are clearly inscribed in the common history of the parties in conflict (such as between the Nazis and the Jews during World War II)? Should we not grasp here for the cat-egories "oppression/liberation"? Is not the moral combat gear the categories provide precisely what we *need*? This brings me to the second problem with the categories of "oppression/liberation." What happens when, armed with the belief in the rightness of its own cause, one side wins? How will the lib-erated oppressed live with their conquered oppressors? "Liberation of the oppressors" is the answer that the "oppression/liberation" schema suggests. But is it persuasive? Does it not betray an ideological blindness because it fails to entertain the idea that when the victims become *liberators* it is they, and not only the oppressors, who might need to change? E. M. Cioran, this "aristocrat of doubt," perceptively noted the perverse fact that the great persecutors are often "recruited among the martyrs not quite beheaded."[9]

8. In its polemic against "Church Theology's" stress on "reconciliation" the *Kairos Document* under-lines that there are "conflicts in which one side is right and the other wrong"; "there are conflicts that can only be described as the struggle between justice and injustice, good and evil, God and the devil." I would certainly not dispute this. I wish only to illustrate the main point I am making. By arguing that the racial conflict in South Africa was a conflict between "good" and "evil," the *Kairos Document* underlines that such clear categorizations are necessary if the language of "oppression/liberation" is to make sense. Robert McAfee Brown, ed., *Kairos: Three Prophetic Challenges to the Church* (Grand Rapids: Eerdmans, 1990), 38.

9. E. M. Cioran, *A Short History of Decay*, transl. Richard Howard (London: Quartet Books, 1990), 4.

To put it somewhat more positively, liberators are known for not taking off
their soldiers' uniforms. "As history progresses," writes Bauman in *Life in
Fragments*,

> injustice tends to be compensated for by injustice-with-role-reversal.
> It is only the victors, as long as their victory stays unchallenged, who
> mistake, or misrepresent, that compensation as the triumph of justice.
> Superior morality is all too often the morality of the superior.[10]

The *categories* "oppression/liberation" seem ill-suited to bring about
reconciliation and sustain peace between people and people groups.
Though the categories themselves are indispensable, we must resist making "oppressed/oppressor" the overarching schema by which to align our
social engagement. As a consequence, we need to reject "freedom" as the
ultimate social goal.[11]

It could be argued that in some cases, reconciliation is not what is
needed, at least not *before* justice is done, as the *Kairos Document* has
insisted.[12] Though the argument has force, will we make progress toward
justice if the ultimate goal is not reconciliation? Is this not the basic insight that led to the formation of the Commission for Truth and Reconciliation after the Apartheid regime had been abolished?

The father of Latin American Liberation Theology, Gustavo Gutiérrez, was right to insist that love, not freedom, is ultimate. The "deepest
root of all servitude," he stressed in the introduction to the revised edition
of his *Theology of Liberation*, "is the breaking of friendship with God and
with other human beings, and therefore cannot be eradicated except by
the unmerited redemptive love of the Lord whom we receive by faith and
in communion with one another."[13] Similarly, for the grandfather of all
liberation theologies, Jürgen Moltmann, the ultimate goal of human beings is not the "kingdom of freedom." Rather, the kingdom of freedom is
a *process* toward the kingdom of God, which is the kingdom of *love*. As he
argued in *The Trinity and the Kingdom*, the freedom of the triune God is

---

10. Zygmunt Bauman, *Life in Fragments: Essays in Postmodern Morality* (Oxford: Blackwell, 1995),
183f.

11. Stanley Hauerwas, *After Christendom? How the Church Is to Behave If Freedom, Justice, and a Christian Nation Are Bad Ideas* (Nashville: Abingdon, 1991), 50ff.

12. Brown, *Kairos*, 38; see also Chapters IV and V below.

13. Gustavo Gutiérrez, *A Theology of Liberation: History, Politics, and Salvation*, 2nd ed., transl. Caridad Inda and John Eagleson (Maryknoll, NY: Orbis, 1988), xxxviii; Nicholas Wolterstorff, *Until Justice
and Peace Embrace* (Grand Rapids: Eerdmans, 1983), 51ff.

neither simply the absence of interference nor self-control but "vulnerable love."[14] It is no different with authentic human freedom. It consists in being a friend of God and partaking in the glory of the triune God who is nothing but pure love.[15]

To make love tower over freedom does not mean abandoning the *project* of liberation, however. The Holy One of Israel, the God of Jesus Christ, is on the side of the downtrodden and poor, a God who listens to the sighs of the voiceless and the cries of the powerless, a God who liberates. But to insist on the primacy of love over freedom means to transform the project of liberation, to liberate it from the tendency to ideologize relations of social actors and perpetuate their antagonisms. We need to insert the project of liberation into a larger framework of what I have called elsewhere "a theology of embrace."[16]

Adieu to the Grand Narratives

Was I not too impatient with the primacy of "freedom"? Could it not be that the culprit is not the primacy of freedom but the Grand Idea of Emancipation? Instead of calling into question the primacy of freedom, should we not critique the pursuit of *universal* emancipation? A chorus of postmodern thinkers, their dissonances notwithstanding, has sung intricate melodies that communicate this message.

Take, for example, Jean-François Lyotard's analysis and critique of modernity (though Michel Foucault or Gilles Deleuze could have served my purposes here as well). He writes:

> The thought and action of the nineteenth and twentieth centuries are governed by an Idea (in the Kantian sense): the Idea of emancipation. It is, of course, framed in quite different ways, depending on what we call the philosophies of history, the grand narratives that attempt to organize this mass of events: the Christian narrative of the redemption of original sin through love; the *Aufklärer* narrative of emancipation from ignorance and servitude through knowledge and egalitarianism; the speculative narrative of the realization of the universal idea through the dialectic of the concrete; the Marxist narrative of emancipation from

---

14. Jürgen Moltmann, *The Trinity and the Kingdom: The Doctrine of God*, transl. Margaret Kohl (San Francisco: HarperCollins 1981), 56.

15. Ibid., 219ff.

16. Miroslav Volf, "Exclusion and Embrace. Theological Reflections in the Wake of 'Ethnic Cleansing,'" *Journal of Ecumenical Studies* 29, no. 2 (1992): 230–48.

exploitation and alienation through the socialization of work; and the capitalist narrative of emancipation from poverty through technological development. Between these narratives there are grounds for litigation and even for difference. But in all of them, the givens arising from events are situated in the course of a history whose end, even if it remains beyond reach, is called universal freedom, the fulfillment of all humanity.[17]

Notice the function of the versions of the "grand idea" or the "grand narrative." It sets up freedom as the single goal of the universal history and then forces the multiple streams of history into the great river that flows toward that goal. For the Grand Idea, the promise of freedom is both the source of legitimation and the horizon of progress.[18]

If modernity feeds on the promise of freedom contained in "the grand narratives," postmodernity is defined by incredulity concerning such narratives.[19] First, every one of the grand narratives has failed. To take but two examples, the dominant grand narrative says that the market, if only left to operate without interference of well-intentioned but wrong-headed social reformers, will free humanity from poverty, but the growing millions of destitute prove the opposite; another grand narrative claims that all the proletarians were communists and all the communists were proletarians, but the tanks in Budapest (1956), Prague (1968), and Beijing (1989) prove the opposite. Second, the grand narratives speak of universal liberation, but they are all formulated from a particular standpoint. The declaration of human rights proclaims the universal ideal of citizenship, for instance, but is promulgated in the name of a particular cultural entity—"We, the French people…"[20]

The *universality* of grand narratives is the main reason for their failure, insists Lyotard. Cultures and subcultures—echoing Ludwig Wittgenstein, he calls them "language games"—are intrinsically plural, heterogeneous, incommensurable. The grand narratives seek to effect the final reconciliation between them and therefore suppress the richness of "language games"—the small narratives—and press them into a single mold. All such attempts "to totalize" language games into "real unity" are universalistic

17. Jean-François Lyotard, *The Postmodern Explained: Correspondence 1982–1985*, transl. Don Barry et al. (Minneapolis: University of Minnesota Press, 1993), 24f.

18. Ibid., 81f.

19. Jean-François Lyotard, *The Postmodern Condition: A Report on Knowledge*, transl. Geoff Bennington and Brian Massumi (Minneapolis: University of Minnesota Press, 1984), xxiv.

20. Lyotard, *The Postmodern Explained*, 31.

illusions whose terrible price is a reign of terror.[21] Instead of scripting grand narratives that feed the nostalgia for the reign of "the whole and the one," we need to guard the heterogeneity of language games: through the practice of "permanent dissent" we should ensure that every consensus remains fluid, never final and universal, always temporal and local.[22] "Let us wage a war on totality," writes Lyotard in *The Postmodern Condition*, "let us be witnesses to the unpresentable; let us activate the differences and save the honor of the name."[23]

When asked in the name of what we should wage the war on totality, Lyotard appeals to "justice"—a value, he claims, "that is neither outmoded nor suspect."[24] But does not justice overarch heterogeneous language games? we may protest. What happened to their principled incommensurability? Does not each language game have its own account of justice? Groping for a nonuniversal, nonconsensual idea of justice, Lyotard insists on "the recognition of the specificity and autonomy of the multiplicity and untranslatability of the entangled language games, the refusal to reduce them; with a rule, which nevertheless would be a general rule, 'let us play... and let us play in peace.' "[25] As we listen to the call to recognize the autonomy of heterogeneity, we hear the back door squeaking open, and what Lyotard has driven out through the front door is rushing back in. Is he not peddling something that looks very much like the Enlightenment's grand narrative of freedom under the label of nonuniversal justice?

At the end of *The Postmodern Condition*, Lyotard dreams of computer technology providing "free access to the memory and data banks," thus giving all players of language games "perfect information at any given moment."[26] Substitute "means of production" for "information" and Lyotard's project to create a public sphere for truly free discussion looks suspiciously like the "kingdom of freedom" of Karl Marx, that incorrigible

---

21. Lyotard, *The Postmodern Condition*, 81.

22. Lyotard suggests that he has learned the strategy of permanent dissent—or "para-logy"—from the way modern science functions; it theorizes "its own evolution as discontinuous, catastrophic, nonrectifiable, and paradoxical" (ibid., 60). The model of science would be that of a *permanent* revolution. Richard Rorty has rightly objected that "to say that 'science aims' at piling paralogy on paralogy is like saying that 'politics aims' at piling revolution on revolution. No inspection of the concern of contemporary science or contemporary politics could show anything of the sort." "Habermas and Lyotard on Post-modernity," *Praxis International* 4, no. 1 (1984): 33.

23. Lyotard, *The Postmodern Condition*, 81f.

24. Ibid., 66.

25. Jean-François Lyotard, *Das postmoderne Wissen,* transl. Otto Pfersmann (Bremen: Passagen Verlag, 1982), 131.

26. Lyotard, *The Postmodern Explained*, 67.

106

scripter of grand narratives.[27] Setting out to erase all grand narratives of emancipation, Lyotard ends up scripting an "anti-grand narrative" that looks like some combination of liberal and socialist projects.

We might not even mind this anomaly—inconsistency, strictly speaking, it is not[28]—were it not for more serious problems that beset Lyotard's idea of emancipation. Consider what happens when one tries to replace the modern schema of "oppression/liberation" with a postmodern model of incommensurable "language games." As Jürgen Habermas has argued, intersecting and sequential language games have the unfortunate characteristic that judgments of validity are not possible *between* them.[29] We are left with a pantheon of gods without hope of knowing how to decide between their competing claims because there are no criteria binding for all (though each god will be able to provide his or her own good *reasons* for engaging in the struggle). In the words of Richard Rorty, who agrees at this point with Lyotard, we can give "no 'theoretical' reason for moving in one social direction rather than another."[30]

Unable to settle their differences by reasoning, the gods will invariably fight. Given the incommensurability of language games we are not surprised to find Lyotard arguing that "to speak is to fight" and assigning speech acts to the "domain of a general agonistics."[31] He interprets, however, this struggle as "play," and places all plays under the general rule that they should be done "in peace."[32] The trouble is that children will not stay in their separate rooms; they play together and—fight. When the play gets serious, when one party breaks what the other party thinks are the rules of fair play and players are being carried off the field, would not continuing to play "in peace" amount to perpetuating injustice? How would the players who (from their perspective) suffered injustice be persuaded to continue playing "in peace"? Why *should* they be persuaded? Does not the peaceful play of differences end up with "big differences" swallowing up the "small differences"? Does not the call to "play in peace" come too close to the Nietzschean kind of affirmation of life, which is a paradise for

27. Albrecht Wellmer, "On the Dialectic of Modernism and Postmodernism," *Praxis International* 4, no. 4 (1984): 358.

28. It is possible to promote the same ends that are legitimized by the grand narratives of emancipation without a recourse to a grand narrative to legitimate these ends.

29. Jürgen Habermas, "The Entwinement of Myth and Enlightenment: Re-reading *Dialectic of Enlightenment*," *New German Critique* 26 (1982): 29.

30. Rorty, "Habermas and Lyotard on Post-modernity," 40.

31. Lyotard, *The Postmodern Condition*, 10.

32. Lyotard, *Das Postmoderne Wissen*, 131.

the strong but a hell for the weak, because it celebrates the way things are, which is to say the way the strong have made them to be?

Lyotard sets out to overcome the violence that the grand narratives do to small narratives but ends up with no resources to prevent the small and big dictators from doing violence to their many victims. "Perfect information at any given moment"[33] for every player is certainly not such a resource. For perfect information will forever remain an unattainable goal, and even if it were ever to be attained, there would remain a disparity between persons' capacity to employ such information to their advantage. Hence the struggle between the strong and the weak will remain, and in the absence of overarching criteria to apply to the struggle, the weak will remain the losers. Against Lyotard's will, a perverse kind of emancipation pops up its ugly head after he has deconstructed the grand narratives of emancipation: the emancipation of the powerful to oppress the powerless with impunity.

Lyotard, however, rightly debunks attempts at final reconciliation based on systematic totalization. The plurality of cultures and subcultures, the plurality of "power/discourse formations" and "language games," is irreducible. But this is not because the language games are in principle incommensurable, as he claims. They are not. Since social actors inhabit a common world, their language games are permeable and communication between them possible.[34] The *incommensurability* is not universal but always local, temporal, and partial, just as the commensurability is. No, what stands in the way of reconciliation is not some inherent incommensurability, but a more profoundly disturbing fact that along with new understandings and peace agreements new conflicts and disagreements are permanently generated.

The crucial question, therefore, is not how to accomplish the final reconciliation. That messianic problem ought not to be taken out of God's hands. The only thing worse than the failure of some modern grand narratives of emancipation would have been their success! Merely by trying to accomplish the messianic task, they have already done too much of the work of the antichrist. In demasking anti-messianic projects that offer universal salvation, Lyotard helps us ask the right kind of question, which is not how to achieve the final reconciliation, but *what resources we need to live in peace in the absence of the final reconciliation.*

33. Lyotard, *The Postmodern Condition*, 67.
34. Walter Reese-Schäfer, *Lyotard zur Einführung* (Wien: Junius Verlag, 1989), 96.

From the postmodern critique of emancipation ("Adieu to the Grand Narratives") we can learn that we must engage in the struggle against oppression, but renounce all attempts at the final reconciliation; otherwise, we will end up perpetuating oppression. From the limitations inherent in the projects of liberation ("The Ambiguities of Liberation") we can learn that the struggle against oppression must be guided by a vision of reconciliation between oppressed and oppressors; otherwise it will end in "injustice-with-role-reversal." Both the modern project of emancipation and its postmodern critique suggest that a *nonfinal reconciliation in the midst of the struggle against oppression* is what a responsible theology must be designed to facilitate. Anything else would amount to a seductive ideology of a false liberation that would prove most unhelpful precisely for those in whose name it has been promulgated and who need it the most.

If the *project* of final reconciliation is clearly mistaken, should then the *hope* for final reconciliation be given up? Is the "grand narrative" about the "great Supper of the Lamb" a dangerous illusion that feeds totalitarian dreams and therefore sustains totalitarian practice? But how could Christian faith live without such metaphors as "the kingdom of God," "the new creation," or "heaven"? And what else could such metaphors designate if not a universal and eternal peace and well-being—shalom—whose loss would provide the final proof that the shamelessly immodest "pretenses" of these metaphors were false? For Christian faith to give up the *hope* for the final reconciliation—for a reconciliation that can neither be surpassed nor undone—would mean to give itself up. Everything depends, however, on how we understand the final reconciliation and its implication for life in a world of enmity. I will offer here only three brief disclaimers. First, the final reconciliation is not a work of human beings but of the triune God. Second, it is not an apocalyptic end of the world but the eschatological new beginning of this world.[35] Third, the final reconciliation is not a self-enclosed "totality" because it rests on a God who is a perfect love. The hope for such "nontotalitarian" final reconciliation is the backdrop against which Christians engage in the struggle for peace under the conditions of enmity and oppression.

Drawing on the resources found in Jesus's proclamation of the reign of God, in his death on the cross, and in the character of the triune God, I will advocate here the struggle for *a nonfinal reconciliation based on a vision of*

---

35. Jürgen Moltmann, *The Coming of God: Christian Eschatology*, transl. Margaret Kohl (Minneapolis: Fortress, 1996), 11ff.

reconciliation that cannot be undone. I will argue that reconciliation with the other will succeed only if the self, guided by the narrative of the triune God, is ready to receive the other into itself and undertake a re-adjustment of its identity in light of the other's alterity. The idea of "re-adjustment" may suggest equal acceptability of all identities and a symmetry of power between them. But to assume such universal acceptability and symmetry as givens would be to fall captive to a pernicious ideology. I will therefore explore what it takes to struggle for nonfinal reconciliation by readjusting dynamic identities under the condition of pervasive inequality and manifest evil.

The Politics of the Pure Heart

One of the most distressing stories from the war in former Yugoslavia comes from a Muslim woman. Here is how she tells it:

> I am a Muslim, and I am thirty-five years old. To my second son who was just born, I gave the name "Jihad." So he would not forget the testament of his mother—revenge. The first time I put my baby at my breast I told him, "May this milk choke you if you forget." So be it. The Serbs taught me to hate. For the last two months there was nothing in me. No pain, no bitterness. Only hatred. I taught these children to love. I did. I am a teacher of literature. I was born in Ilijash and I almost died there. My student, Zoran, the only son of my neighbor, urinated into my mouth. As the bearded hooligans standing around laughed, he told me: "You are good for nothing else, you stinking Muslim woman...." I do not know whether I first heard the cry or felt the blow. My former colleague, a teacher of physics, was yelling like mad, "Ustasha, ustasha..." And kept hitting me. Wherever he could. I have become insensitive to pain. But my soul? It hurts. I taught them to love and all the while they were making preparations to destroy everything that is not of the Orthodox faith. Jihad—war. This is the only way....[36]

A Serbian journalist, Željko Vuković, from whose book *The Killing of Sarajevo* I take this story, comments: "How many mothers in Bosnia have sworn to teach their children hate and revenge! How many little Muslims, Serbs, and Croats will grow up listening to such stories and learning such lessons!"[37] How many children around the globe, we could continue to

36. Vuković, *Ubijanje Sarajeva*, 134.
37. Ibid.

ask, are growing up with "jihad," "war," "crusade," "revenge," "hatred" not only inscribed in their names but woven into the very fabric of their lives! For reconciliation to take place, the inscriptions of hatred must be carefully erased and the threads of violence gently removed. This, I think, is one important lesson of Jesus's proclamation of the reign of God. Let me explicate.

Though the addressees of Jesus's message were clearly not only the masses of the destitute and powerless who made up the lowest strata of Palestinian society, there is little doubt that most of them had good reasons to consider themselves the innocent "victims" of oppression.[38] Politically, the Palestinian population suffered under the loss of national sovereignty to the Romans, as well as under a tense relationship between the Jewish aristocracy, the Herodian monarchy, and the Roman occupying forces. Economically, the majority was caught between the Roman and the domestic elites, each competing with the other to expand its fortune, partly by exploiting large segments of the population by a burdensome, heavy taxation. Finally, with the political rule of the Romans came the pressure to assimilate to a foreign culture. The Jews, who rightfully boasted a long-standing and noble religious tradition and expected the future conversion of all Gentiles, must have resented profoundly the forced incursions of Hellenistic culture into their religious and cultural space. Dominated, taken advantage of, and threatened in their cultural identity, the majority of the inhabitants of Palestine were victimized, whether they belonged to the lower or middle classes.

Given the context of pervasive oppression, it is not surprising that Jesus's proclamation of God's kingdom found an extraordinary echo. Political, economic, and cultural frustrations and aspirations united to fill the concept of God's kingdom with extraordinary social potency. God will bring foreign occupiers and domestic elites down from their thrones; God will liberate the people from all oppression and make an end to every earthly rule. Dreams of a future in which God alone will rule in truth and justice were nourished by the hard realities of domination, exploitation, and cultural suppression. By making the "kingdom of God" the central feature of his message and "the poor" the main recipients of his good news,[39] Jesus gave an unmistakably political edge to his whole ministry.

---

38. Gerd Theissen, *Sociology of Early Palestinian Christianity*, transl. John Bowden (Philadelphia: Fortress, 1978), 31–76.

39. Joachim Jeremias, *New Testament Theology: The Proclamation of Jesus*, transl. John Bowden (New York: Scribners, 1971), 103–21.

111

How could his hearers have failed to register the political overtones of his programmatic sermon in which he asserted that the spirit of God has anointed him "to proclaim release to the prisoners and recovery of sight to the blind, to liberate the oppressed, and to proclaim the year of the Lord's favor" (Luke 4:18-19 CEB)!?

Truly surprising and new in Jesus's ministry, however, were neither the political overtones of his message nor the special interest he displayed toward "the poor." Such interest is precisely what we would expect from any half-witted political leader from the margins; to be a leader you need social power, to have social power you need a following, and to have a following you must take on the cause of the disgruntled, which in Jesus's case would have been the great majority at the bottom of the heap of society. But Jesus had no aspirations to political leadership[40] and he did more, much more, than what we would expect of a politician. No doubt, he kindled hope in the hearts of the oppressed and demanded radical change of the oppressors, as any social reformer would. But he also built into the very core of his "platform" the message of God's unconditional love and the people's need for repentance.[41] From the perspective of contemporary Western sensibilities, these two things together—divine love *and* human repentance—*addressed to the victims* represent the most surprising and, as political statements, the most outrageous and (at the same time) most hopeful aspects of Jesus's message.

What disturbs us, of course, is not the unconditional love, which we have come to expect, but the call to *repentance*.[42] Were Jesus simply demanding "a radical alteration of the course and direction of one's life, its basic motivations, attitudes, objectives,"[43] as repentance is sometimes described, we might not even object, though we would insist that he should have spared the unfortunate and challenged the mighty. But he demanded

---

40. Gerd Theissen, *The Shadow of the Galilean: The Quest for the Historical Jesus in Narrative Form*, transl. John Bowden (London: SCM Press, 1987), 95.

41. E. P. Sanders has argued that "repentance" was not part of Jesus's original proclamation but "must be read into" his message (*Jesus and Judaism* [Philadelphia: Fortress, 1985], 111). Bruce Chilton and J. I. H. McDonald responded that "penitent renunciation" is "implicit within a positive response to the Kingdom as supremely valuable" (*Jesus and the Ethics of the Kingdom* [Grand Rapids: Eerdmans, 1987], 41). My larger theological point about the significance of repentance does not depend, however, on the place of repentance in the preaching of the historical Jesus. Provided one can construe *the audience of the Gospels* as "oppressed," the same kinds of theological implications would follow from the later editorial insertion of repentance into the proclamation of Jesus.

42. The call to repentance has not disturbed Jesus's contemporaries as it disturbs us in the twenty-first century, since repentance was "an aspect of conventional theology of early Judaism" (McDonald, *Jesus and the Ethics of the Kingdom*, 41).

43. James D. G. Dunn, *Jesus' Call to Discipleship* (Cambridge: Cambridge University Press, 1992), 20.

more than a radical alteration. To repent means to make a turnabout of a profound moral and religious import. Repentance implies not merely a recognition that one has made a bad mistake but that one has *sinned*. Jesus stated explicitly that he came "to call not the righteous but sinners" (Mark 2:17) and the evangelists report that he was engaged in the practice of "forgiving sins" (Mark 2:5).

Jesus's claim that the kingdom belongs uniquely to the poor notwithstanding, his talk of them as sinners triggers in us an eruption of suspicion. Does he not have anything more comforting and constructive to say to "the poor" than to insult them by calling them sinners? How different is he from the "ascetic priest" of Nietzsche's *Genealogy of Morals*, who makes himself into a healer "of the sick flock" by poisoning their minds with the belief that they are to blame for their woes?[44] Would not the proper first step in healing *this* flock have been a resounding message that the flock *has been made* sick? Instead of calling sinners to repentance, should Jesus not have demasked the ideological construals of "the poor" as sinners and challenged the oppressive practices these construals served to legitimate?

Notice that Jesus did not fail to do precisely that: he lashed out against religious mechanisms, which produced sinners where there were none. His rejection of the laws of purity (Mark 7:1-23), for instance, "cuts to the heart of the sectarian classification into the righteous and sinner."[45] Symbolic boundaries drawn by false religious beliefs that ascribe sinfulness to what is innocent must come down, Jesus insisted. Moreover, he showed an extraordinary sensibility to the fact that people suffer not only because they commit sin but also because sin is committed against them. His programmatic sermon, for instance, mentions explicitly "captives" who need to be released (because they were *wrongly* incarcerated) and "oppressed" who need to be let go (because they were treated *unjustly*). He did not add to the sufferers' misery by burdening them with blame for their own suffering. To take up Nietzsche's terminology, Jesus was no cunning "ascetic priest" who exploited the misfortunes of others, but a prophet who denounced oppression and its ideological legitimations (cf. Matt 23). In a limited but important sense, the gospel Jesus proclaimed was good news for "the sinned-against."[46]

---

44. Friedrich Nietzsche, *The Birth of Tragedy and The Genealogy of Morals*, transl. Francis Golffing (Garden City: Doubleday, 1956), 262ff.

45. Dunn, *Jesus' Call to Discipleship*, 75.

46. Raymond Fung, "Good News to the Poor—A Case for a Missionary Movement," *Your Kingdom Come: Mission Perspectives* (Geneva: World Council of Churches, 1980), 85ff.

Yet Jesus called to repentance not simply those who falsely pronounced sinful what was innocent and sinned against their victims, but *the victims of oppression themselves*. It will not do to divide Jesus's listeners neatly into two groups and claim that for the oppressed repentance means new hope whereas for the oppressors it means radical change. Nothing suggests such a categorizing of people in Jesus's ministry, though different people ought to repent of different kinds of sins. The truly revolutionary character of Jesus's proclamation lies precisely in the *connection between the hope he gives to the oppressed and the radical change he requires of them*. Though some sins have been imputed to them, other sins of theirs were real; though they suffered at the sinful hand of others, they also committed sins of their own. It is above all to *them* that he offered divine forgiveness. Significantly enough, it is also they, not the self-righteous members of the establishment, that responded to his offer. For as a rule, the kingdom of God enters the world through the back door of servants' shacks, not through the main gate of the masters' mansions.

Why does the call to repentance include the oppressed (in addition to the oppressors who are incomparably greater transgressors)? Why the talk of *their* sin and forgiveness? Because little "Jihads" along with their mothers and fathers need not only material and psychological help but release from the understandable but nonetheless inhumane hatred in which their hearts are held captive. Put more generally and more theologically, victims need to repent because social change that corresponds to the vision of God's reign—God's new world—cannot take place without a *change of their heart and behavior*. Granted, many a false prophet used the message of repentance to stabilize the order of oppression: "the religion of the sinful soul" served to divert attention from "the economics of dirty deals" and "politics of ruthless power." We would be unwise, however, to let this outrageous misuse blind us to the extraordinary social significance of the victim's repentance. If it did, in our own way we would be guilty of the same sin the false prophets are guilty of—we would perpetuate the old order of oppression while self-righteously declaring ourselves the vanguard of the new order of liberty. Let me elaborate on what may be called "the politics of the pure heart."

It is not easy to know from what Jesus called his hearers to repent; he speaks often of sinners, but rarely of their sins. The social consensus of his contemporaries about what counted as sin is not of much help; we cannot assume that he shared the widespread notions of sin, because we know

114

that he challenged his contemporaries on that very issue. So we have to infer from what he wanted people to repent by looking at how he wanted them to live; sin appears here as a failure to live the life of discipleship as described in the Sermon on the Mount.[47] This is not the place to give a full-fledged account of Jesus's implicit theology of sin. Two prominent foci of his message, however, illustrate well the social relevance of repentance—his teaching on wealth and violence. Jesus said, "You cannot serve God and wealth," and "Love your enemies and pray for those who persecute you" (Matt 6:24; 5:44). Devotion to wealth and hatred of the enemy are sins of which the followers of Jesus must repent. Especially for the powerless victims of oppression—who have limited means of serving wealth because they possess none and can hardly make use of a sword because there are not enough swords around—the two injunctions translate into a critique of *envy* and *enmity*. One could be tempted to object: What possible political significance could these seemingly private attitudes of the disprivileged and powerless have? These unfortunate people may be "healthier" if they got rid of their negative feelings, a psychiatrist might counsel. But why would a prophet admonish the disprivileged to *repent* of them? More specifically, what possible social import could such repentance have?

In the course of his critique of the self-perpetuating character of modernity, Zygmunt Bauman points to the tendency of conflicts that are born under the conditions of inequality to breed jealousy in the privileged and envy in the disprivileged. Commenting in *Postmodern Ethics* on the social significance of *envy* he writes:

> The most seminal impact of envy consists...in transforming "the ideas of the dominant" into the "dominant ideas." Once the link between the privileged position and certain values has been socially constructed, the disprivileged are prompted to seek redress for their humiliation through demanding such values for themselves—and thereby further enhancing those values' seductive power.[48]

Bauman's astute observation about envy applies equally well to enmity. The most seminal impact of enmity, we might argue, using Bauman's vocabulary, consists in transforming the violent practices of the dominant into dominant practices. Once the link between violence and social status has been established, victims are prompted to seek redress for their

---

47. Joachim Gnilka, *Jesus von Nazaret: Botschaft und Geschichte* (Freiburg: Herder, 1993), 212.
48. Bauman, *Postmodern Ethics*, 216.

oppression with violent means. The social impact of envy and enmity, singly and in combination, is to reinforce the dominant values and practices that cause and perpetuate oppression in the first place. Envy and enmity keep the disprivileged and weak chained to the dominant order—even when they succeed in toppling it! All too often, of course, they do not want to topple the dominant order; as Bauman says, they "demand the reshuffling of cards, not another game. They do not blame the game, only the stronger hand of the adversary."[49] The dominant values and practices can be transformed only if their hold on the hearts of those who suffer under them is broken. This is where repentance comes in. To repent means to resist the seductiveness of the sinful values and practices and to let the new order of God's reign be established in one's heart.[50] For a victim to repent means not to allow the oppressors to determine the terms under which social conflict is carried out, the values around which the conflict is raging, and the means by which it is fought. Repentance thus empowers victims and disempowers the oppressors. It "humanizes" the victims precisely by protecting them from either mimicking or dehumanizing the oppressors. Far from being a sign of acquiescence to the dominant order, repentance creates a haven of God's new world in the midst of the old and so makes the transformation of the old possible. From what sins, then, should the victims be delivered? What should the Muslim woman who named her son "Jihad" repent of? She should certainly not repent of the violence and humiliation she has suffered, as if she were to blame for being brutally violated and utterly humiliated; the perpetrators, and only they, must repent of that terrible deed. If anything, along with most victims, she may need help in learning how to resist the tendency to blame herself. But she and many other victims—most of us when we are victims—need to repent of what the perpetrators do to our soul. Victims need to repent of the fact that all too often they mimic the behavior of the oppressors, let themselves be shaped in the mirror image of the enemy. They need to repent also of the desire to excuse their own reactive behavior either

---

49. Ibid.

50. The early church was surprisingly successful in resisting dominant values, such as the obsession with wealth and power. Gerd Theissen has noted a "democratization" of the ancient charitable practices in the early church: the poorest of the poor acted not simply as recipients but as *subjects* of charitable help. They worked hard, even fasted, to meet the needs of *others*, an achievement impossible without a sovereign freedom from the seduction of wealth. The same remarkable signs of God's reign are visible in many impoverished Christian communities around the world today. "'Geben ist seliger als nehmen' (Apg 20:35): Zur Demokratisierung antiker Wohltätermentalität im Urchristentum," *Kirche, Recht und Wissenschaft: Festschrift für Oberkirchenrat i. R. Prof. Dr. Albert Stein zum siebzigsten Geburtstag*, ed. Andrea Boluminski (Neuwied: Luchterhand Verlag, 1995).

by claiming that they are not responsible for it or that such reactions are a necessary condition of liberation. Without repentance for these sins, the full human dignity of victims will not be restored and needed social change will not take place.

One could object that victims should no more repent for what the perpetrators have done to the moral makeup of their souls than they should repent for what the perpetrators have done to the integrity of their bodies. Have not "the Serbs... taught" the Muslim woman to hate, as she put it? In an important sense, they did; the kind of violence and disgrace she has suffered creates hate. And yet even under the onslaught of extreme brutality, an inner realm of freedom to shape one's self must be defended as a sanctuary of a person's humanity. Though victims may not be able to prevent hate from springing to life, for their own sake they can and must refuse to give it nourishment and strive to weed it out. If victims do not repent today, they will become perpetrators tomorrow who, in their self-deceit, will seek to exculpate their misdeeds on account of their own victimization.[51]

Of course, something much more than a change in the hearts of the disadvantaged needs to happen for the dominant order to change. How could we forget the lessons about the structural dimensions of sin that the Marxist tradition discovered and that have now become received social wisdom? Moreover, the vise-grip of the dominant values and practices must be broken also in the hearts of the privileged; *they* certainly need to repent. This seems so obvious, however, that it could almost be left unsaid were it not for the ideological machinery that the privileged use to script narratives that shift the blame away from themselves. The Gospels insist that repentance is not only necessary for the oppressor, but that for them it means more than just purifying desire and mending ways, more even than making restitution to those they have wronged. As the story of Zacchaeus hyperbolically states, repentance entails for them paying back "four times as much" and giving half of their possession to the poor (Luke 19:8). A genuine repentance of the oppressors will lead to the "injustice"

51. Sharon Lamb, *The Trouble with Blame: Victims, Perpetrators, and Responsibility* (Cambridge: Harvard University Press, 1996), 54. As a whole, Lamb concentrates not on what the perpetrator's violation does to the moral character of the victim, as I do here, but on retrieving the capacity of perpetrators and victims alike to take responsibility and blame. Her argument, premised on the belief that "we do not hold perpetrators responsible enough for the harms they inflict," is that "when we begin to hold perpetrators responsible for their actions (and they begin to hold themselves responsible), victims can then take a realistic look at themselves, and we can feel free to acknowledge some of the assertion, free will, and yes, blame, that also belong to victims" (ibid., 8).

of superabundant restitution, which seeks to offset the injustice of the original violation.

From the perspective developed here, talk about the sinfulness and repentance of victims has nothing to do with the ascription of blame that legitimizes corresponding political actions. It clearly *does not* imply, for instance, that it is simply "bad family values" that keep the poor enslaved to poverty (as though economic and political structures had nothing to do with the cycle of poverty) or that in helping the poor we ought to distinguish between the worthy, who ought to be helped, and the unworthy, who ought not to be (as though people need to deserve their own survival by the quality of their character). Rather, talk about the need for the victim's repentance has to do with creation of the kind of social agents that are shaped by the values of God's kingdom and therefore capable of participating in the project of authentic social transformation.[52] The significance of the character of social agents is an important *political* lesson we can learn from Jesus's theological claim that the first act of any human being in response to the coming kingdom of God is to have their own heart made pure, a response whose effect may be a salutary political change but whose profound reason lies in God's saving grace.

In *The Scapegoat* René Girard argued that the identification of the victim as an innocent scapegoat in the Gospels has the significance of revelation.[53] Without wanting to minimize the singular importance of the discovery that oppressors often engage in scapegoating, I want to submit that from the perspective of the Gospels, Girard's more general argument about the innocence of the victim has the significance of obfuscation. What does have the significance of revelation is Jesus's insistence on the need for repentance *both on the part of the oppressors and the oppressed*—at least his insistence has such significance in contemporary societies. Jesus combines a deep commitment to seeing "the oppressed go free" with an acute awareness that the oppressed—that *we!*—need repentance, a radical reorientation of basic attitudes and actions in response to God's coming salvation. "Blessed are the poor" and "Blessed are the pure" belong inseparably together (Matt 5:3, 8). Without a "politics of the pure heart" every

---

52. The idea that the transformation of people rather than the proper ascription of blame is at the heart of repentance mirrors the fact that Jesus's proclamation of repentance was motivated not so much by fear of the coming final judgment as by joy over the nearness of God's reign (see Matt 13:44). Peter Stuhlmacher, *Biblische Theologie des Neuen Testaments. Grundlegung: Von Jesus zu Paulus*, vol. 1 (Göttingen: Vandenhoeck & Ruprecht, 1992), 95.

53. René Girard, *The Scapegoat*, transl. Yvonne Freccero (Baltimore: Johns Hopkins University Press, 1986). See also below, Chapter VII.

politics of liberation will trip over its own feet—the son who was named "Jihad" will infuse another mother with a hatred so pure that she too will inscribe "revenge" into the very identity of her offspring.[54]

The Practice of Forgiveness

Genuine repentance may be one of the most difficult acts for a person, let alone a community, to perform. For good reasons, Christian tradition thinks of genuine repentance not as a human possibility but as a gift of God. It is not just that we do not like being wrong, but that almost invariably the others are not completely right either. As Carl Gustav Jung observed after World War II, most confessions come as a mixture of repentance, self-defense, and even some lust for revenge.[55] We admit wrongdoing, justify ourselves, and attack, all in one breath.

When we are clearly the aggressors, no matter how great our offense— if we only admit it—we will want to point out the noninnocence of the side we have victimized and seek to drag them into the swamp of common undifferentiated sinfulness that requires a balanced reciprocal confession of sin. The difficulty with which the Evangelical Church in Germany made its rather lame confession after World War II (the Stuttgart Declaration of Guilt, adopted on October 18–19, 1945) is a good example. Resistance to repentance will be even greater if we see ourselves as disprivileged and powerless victims. How will we be able to confess our wrongdoing without seeking to justify ourselves by pointing to the wrongdoing we have suffered, a wrongdoing that both dwarfs any wrongdoing that we might have committed and provides a good deal of explanation for why we committed it? Whether we are aggressors or victims, genuine repentance demands that we take ourselves, so to say, out of the mesh of small and big evil deeds that characterize so much of our social intercourse, that we refuse to explain our behavior and accuse others, and that we simply take our wrongdoing upon ourselves: "*I* have sinned in my thoughts, in my words, and in my deeds," as the Book of Common Prayer puts it.

Commenting on the Stuttgart Declaration of Guilt, Jürgen Moltmann points out both the pain and the promise of a genuine confession:

---

54. Geiko Müller-Fahrenholz, *Vergebung macht frei: Vorschliige für eine Theologie der Versöhnung* (Frankfurt: Otto Lembeck, 1996), 129ff. Müller-Fahrenholz uses this story to point out the necessity of forgiveness, not of repentance, as I do

55. Carl Gustav Jung, "Epilogue to 'Essay on Contemporary Events,'" *Collected Works of C. G. Jung*, ed. H. Read et al. (New York: Pantheon Books, 1964), 240f.

A person who thus admits his guilt and complicity renders himself defenseless, assailable and vulnerable. He stands there, muddied and weighed down. Everyone can point at him and despise him. But he becomes free from alienation and the determination of his actions by others; he comes to himself, and steps into the light of a truth which makes him free....[56]

Liberation through confession—liberation from "the suppression of guilt, and from an obtuse belief in destiny," from "the armor of insensibility and defiance in which we had encased ourselves," as Moltmann describes it[57]—might be among the most painful of all liberations. But when we have made this first difficult step of repentance we have traveled a good distance on the road to reconciliation. The next step is forgiveness.[58]

But is forgiveness any easier? Deep within the heart of every victim, anger swells up against the perpetrator, rage inflamed by unredeemed suffering. The imprecatory Psalms seem to come upon victims' lips much more easily than the prayer of Jesus on the cross. If anything, they would rather pray, "Forgive them not, Father, for they knew what they did!" The powerful emotional pull of revenge is not the only reason we resist forgiving, however. Our cool sense of justice sends the same message: the perpetrator *deserves* unforgiveness; it would be unjust to forgive. As Lewis Smedes puts it in *Forgive and Forget*, forgiveness is an outrage "against straight-line dues-paying morality."[59] If perpetrators were repentant, forgiveness would come more easily. But too often they are not. And so both victim and perpetrator are imprisoned in the automatism of mutual exclusion, unable to forgive or repent and united in a perverse communion of mutual enmity. Instead of wanting to forgive, we instinctively seek revenge. An evil deed will not be owed for long; it demands instant

---

56. Jürgen Moltmann, "Forty Years after the Stuttgart Declaration," *Case Study 2: The Forgiveness and Politics Study Project*, ed. Brian Frost (London: New World Publications, 1987), 43.

57. Ibid.

58. I am not suggesting that there is a necessary temporal sequence between repentance and forgiveness such that, say, one first repents and then offers or receives forgiveness. In fact, theologically one will do well to insist on the priority of forgiveness: forgiveness must be already at work before repentance can take place, as Kyle A. Pasewark has argued in his review of Shriver's *An Ethic for Enemies* ("Remembering to Forget: A Politics of Forgiveness," *Christian Century* 112 [July 5–12, 1995]: 685). My interest here is not so much to analyze the sequence of the steps in the cycle of reconciliation, as to indicate various elements of this cycle. Moreover, the terminology of "steps" should not mislead one to think that repentance and forgiveness are one-time acts, done once and for all. In *Embodying Forgiveness: A Theological Analysis* (Grand Rapids: Eerdmans, 1995), L. Gregory Jones has rightly argued for forgiveness as a "craft," "a way of life."

59. Lewis B. Smedes, *Forgive and Forget: Healing the Hurts We Don't Deserve* (San Francisco: Harper & Row, 1984), 124.

repayment in kind. The trouble with revenge, however, is that it enslaves us. As Hannah Arendt pointed out in *The Human Condition,* vengeance

> acts in the form of reacting against an original trespassing, whereby far from putting an end to the consequences of the first misdeed, everybody remains bound to the process, permitting the chain reaction contained in every action to take its unhindered course;...[vengeance] encloses both doer and sufferer in the relentless automatism of the action process, which by itself need never come to an end.[60]

The endless turning of the spiral of vengeance—"violence feeds on revenge; revenge, on violence"[61]—has its own good reasons that seem woven into the very fabric of social realities. The one reason has to do with a lack of sync between the perspectives of social actors. When one party sees itself as simply seeking justice or even settling for less than justice, the other may perceive the same action as taking revenge or perpetrating injustice. As the intended justice is translated by the other party into actual injustice, a "just" revenge leads to a "just" counter-revenge. We may call this first reason for the spiral of vengeance "the predicament of partiality"—the inability of the parties locked in conflict to agree on the moral significance of their actions.

The other reason for the spiral of vengeance lies in the temporal sequence in which our acts are necessarily embedded. Hannah Arendt has called it "the predicament of irreversibility"—an inability "to undo what one has done though one did not, or could not, have known what he was doing."[62] If our deeds and their consequences could be undone, revenge would not be necessary. The undoing, if there were a will for it, would suffice. But our actions are irreversible. Even God cannot alter them. And so the urge for vengeance seems irrepressible. The only way out of the predicament of irreversibility, Arendt insisted, is through *forgiveness.* Forgiveness is also the only way out of the predicament of partiality, I would add. A genuinely free act that "does not merely re-act,"[63] forgiveness breaks the power of the remembered past and transcends the claims of the affirmed

60. Hannah Arendt, *The Human Condition: A Study of the Central Dilemmas Facing Modern Man* (Garden City: Doubleday, 1959), 216.

61. Donald W. Shriver Jr., *An Ethic for Enemies: Forgiveness in Politics* (New York: Oxford University Press, 1995), 19.

62. Arendt, *The Human Condition*, 212f.

63. Ibid., 216.

justice and so makes the spiral of vengeance grind to a halt. This is the social import of forgiveness.

"The discoverer of the role of forgiveness in the realm of human affairs was Jesus of Nazareth," claimed Hannah Arendt.[64] Appropriate or not, the title of "discoverer" correctly underlines the centrality of forgiveness in Jesus's proclamation. The climate of pervasive oppression in which he preached was suffused with the desire for revenge. The principle "If anyone hits you, hit back! If anyone takes your coat, burn down his house!" seemed the only way to survive;[65] Lamech's kind of revenge, which returns seventy-seven blows for every one received, seemed, paradoxically, the only way to root out injustice (Gen 4:23-24). Turning Lamech's logic on its head, however, Jesus demanded his followers not simply to forego revenge but to forgive as many times as Lamech sought to avenge himself (Matt 18:21). The injustice of oppression must be fought with the creative "injustice" of forgiveness, not with the aping injustice of revenge.

Hanging on the cross where he was sent by an unjust judge, Jesus became the ultimate example of his own teaching. He prayed, "Father, forgive them..." (Luke 23:34). Commenting on this prayer, Jürgen Moltmann writes,

> With this prayer of Christ the universal religion of revenge is overcome and the universal law of retaliation is annulled. In the name of the Crucified, from now on only forgiveness holds sway. Christianity that has the right to appeal to him is a religion of reconciliation. To forgive those who have wronged one is an act of highest sovereignty and great inner freedom. In forgiving and reconciling, the victims are superior to the perpetrators and free themselves from compulsion to evil deeds.[66]

Is Moltmann not setting up false alternatives, however? Is there nothing besides the choice between vengeance and forgiveness? Why not simply forego *both* and opt for justice—repaying the offenders neither more (as vengeance would want) nor less (as forgiveness would require) than their offense? Why not an eye for an eye, a tooth for a tooth, as the *lex talionis* says, that principle that seeks to limit conflict by imposing the

---

64. Ibid., 214f.
65. Theissen, *The Shadow of the Galilean*, 88.
66. Jürgen Moltmann, *Das Kommen Gottes: Christliche Eschatologie* (Gütersloh: Christian Kaiser, 1995), 29.

exact extent of the "repayment"? Notice, however, that the very idea of forgiveness implies an affirmation of justice. The Lord's Prayer makes this plain. When we pray, "forgive us our debts, as we also have forgiven our debtors" (Matt 6:12), we imply that we *owe* God something and that other people *owe* us something. What we owe and what is owed to us can be established only by applying the principle of justice. Hence: no justice, no forgiveness.

But if justice, then why forgiveness? Because strict restorative justice can never be satisfied. If the predicament of partiality puts the lid on the coffin of such justice, the predicament of irreversibility screws the lid tightly down. Since "no deed can be annihilated," as Nietzsche said, at the very least the original offense remains. Within the framework of justice, guilt is eternal and therefore, concludes Nietzsche, "all punishments, too, must be eternal."[67] And yet even an eternal hell for the tormentors that Nietzsche's logic demanded could not set things right for those who have been tormented, as Dostoevsky's sagacity perceived.[68] We can think of nothing that can rectify the original offense. Moreover, as soon as we step outside the realm of pure thought into the realm of concrete social intercourse, as a rule, much more remains unrectified than the original offense. In this realm offenses exist for which no possible restitution can be made, and even when restitution can be made the disputes about what kind of restitution is appropriate make restitution unlikely and its justice contested. In the framework of strict restorative justice, no reconciliation is possible. On the contrary, the pursuit of such justice will deepen the conflict and reinstate the "compulsion to evil deeds." Hence the need for forgiveness.

Again, forgiveness is not a substitute for justice. Forgiveness is no mere discharge of a victim's angry resentment and no mere assuaging of a perpetrator's remorseful anguish, one that demands no change of the perpetrator and no righting of wrongs. On the contrary: every act of forgiveness enthrones justice; it draws attention to its violation precisely by offering to forego its claims.[69] Moreover, forgiveness provides a framework in

67. Friedrich Nietzsche, *Thus Spoke Zarathustra: A Book for Everyone and No One*, transl. R. J. Hollingdale (London: Penguin, 1969), 162.

68. Fyodor Dostoevsky, *The Brothers Karamazov*, transl. R. Pevear and L. Volokhonsky (San Francisco: North Point, 1990), 245.

69. Michael Welker, "Gewaltverzicht und Feindesliebe," *Einfach von Gott reden: Ein theologischer Diskurs. Festschrift für Friedrich Mildenberger zum 65. Geburtstag*, ed. Jürgen Roloff and Hans G. Ulrich (Stuttgart: W. Kohlhammer, 1994), 246.

which the quest for properly understood justice can be fruitfully pursued. "Only those who are in a state of truthfulness through the confession of their sin to Jesus are not ashamed to tell the truth wherever it must be told," maintained Dietrich Bonhoeffer in *The Cost of Discipleship*.[70] Only those who are forgiven and who are willing to forgive will be capable of relentlessly pursuing justice without falling into the temptation to pervert it into injustice, we could add.

How do we find the strength to forgive, however? Should we try to persuade ourselves that forgiveness is invariably good for mental and spiritual health whereas vindictiveness is bad? Should we tell ourselves that, given the nature of our world, it is wiser to forgive than to fall prey to the spinning spiral of revenge? Even if valid, will these arguments get at such a powerful emotion as the desire for revenge? More significantly, do they take sufficient note of the fact that the desire for revenge, far from being just an irrational passion of a sick or maladjusted psyche, flows "from a need to restore 'something missing'—a sense of physical and emotional integrity that is shattered by violence," as Susan Jacoby rightly argued in *Wild Justice*?[71] How will we satisfy our thirst for justice and calm our passion for revenge so as to practice forgiveness?

In the imprecatory Psalms, torrents of rage have been allowed to flow freely, channeled only by the robust structure of a ritual prayer.[72] Strangely enough, they may point to a way out of slavery to revenge and into the freedom of forgiveness. This suggestion will not work, of course, if we see the imprecatory Psalms as publicly pronounced indirect threats to powerful enemies who could not be confronted directly—moments "in a larger web of intriguing words and actions in which the Psalmist is fully involved," as Gerald T. Sheppard has argued.[73] Partly out of a false concern that these Psalms may "dissipate and neutralize the desire actually to retaliate, to punish, or to take power from another person,"[74] Sheppard misreads the specific character of the Psalms as discourse. They are *prayers*. And everybody except moderns for whom God does not matter knows that the primary addressee of prayers is God. Whatever else these Psalms might have done

---

70. Dietrich Bonhoeffer, *The Cost of Discipleship*, transl. R. H. Fuller (New York: Macmillan, 1963), 155.

71. Susan Jacoby, *Wild Justice: The Evolution of Revenge* (New York: Harper & Row, 1983), 298.

72. Cristoph Barth, *Introduction to the Psalms* (New York: Scribners, 1966), 43ff.

73. Gerald T. Sheppard, "'Enemies' and the Politics of Prayer in the Book of Psalms," *The Bible and the Politics of Exegesis*, ed. D. Jobling et al. (Cleveland: Pilgrim, 1992), 74.

74. Ibid., 71.

to those who listened (and I do not doubt that they functioned at that level too), they brought the puzzlement and rage of the oppressed over injustice into the presence of the God of justice who is the God of the oppressed.[75]

For the followers of the crucified Messiah, the main message of the imprecatory Psalms is this: rage belongs before God[76]—not in the reflectively managed and manicured form of a confession, but as a pre-reflective outburst from the depths of the soul. This is no mere cathartic discharge of pent up aggression before the Almighty who ought to care. Much more significantly, by placing unattended rage before God we place both our unjust enemy and our own vengeful self face-to-face with a God who loves and does justice. Hidden in the dark chambers of our hearts and nourished by the system of darkness, hate grows and seeks to infest everything with its hellish will to exclusion. In the light of the justice and love of God, however, hate recedes and the seed is planted for the miracle of forgiveness. Forgiveness flounders because I exclude the enemy from the community of humans even as I exclude myself from the community of sinners. But no one can be in the presence of the God of the crucified Messiah for long without overcoming this double exclusion—without transposing the enemy from the sphere of monstrous inhumanity into the sphere of shared humanity and himself or herself from the sphere of proud innocence into the sphere of common sinfulness. When one knows that the torturer will not eternally triumph over the victim (Chapter VII), one is free to rediscover that person's humanity and imitate God's love for him or her. And when one knows that God's love is greater than all sin, one is free to see oneself in the light of God's justice and so rediscover one's own sinfulness.[77]

In the presence of God our rage over injustice may give way to forgiveness, which in turn will make the search for justice for all possible (see Chapter V). If forgiveness does take place it will be but an echo of the forgiveness granted by the just and loving God—the only forgiveness that ultimately matters because, though we must forgive, in a very real sense no one can either forgive or retain sins "but God alone" (Mark 2:7).

75. Patrick D. Miller, *They Cried to the Lord: The Form and Theology of Biblical Prayer* (Minneapolis: Fortress, 1994), 106ff. Bernd Janowski has persuasively argued that the "enemy" in the Psalms is not just "a personal opponent" but "a representative of a chaotic power" ("Dem Löwen gleich, gierig nach Raub: Zum Feindbild in den Psalmen," *Evangelische Theologie* 55, no. 2 [1995]: 163ff). The imprecatory Psalms are therefore less after personal vengeance than after justice.

76. Ibid., 173.

77. Situating ourselves in the presence of God is, of course, not all we need to do in order to learn to forgive. We also need to situate ourselves in a community of forgiveness, a community that will help us learn the craft of forgiveness (Jones, *Embodying Forgiveness*). The praying of the Psalms in fact does some of this communal situating, for they are the ritual prayers of the people of God.

Space for the Other: Cross, Trinity, Eucharist

"Forgiveness" sums up much of the significance of the cross[78]—for Christians the ultimate symbol at the same time of the destructiveness of human sin and of the greatness of God's love. Though Jesus may never have uttered the prayer, "Father, forgive them; for they do not know what they are doing" (Luke 23:34)[79] these words are indelibly inscribed in the story of his passion, indeed in his whole life that leads to the cross. As that prayer makes plain, Christ's crucifixion was more than simply another instance of an innocent person's suffering. The suffering of the innocent *as such* has no redemptive value, either for the sufferers themselves or for anybody else; it is tragic, rather than redeeming, because it only swells the already overbrimming rivers of blood and tears running through human history. More than just the passive suffering of an innocent person, the passion of Christ is the agony of a tortured soul and wrecked body offered as *a prayer for the forgiveness of the torturers*. No doubt, such prayer adds to the agony of the passion. As Dietrich Bonhoeffer saw clearly, forgiveness itself is a form of suffering;[80] when I forgive I have not only suffered a violation but also suppressed the rightful claims of retributive justice. Under the foot of the cross we learn, however, that in a world of irreversible deeds and partisan judgments redemption from the passive suffering of victimization cannot happen without the active suffering of forgiveness.

Forgiveness is necessary, but will it suffice? Forgiveness is the boundary between exclusion and embrace. It heals the wounds that the power-acts of exclusion have inflicted and breaks down the dividing wall of hostility. Yet it leaves a distance between people, an empty space of neutrality, that allows them either to go their separate ways in what is sometimes called "peace" or to fall into each other's arms and restore broken communion. "Going one's own way" is the boldest dream many a person caught in the vortex of violence can muster the strength to dream. "Too much injustice was done for us to be friends; too much blood was shed for us to live together," are the words that echo all too often in regions wrecked with conflict. A clear line will separate "them" from "us." They will remain "they"

---

78. This is no place to develop a full-blown theology of the cross; I only draw on some features of the New Testament witness to the death of Christ. In particular, I will eschew here all attempts to explain the "logic" of redemption (see Chapter VII). I am interested here in elaborating on the social significance of some aspects of what happened on the cross, not in explaining why and precisely how it happened.

79. Important ancient manuscripts do not contain the words.

80. Bonhoeffer, *The Cost of Discipleship*, 100.

and we will remain "we," and we will never include "them" when we speak of "us." Such "clean" identities, living at safe distances from one another, may be all that is possible or even desirable in some cases at certain junctures of people's mutual history. But a parting of the ways is clearly not yet peace. Much more than just the absence of hostility sustained by the absence of contact, *peace is communion between former enemies.* Beyond offering forgiveness, Christ's passion aims at restoring such communion—even with the enemies who persistently refuse to be reconciled.

At the heart of the cross is Christ's stance of not letting the other remain an enemy and of creating space in himself for the offender to come in. Read as the culmination of the larger narrative of God's dealing with humanity, the cross says that despite its manifest enmity toward God humanity belongs to God; God will not be God without humanity. "While we were enemies, we were reconciled to God through the death of his son," writes the Apostle Paul (Rom 5:10). The cross is the giving up of God's self in order not to give up on humanity; it is the consequence of God's desire to break the power of human enmity without violence and receive human beings into divine communion. The goal of the cross is the dwelling of human beings "in the Spirit," "in Christ," and "in God." Forgiveness is therefore not the culmination of Christ's relation to the offending other; it is a passage leading to embrace. The arms of the crucified are open—a sign of a space in God's self and an invitation for the "enemy" to come in.

As an expression of the will to embrace the enemy the cross is no doubt a scandal in a world suffused with hostility. We instinctively reach for a shield and a sword, but the cross offers us outstretched arms and a naked body with a pierced side; we feel we need the cunning wisdom of serpents, but the cross invites us to the foolishness of innocent doves (1 Cor 1:18ff.). Scandalous as they may be, such cruciform vulnerability and innocence do not tell, however, of "the *inability* for enmity," as Nietzsche suggested in *The Anti-Christ*.[81] Rather, they bespeak the kind of *enmity* toward enmity, which rejects all enmity's services. Instead of aping the enemy's act of violence and rejection, Christ, the victim who refuses to be defined by the perpetrator, forgives and makes space in himself for the enemy. Hence precisely as a victim Christ is the true judge: by offering to embrace the offenders, he judges both the initial wrongdoing of the perpetrators and the reactive wrongdoing of many victims. Enmity toward

81. Friedrich Nietzsche, *Twilight of the Idols and The Anti-Christ*, transl. R. J. Hollingdale (London: Penguin, 1990), 153.

127

enmity achieves what neither enmity itself nor the inability for enmity could accomplish. Embrace *transforms* the relation between the victim and the perpetrator, whereas enmity would merely invert it and the inability for enmity leave it untouched.[82]

Yet even as a judgment against enmity, the cross remains an offense in a world of violence. Will not such peaceful agonism lead to an unbearable agony of Christ's followers?[83] Will not the heavy weight of the cross crush the weak—those who have no platform of power on which to step when the strategy of making space in the self for the enemy fails? Will not such a "word of the cross" be all too good news for the perpetrator? Elsewhere in the book I will address these profoundly disturbing questions (see Chapters V–VII). Here I want to underline that the offense of the cross—and whoever thinks the cross is *not* an offense has never followed the Crucified to Gethsemane let alone to Golgotha—lies deeper than the theology of the cross. If the fate of the Crucified and his demand to walk in his footsteps disturb us, then we will also be disturbed by the *God* of the Crucified. For the very nature of the triune God is reflected on the cross of Christ. Inversely, the cross of Christ is etched in the heart of the triune God; Christ's passion is God's passion.[84] As Rowan Williams puts it, "the inconceivable self-emptying of God in the events of Good Friday and Holy Saturday is no arbitrary expression of the nature of God: this is what the life of the Trinity is, translated into the world."[85] A trinitarian theology of the cross leads us to ask, therefore, what "the life of the Trinity" untranslated into the world is, and how it should shape our relations to the other.

Note first the two dimensions of the passion of Christ: self-giving love that overcomes human enmity and the creation of space in himself to receive estranged humanity. This same giving of the self and receiving of the other are the two essential moments in the internal life of the Trinity; indeed, with the triune God of perfect love they are identical. Both those who espouse a hierarchical view of the trinitarian relations, following the tradition, and those who join more recent trends and advocate a

---

82. See Rowan Williams, *Resurrection: Interpreting the Easter Gospel* (London: Darton, Longman & Todd, 1982), 11ff.

83. On the issue of "vulnerability" see Sarah Coakley's important essay "*Kenosis* and Subversion: On the Repression of 'Vulnerability' in Christian Feminist Writing" (*Powers and Submissions: Spirituality, Philosophy, and Gender* [Oxford: Blackwell, 2002]); she argues for "the normative concurrence in Christ of nonbullying divine 'power' *with* 'self-effaced' humanity" (31).

84. Moltmann, *The Trinity and the Kingdom*, 21ff.

85. Rowan Williams, "Barth on the Triune God," *Karl Barth: Studies of His Theological Method*, ed. S. W. Sykes (Oxford: Clarendon, 1979), 177.

nonhierarchical view of trinitarian relations, agree that the life of God is a life of self-giving and other-receiving love. As a consequence, the identity of each trinitarian person cannot be defined apart from other persons. The Johannine Jesus says: "The Father is in me and I am in the Father" (John 10:38). The one divine person is not that person only, but includes the other divine persons in itself; it is what it is only through the indwelling of the others. The Son is the Son because the Father and the Spirit indwell him; without this interiority of the Father and the Spirit, there would be no Son. Every divine person *is* the other persons, but he is the other persons in his own particular way. This is what the patristic idea of divine *perichoresis* sought to express—"co-inherence in one another without any coalescence or commixture."[86]

Everything in the idea of *perichoresis*—or "mutual interiority," as I prefer to put it—depends on success in resisting the slide into pure identity. Building on an Augustinian and Thomist understanding of the trinitarian persons as relations, Joseph Ratzinger has argued that personhood consists in *pure relations*[87]—"persona est relatio."[88] Appealing to such statements of the Johannine Jesus as "My teaching is not mine but his who sent me" (John 7:16), Ratzinger claims that in the Son there "is nothing in which he is just he, no kind of fenced-off private ground,"[89] but that his whole being consists in being completely transparent for the Father. Hence Jesus can say: "Whoever has seen me has seen the Father" (14:9). But how is such a radical transparency of the Son for the Father different from the dissolution of the Son in the Father? Even more, if *no* person has anything of their own, the three divine persons collapse into the one undifferentiated divine substance and their "mutual interiority" is lost. Instead of identifying "persons" and "relations" it seems better, with Jürgen Moltmann, to understand them "in a reciprocal relationship."[90] The Son is now not completely transparent for the Father, but both are now conceived as "in" one another: "the Father is in me and I am in the Father" (John 10:38). This mutual interiority born out of love—"I am not just I, the

---

86. G. L. Prestige, *God in Patristic Thought* (London: SPCK, 1956), 298.

87. Joseph Ratzinger, *Introduction to Christianity*, transl. J. R. Foster (New York: Herder and Herder, 1970), 131.

88. Aquinas, *Summa Theologica*, transl. Fathers of the English Dominican Province (New York: Benzinger, 1948), I, 40, 2.

89. Ratzinger, *Introduction to Christianity*, 134.

90. Moltmann, *The Trinity and the Kingdom*, 172.

other belongs to me too"—describes both the identity and the relations of the divine persons from eternity to eternity.[91]

When the Trinity turns toward the world, the Son and the Spirit become, in Irenaeus's beautiful image, the two arms of God by which humanity was made and taken into God's embrace.[92] That same love that sustains nonself-enclosed identities in the Trinity seeks to make space "in God" for humanity. Humanity is, however, not just the other of God, but the beloved other who has become an enemy. When God sets out to embrace the enemy, the result is the cross. On the cross the dancing circle of self-giving and mutually indwelling divine persons opens up for the enemy; in the agony of the passion the movement stops for a brief moment and a fissure appears so that sinful humanity can join in (see John 17:21). We, the others—we, the enemies—are embraced by the divine persons who love us with the same love with which they love each other and therefore make space for us within their own eternal embrace.[93]

The Eucharist is the ritual time in which we celebrate this divine "making-space-for-us-and-inviting-us-in." By eating the bread and drinking the wine, we remember the body broken "for us" who were God's enemies, and the blood spilled to establish a "new covenant" with us who have broken the covenant (1 Cor 11:24-25). We would most profoundly misunderstand the Eucharist, however, if we thought of it only as a sacrament of God's embrace, of which we are simply the fortunate beneficiaries. Inscribed on the very heart of God's grace is the rule that we can be its recipients only if we do not resist being made into its agents; what happens to us must be done by us. Having been embraced by God, we must make space for others in ourselves and invite them in—even our enemies. This is what we enact as we celebrate the Eucharist. In receiving Christ's broken body and spilled blood, we, in a sense, receive all those whom Christ received by suffering.

Both Catholic and Orthodox theology have a long tradition of reflecting on what they call a "catholic personality," centered around the mystery of the Eucharist. Take John Zizioulas's formulation of this notion, though

---

91. Ibid., 191f.; Jürgen Moltmann, *In der Geschichte des dreieinigen Gottes: Beiträge zur trinitarischen Theologie* (München: Kaiser, 1991); Miroslav Volf, *After Our Likeness: The Church as the Image of the Trinity* (Grand Rapids: Eerdmans, 1998), ch. 4.

92. See Irenaeus, *Against Heresies*, 5, 6, 1.

93. The plural here is by no means a slippage into polytheism. As the plural in John 17:21 ("they"—those who will believe—in "us"—the Father and the subject of the high priestly prayer) suggests, one cannot speak of the triune God simply in the singular (though, of course, one of the basic rules of language about the Christian God is that one cannot speak of the triune God simply in the plural either)!

one could equally well take, say, Hans Urs von Balthasar's.[94] Since in the Eucharist the "whole Christ"—the head and the body—is received by each communicant, each is made into an *ecclesial person* and all are *internal to the very being of each*.[95] Even if one objects to the organicistic character of Zizioulas's thought—the one and whole Christ comprised of the head and the body is present in each member[96]—the idea of an *ecclesial person* or *catholic personality* (as Zizioulas prefers to formulate) is both profound and fruitful. By breaking the bread we share not only in the body of the crucified and resurrected Lord but also in the multi-membered body of the church. The Eucharist tells us that each member is not external to the other members. A discrete individual person is also a unique nodal point, the sediment of the internalized relations to other members of the body of Christ. As I have argued earlier (Chapter III), properly understood, the notion of the catholic personality takes us even beyond the boundaries of the church. By the Spirit we are not only baptized into the one body but also made "a new creation." Hence the Spirit opens us up to anticipate that final gathering of God's people in God's new world and sets us on the road to becoming truly catholic personalities—personal microcosms of the eschatological new creation. In the Eucharist, then, we celebrate the giving of the self to the other and the receiving of the other into the self that the triune God has undertaken in the passion of Christ and that we are called and empowered to live such giving and receiving out in a conflict-ridden world.

At the height of the liturgical life of the Orthodox church, during the celebration of the "feast of feasts" at the end of paschal Matins and just before the beginning of the Divine Liturgy, the choir sings the following words:

Pascha of beauty,
The Pascha of the Lord,
A Pascha worthy of all honor has dawned for us.
Pascha!

---

94. Hans Urs von Balthasar, *Katholisch: Aspekte des Mysteriums*. Kriterien 36 (Einsiedeln: Johannes, 1975), 8.

95. John Zizioulas, "L'eucharistie: quelques aspects bibliques," *L'eucharistie*, ed. J. Zizioulas et al. (Paris: Marne, 1970), 69; Zizioulas, "Die pneumatologische Dimension der Kirche," *Communio* 2 (1973): 142; Zizioulas, *Being as Communion: Studies in Personhood and the Church* (Crestwood: St. Vladimir's Seminary Press, 1985), 58.

96. A more extensive discussion of this issue in Catholic and Orthodox tradition and an attempt at its appropriation within the framework of Protestant thought is found in my *After Our Likeness: The Church as the Image of the Trinity* (Grand Rapids: Eerdmans, 1998).

Let us embrace each other joyously.
O Pascha, ransom from affliction.

And then again, after the verse gives glory to the triune God, "to the Father, and to the Son, and to the Holy Spirit, now and ever, and unto ages of ages," the choir sings again:

This is the day of resurrection.
Let us be illumined by the feast.
Let us embrace each other.
Let us call "Brothers" even those that hate us,
and forgive all by the resurrection.[97]

Much of the meaning of the death and resurrection of Christ is summed up in this injunction, "Let us embrace each other." As the choir clearly states, the other, who ought to be embraced by those for whom "a Pascha worthy of all honor has dawned," is not just the "brother" or "sister" inside the self-enclosed ecclesial community. The other is also the enemy outside—"those that hate us" and "all"—who is taken into the embrace by being forgiven and *called* "brother" and "sister."

In a sense, this liturgical call to embrace each other marks the boundary between the space and time of the Paschal ritual and the space and time of everyday life. In obedience to the call "to embrace each other" the Paschal mystery is lived out in the world. We who have been embraced by the outstretched arms of the crucified God open our arms even for the enemies—to make space in ourselves for them and invite them in—so that together we may rejoice in the eternal embrace of the triune God.

Paradise and the Affliction of Memory

After we have repented and forgiven our enemies, after we have made space in ourselves for them and left the door open, our will to embrace them must allow the one final, and perhaps the most difficult act to take place, if the process of reconciliation is to be complete. It is the act of forgetting the evil suffered, a *certain kind of forgetting* I hasten to add.[98] It

97. John Erickson and Paul Laraz, eds., *The Paschal Service* (Wayne: Orthodox Christian Publications Center, 1990).

98. In *Forgive and Forget: Healing the Hurts We Don't Deserve* (San Francisco: Harper & Row, 1984), Lewis B. Smedes, one of the few contemporary writers who does not simply dismiss forgetting as inhumane, has some very sensible pastoral things to say about why and how we ought to forget (38–40, 108, 134–37).

is a forgetting that assumes that the matters of "truth" and "justice" have been taken care of (see Chapters V and VI), that perpetrators have been named, judged, and (hopefully) transformed, that victims are safe and their wounds healed (see Chapter VII), a forgetting that can therefore ultimately take place *only together with* the creation of "all things new."

Could I be serious in suggesting "forgetting" as the final act of *redemption*? Do not the victims have excellent reasons for *never forgetting* the injustices suffered and hurts endured? There is no need to look far to find reasons. The subdued joy of the perpetrators over the loss of memory is the best argument for inscribing the narratives of their misdeeds in stone. Building in part on the work of Elie Wiesel, later in the book I will argue strenuously for the obligation to know, to remember, and not to keep silent (see Chapter VI). If the victims remember rightly, the memory of inhumanities past will shield both them and all of us against future inhumanities; if the perpetrators remember rightly, the memory of their wrongdoing will help restore their guilty past and transform it into the soil on which a more hopeful future can grow.[99] Yet, if we must remember wrongdoings in order to be safe in an unsafe world, we must also let go of their memory in order to be finally redeemed, or so I want to argue here, and suggest that only those who are willing ultimately to forget will be able to remember rightly.

My argument will make sense only if we give up the prejudice that "remembering" is always good and "nonremembering" always bad. The prejudice is understandable because remembering does the kind of work for us in day-to-day living that forgetting could never do. "Don't you remember!?" may be a legitimate reproach, whereas "didn't you *fail to remember*!?" strikes us as nonsensical. Should we conclude that the less we forget the better? When it comes to such things as names of our acquaintances or items on a grocery list, this is indeed so. But when it comes to the complex and ongoing relationship between friends, complete restitution of the past is not only impossible; its very thought is terrifying. Memory is much more complex than simple retention; its opposite is not oblivion. Instead, retention and oblivion function as two interrelated aspects of the larger phenomenon of memory; remembering some things entails forgetting others, and forgetting some things often takes place by remembering others. We remember what matters to us and forget what does not; and only what we remember can matter to us whereas what we forget cannot. Within the framework of historical memory, "remembering" and

---

99. See Williams, *Resurrection*, 28–51.

"nonremembering" are two intertwined ways of reconstructing our past and thereby forging our identities.[100] Forgetting is itself therefore not so much our enemy; rather, it is those who would rob us of the right to decide for ourselves what to forget and what to remember, as well as when to do so.[101]

How might "forgetting" (the evil suffered) shape our identity and our relation to the other? In what way can forgetting be redemptive? Memory of evil is a shield against evil, I said. Notice, however, the double function of the shield: it protects from violence by inserting itself between me and the enemy; it shelters by redoubling the boundary between the self and the other. The memory of wrongdoing superimposes on the image of the other a narrative of transgression; even a forgiven sinner *is still* a *past* sinner if his or her sins are not forgotten. If the wrongdoing does not recur, the narrative of transgression will recede into the background, and allow the human face of the other to emerge, which will in turn cast the narrative of past sin in a new light. But as soon as a new wrongdoing occurs, the narrative of transgression will spring into the foreground, its large letters, printed in bold, eclipsing the human face of the other. Vivid or clouded, the memory of exclusion suffered is itself a form of exclusion—a protective one to be sure, but an exclusion nonetheless. In my memory of the other's transgression, the other is locked in unredemption and we are bound together in a relationship of nonreconciliation.

The memory of the wrong suffered is also a source of my own nonredemption. As long as it is remembered, the past is not just the past; it remains an aspect of the present. A remembered wound is an experienced wound. Deep wounds from the past can cause so much pain in our present that, as Toni Morrison puts it in *Beloved*, the future becomes "a matter of keeping the past at bay."[102]

"All things and all manner of things" cannot be well with me today, if they are not well in my memory of yesterday. Even remaking the whole world and removing all sources of suffering will not bring redemption if it does not stop incursions of the unredeemed past into the redeemed present through the door of memory. Since memories shape present identities,

---

100. Jan Assmann, *Das kulturelle Gedächtnis: Schrift, Erinnerung und politische Identität in frühen Hochkulturen* (München: C. H. Beck, 1992), 29–86.

101. Tzvetan Todorov, "The Abuses of Memory," *Common Knowledge* 5, no. 1 (1996): 326.

102. Toni Morrison, *Beloved* (New York: Signet, 1991). L. Gregory Jones gives a helpful theological analysis of the politics of memory in Toni Morrison's *Beloved* (*Embodying Forgiveness*, 279ff.), though, except for one brief moment (147), he ascribes only a negative function to forgetting.

neither I nor the other can be redeemed without the redemption of our remembered past. "To redeem the past . . . that alone do I call redemption," remarked Nietzsche profoundly in *Thus Spoke Zarathustra*.[103]

But how can the past be redeemed when "time does not run back"? How can we undo our *past* wounds so as to transform our broken selves into whole ones? How can we separate evildoers from their *past* evil deeds and be reconciled with them? "Powerless against that which has been done," how will we roll away the stone called "That which was," we could ask, using Nietzsche's image?[104] To accomplish the redemption of the past, Nietzsche himself suggested the superhuman act of transforming every "It was" into an "I willed it thus" by the force of "the creative will."[105] Yet the kind of metaphysical miracle Nietzsche has to perform in order to teach the will to "will backwards" and "be reconciled with time" will strike most as a failed trick of a magician. In order to enable the will to "break time and time's desire"[106] he must devise a whole dark theory of the eternal recurrence of all things,[107] that makes even Zarathustra look "like a man seized by extremist terror!"[108] No, for the will—even for the kind of "creative will" that Nietzsche celebrates—the past will forever remain its "most lonely affliction."[109]

The more customary way of redeeming the past is not by willing but by thinking, by an interpretative act of inscribing the tragedy of the past into the precondition of a nontragic future. Redemption of the past is here modeled on theodicies. In the trajectory of Augustinian thinking, for instance, one could reason something like this: much like all the dark shadows in the world "harmonize" with patches of light and contribute to the beauty of the world when the whole is seen from the ultimate perspective of the Creator, so also all the ugliness in my life contributes in some inexplicable way to its future beauty. Evil serves some larger good and we "no longer desire a better world," as Augustine puts it in the *Confessions*.[110] Yet none of the attempts at redeeming past suffering through thinking are able to redeem all such suffering, and most have the odious consequence of making the suffering itself appear to be all the more justified (or at

---

103. Nietzsche, *Thus Spoke Zarathustra*, 161.
104. Ibid.
105. Ibid., 163.
106. Ibid., 161.
107. Ibid., 331ff.
108. Ibid., 163.
109. Ibid., 161.
110. Augustine, *Confessions*, transl. Albert Outler (Philadelphia: Westminster, 1955), bk. vii, 13.

least sanctioned), the more successful they are.[111] More important, even if thinking can deny evil, it cannot remove pain; it triumphs not "over real evil but only over its aesthetic phantom," as Paul Ricoeur puts it.[112] The problem of suffering, whether past or present, cannot be addressed as a speculative question. Life in this world, says Jürgen Moltmann in *The Trinity and the Kingdom*, means living with the "open question" of suffering which springs from the "open wound of life in this world"—and "seeking the future in which the desire for God will be fulfilled, suffering will be overcome, and what has been lost will be restored."[113] The only adequate response to suffering is *action*.

But though action can do much about suffering in the present, it can do nothing about the past experience of suffering. When the tears have dried up and death and pain are no more, what will happen with the *memories* of the wounds suffered and of the inhumanity of those who inflicted them? When God restores what has been lost, how will the *experience* of loss be restored? As long as we remember the injustice and suffering we will not be whole, and the troubling and unanswerable "open question" that craves resolution in an impossible harmony will keep resurfacing. The response of action, even the eschatological transformation, to the problem of past suffering will not suffice. Even in God's new world, we will either have to look back and see "sense" by making the impossible claim that all suffering was justified, or be deeply troubled by the "nonsense" of evil. Will we be able to see "sense"? No, the "nonsense" of at least some suffering is eternal; all the "work of thinking" must finally fail and evil remain a "permanent aporia."[114] Yet in the glory of God's new world—especially there!—the "nonsense" of past suffering will be insufferable—as insufferable as would be its "sense."

If both "nonsense" and "sense" are unacceptable as noetic stances, could then the only way to "solve" the problem of *past* suffering be the *nontheoretical act of nonremembering*[115] just as the only way to overcome

---

111. Emmanuel Lévinas, *Entre nous: Essais sur le penser-à-l'autre* (Paris: Grasset & Fasquelle, 1991); Kenneth Surin, *Theology and the Problem of Evil* (Oxford: Basil Blackwell, 1986); Terrence Tilley, *The Evils of Theodicy* (Washington: Georgetown University Press, 1991).

112. Paul Ricoeur, "The Hermeneutics of Symbols and Philosophical Reflection: I," *The Conflict of Interpretations*, ed. Don Ihde (Evanston: Northwestern University Press, 1974), 312.

113. Moltmann, *The Trinity and the Kingdom*, 49.

114. Paul Ricoeur, "Evil, A Challenge to Philosophy and Theology," *Journal of the American Academy of Religion* 53, no. 3 (1985): 644.

115. Even if suffering inflicted is *forgiven* and the kind of "higher harmony," which Dostoevsky's Ivan Karamazov "absolutely renounces," is established (Dostoevsky, *The Brothers Karamazov*, 245), the "nonsense" of *past* suffering and therefore a "disharmony" in the present would still remain. This disharmony

the present experience of suffering is the nontheoretical act of recreating? After arguing for the "aporetic aspect of thinking about evil" and suggesting "the response of action to the challenge of evil," in his essay "Evil, a Challenge to Philosophy and Theology," Paul Ricoeur immediately adds that "the action alone is not enough" because suffering keeps rekindling the questions "Why?" "Why me?" and "Why my beloved child?" To deal with these persisting questions he suggests that we do the "work of mourning."[116]

The suggestion is helpful, but does not go far enough. Even after the work of mourning is done, the questions will remain if the memory remains. Passing through the stages of mourning, we must ultimately reach the stage of nonremembering—in the arms of God. For Ricoeur, however, the final stage of mourning is not forgetting but "loving God for naught." If we reached that point, he argues, we would "escape completely the cycle of retribution to which the lamentation still remains captive, so long as the victim bemoans the injustice of his or her fate."[117] But would we be fully redeemed? Since "loving God for naught" would not remove the pain from the past or right the injustice already committed—no heaven can *rectify* Auschwitz[118]—we would love God *in spite* of such pain and injustice. And if the suffering remains in the past, the lament over the suffering will remain, at least in the form of an unredeemed sadness over injustice that could not be undone. Only nonremembering can end the lament over suffering which no thought can think away and no action undo.[119]

In a nutshell, my argument is this: since no final redemption is possible without the redemption of the past, and since every attempt to redeem the past through reflection must fail because no theodicy can succeed, the final redemption is unthinkable without a certain kind of forgetting. Put starkly, the alternative is: either heaven *or* the memory of horror. Either heaven will have no monuments to keep the memory of the horrors alive, or it will be closer to hell than we would like to think. For if heaven cannot rectify

---

cannot be resolved either through thought, or through action, or through forgiveness, because none of these can make the deed undone.

116. Paul Ricoeur, "Evil," 646–48.

117. Ibid., 647.

118. Dorothee Soelle, *Suffering*, transl. Evert R. Kalin (Philadelphia: Fortress, 1975), 149.

119. Even the impossible act of undoing what was done would not suffice to achieve the final redemption because the memory of what was done, unless erased, would still remain to afflict the person. Only a much more radical act of "making what happened *not to have happened*" would do, because if what happened was made not to have happened, then what was remembered would have been made *not to have been remembered* too. Which is to say, to have final redemption one may want more than "the transformation of the world plus the loss of the memory of suffering," but one cannot want less.

Auschwitz, then the memory of Auschwitz must undo the experience of heaven. Redemption will be complete only when the creation of "all things new" is coupled with the passage of "all things old" into the double *nihil* of nonexistence and nonremembrance. Such redemptive forgetting is implied in a passage in Revelation about the new heavens and the new earth. "Mourning and crying and pain" will be no more not only because "death will be no more" but also because "the former things have passed away" (Rev 21:4 CEB)—from experience as well as from memory, as the text in Isaiah from which Revelation quotes explicitly states: "the former things shall not be remembered or come to mind" (Isa 65:17; cf. 43:18).[120]

But what about God's memory? Will not God remember? Is not God's memory, as Rowan Williams puts it in *Resurrection*, the long memory of the victim, even if it is a memory of "the victim who will not condemn"?[121] Commenting on the encounter between the resurrected Lord and Peter, Williams argues beautifully that God, resisting the endemic forgetfulness of offenders, restores to them their guilty past, though not so as to condemn them but as to make the restored past "the foundation for a new and extended identity."[122] What will happen, however, after God has narrated the history of the offender's sin in the context of grace[123] and has given the offender a new identity? The answer is so simple and we are so used to hearing it that we miss its profundity: God, to whom all things are present, will *forget* the forgiven sin. The God of Israel, who is about "to do a new thing" and who calls people "not to remember the former things," promises to blot their transgression out of God's own memory (Isa 43:18-19, 25; cf. 65:17). "I will forgive their wrongdoing and never again remember their sins" (Jer 31:34 CEB).

I will return at the end of this section to the modus of God's nonremembrance. Here I want to explore why God "forgets" and what the

---

120. It could be objected that without the memory of the evil or wrongdoing suffered, a person would not be himself or herself. But this would be an odd argument, the fact that our history forms part of our identity notwithstanding. For clearly, we remember now neither everything that has happened to us nor everything we once remembered as having happened to us, and yet we are, arguably, ourselves. Indeed, we are now who we are precisely *because* we do not remember everything but remember this or that and remember it in this or that way. Why, then, would we not be able to be ourselves if the memory of wrongdoing and evil we suffered receded into oblivion? True, our identity would have been reconstituted with such nonremembrance, but it is *our* identity that would be thus reconstituted, much like it is being reconstituted daily. Would it not be strange to assert, for instance, that my mother would not be who she is without the memory of my little brother Daniel's fatal accident, when now as she remembers the accident she wishes with all of her being that it had not happened?

121. Williams, *Resurrection*, 23.

122. Ibid., 35.

123. Jones, *Embodying Forgiveness*, 147.

implications of God's "forgetting" of sins may be for human forgetting of evil and wrongdoings. In seeking an answer to the meaning of God's forgetting, we must pay attention to the complex and multilayered dynamic of divine remembering and nonremembering. God remembers iniquities, remembers them well (Rev 18:5). Yet God also forgets them. God remembers iniquities just to forget them after they have been named as iniquities and forgiven. Why both remembering and forgetting? Because of another divine memory, much more important and powerful than the memory of the offense, a memory that defines the very identity of the God of Israel. Just as a woman cannot forget her nursing child, so God cannot forget Israel. Inscribed on the palms of God's hands, Israel is unforgettable even when she has offended and forgotten God (Isa 49:15-16). The memory of sin must be kept alive for a while, as long as it is needed for repentance and transformation of the wrongdoer to occur. But then it must be let die, so that the fractured relationship of the divine mother and her all too human child may be fully healed. The memory of offense, sustained beyond repentance and transformation of the wrongdoer, clouds both the memory of past love and the vision of future reconciliation. The loss of this memory—the memory of iniquities—brings back the child into the mother's arms, already outstretched toward the baby, because she would not lose the memory of their embrace.

But how dare God forget, we may protest! Let God "forgive and forget" the insults God has suffered, but what "right" does God have to forget all the brutalities done to so many human victims? Would not a loss of *this* memory amount to an embrace between the perpetrator and God—a collusion of the perpetrator's short memory and God's forgetting—that would blur over suffering and death and leave the victims forgotten? Indeed, if God is the God of the victims (which is what the cross tells us God is), God cannot forget as long as the victims remember. With a loud voice the souls of those who have been slaughtered keep reminding God: "Holy and true Master, how long…" (Rev 6:10 CEB). But how long should victims remember? Must victims remain eternally enslaved by what Nietzsche called "the spirit of revenge"?[124] Should not *they too* forget in the end, so that they themselves can be redeemed, the former, transformed perpetrators dressed in white robes, and both reconciled to each other? What speaks so loudly against the victim's forgetting is, of course, the thought—an abysmal thought—of "dressing the former perpetrator in a

124. Nietzsche, *Thus Spoke Zarathustra*, 162.

139

white robe." I wrote these words down drawn by the Pauline vision of justified *sinners*—and immediately erased them. My mind flooded with the images of burned villages, destroyed cities, and raped women from the history of my native country Croatia. It seems impossible for me to embrace a četnik with bloody hands just as it seems impossible for a Jew to embrace a Nazi or that mother to embrace the tormentor who let his dogs tear her son to pieces![125] No redeemed future is imaginable in which perpetrators—even judged and transformed perpetrators!—are dressed in white robes. Everything in us rebels against the image. Yet everything we know about the God of the cross demands that we seriously entertain it. If we do, the question will no longer be how dare God forget, but how can God, without forgetting the victims, help heal their memories.

Consider, first, the eschatological side of the answer. In what strikes one as an "anti-theodicy" of sorts—an abandonment of all speculative solutions to the problem of suffering—the Apostle Paul writes: "I consider that the sufferings of this present time are not worth comparing with the glory about to be revealed to us" (Rom 8:18). The logic is as simple as it is profound. If something is not worth comparing, then it will not be compared, and if it will not be compared then it will not have been remembered. For how would one fail to compare suffering with glory if one remembered the suffering while experiencing the glory?[126]

When we reach the other side, and the bridge connecting the new to the old is destroyed so as to prevent the old from ever invading the new, the last part of the bridge to disappear will be the *memory* of the old. Enveloped in God's glory we will redeem ourselves and our enemies by one final act of the most difficult grace made easy by the experience of salvation that cannot be undone—the grace of nonremembering. When not born out of resentment, the memory of inhumanity is a shield against inhumanity. But where there are no swords, no shields will be necessary. Freed by the loss of memory of all unredeemed past that unredeems every present and separated only by the boundaries of their identities, the former enemies will embrace each other within the embrace of the triune God. "That alone do I call redemption," we might say echoing Nietzsche but referring to a quite different redemption.[127]

125. Dostoevsky, *The Brothers Karamazov*, 245.

126. I do not read Paul's claim "We know that all things work together for good for those who love God" (Rom 8:28) as an attempt to justify God by justifying "all things" but to describe a function of "unjustifiable" things in the lives of "those who love God."

127. Nietzsche, *Thus Spoke Zarathustra*, 161.

Does this vision of the *final* redemption whose *last act* is "nonremembering"—a redemption that has nothing to do with reconciliation through "systematic totalization"[128]—have any bearing on our life in a world where swords abound and shields must be used? It does—provided we do not forget that, as long as the Messiah has not come in glory, for the sake of the victims, we must keep alive the memory of their suffering; we must know it, we must remember it, and we must say it out loud for all to hear (see Chapter VI). This indispensable remembering should be guided, however, by the vision of that same redemption that will one day make us lose the memory of wrongs and hurts suffered and offenses committed. For ultimately, forgetting the suffering is better than remembering it, because wholeness is better than brokenness, the communion of love better than the distance of suspicion, harmony better than disharmony. We remember now in order that we may forget then; and we will forget then in order that we may love without reservation. Though we would be unwise to drop the shield of memory from our hands before the dawn of the new age, we may be able to move it cautiously to the side by opening our arms to embrace the other, even the former enemy.

In the well-known story in the book of Genesis, Joseph was ready to undertake the difficult journey of reconciliation with his brothers who sold him into slavery because, as he put it, "God has made me forget all my hardship and all my father's house" (Gen 41:51). Before coming to an end, the journey of reconciliation entailed a good deal of remembering, however. Joseph himself was reminded of the suffering his brothers had caused, and subtly but powerfully he made them remember it too (Gen 42:21-23; 44:27ff.). Yet, like the distant light of a place called home, the divine gift of forgetting what he still remembered—"backgrounding" the memory might be the right term[129]—guided the whole journey of return. Wanting to ensure that the precious gift be lost neither on him nor on his posterity, Joseph inscribed it into the name of his son, Manasseh—"one who causes to be forgotten." A paradoxical memorial to forgetting

128. Ricoeur, "Evil," 635.
129. Philip Clayton has suggested this term to me. It could be argued that what I should be after in this whole section is "backgrounding" or "*Aufhebung*" of the memories of horrors. Both "backgrounding" and "*Aufhebung*" keep the memory of horrors alive, and therefore require a successful theodicy if they are not to undo the final reconciliation. Since I do not see (yet) how a theodicy can succeed, I continue to believe that all those who want heaven cannot want the memory of horrors. "Backgrounding" and "*Aufhebung*" is, however, appropriate as a way of dealing with the memories of horrors within history; they are the preeschatological anticipations of the eschatological nonremembering; or, to put it the other way around, eschatological nonremembering is backgrounding the horrors into oblivion.

(how can one be reminded to forget without being reminded of what one should forget?), Manasseh's presence recalled the suffering in order to draw attention to the loss of its memory. It is this strange forgetting, still interspersed with indispensable remembering, that made Joseph, the victim, able to embrace his brothers, the perpetrators (Gen 45:14-15)—and become theirs and his own savior (Gen 46:1ff.).

In summary, recall divine "forgetting" and its relation to human forgetting. How can God forget the wrongdoings of human beings? Because at the center of God's all-embracing memory there is a paradoxical monument to forgetting. It is the cross of Christ. God forgets humanity's sins in the same way God forgives humanity's sins: by taking sins away from humanity and placing them upon Godself. How will human beings be able to forget the horrors of history? Because at the center of the new world that will emerge after "the first things have passed away" there will stand a throne, and on the throne there will sit the Lamb who has "taken away the sin of the world" and erased their memory (Rev 22:1-4; John 1:29).

The Drama of Embrace

As fruit of both the suffering of Christ and the glory of God's new world, eschatological forgetting finally removes the memory of injury as the last obstacle to an unhindered embrace. But what is an embrace? In what sense can it function as a metaphor for reconciliation, even suggest more than is contained in the notion of reconciliation itself? Looking partly back, especially at the section "Space for the Other," I want to sketch a "phenomenology of embrace" in order to suggest a way of thinking about identity—personal as well as communal—in relation to the other under the conditions of enmity. For this purpose I will first draw attention to the essential structural elements of embrace and then elaborate on some of its key features. But first two introductory comments.

First, as I was writing the following "drama of embrace" I kept casting a glance (mostly a disagreeing one!) at the "drama of reciprocal recognition" between the "master" and the "slave" in *The Phenomenology of Spirit*, where Hegel develops his "first and basic model of the recognition of oneself in others."[130] Just as in Hegel's famous and influential text, metaphorical language about "master" and "slave" glides into the nonmetaphorical and back, so also in the following analysis of the self and the other

---

130.   Charles Taylor, *Hegel* (Cambridge: Cambridge University Press, 1975), 152f.

centered around "embrace" metaphor and concept are intertwined.[131] Second, my choice to take embrace as "a metonymy" for the whole realm of human relations in which the interplay between the self and the other takes place[132] might strike people in some cultures (such as Asian and North European) as too intimate; for them, the handshake might be more appropriate, which again in other cultures (such as African or American) might seem too cold and distant. What I say about embrace could equally well be said of a handshake, however, which Gurevitch has appropriately called "a mini-embrace."[133] In fact, there is a range of embraces—"from finger holding finger, palm holding palm, hand holding arm, to hands over shoulders while walking, sitting, or lying side by side."[134] In any case, I am not interested here so much in the physical embrace itself as in the dynamic relationship between the self and the other that embrace symbolizes and enacts.

The four structural elements in the movement of embrace are opening the arms, waiting, closing the arms, and opening them again. For embrace to happen, all four must be there and they must follow one another on an unbroken timeline; stopping with the first two (opening the arms and waiting) would abort the embrace, and stopping with the third (closing the arms) would pervert it from an act of love to an act of oppression and, paradoxically, exclusion. The four elements are then the four essential steps of an integrated movement.

Act one: *opening* the arms. Open arms are a gesture of the body reaching for the other. They are a sign of discontent with my own self-enclosed identity, a code of *desire* for the other. I do not want to be myself only; I want the other to be part of who I am and I want to be part of the other. A herald of nonself-sufficiency and nonself-enclosure, open arms suggest the pain of other's absence and the joy of the other's anticipated presence. Both the pain of absence and the joy of anticipated presence underscore the fact that even before the self opens its arms, the other is in a sense already part of it. Unlike the "self-consciousness" of *The Phenomenology of the Spirit*, the self does not appear first as "self-equal through the exclusion

131.   Unlike my use of "embrace," Hegel's language of "master" and "slave" is not purely metaphorical, but conditioned by his, from my perspective impossible, attempt at a historical reconstruction of the Spirit's development.

132.   Z. D. Gurevitch, "The Embrace: On the Element of Non-Distance in Human Relations," *Sociological Quarterly* 31, no. 2 (1990): 187–201. I have written my text before this important essay came to my attention.

133.   Ibid., 192.

134.   Ibid., 194.

from itself of everything else."[135] From the very start, it is inhabited by various others, who can be excluded from the self only at the price of losing the self.[136] It is the void, created by the absence of what in some sense is already present as a structuring element of the self, that generates the desire for the other.

More than just a code for desire, open arms are a sign that I have *created space* in myself for the other to come in and that I have made a movement out of myself so as to enter the space created by the other. To stretch the arms toward the other, the self must at the same time withdraw from itself, pull itself back, so to speak, away from the limits of its own boundaries; the self that is "full of itself" can neither receive the other nor make a genuine movement toward the other. In opening its arms, the self makes room for the other and sets on a journey toward the other in one and the same act. Third, open arms suggest a *fissure* in the self. They signify an aperture on the boundary of the self through which the other can come in. The desire for the other can be fulfilled and the space for the other created by self-emptying occupied only if the boundaries are passable.

Finally, open arms are a gesture of *invitation*. Like a door left opened for an expected friend, they are a call to come in. No knock is necessary, no question on the part of the other whether he or she can come in is needed, just the announcement of arrival and stepping over the threshold. If the friendship is damaged, even turned into enmity, the invitation will be conditional—in the sense that certain conditions need to be fulfilled not before the invitation can be issued but before "entering in" can take place. In fact, the invitation is *always* conditional in this limited sense— dirty shoes must stay outside!—only that friends, being friends, tend to fulfill the conditions. Unlike the open door, however, open arms are more than just a gesture of invitation for the other to come in. They are also a *soft knock* on the other's door. The desire to enter the space of the other has been signaled by the very same act by which the self has opened itself up for the other to come in.

Act two: *waiting.* The open arms reach out but stop before touching the other. They wait. By opening the arms, the self has initiated the movement toward the other, a movement for whose justification no invitation from the other is needed and no reciprocation on the part of the other

---

135. Georg Wilhelm Friedrich Hegel, *Phenomenology of the Spirit*, transl. A. V. Miller (Oxford: Oxford University Press, 1977), 113.

136. Charles Taylor, "The Politics of Recognition," *Multiculturalism: Examining the Politics of Recognition*, ed. Amy Gutmann (Princeton: Princeton University Press, 1994), 32ff.

necessary, a movement that is itself an invitation to the other and for whose justification therefore the simple desire of the self not to be without the other suffices. But the initiated movement of embrace is not "an act of invasion," not even a "tentative and exploratory" one, as Bauman said of "caress" as a metaphor for morality.[137] After creating space in itself and coming out of itself, the self has "postponed" desire and halted at the boundary of the other. Before it can proceed, it must wait for desire to arise in the other and for the arms of the other to open. Using Hegel's understanding of labor as "desire held in check,"[138] we can describe waiting as the labor of the desiring self on itself for the sake of the integrity of the other—the other, who may not want to be embraced but left alone,[139] perhaps because of the painful memory that once what started as an embrace ended in violation or even rape (as with those women who were liberated at the end of World War II just to be raped by their liberators).

The halted movement of the arms outstretched toward the other has its own proper power, of course. This one-sidedness of action is not "useless," as Hegel suggests.[140] The waiting self *can* move the other to make the movement toward the self, but its power to do so is the power of signaled desire, of created space, opened boundary of the self, and enacted respect for the other, not the power that breaks the boundaries of the other and forces the fulfillment of desire. The other cannot be coerced or manipulated into an embrace; violence is so much the opposite of embrace that it undoes the embrace. If embrace takes place, it will always be because the other has desired the self just as the self has desired the other. This is what distinguishes embrace from grasping after the other and holding the other in one's power. Waiting is a sign that, although embrace may have a one-sidedness in its origin (the self makes the initial movement toward the other), it can never reach its goal without reciprocity (the other makes a movement toward the self).

Act three: *closing* the arms. This is the goal of embrace, the embrace proper, which is unthinkable without *reciprocity*; "each is both holding and being held by the other, both active and passive."[141] It takes *two* pairs of arms for *one* embrace; with one pair, we will either have merely an

---

137. Bauman, *Postmodern Ethics*, 93.
138. Hegel, *Phenomenology of the Spirit*, 118.
139. Marjorie Hewitt Suchocki, *The Fall to Violence: Original Sin in Relational Theology* (New York: Continuum, 1995), 146f.
140. Hegel, *Phenomenology of the Spirit*, 112.
141. Gurevitch, "The Embrace," 194.

invitation to embrace (if the self respects the other) or a taking in one's clutches (if there is no such respect). In an embrace a host is a guest and a guest is a host. Though one self may receive or give more than the other, each must enter the space of the other, feel the presence of the other in the self, and make its own presence felt. Without such reciprocity, there is no embrace. Hegel puts it precisely: the action is "two-sided" because it is "the action of the one as well as the other."[142]

For such free and mutual giving and receiving to take place, in addition to reciprocity, a *soft touch* is necessary. I may not close my arms around the other too tightly, so as to crush the other and assimilate him or her, otherwise I will be engaged in a concealed power-act of exclusion; an embrace would be perverted into a "bear-hug." Similarly, I must keep the boundaries of my own self firm, offer resistance, otherwise I will be engaged in a self-destructive act of abnegation. At no point in the process may the self deny either the other or itself. The embrace itself depends on success in resisting the vortex of de-differentiation through active or passive assimilation, yet without retreating into self-insulation. In an embrace the identity of the self is both preserved and transformed, and the alterity of the other is both affirmed as alterity and partly received into the ever-changing identity of the self.

To preserve the alterity of the other in the embrace it is essential to acquire the unusual ability *not* to understand the other. In an important essay "The Power of Not Understanding," Z. D. Gurevitch has argued against the simple schema that posits a movement from "the inability to understand" to "the ability to understand." This schema diverts attention from the fact that the initial "inability to understand" may be tacitly predicated on the desire to understand the other on the self's own terms, within the framework of its own reflexivity, whereas the other may not be understandable within the self's framework precisely on account of being the other. "The-inability-not-to-understand" may be, paradoxically, a hindrance to understanding. Hence Gurevitch argues that "the-ability-not-to-understand"—"the ability to recognize and behold the other (or the self) as an other"—is essential.[143] In concrete encounters with the other, at "the moment of not understanding" the self understands that what there is to understand about the other can "only be addressed as a question."[144]

142. Hegel, *Phenomenology of the Spirit*, 112.
143. Z. D. Gurevitch, "The Power of Not Understanding: The Meeting of Conflicting Identities," *The Journal of Applied Behavioral Science* 25, no. 2 (1989): 163.
144. Ibid., 168.

The emergence of *the other as a question* right in the midst of an embrace represents a *productive refusal to occultate the opacity of the other*, a refusal that opens possibilities of new and better understanding: the self sees both itself and the other in a new light. Within the movement of embrace, the nonunderstanding, which seems like a defeat is in fact a small triumph—"yet this is not the triumph of the self, but of the other as other for the self."[145] Without the framework of embrace, the ability-not-to-understand is sterile; but without the ability-not-to-understand a genuine embrace is impossible.

Act four: *opening* the arms again. Embrace does not make "two bodies one" by "transforming the boundary between bodies into the seam that holds together one body," as Bauman writes of love's desire.[146] What holds the bodies together in an embrace is not their welded boundary but the arms placed around the other. And if the embrace is not to cancel itself, the arms must open again.[147] The mutual indwelling of the selves that embrace signifies must not end in "this absolute substance that is the unity of the different independent self-consciousnesses, which, in their opposition, enjoy perfect freedom and independence: 'I' that is 'We' and 'We' that is 'I,'" as Hegel describes the Spirit.[148] Were this to happen, embrace would signal the final "disappearance of the 'I' into the 'we'" that is characteristic not only of totalitarian regimes but of many cultural movements and family relations.[149] As the final act of embrace, the opening of the arms underlines that, though the other may be inscribed into the self, the alterity of the other may not be neutralized by merging both into an undifferentiated "we" (though, arguably, "de-differentiation" is not what Hegel intended). The other must be let go so that his or her alterity—his or her genuine dynamic identity—may be preserved; and the self must take itself back into itself so that its own identity, enriched by the traces that the presence of the other has left, may be preserved.

The other must be let go, finally, so that "the negotiation of difference," which can "never produce a final settlement," may be continued.[150] The open arms that in the last act let the other go are the same open arms

---

145. Ibid., 172.

146. Bauman, *Postmodern Ethics*, 94.

147. Gurevitch, "The Embrace," 194.

148. Hegel, *Phenomenology of the Spirit*, 110.

149. Todorov, *The Conquest of America: The Question of the Other*, transl. Richard Howard (New York: HarperCollins, 1984), 251.

150. Michael Walzer, *Thick and Thin: Moral Arguments at Home and Abroad* (Notre Dame, IN: University of Notre Dame Press, 1994), 83.

that in the first act signal a desire for the other's presence, create space in oneself, open up the boundary of the self, and issue an invitation for the other to come. They are the same arms that in the second act wait for the other to reciprocate, and that in the third act encircle the other's body. The end of an embrace is, in a sense, already a beginning of an embrace, even if that other embrace will take place only after both selves have gone about their own business for a while. Though embrace itself is not terminal, the movement of the self to the other and back has no end. This movement is circular; the actions and reactions of the self and the other condition each other and give the movement both meaning and energy.[151]

These then are the essential structural elements of embrace; without them there could be no genuine embrace. Now I want to look at the four notable features of a successful embrace, some of which are implied in the logic of the embrace itself, and some of which are inscribed in God's embrace of humanity on the cross and should characterize our desire for embrace under the conditions of enmity. The first is the *fluidity of identities*. In *Culture and Imperialism,* Edward Said points out that "all culture is hybrid... and encumbered, or entangled with what used to be regarded as extraneous elements."[152] The same is true of the individual selves that inhabit encumbered cultures; the selves are internally differentiated through the various roles they play, communities with which they identify, and principles and values they espouse.[153] There are always strangers within our personal and communal gates and we ourselves never belong completely to a given group but only in part. As individuals and communities, we live in overlapping social territories. Our selves and our communities are like our domiciles in which we feel at home, and yet keep remodeling and rearranging, taking old things out and bringing new things in, often objects acquired on visits to near and distant places, objects that symbolize that we can never be the same after we have ventured out of our home, that things we encounter "outside" become a part of the "inside."

Second, the *nonsymmetricity* of the relationship. Embrace, I propose, should not just be seen as a metaphor for the factual or desirable "merging" and "diverging" of various streams that take place in every self and every community. It describes also a *moral* stance of the selves that are in fact never simply "merging" and "diverging" but are inserted into a

151. Helm Stierlin, *Das Tun des Einen ist das Tun des Anderen: Eine Dynamik menschlicher Beziehungen* (Frankfurt: Suhrkamp, 1976), 67f.

152. Edward W. Said, *Culture and Imperialism* (New York: Alfred A. Knopf, 1993), 317.

153. Walzer, *Thick and Thin*, 85f.

permanent struggle in which the strong oppress the weak and the weak seek to subvert the power of the strong. Emmanuel Lévinas has emphasized that, properly speaking, a moral stance entails eschewing symmetricity. In *Otherwise than Being* he writes,

> The knot of subjectivity consists in going to the other without concerning oneself with his movement toward me. Or, more exactly, it consists in approaching in such a way that, over and beyond all the reciprocal relations that do not fail to get set up between me and the neighbor, I have always taken one step more toward him.[154]

"One step more" toward the neighbor, and the first step—maybe even the second and the third—toward the enemy! As a metaphor, embrace implies that the self and the other belong together in their mutual alterity. For the self shaped by the cross of Christ and the life of the triune God, however, embrace includes not just the other who is a friend but also the other who is the enemy. Such a self will seek to open its arms toward the other even when the other holds a sword. The other will, of course, have to drop the sword, maybe even have the sword taken out of his or her hand, before the actual embrace can take place. Yet even the struggle over the sword will be undergirded by the will to embrace the other and be embraced in return.

In the context of enmity, if reciprocity between the self and the other is established, it will not be simply through the "struggle for recognition" between "the master" and "the slave," which eventually ends in a reciprocal recognition among equals, as Hegel thought.[155] The reciprocal embrace of equals, to return to my terminology, is a fruit of self-giving that already *presupposes recognition of the other*, not of struggle through which the self and the other must earn recognition. Except for a naïve philosophy of history, the struggle leads to struggle and hierarchizes relationships rather than equalizing them because it generates ever-new versions of the "master"–"slave" polarity. Hierarchies cannot be simply leveled, least of all through struggle; they must be inverted: the Lamb is the Shepherd (Rev 7:17) and the Kings are the Servants (Rev 22:1-5).[156] The equality and

---

154. Emmanuel Lévinas, *Otherwise Than Being, or Beyond Essence*, transl. A. Lingis (The Hague: Martinus Nijhoff, 1981), 84.

155. Hegel, *Phenomenology of the Spirit*, 111ff.

156. Daniel Boyarin rightly pleads for a conception of identity "in which there are only slaves but no masters, that is, an alternative to the model of self-determination which is, after all, in itself a western, imperialist imposition" (*A Radical Jew: Paul and the Politics of Identity* [Berkeley: University of California Press, 1994], 249).

reciprocity that are at the heart of embrace can be reached only through self-sacrifice (Mark 10:41-45), even if self-sacrifice is not a positive good but a necessary *via dolorosa* in a world of enmity and indifference toward the joy of reciprocal embrace. Such self-sacrifice is modeled on Christ's self-sacrifice, which is nothing but the mutuality of trinitarian self-giving in encounter with the enemy.[157]

Third, the *underdetermination of the outcome*. Built into the very structure of embrace is a "multifinality" that rests on the systematic underdetermination of outcomes. Given the structural element of waiting, nothing can guarantee that embrace will take place; the only power that can be used to bring it about is the power of embrace's own allure. Though each may open the arms toward the other, each has the right to refuse the embrace, to close himself or herself off and stay outside the exchange of mutual giving and receiving. And once the embrace has taken place, nothing can guarantee a particular outcome. Given the structural element of gentleness, we can never know in advance how the reshaping of the self and the other will take place in embrace. Though the self may try to reconfigure the other, no outcome can be preprogrammed (as in a good barter where both get roughly the same value of the goods as they give), and (as in a good intellectual exchange) all outcomes are in principle possible, even if many are not likely, given the previous history of the selves. Only one outcome is not possible: a genuine embrace cannot leave both or either completely unchanged.[158]

Finally, there is the *risk of embrace*. The risk follows both from nonsymmetricity and systematic underdetermination. I open my arms, make a movement of the self toward the other, the enemy, and do not know whether I will be misunderstood, despised, and even violated, or whether my action will be appreciated, supported, and reciprocated. I can become a savior or a victim—possibly both. Embrace is grace, and "grace is gamble, always."[159]

---

157. In dialogue with many recent interpreters of the doctrine of the Trinity, Anthony C. Thiselton has argued in *Interpreting God and the Postmodern Self: On Meaning, Manipulation and Promise* (Grand Rapids: Eerdmans, 1995) for taking trinitarian self-giving as a model for the relation of the human self to the other (153ff.).

158. In the debate about the relative value of cultures, for instance, we can neither say in advance that we owe equal respect to all cultures nor that some cultures are excluded as possible candidates for equal respect. Responsible judgment will be made only after the encounter, an encounter which could alter not only our initial suspicions but also transform the *standards* by which we make judgments (Taylor, "The Politics of Recognition," 66–73).

159. Smedes, *Forgive and Forget,* 137.

Contract, Covenant, Embrace

Without a certain kind of "gamble"—a gamble on account of "grace"—truly human life would be impossible. Yet "gambling party" would be a singularly ill-suited metaphor for social life as a whole. Awash in the sea of contingency and threatened by enmity, human beings need much more predictability than the fickle play of the dice tends to provide.[160] Would then the combination of (initial) nonsymmetricity and systematic underdetermination of outcomes that make embrace a risky endeavor undo the political usefulness of embrace? No, but the need for basic predictability demands that we complement the risky "grace" of embrace with some form of mutually binding "law"; or rather, to frame the "law" regulating social relations by the "grace" of embrace so as to both affirm the "law" and keep transforming it from within. I will explore two dominant metaphors for regulating social life in contemporary societies that seek to ensure predictability—"contract" and "covenant"—and then suggest how the prevalent understanding of social covenant might be enriched by the preceding reflection on embrace.

One powerful contemporary metaphor for social life designed to guarantee a great deal of predictability—even strict calculability—is the metaphor of "contract." Political liberalism, which conceives life as essentially a business of individual self-interest, has promoted "contract" as the master metaphor of social life. Plagued by fear of harm and driven by desire for comfort, individuals enter "contracts" that favor them with "security and gain."[161] Contracts let each achieve with the help of others what none could achieve alone. Civil society emerges as the offspring of such contractual interaction. Are the shoulders of "contract" broad enough, however, to carry the social burden placed on it?

Consider the following three notable features of contracts. First, they are *performance oriented*. Though conviviality may be a pleasant side-benefit, the point of a contract is to ensure that a task is accomplished, say, a commodity produced or a service rendered. The task done, the relationship dissolves—insofar as it was regulated by contract. Second, contracts are marked by *limited commitment*. In the words of Philip Selznick, who underscores this feature of contractual relations,

---

160. Arendt, *The Human Condition*, 219ff.
161. William M. Sullivan, *Reconstructing Public Philosophy* (Berkeley: University of California Press, 1982), 13.

terms and conditions are specified closely, and the cost of nonperformance is calculable. Furthermore, with some exceptions, the moral or legal obligation is not necessarily to *fulfill* the agreement, but only to make good losses that may be incurred in case of an unjustified breach.[162]

The contract obliges only to what it explicitly or implicitly states, no less and certainly no more; it secures an attachment "until a better return is available elsewhere," as Michael Luntley describes what he calls "mercantile belonging."[163] Third, contracts are strictly *reciprocal.* The consent of both parties is needed to oblige both; obversely, the transgression of the one dis-obliges the other. In an important sense, the contract is designed to make the parties mirror each other's behavior. As Bauman puts it, "the 'duty to fulfill the duty' is for each side dependent on the other side's record. I am obliged to abide by the contract only as long, and in as far, as the partner does the same."[164]

Given the contract's strict reciprocity, limited commitment, and performance-orientation it is easy to see why it would emerge as the master metaphor for social relations in contemporary societies. In a typically modern way, our lives are organized around the roles we play, and we like to think that we are free to choose which roles to play and how long to play them. We offer services in exchange for services, but keep our options open for a better deal or a more desirable benefit. Contracts make relations binding but not inflexible; they commit without enslaving. Tailor-made for interaction between social actors who see themselves as separate units and whose most sacred good is freedom to decide what they want and how long they want it, contracts both stabilize commitments and keep them fluid. They seem the perfect structuring principle of an order typical of contemporary societies, always "local, emergent, and transitory."[165]

The social utility of contracts is indisputable; without them life in detraditioned and differentiated societies would be nearly impossible. But will "contract" do as the master metaphor for social life as a whole? Can it offer more than just a "descriptive code" for what we do in one important segment of our lives? Does it suggest a vision of how we *should* live, a vision of the good life? Hardly. In a contractual model of society, the three salient

---

162. Philip Selznick, *The Moral Commonwealth: Social Theory and the Promise of Community* (Berkeley: University of California Press, 1992), 479.

163. Michael Luntley, *Reason, Truth and Self: The Postmodern Reconditioned* (London: Routledge, 1995), 190.

164. Bauman, *Postmodern Ethics*, 59.

165. Zygmunt Bauman, *Intimations of Postmodernity* (London: Routledge, 1992), 189.

features of contracts are three important ways of misconstruing human life. First, human beings are not "autonomous individuals" who associate only to perform tasks that advance their self-interests; relations to other people penetrate below the surface of the self. To give but one example, even with a contract in hand, a patient wants more from a doctor than competent technical performance; functional relations between them feed on "irrational" and nonspecifiable emotional bonds.[166] Second, at many levels mutual commitments cannot be limited by terms and conditions clearly specified in advance. Often human beings are bound by something like a common destiny, not just by mutual utility. As the example of divorce shows (even a "successful" one), it is impossible strictly speaking to make good losses incurred by a breach of such close fellowship. Finally, we have obligations to our neighbors that are not invalidated by our neighbor's failure to fulfill corresponding obligations to us; our relationships are not strictly reciprocal. If my neighbor breaks trust, I am not entitled to do the same, as I would be entitled not to pay her for a service she did not render. As the master metaphor for social relations, the contract is deeply flawed because human beings are socially situated, their lives intertwined, and their interchange morally encumbered.[167]

Troubled by the dominance of contractual relations in contemporary societies, "which leave every commitment unstable"[168] and undermine community, some social philosophers have advocated retrieval of covenant as the alternative master metaphor of social life.[169] With its original home in the world of religious commitments rather than business transactions,[170] covenant promises better to express the communal and moral dimensions of human life. In contrast to contract, argues Selznick in *Moral Commonwealth*,

---

166. Stierlin, *Das Tun des Einen ist das Tun des Anderen*, 24ff.

167. In *The One, the Three and the Many* (Cambridge: Cambridge University Press, 1993), Colin Gunton defends the metaphor of "social contract" on the grounds that "the language of contract is a metaphorical way of speaking of the social" (222). The response must surely be that "contract" is a bad *metaphor*.

168. Robert Bellah et al., *Habits of the Heart: Individualism and Commitment in American Life* (New York: Harper, 1985), 130.

169. Robert Bellah, *The Broken Covenant: American Civil Religion in Time of Trial* (New York: Seabury, 1975); Sullivan, *Reconstructing Public Philosophy*.

170. In *The Heavenly Contract: Ideology and Organization in Pre-Revolutionary Puritanism* (Chicago: The University of Chicago Press, 1985), David Zaret has, however, argued that the prominence of the theme of covenant in the Puritan theology of the sixteenth and seventeenth centuries owes much to the fact that from 1500 to 1640 "contractual interactions in pursuit of profit became a familiar feature of everyday economic life" (165).

Covenant…suggests an indefeasible commitment and a continuing relationship. The bond is relatively unconditional, relatively indissoluble…. The bond contemplates open-ended and diffuse obligations, implicates the whole person or group, and creates a salient status.[171]

As a communitarian liberal, Selznick refuses to give up either on the modern "autonomous individual"[172] or on the "relatively unconditional" bonds and "moral ordering" of social life.[173] Covenant, he claims, allows him to hold on to both. It speaks both of autonomy and belonging, of individual commitments and ongoing social situatedness; "covenant" contains "vital elements of voluntarism and consent" and creates obligations that "derive from the nature and history of the relationship" and cannot be "fully specified in advance."[174] Unlike contract, which defines a limited and reciprocal commitment, covenant structures an open-ended and morally ordered relationship.

But what is the nature of the relationship that the covenant structures? What kind of common history does it create? Why should this relationship not be exclusive, for instance, designed to promote the interests of a community of destiny that is morally ordered in deeply *immoral* ways? Was not Apartheid based on the covenant idea too? Covenant may morally structure communal life, but the decisive question is surely *what will morally structure the covenant itself* so as to make it a covenant of justice rather than oppression, of truth rather than deception, of peace rather than violence. Selznick makes the principle that "all men are created equal" the chief "covenantal premise." But he arrives at the principle not through the idea of covenant but through "a leap of faith," "a self-defining commitment," "a venture in constitution-making." In other words, the theory of covenant works as "a theory of moral ordering" only because he *adds* to the formal structure of the covenant as a pattern of social relations the commitment to certain "self-evident principles."[175] Covenant has no sufficiently strong moral legs of its own but must rest on substantive values that come from elsewhere. These substantive values do much more social work than the formal notion of the covenant.

---

171. Selznick, *The Moral Commonwealth*, 479.
172. Ibid., 482ff.
173. Ibid., 477.
174. Ibid., 480.
175. Ibid., 482f.

In today's political discourse the notion of covenant draws much of its potency from the fact that the United States of America was "a nation formed by a covenant."[176] A covenant could form a nation, of course, only because the so-called Calvinist "monarchomachians" first formed *a covenantal idea of nation*.[177] For them, however, the covenant of human beings with one another was "based on and preserved by God's covenant with them";[178] the covenant's moral legs were supplied by the covenant-making God. The duties of human beings as God's covenant partners were expressed in the "moral law," the Decalogue, that federal theologians considered universally binding. It mapped a moral order that extended as far as the rule of the one God reached; it encompassed the whole of human community. Covenant could become a useful political category because it was first a *moral* category, and it became a moral category because it was at its core a *theological* category. All particular human covenants, from family and neighborhood to state, must be subordinate to the inclusive covenant that encompasses the whole of humanity and is guided by substantive values, the universal "holding on to each other" in solidarity.[179] Without some such universal substantive values to form its premises, covenant may well serve as the bond of political community, but the political community will be no better than the values it espouses. By itself, the covenant will certainly not provide an adequate standard by which a political community can judge itself.[180]

Beyond the stress on the universality of covenant and the substantive values stemming from God's covenant with humanity, what can theology bring to the reflection about covenant as the master metaphor for social life? In the article "Covenant or Leviathan" Jürgen Moltmann has followed the early federalist "political theologians" and underscored the freedom that people united by a covenant under God acquire to resist "the

---

176.   John Schaar, *Legitimacy and the Modern State* (New Brunswick: Transaction Books, 1981), 291.

177.   Charles McCoy and J. Wayne Baker, *Fountainhead of Federalism: Heinrich Bullinger and the Covenantal Tradition* (Louisville: Westminster John Knox, 1991), 45ff., 94ff.

178.   Jürgen Moltmann, "Covenant or Leviathan? Political Theology for Modern Times," *Scottish Journal of Theology* 47, no. 1 (1994): 25.

179.   Sander Griffioen, "The Metaphor of the Covenant in Habermas," *Faith and Philosophy* 8, no. 4 (1991): 534ff.

180.   If we are to believe John Schaar, Abraham Lincoln's notion of covenant echoed something of the original federal tradition because it was centered around universal commitments—a covenant to "uphold and advance certain commitments among ourselves and throughout the world"—and could therefore serve not simply as "the bond of political community" but as "the standard by which the nation must judge itself" (Schaar, *Legitimacy and the Modern State*, 291).

great Leviathan"—a tyrannical government.[181] He analyzed the vertical relation of the covenanting people to the state; his concern was the nature of consent and the limits of political authority. I want to supplement his analysis by looking at the horizontal relation between covenanting people themselves; my concern is the nature of commitments and the conditions for communal flourishing.[182]

Contemporary societies are threatened as much, if not more, by the incapacity of people to keep covenant with one another as by the tendency of tyrannical governments to break covenant with them. The two threats are related. If you do not attend to the capacity of people to keep their covenant you will have to contend with the tendency of the government to break the covenant with the people. This is the negative lesson of Hobbes's political philosophy: the more society consists of self-centered egoists, the greater the need for Leviathan—a tightly organized and centralized state apparatus.[183] The close kinship between individualism and absolutism[184] works in the other direction too: the less people are able to claim the right of resistance against the great Leviathan, the more they will want to see themselves as autonomous individuals engaged in pursuit of their own interests only.

"By mutual covenants one with another," says Thomas Hobbes in *Leviathan,* people transfer "authority" to the state and thus give birth to "that great Leviathan (or rather, to speak more reverently...*mortal god*), to which we owe under the *immortal God,* our peace and defense."[185] The transfer of power in the moment of the unanimity of "every man with every man" is necessary to end the persisting war of "everyone against everyone." Incapable of forming and keeping covenants between themselves, people need Leviathan—who, according to the biblical witness, makes covenants with no one (Job 41:4)—so that by "terror" of his power and strength he may "form the wills of them all" and thereby ensure "peace at home and mutual aid against their enemies abroad." Leviathan emerges out of the murky and chaotic waters of negative anthropology. In contrast,

---

181. Moltmann, "Covenant or Leviathan?"

182. Moltmann has since addressed the horizontal dimensions of the covenant with the help of the category of "promise" ("Christianity and the Values of Modernity and of the Western World," Unpublished paper, 1996).

183. Sullivan, *Reconstructing Public Philosophy,* 20.

184. John Milbank, *Theology and Social Theory: Beyond Secular Reason* (Oxford: Blackwell, 1990), 12ff.

185. Thomas Hobbes, *Leviathan,* The Library of Liberal Arts, ed. Oskar Piest (Indianapolis: Bobbs-Merrill, 1967), Part 2, Chapter 17.

covenant presupposes a more positive anthropology. As Moltmann has argued, trust in the God who enters into covenant with human beings grounds the trust in their ability to form covenants.[186]

Yet the indisputable human capacity to make covenants is matched by their incontestable capacity to break them. The cumulative message of the biblical covenantal traditions is that both "capacities" are in fact the two intertwined ways of communal living: human beings continuously make and break covenants. And behind the tumult of "making" and "breaking" lies an anthropological constant: human beings are *always already in the covenant* as those who have *always already broken the covenant*. Reflection on the intricate dynamics of making and breaking covenants should therefore supplement (not substitute!) interest in the alternative between negative and positive anthropology.

For theological reflection on social matters, much more significant than the "original covenant" on which the federalist tradition builds, is the "new covenant," which remains almost completely neglected as a resource for political thought. What are the social implications of the new covenant? The new covenant also presupposes the capacity of humans to form covenants. Yet it situates this capacity in the midst of a history of conflict not simply between the people and the state but among the covenanting people themselves. For one, the new covenant is a response to a persistent pattern of breaking the covenant. In social terms, it emerges against the backdrop of enmity, understood not as some fictive "state of nature" to be rectified by an equally fictive "covenant," but as a pervasive social dynamic between the people who already belong to the covenant but fail to keep it. Second, the new covenant raises the fundamental issue of how to take the covenantal promises from stone tablets and put them within the people and engrave them onto their hearts (Jer 31:31ff.). Above and beyond persuading people to resist tyrants by entering and keeping covenants, a key political task must be to nurture people whose very identity should be shaped by the covenants they have formed so that they do not betray and tyrannize one another. To place the new covenant at the center of theological reflection on social issues means for a Christian theologian to inquire about the relation between *the cross and the covenant*. On the cross we see what God has done to renew the covenant that humanity has broken. Drawing partly on my earlier discussion ("Space for the Other: Cross, Trinity, Eucharist"), I want to point out briefly what can be learned from

---

186. Moltmann, "Covenant or Leviathan?" 25.

the cross about how to renew the covenant—renew in the triple sense of strengthening the covenants that are fragile, repairing the covenants that are broken, and keeping the covenants from being completely undone.

First, on the cross God renews the covenant by *making space* for humanity in God's self. The open arms of Christ on the cross are a sign that God does not want to be a God without the other—humanity—and suffers humanity's violence in order to embrace it. What could this divine "making-space-in-oneself" imply for social covenants?

Unlike contract, covenant is not simply a relationship of mutual utility but of moral commitment, I argued earlier, agreeing with the critics of the contractual model of society. We have to go a step farther, however. For covenant partners are not simply moral agents who have certain duties to one another within the framework of a long-standing relationship. Precisely because covenant is lasting, the parties themselves cannot be conceived as individuals whose identities are external to one another and who are related to one another only by virtue of their moral will and moral practice. Rather, the very *identity* of each is formed through relation to others; the alterity of the other enters into the very identity of each.

Under these conditions, to renew the covenant means to "transcend the *perspective* of the one side and take into account the complementary dispositions of the other side."[187] Even more, to renew the covenant means to attend to the shifts in the *identity* of the other, to make space for the changing other in ourselves, and to be willing to renegotiate our own identity in interaction with the fluid identity of the other.[188] Each party in the covenant must understand its own behavior and identity as complementary to the behavior and identity of other parties. Without such complementarity and continual readjustments of dynamic identities, moral bonds will not suffice as protection against the pressure on the covenant in a pluralistic context, and the door will open for Leviathan's return. Sustaining and renewing covenants between persons and groups requires the work of mutual "making space for the other in the self" and of rearranging the self in light of other's presence.

Second, renewing the covenant entails *self-giving*. On the cross the new covenant was made "in blood" (Luke 22:20). Notice that the blood of the new covenant was not the blood of a third party (an animal), shed

---

187. Aleida Assmann and Jan Assmann, "Aspekte einer Theorie des unkommunikativen Handelns," *Kultur und Konflikt*, ed. Jan Assmann and Dietrich Harth (Frankfurt: Suhrkamp, 1990), 36.

188. See Michael Welker, *Kirche im Pluralismus* (Gütersloh: Christian Kaiser, 1995), 54ff.

to establish a fictive blood relation between the parties of the covenant and dramatize the consequences of breaking it. In this respect the new covenant is profoundly different from the first covenant God made with Abraham (Gen 15).[189] Abraham cut the sacrificial animals in two, and "a smoking fire pot and a flaming torch"—both symbols of theophany—passed between the halves (15:17). The unique ritual act performed by God was a pledge that God would rather "die" than break the covenant, much like the animals died, through which God passed.[190] The thought of a living God dying is difficult enough—as difficult as the thought of a faithful God breaking the covenant. At the foot of the cross, however, a veritable abyss opens up for the former thought. For the narrative of the cross is not a "self-contradictory" story of a God who "died" because God broke the covenant, but a truly incredible story of God doing what God should neither have been able nor willing to do—a story of God who "died" because God's all too human *covenant partner* broke the covenant.

The "blood" in which the new covenant was made is not simply the blood that holds up the threat of breaking the covenant or that portrays common belonging; it is the blood of self-giving, even self-sacrifice. One party has broken the covenant, and the other suffers the breach because it will not let the covenant be undone. If such suffering of the innocent party strikes us as unjust, in an important sense it *is* unjust. Yet this "injustice" is precisely what it takes to renew the covenant. One of the biggest obstacles to repairing broken covenants is that they invariably entail deep disagreements over what constitutes a breach and who is responsible for it. Partly because of the desire to shirk the responsibilities that acceptance of guilt involves, those who break the covenant do not (or will not) recognize that they have broken it. In a world of clashing perspectives and strenuous self-justifications, of crumbly commitments and strong animosities, covenants are kept and renewed because those who, from their perspective, have not broken the covenant are willing to do the hard work of repairing it. Such work *is* self-sacrificial; something of the individual or communal self dies performing it. Yet the self by no means perishes but is renewed as

---

189. For my purposes here it is of little significance whether Genesis 15 is about "covenant" or "oath" (Claus Westermann, *Genesis 12–36: A Commentary,* transl. John J. Scullion [Minneapolis: Augsburg, 1985], 215).

190. Joseph Ratzinger, "Der Neue Bund: Zur Theologie des Bundes im Neuen Testament," *Internationale Katholische Zeitschrift Communio* 24, no. 3 (1995): 205f.

the truly communal self, fashioned in the image of Christ and the triune God who will not be without the other.

Third, the new covenant is *eternal*. God's self-giving on the cross is a consequence of the "eternality" of the covenant, which in turn rests on God's "inability" to give up the covenant partner who has broken the covenant. "How can I hand you over, O Israel?" asks rhetorically Hosea's God, whose "compassion grows warm and tender" (11:8), because God is bound to Israel with unbreakable "bonds of love." God's commitment is irrevocable and God's covenant indestructible.[191] Analogously, though any given political covenant may be dissolved, being *"relatively unconditional*,"[192] the broader social covenant is *strictly unconditional* and therefore "eternal." It can be broken, but it cannot be undone. Every breach of the covenant still takes place *within* the covenant; and all the struggle for justice and truth on behalf of the victims of the broken covenant takes place *within* the covenant. Nobody is outside the social covenant; and no deed is imaginable which would put a person outside of it.

The readjustment of complementary identities, the repairing of the covenant even by those who have not broken it, and the refusal to let the covenant ever be undone—these are the key features of a social covenant conceived in analogy to a Christian theology of the new covenant. The three features correspond closely to the sense I have given in this chapter to "embrace"—a metaphor that seeks to combine the thought of reconciliation with the thought of dynamic and mutually conditioning identities. The new covenant is *God's embrace* of the humanity that keeps breaking the covenant; the social side of that new covenant is *our way of coming to embrace* one another even under the conditions of enmity. Reflection on social relations from the perspective of the new covenant ("embrace") is not meant to replace but to supplement reflection from the perspective of the old covenant (covenant), I said earlier. What is the relation between the two? Embrace is the inner side of the covenant, and covenant is the outer side of the embrace.[193]

---

191. Cf. Assmann, *Das kulturelle Gedächtnis*, 256f.

192. Selznick, *The Moral Commonwealth*, 479.

193. I received important stimuli for the section "Contract, Covenant, Embrace" during the Tübingen consultation on "Covenant" (October 20–22, 1995) organized by Charles S. McCoy and Jürgen Moltmann. I have learned much in these discussions, especially with Amitai Etzioni, Dieter Georgi, Walter Grois, Philip Selznick, and Wolfgang Graf Vitzthum.

The Open Arms of the Father

It was the profound and singularly fecund story of the prodigal son (Luke 15:11-32) that originally suggested to me the idea for a "theology of embrace." The whole present chapter—and, in a sense, the whole book—is but an attempt to draw out its social significance. In conclusion, after a long journey into what I hope was not a distant country, I want to return to the story from which I never departed, and read it in the light of the theology to which it gave birth.

Two main features of the story are also the two central themes of this whole chapter: the father's giving himself to his estranged son and his receiving that son back into his household. Picking up these two themes, I will take the basic argument of this chapter an important step further by *pursuing the question of how identities need to be constituted if broken relationships are to be restored*. Between the lines of my text, an intensive dialogue is going on with the relational feminists' critique of "separate" selves and the postmodern critique of "stable identities."[194] Hermeneutically, I will proceed in the following way: rather than translating the story first into a theological principle about God, the strayed, and the not-so-strayed sinners, and then translating the principle back into the world of social relations, I will simply *read the story at the social level*, looking at one after the other of its main actors and concentrating on the character of their relations and identities.

First, *the younger son*. A typically modern way to read the desire of the younger son to receive an early inheritance and leave home is to see him breaking out of the confines of a patriarchal home in order to find his authentic self and become an individual. Departure is now not a transgression. To the contrary, a "good" son who stays in the world that others have constructed is a *bad* individual who betrays his authenticity. In this modern reading, the story is about a young man who fails to make something out of himself and implicates unfairly others in his failure. The background is a monologically constructed self made miserable by a combination of stupidity ("squandering," 15:13) and bad luck ("severe famine," 15:14). Correspondingly, the return of the younger son can only be a matter of coming back to find work ("hired hands," 15:19) in order to have something to eat ("bread," 15:17). For, much like the son in Franz

---

194. Allison Weir, *Sacrificial Logics: Feminist Theory and the Critique of Identity* (New York: Routledge, 1996).

Kafka's "Heimkehr,"[195] instead of "home" he will find a *house*—his father's house. Back among his own, he will still remain in a distant country.[196]

But the story does not quite work against the backdrop of modern restless "adolescence" in which the self forges its identity by constructing itself as alterity over against its origins.[197] Instead, we must presuppose a situated self that has already reached "adulthood" (or will never get to the kind of independence we call "adulthood"). For premodern[198] and non-Western[199] commentators, the younger son has already done wrong by demanding the parceling out of the inheritance and deciding to depart. For one, he broke the ancient household solidarity, whose basic ethos was protecting and increasing, not dividing and diminishing.[200] Equally significantly, he cut himself off from the relations which constituted his very identity. Each of the characters is identified by a relational designation—"father," "son," "brother"—and all designations are interrelated through possessive pronouns—such as "*his* father" (15:11) and "*your* brother" (15:27). The very identity of each character is unthinkable without the others.

The younger son's breach with the family was total. He gathered "*all* he had," traveled to "a *distant* country"; no property of his should remain with them, because as long as what belongs to him is with them, he is, in a sense, with them and they are with him. And in the distant country he did exactly the opposite of what a member of a good household should do: he "*squandered*" the inheritance in "*dissolute* living" (15:13). All behavioral patterns learned at home must be put aside, because as long as he behaves like a son he is a son, and home is with him and he is, in a sense, at home. His project was to "un-son" himself; there was no place in him for the place called home. That the father considered him "lost," even "dead" (15:24) confirms this. Departure was not an act of separation required for

195. Franz Kafka, "Heimkehr," *Sämtliche Erzählung* (Frankfurt am Main: Fischer Taschenbuch, 1972).

196. Cf. Werner Brettschneider, *Die Parabel vom verlorenen Sohn: Das biblische Gleichnis in der Entwicklung der europäischen Literatur* (Berlin: Erich Schmidt, 1978), 53ff.; Peter Pfaff, "Einspruch gegen Landwirtschaft: Kafkas 'Heimkehr': Die Parabel zu Parabel," *Die Sprache der Bilder: Gleichnis und Metapher in Literatur und Theologie,* ed. Hans Weder (Gütersloh: Gütersloher Verlagshaus Gerd Mohn, 1989).

197. Another way to construe the coming back of the Prodigal against the background of a monologically constructed self is to speak about the return of the self to itself (Jill Robbins, *Prodigal Son/Elder Brother* [Chicago: The University of Chicago Press, 1991]). Then the departure would entail a loss of the self and return would constitute a regaining of the self. The basic trouble with this reading is that in the story the self is not monologically constructed.

198. Brettschneider, *Die Parabel vom verlorenen Sohn,* 19–40, 62.

199. Kenneth E. Bailey, *Finding the Lost: Cultural Keys to Luke 15* (St. Louis: Concordia, 1992), 112ff.

200. Wolfgang Pöhlmann, *Der verlorene Sohn und das Haus: Studien zu Lukas 15, 11–32 im Horizont der antiken Lehre von Haus, Erziehung und Ackerbau* (Tübingen: J. C. B. Mohr [Paul Siebeck], 1993), 186.

the formation of a distinct identity but an act of exclusion by which the self pulls itself out of the relationships without which it would not be what it is. The self cuts itself off from responsibilities to others and places itself in conflictual relation to them.

For the self, nothing is more difficult than a radical breach, a thoroughgoing alterity. The younger son's failure was preprogrammed in the radicality of the departure. The "severe famine" serves as a narrative device that puts him where the logic of the story demands that we find him. Since he has abdicated his responsibilities and cut himself off from relations that constituted his very identity, he must "cleave" to a foreigner and herd his pigs (15:15); he is hungry (15:16) and alienated from his proper self (in the fields with the pigs, 15:15). At the end of the road of pushing others out of the self he finds himself, paradoxically, "away from himself."

Correspondingly, when he "comes to himself"[201] he remembers the other whom he wanted to push out of his world but to whom he found himself still belonging: "How many of *my father's* hired hands have bread enough...." (15:17). Through departure he wanted to become a "non-son"; his return begins not with repentance but with something that makes the repentance possible—the memory of sonship. There is no coming to oneself without the memory of belonging. The self has been constructed in relation to others, and it can come to itself only through relationship to others. The first link with the other in a distant country of broken relationships is memory.

For him whose project was to "un-son" himself and who is still in a distant country, "sonship" can only be a memory, but it is a memory that defines his present so much that it sets him on a journey back. The memory of sonship gives hope, but it also reminds of failure; the bridge that the memory builds is a testimony to the chasm created by departure. The one who *remembers* sonship can no longer be a son pure and simple; he has been shaped by the history of the departure, which cannot be erased. As the younger son states twice—once to himself and once to the father—he is now the "son-no-longer-worthy-to-be-called-a-son" (15:18, 21). He will request to be treated as one of the hired hands. From the son's perspective, the relationship should be reestablished, but the history of betrayal will have changed the identities and reconfigured obligations and

---

201. My point is independent of whether the use of "coming to himself" is merely idiomatic and means no more than "come to his senses" (John Nolland, *Luke 9:21–18:34*, Word Biblical Commentary, vol. 35B [Dallas: Word Books, 1993], 783) or whether the language implies a certain rediscovery of the proper self.

expectations. With an identity constructed out of the shell of the original identity as a son and the broken pieces of the attempted identity as a "non-son," the prodigal sets out on the journey home.

Second, *the father*. The first surprise of the story is the audacity of the younger son to request the inheritance. The second surprise is the father's permission to leave with "all he had" (15:13). Sound reason and a venerable tradition (see Sirach 33:19-23) counseled the father to do otherwise.[202] The most significant aspect of the story is, however, that the father who lets the son depart *does not let go of the relationship between them*. The eyes that searched for and finally caught sight of the returning son in "the distance" (15:20) tell of a heart that was with the son in "the distant country" (15:13). Away from home, the son remained still in the father's heart. Against the force of the wrongdoing suffered and the shame endured that sought to push the son out, the father kept the son in his heart as an absence shaped by the memory of the former presence. Since he would not give the departed son up, he became a father of the "lost" son, of the "dead" son (15:24). When the son's attempt to "un-son" himself changed the son's identity, the father had to renegotiate his own identity as a father.

The same holding on to the son in memory that directed the father's expectant gaze toward the distant land filled the father's heart with compassion when he saw the son returning; it made the father run, put his arms around the prodigal, and kiss him (15:20). Without the father's having kept the son in his heart, the father would not have put his arms around the prodigal. No confession was necessary for the arms to open up and the offer of embrace to be extended for the simple reason that the relationship did not rest on moral performance and therefore could not be destroyed by immoral acts. The son's return from "the distant country" and the father's refusal to let the son out of his heart sufficed.

The son's strategy of return had events arranged in a different sequence: going up to the father—confession—acceptance into service (15:18-19). The father's welcome, however, interrupted the sequence ("but," 15:20). Confession *followed* acceptance (15:21). But it did follow, without interruption. For though the relationship was not grounded in uprightness, after the son's departure the relationship was infected by a transgression and therefore had to be healed by a confession. For the embrace to be

---

202. Joseph A. Fitzmyer, *The Gospel According to Luke (X-XXIV): Introduction, Translation, and Notes*, Anchor Bible 28A (New York: Doubleday, 1985), 1087.

complete—for the celebration to begin—a confession of wrongdoing had to be made.

The father interrupted the son's strategy of return a second time. The first interruption enacted an unconditional acceptance; the second performed a transformation. After failure in the distant country, the son reconstructed his identity as a "son-not-worthy-to-be-called-a-son." By the sheer joy of his father's embrace, without a word, his identity starts to be changed again. The son made his confession, but right at the point where his strategy dictated that he inform the father about the new identity he had constructed for himself in the light of his transgression ("a hired hand," 15:19), the father interrupts him again ("but" and "quickly," 15:22). The confession made to the father who embraced him has taken his identity in relation to the father out of his hands and placed it into the hands of the father. With a command to the slaves, the father reconstructed the prodigal's identity. He ordered a robe—the best one—put on him, a ring placed on his finger, and sandals on his feet, and then, as the prodigal was transformed before the eyes of those present, he called him "son of mine." First he symbolically *remade* the "son-not-worthy-to-be-called-a-son" into a "son-he-could-be-proud-of," and then *called* him "my son." The secret of the son's transformation is the same as the secret of his unconditional acceptance: the father would not let his son—the "lost" and the "dead" son (15:24, 32)—out of his heart's embrace.

Ever suspicious of belonging, moderns may ask, but what if the younger son did not want his identity reconstructed by the father's embrace? After all, the son was not asked, not even spoken to! The father was all action and no communication. Have we not witnessed an oppressive act of a domineering father exploiting the weakness of a son who failed, an act that only such a father could mistake for genuine love? Is not love in a parental home, a love which "understands" and "forgives," beset with the danger of erasing difference, as Rainer Maria Rilke suggests in *The Notebooks of Malte Laurids Brigge*?[203] But what makes us suspicious where the original readers would probably not have been? Might we not fear erasure of difference partly because we cannot stop oscillating between the polarities of "difference" and "domestication," of "self-constructed" and "imposed" identities? Are we suspicious because we have forgotten the art

203. Rainer Maria Rilke, *The Notebooks of Malte Laurids Brigge*, transl. Stephen Mitchell (New York: Random House, 1982), 252ff.

of negotiating fluid identities within a relationship? Is it because we are too much like the older brother and much too little like the father?

Third, *the older brother*. The older brother did not like the music and dance around the prodigal's return. He was angry and would not come in (15:28). The spatial distancing was an outward sign of inner exclusion. The prodigal is no longer *his brother*; he is "this son of yours" (15:30). The pejorative "this,"[204] "son" instead of "brother," and "yours" instead of "mine" bespeak the radicality of exclusion. Unlike the father, the older brother did not keep the younger brother in his heart while this one was in the far country. He refused to readjust his identity to make space for a brother blemished by transgression; the brother's transgression, not the memory of his former presence, has come to occupy the space vacated by the brother's departure. The older one will not be the "brother-of-the-prodigal," and hence for him the prodigal is not "my brother." As a consequence, after the father had embraced the prodigal, the older brother had to "un-son" himself. For the first time in the whole story, in the older brother's explanation of his anger, the father is not addressed as "father." He has become just another "you" (15:29-30). As long as the younger brother and the father have a relationship ("this son of yours" [v. 30]) he will exclude himself from the relationship with the father. The younger brother has become a "non-brother" because he was not the brother he should have been; the father has become a "non-father" because he acted as a father should not—he failed to disown a rebellious son (Deut 21:18-21).[205]

The anger, the refusal to enter and celebrate, the "un-fathering" of the father, all of this is only a moment in the older brother's story, however, not his whole identity. He is now "outside" (v. 28), and yet the mode of his being outside is intelligible only against the backdrop of his more fundamental being "inside"—of being "always with the father" and "all" that is the father's being his (15:31). He must *refuse* to enter (15:28) because he already belongs inside; he must "un-father" the father, because he *is* his son. The older brother may not have as adventurous of a story as the younger one, but he does not "exist in a dreary present" with no "temporal destiny" and "no story" but the story outside the story, as Jill Robbins claims in *Prodigal Son/Elder Brother*.[206] To the contrary, the older brother's

---

204. Fitzmyer, *The Gospel According to Luke*, 1091.

205. Darrell Bock, *Luke 9:51–24:53*, Baker Exegetical Commentary on the New Testament (Grand Rapids: Baker, 1996), 1319.

206. Robbins, *Prodigal Son/Elder Brother*, 36.

Embrace

being "outside" is a segment "inside" a story that he shares with the father and the younger brother.

Why this undoing of the relationships? The older brother is not just insulted because he behaved better but was treated worse (15:29-30). Neither is he simply acting out his fear over his inheritance[207] that he now may be obliged to share. Instead, he is angry because some basic rules have been broken—not oppressive rules that destroy life but rules without which no civil life would be possible.[208] The one who works (15:29) deserves more recognition than the one who squanders; celebrating the squanderer is squandering. The one who obeys where obedience is due (15:29) deserves more honor than the one who irresponsibly breaks commands; honoring the irresponsible is irresponsible. The one who remains faithful should be treated better than the one who excludes others; preference for the excluding one is tacit exclusion of the faithful one. When squandering becomes better than working and the breach of relationships better than faithfulness, justice will be perverted and the household will fall apart; there will be no place from which a prodigal could depart and no place to which he could return; we *all* will be in a "distant country" dreaming about filling our emaciated bodies with "the pods" for the pigs (15:16). Powerful arguments demanded that the one who excludes others be excluded, the one who disobeyed do penance, the one who squandered repay. The prodigal may be received back as "a hired hand," but *not* as a son. For all their differences, the two brothers—the one in a distant country and the other at home—were so much alike; the expectations of the one and the demands of the other were governed by the same logic.[209]

Who could object to that logic? And yet the objection emerges from between the lines of the very discourse that makes the need for clear-cut rules of inclusion and exclusion so plausible. The rules are necessary to preserve social ties, the older brother says. But in addition to separating him from the father and the brother, his anger over the transgression of rules makes *him* break some rather significant rules. He insists

207. Bailey, *Finding the Lost*, 184.

208. John Nolland has sought to counter the tendency to portray the "older brother" in the worst possible light (Nolland, *Luke 9:21–18:34*, 787ff.). He rightly points out that "the interpretations that are highly critical of the elder brother cannot begin to do justice to this verse [v. 31]" (788).

209. Jill Robbins suggests that the prodigal's actual return home, not just his intended way of returning, is "ultimately economic, part of a loss and gain in a system of exchanges," because it is organized around the scheme of "departure *and* return" (Robbins, *Prodigal Son/Elder Brother*, 72). But such interpretation is way too schematic and abstract, misled by the formal structure of "departure and return" to disregard the complex texture of the concrete nature of both departure and return as narrated in the story.

that he worked like a slave for the *father* (15:29), but fails to mention that he also worked *for himself* as the heir of two-thirds of the property. He claims that his brother devoured the *father's* property (15:30), but fails to tell that what the younger brother "devoured" *belonged* also to the younger brother. Most significantly, he projects onto his brother evil that his brother did not commit: the brother's "dissolute" living, which in the original seemingly implies no immorality,[210] he makes into "devouring the property with prostitutes" (v. 30).

Obsession with the rules—not bad rules, but salutary rules!—encourages self-righteousness and the demonization of others. To make the rules stick, one must reduce moral ambiguity and the complexity of social agents and their interaction. Insistence on observance of the rules fosters polarities where none are to be found and heightens them where they do exist. As a result, one is either completely "in" (if no rule was broken) or completely "out" (if a rule has been broken). The younger brother clearly did break rules and he was therefore "out," excluded from the relationship.

That the inability to take account of ambiguity and complexity results in inappropriate and oppressive exclusion is a serious charge against the account of social relations expressed by the powerful self-defense of the older brother. Even if persuasive, the charge will not stick, however, without a plausible alternative vision. Such a vision is inscribed in the behavior of the father.

Fourth, *the father again*. Who is this strange father? A sentimental old man with a weakness for his own "Benjamin" and an inability to endure conflict? A tragic, even pitiful, figure, enslaved by an irrational compulsion to embrace the prodigal (15:20) and placate his angry sibling (15:28), by the need to make a "son" again out of the one who squandered all he had and tenderly call "(my) child" (15:31) the one who in anger refused to address him as "father"? A representative of an order that must appear insane from the perspective of any responsible guardian of the household precisely because it is bound to destroy the household? The images are clearly wrong; they make sense only if one takes the skewed perspective of the older brother and constructs the father as his opposite. But the father is not a mirror image of the older brother. If he were, the older brother would have won, at least until the "kingdom came in glory." For then the father would be locked in safe "heavenly" irrelevance, and the affairs of the world would be handed over to "older brothers."

210. Bailey, *Finding the Lost*, 124.

Notice that the father has *not* reinstated the younger son exactly into all his former privileges. Clearly, if the father can tell the older son "*all that is mine is yours*" (15:31), then the younger son will get no second inheritance; the ring he received is a sign of the father's generosity, not of the son's disposition over all property.[211] Though the father has made the prodigal into his son again, the prodigal is not simply a son as he was before his departure but a "son-that-was-dead-and-is-alive-again" (15:32)— even if only for a while. Transformed into a son, he is a "son-again"; an embrace and a meal around a fatted calf do not simply undo the past. Similarly, if the father was setting the order of the household completely aside, he would have had to "un-son" the older son, who in the second half of the story emerges as the representative of this order.[212] But though the older son "un-fathers" the father, the father not only holds on to him (as he held onto the prodigal while the prodigal was in the distant country), but states clearly that the relationship has not been broken. Neither the embrace of the prodigal nor the older brother's anger changes the fact that the older one "is always" with the father, indeed that he is his father's dear "child" and that "all" that belongs to the father belongs also to the son (15:31). Far from completely discarding the order of the "household," the father continues to uphold it. What the father did was to "reorder" the order! He inserted into the "must" of that order another "must" (15:32)— the "must" of embracing the returning transgressor and making him a son again, rather than locking him out of fellowship! There is a "must" of following salutary rules; but there is a "must" of receiving back the one who has broken these rules. In addition to celebrating with those who are already "in" ("friends," 15:29), one must celebrate with those who want to return.

What is so profoundly different about the "new order" of the father is that it is not built around the alternatives as defined by the older brother: either strict adherence to the rules or disorder and disintegration; either you are "in" or you are "out," depending on whether you have or have not broken a rule. He rejected this alternative because his behavior was governed by the one fundamental "rule": relationship has priority over all rules. Before any rule can apply, he *is* a father to his sons and his sons *are* brothers to one another. The reason for celebration is that "this son of mine" (15:24) and "this brother of yours" (15:32) has been found and

---

211. Fitzmyer, *The Gospel According to Luke*, 1090; Nolland, *Luke 9:21–18:34*, 785.
212. Pöhlmann, *Der verlorene Sohn und das Haus*, 188f.

has come alive again. Notice the categorical difference between how the father and how the older brother interpret the prodigal's life in the "distant country." The older brother employs *moral categories* and constructs his brother's departure along the axis of "bad/good" behavior: the brother has "devoured your property with prostitutes" (15:30). The father, though keenly aware of the moral import of his younger son's behavior, employs *relational categories* and constructs his son's departure along the axis of "lost/found" and "alive (to him)/dead (to him)." Relationship is prior to moral rules; moral performance may *do something* to the relationship, but relationship is *not grounded* in moral performance. Hence the *will* to embrace is independent of the quality of behavior, though at the same time "repentance," "confession," and the "consequences of one's actions" all have their own proper place. The profound wisdom about the priority of the relationship, and not some sentimental insanity, explains the father's kind of "prodigality" to both of his sons.[213]

For the father, the priority of the relationship means not only a refusal to let moral rules be the final authority regulating "exclusion" and "embrace" but also a refusal to construct his own identity in isolation from his sons. He readjusts his identity along with the changing identities of his sons and thereby reconstructs their broken identities and relationships. He suffers being "un-fathered" by both, so that through this suffering he may regain both as his sons (if the older brother was persuaded) and help them rediscover each other as brothers. Refusing the alternatives of "self-constructed" versus "imposed" identities, difference versus domestication, he allows himself to be taken on the journey of their shifting identities so that he can continue to be their father and they, each other's brothers.

213. Since the father does not ground the relationship in moral performance, he can avoid simply *inverting* the moral categories of the older brother. No, for the father the one who confesses transgression is *not* better than the one who obeys and works (ibid., 141). From the perspective of the father such a claim is nonsensical; it would elicit exactly the response that the father gave to the older brother (Gen 15:31-32), the passage that Pöhlmann, strangely enough, does not address in his concluding reconstruction of the "world of the household and the kingdom of God in the parable" (183–89). Similarly, the father does not *"favor* those who forsake their duty and subsequently return" (E. P. Sanders, *The Historical Figure of Jesus* [London: Penguin, 1993], 198). To make such a claim, one must take the perspective of the *older brother* and then *affirm what the older brother denies*. For the father, the sons cannot be placed on a moral scale and then the returning prodigal, on account of his confession, pronounced better and accepted but the older brother pronounced worse and rejected. The nonprodigal is good in that he has remained, worked, obeyed, but he is *bad* in that he was too concerned with the "rules" and has not received his brother back and rejoiced. The prodigal is *bad* in that he has gone and *good* in that he has returned and confessed. Both are loved, however, irrespective of their goodness or badness, and therefore the goodness and badness of each can be evaluated in a nonschematic and differentiated way.

Why does he not lose himself on the journey? Because he is guided by indestructible love and supported by a flexible order.

Flexible order? Changing identities? The world of fixed rules and stable identities is the world of the older brother. The father destabilizes this world—and draws his older son's anger upon himself. The father's most basic commitment is not to rules and given identities but to his sons whose lives are too complex to be regulated by fixed rules and whose identities are too dynamic to be defined once for all. Yet he does not give up the rules and the order. Guided by the indestructible love, which makes space in the self for others in their alterity, which invites the others who have transgressed to return, which creates hospitable conditions for their confession, and rejoices over their presence, the father keeps reconfiguring the order without destroying it so as to maintain it as an order of embrace rather than exclusion.

Part Two

CHAPTER V
Oppression and Justice

Justice Against Justice

In 1843 General Charles Napier conquered Sind and installed the order of British colonial rule, no doubt to bring the blessings of civilization to the "inferior races." When the British came, one of the colonial impositions they instituted was the prohibition of *sati*—of widows being cremated on their husbands' funeral pyres. They were shrewd enough to tolerate a number of native peculiarities, but not the burning of widows. The Brahmans of Sind, however, defended *sati* as an age-old custom. General Napier's response was as simple as it was arrogant: "My nation also has a custom. When men burn women alive, we hang them. Let us all act according to national custom!"[1]

Sometimes this story is told as a polemical tool to underline the clear moral superiority of certain practices over others. It is possible, however, to see it as an extreme case of competing, indeed clashing, justices. There is a justice of the Brahmans, which found nothing wrong with the burning of widows. Women by nature belong to men—to fathers or husbands (and possibly sons). When a husband dies, his wife continues to belong to him and can therefore be cremated on his funeral pyre, presumably feeling no pain because the power of *sati* has descended upon her. To offset the damage, she might be worshipped as a goddess.[2] An alternative apology for the

---

1. Peter Berger, *A Far Glory: The Quest for Faith in an Age of Credulity* (New York: Free Press, 1992), 71.
2. See Lourens P. Van den Bosch, "A Burning Question: Asti and Sati Temples as the Focus of Political Interest," *Numen* 37, no. 2 (1990): 174ff.

custom went something like this: "By following her deceased husband in the flames of his funeral pyre, she frees him and herself of all sin, and the couple will experience eternal bliss in Heaven."[3] Was *sati* unjust? Not by the standards of the Brahmans.

General Napier's justice operated with different standards, however, which were embedded in a different culture. The most basic creed of Napier's Western democratic culture taught that every human being has singular worth, that there is nothing more sacred than the life of an individual. If you brutally violate the life of a person, your life must be violated. The logic of justice demanded hanging, or some similar punishment. If the general had been a woman, he could have easily brushed aside the apology for *sati* as a rationalization of a practice which was "entirely a political scheme intended to insure the care and good offices of wives to their husbands," as Eliza Fay, an Englishwoman living in India in 1779, insisted with disapproval.[4] Where does the confrontation between Sind Brahmans and a British general leave us? Culture against culture? Justice against justice? If so, then the justice of imperial generals will always win over the justice of sages and priests—at least for the time being.

From the distance of a century and a half, postcolonial sensibilities make us see things somewhat differently from either the Brahmans of Sind or the General Napier. On the one hand, much like Napier we are persuaded that widows must not be burned. *Sati* is inhumane; it is unjust. If anyone were barbaric enough not to condemn the practice, we would insist that he be at least civilized enough not to discriminate against women! With a macabre but compelling logic we would demand that if widows burn, widowers should burn too; anything else would be unjust. On the other hand, much like the Brahmans, most of us would hold that the violence with which colonial powers imposed their rule and their values on native populations was profoundly unjust. Were not the so-called "barbarities" of "inferior races" an excuse for Spain's brutal conquest of America? We easily resonate with the "moral paradoxes" of colonization, as Tzvetan Todorov calls them in *The Conquest of America*: "The Christians are disgusted by cases of cannibalism. The introduction of Christianity involves their suppression. But, in order to achieve this suppression, men

---

3. Paul Pederson, "Ambiguities of Tradition: Widow Burning in Bengal in the Early Nineteenth Century," *Religion, Tradition, and Renewal*, ed. A. W. Geertz and J. S. Jensen (Aarhus: Aarhus University Press, 1991), 68.

4. Claire Herman, "The Widow's Gesture," *Times Literary Supplement* (July 12, 1996): 29.

are burned alive!"[5] Today, Todorov observes dryly, "we scarcely perceive the difference in 'civilization' between being burned alive and eaten dead."

Postcolonial sensibilities tell us that both Napier and the Brahmans were unjust in their own way. Why do we think so? We have our own fabric of practices and values of which our conception of justice is a part. Unlike the representatives of the highest sacerdotal caste in nineteenth-century India and unlike Victorian imperialists, we affirm as values *both* the inviolability of individual life and the plurality of cultures. But where does this leave us? Our *superior* culture against theirs? Our *superior* justice against theirs? We may hesitate to put things quite this way, fearful that our democratic and postcolonial sensibilities might emerge as a covert form of colonialism. But do we hesitate to *think* this way?

The tacit assumption that our own justice is superior is challenged when we face the concrete other today. Unlike Brahmans and colonial generals, our other will talk back, contending that our justice might not be as just as we think. Consider the war in Bosnia during the 1990s, although the same point could be made by examining many other situations. Outsiders are baffled, unable to construe a moral narrative, incapable of telling the story of Croats, Muslims, and Serbs as a story of manifest rights and wrongs. And, as Michael Ignatieff observes, "where empathy fails to find the blameless victim…the conscience finds comfort in shallow misanthropy."[6] The conclusion seems compelling: justice is trampled upon left and right; they are all out of their minds, they are all barbarians (which, of course, indirectly confirms that we Westerners are just, sane, and civilized).

Ask any of the warring parties in Bosnia, however, and they will tell you who the real barbarian is. You might be surprised to find on the Serb list not only Croats and Muslims but also the whole West. That same decadent civilization that destroyed millions of native peoples, colonized cultures, and concocted "the final solution" is showing once again its ugly face by imposing sanctions against us, the Serbs, whose only crime is that we are defending our homes, our wives, and children against murderous Croats and Muslims who want to take what is rightfully ours. Or, listen to the following variation on this indictment. This time the accusers are the Muslims: "How can the Christian West just sit and watch us

5. Tzvetan Todorov, *The Conquest of America: The Question of the Other*, transl. Richard Howard (New York: HarperCollins, 1984), 179.

6. Michael Ignatieff, "Is Nothing Sacred? The Ethics of Television," *Daedalus* 114, no. 4 (1985): 68.

be slaughtered by the thousands? How can they refuse to let us at least arm ourselves?" For the Serbs and Muslims, the Western and Christian rhetoric of civilization and justice only masks barbaric and unjust practice. Where does *this* exchange between the West and the warring parties in Bosnia leave us? Muslim justice against Western barbarity? Western justice against Serb barbarity? Or is it Balkan barbarity against Western barbarity?

In reflecting on Indian and Bosnian exchanges about justice, my purpose was not to suggest that all protagonists are equally right or equally wrong and that no account of justice is better than the other. This is certainly not the case, at least not from my perspective. The Brahmans of Sind were wrong about *sati*; the Serbian critique of the West is devious and self-justifying propaganda. The examples should rather illustrate that when competing accounts either of what is just or what justice means clash, one person's justice is another person's barbarity and society is threatened with the chaos of violence. To use images from the prophet Micah, only if there is consensus on justice can people hope "to sit under their own vines" and "under their own fig trees," and enjoy the fruit of their labor in peace (4:4); if not, they must fear that their vineyards will be trampled by soldiers' boots and their orchards soaked with blood and the work of their hands reduced to ashes. This is not to suggest that "order" and "stability" are impossible without agreement on justice. But what kind of order and stability will they be? They will be born of violence. To have "peace" without justice you will have to keep "breaking the bow," "shattering the spear," and "burning chariots" (Ps 46:9 CEB). For peace to be the fruit of freedom—for the people to "beat their swords into plowshares and spears into pruning hooks" (Mic 4:3) on their own accord—agreement on justice is needed. Justice creates a sphere of mutual obligations that extends through the whole community, rulers no less than subjects, rich and powerful no less than weak and poor, one culture no less than the other. Justice forms the basis for cohesion and solidarity.[7] Without justice, meaning threatens to give way to absurdity, social order is endangered by disorder, and peace is menaced by violence. Is there a way out of the land of chaos in which justice struggles against justice and therefore injustice is perpetrated in the name of justice?

One would think that if we left the generals aside and turned to philosophers, we would find a solution to the problem of clashing justices.

---

7. Jan Assmann, *Das kulturelle Gedächtnis: Schrift, Erinnerung und politische Identität in frühen Hochkulturen* (München: C. H. Beck, 1992), 232ff.

But everyone who asks a philosopher today, "What is just?" must reckon with the counter question, "Whose justice?" "Which justice?" The one asking the counter question need not be a radical postmodern thinker who insists, as Michel Foucault does, that "justice," like "truth," is "a thing of this world...produced by multiple forms of constraint."[8] A different version of the counter question can also come from a conservative communitarian. He or she will tell you that every account of justice is situated within a given tradition of moral inquiry and that therefore there are as many "justices" as there are traditions of moral inquiry.[9] Both a postmodern thinker and a communitarian will, of course, have a great deal to say about how to escape the morass of clashing justices. But their advice would clash. Like the world of generals, the world of philosophers is a world of competing justices.

We seem to be trapped in the iron logic of a syllogism of despair. Premise one: conceptions of justice depend on particular cultures and traditions. Premise two: peace depends on justice *between* cultures and traditions. Conclusion: violence between cultures will never stop. Must we, however, concede the disturbing thought that the justice backed by the most able and best equipped generals or propounded by the most effective propaganda will reign? That the justice of the dominant is the dominant justice? That the price of peace is suppression of "difference"?

That violence will rule under the label of "peace"? Is there a way out of the violence of an unjust justice to a place where just judgments can be made in the struggle of justice against justice?

I will first examine three dominant ways of dealing with the issue of clashing justices—the universalistic affirmation that justice is one, the postmodern claim that justice bears many names, and the communitarian placing of justice within a tradition. Building on the critique of these positions, I will offer my own proposal suggesting that agreement on justice depends on the will to embrace the other and that justice itself will be unjust as long as it does not become a mutual embrace. The chapter ends with a reflection on the "justice" of Pentecost against the backdrop of the injustice of Babel. Throughout the text, my intention is not so much to specify what justice is as to propose how we should go about seeking and pursuing justice in the context of plurality and enmity.

8. Michel Foucault, *Power/Knowledge: Selected Interviews and Other Writings 1972–1977*, transl. Colin Gordon et al. (New York: Pantheon Books, 1980), 131.

9. Alasdair MacIntyre, *Whose Justice? Which Rationality?* (Notre Dame, IN: University of Notre Dame, 1988).

The One and the Only Justice

When justice struggles against justice, at least one must be false. How can there be two, three, or more justices? No doubt, there can be and there are numerous *accounts* of what is just. Only one of them can be correct, however. Like truth, justice is one and universal, valid for all times and all places, or it is no justice at all. Make that one justice reign, and you will have peace. It would seem that the only genuine problem is how to make that one justice reign. But is this in fact the case?

Traditionally, Christian theologians have grounded the belief in one universal justice in convictions about God. Consider the following three beliefs together: God is all-knowing; God is perfectly just; God is not a tribal deity. All three accepted, it follows that what God holds to be just must be just for every person and every culture, apart from how any person construes justice. If God is the God of all peoples, the justice of God must be the justice for all peoples. Universal peace will be the fruit of universal divine justice. This kind of theological reasoning lies behind the famous vision of the prophet Micah (4:2-4; cf. Isa 2:2-4). Peace rests on justice, and justice is sustained by the God of all nations. God "shall judge between many peoples and shall arbitrate between strong nations far away" (Mic 4:3). Nations are not their own last court of appeal; there is a justice that transcends cultural construals of justice. And when this justice reigns, war will cease, terror will be no more, armament industries will be transformed into peace industries, and military academies dismantled (4:3).

From the perspective of the classic Christian faith, the argument from the character of God to universal justice and universal peace is incontrovertible. To be a follower of Jesus Christ means both to affirm that God's justice transcends all cultural construals of justice and to strive for that justice (Matt 6:33). But does the pursuit of divine justice make an end to the struggle between justices? Does it not rather intensify the struggle? Notice that Micah's vision of just peace does not describe the present but predicts a future, "the days to come" (4:1). The realities of Micah's day were not much different from the realities of any age. He writes,

> Each of the peoples walks in the name of their own god;
> but as for us, we will walk
> in the name of the LORD our God forever and always. (Mic 4:5 CEB)

180

Each people walks in the name of its god, and each construes its own account of justice and barbarity. There is no one to judge among them. Not even the God of Israel! As Israel stands alongside the other nations, so also the God of Israel, who "in the days to come" will judge between nations, now stands alongside the other gods. God's divinity is contested and therefore God's justice is disputed.

Together with Israel, Christians claim that their God is the only true God, and that the justice of this God is the only true justice—now, when it is disputed, no less than in the world to come, when it will be affirmed by all. Yet with this claim they are not alone; the devotees of other gods and the presumed followers of no god make similar claims. The question is not whether from a Christian perspective God's justice is universal, whether God can infallibly judge among cultures irrespective of their differences. The question is whether *Christians* who want to uphold God's universal justice can judge among cultures with divine infallibility. The answer is that they cannot.

For one, Christians stand inside a culture, inside a tradition, inside an interest group. Unlike God's knowledge, their knowledge is limited and distorted. Their judgments about what is just in concrete situations are inescapably particular. Hence Croatian Christians can disagree as much with Serbian Christians as they do with Muslims about whether a particular political stance or military action was just. Inversely, Croatian Christians may agree more with, say, Croatian atheists on what is just than with Serbian Christians. Second, well-meaning Christians disagree profoundly about the nature of justice. Western Christian fundamentalists disagree with liberation theologians about the very notion of justice, the claim that their account of justice is true because it is God's justice notwithstanding. And non-Western conservative Christians may agree more with liberation theologians than with Western fundamentalists. We must therefore distinguish between our ideas of God's justice and God's justice itself. Even within the Christian tradition justice struggles against justice, and there is no final court of appeal in advance of that day when all will "appear before the judgment seat of Christ" (2 Cor 5:10).

From the basic distinction between God's justice and the human idea of God's justice, it follows that all Christian accounts of justice are particular and that they must make judgments about what is just in a provisional way.[10] Especially in the seventeenth century, Christians in Europe were not at all inclined to be provisional. They fought one another bitterly over the beliefs they claimed were directly revealed by God. Partly against the background of Christian inability to settle differences in peace by appeal to God, Enlightenment thinkers argued that the only impartial court of appeal is *reason*, freed from the ballast of tradition.[11] In post-industrial societies today, wars of religion are no longer a major threat, though a religious component of many conflicts should not be underplayed and though for some religious differences continue to be a sufficient reason for violence. The plurality of competing Christian confessions has given way to a much more complex plurality of incompatible religious, political, and moral traditions. As John Rawls puts it in *Political Liberalism*, the problem now is "how is it possible that there may exist over time a stable and just society of free and equal citizens" under conditions of such plurality?[12] Today, as in the seventeenth century, one dominant solution offered is a rational theory of justice. Iris Young, who rejects universalist accounts of justice based on reason, explains why such accounts are so alluring.

Without a rational theory that would be "independent of actual social institutions and relations" people could not "distinguish legitimate claims of justice from socially specific prejudices or self-interested claims to power."[13] A principle of justice based on reason and nothing but reason would lead all reasonable human beings eventually to agree on what is just, provided they are willing to reflect on the issues with a measure of disinterested objectivity.

Immanuel Kant, the greatest proponent of a universalist account of justice based on reason, insisted in the essay "Perpetual Peace" that political maxims will be just only if derived from "the pure concept of the duty of right, from the *ought* whose principle is given a priori by pure reason."[14] As the terms "a priori" and "pure reason" indicate, Kant's justice cuts through cultural differences because it rests on something independent of any culture. Justice is blind to differences among human beings; it

10. Richard J. Mouw and Sander Griffioen, *Pluralism and Horizons: An Essay in Christian Public Philosophy* (Grand Rapids: Eerdmans, 1993), 158ff.

11. Stephen Toulmin, *Cosmopolis: The Hidden Agenda of Modernity* (New York: The Free Press, 1990).

12. John Rawls, *Political Liberalism* (New York: Columbia University Press, 1993), xvii.

13. Iris Marion Young, *Justice and the Politics of Difference* (Princeton: Princeton University Press, 1990), 4.

14. Immanuel Kant, *On History*, transl. Lewis White Beck et al. (Indianapolis: Bobbs-Merrill, 1963), 127; cf. Immanuel Kant, *The Metaphysical Elements of Justice: Part I of The Metaphysics of Morals*, transl. J. Ladd (Indianapolis: Bobbs-Merrill, 1965), 33f.

determines how *any and every* freely choosing, autonomous person should act. And in Kant's account, the gist of what justice tells an autonomous person is to treat other human beings as autonomous persons, as subjects rather than objects, as ends rather than means. This done, justice will be done.

For some time now, the idea of "pure reason" has fallen into disrepute. In place of Kantian pure reason, in *Political Liberalism* John Rawls has suggested the idea of "reasonableness"[15]—a suggestion that entailed giving up Rawls's own earlier major endeavor in *A Theory of Justice* to ground justice in the dictates of reason alone.[16] By reasonableness he means "the willingness to propose fair terms of cooperation and to abide by them provided others do."[17] To ensure that those who wish to be reasonable will be fair, Rawls invokes his famous "veil of ignorance."[18] Situated behind the veil of ignorance, a person will propose fair terms if that person does not know where and when he or she will enter the world, whether he or she will be male or female, black or white, speak Mandarin or Tamil, be rich or poor. What is just is determined when reasonable people make judgments "from the point of view of everybody."[19] Such a "procedure" in place, Rawls hopes that what he calls an "overlapping consensus" among people espousing "reasonable comprehensive doctrine" will emerge, a consensus that insures justice for the whole society.[20]

The benefits of a universal justice based on reason (Kant) and of the consensus of all reasonable people about justice (Rawls) would be considerable. But will the proposals work? With some daring I will simply assume here that, contrary to his assumption, Kant's account of justice is laden by historical and cultural particularities, and engage only Rawls's proposal. Critics have been quick to point out that what seems a neutral account of justice capable of being shared by all reasonable people, constitutes in fact a whole "way of life." As Michael Walzer puts it in *Thick and Thin*,

> Men and women who acknowledge each other's equality, claim the rights of free speech, and practice the virtues of tolerance and mutual respect, don't leap from the philosopher's mind like Athena from the

---

15. Rawls, *Political Liberalism*, 48–66.
16. John Rawls, *A Theory of Justice* (Cambridge: Harvard University Press, 1971).
17. Rawls, *Political Liberalism*, 54.
18. Rawls, *A Theory of Justice*, 136ff.
19. Susan Moller Okin, "Reason and Feeling in Thinking about Justice," *Ethics* 99, no. 1 (1989): 248.
20. Rawls, *Political Liberalism*, 133ff.

head of Zeus. They are creatures of history; they have been worked on, so to speak, for many generations; and they inhabit a society that "fits" their qualities and so supports, reinforces, and reproduces people very much like themselves.[21]

One may endorse a way of life that informs Rawls's proposal or one may not. What one should not do is mistake it for being neutral, disconnected from a particular culture, simply "reasonable."[22] Rawls himself says as much. His account of justice is reasonable to the citizens of modern liberal democracies.

Chantel Mouffe has argued that Rawls's distinction between "reasonable" and "unreasonable" serves simply arbitrarily to draw the line between those who accept liberalism and those who do not; only "liberals" are "reasonable."[23] Behind the consignment of nonliberals to the murky regions of "non-reason" she sees the specter of "totalitarianism" emerging.[24] She exaggerates. But the overdrawn objection contains a correct insight. As Charles Taylor pointed out, the liberal notion of justice gives systematic preference to the view of life in which "human dignity consists in autonomy, that is, in the ability of each person to determine for himself or herself a view of the good life."[25] The proposal that set out to give an account of justice that could unite "deeply opposed though reasonable comprehensive doctrines"[26] ends with a conception of justice that is itself an aspect of a particular comprehensive doctrine. This objection does not defeat the liberal understanding of justice. It is possible to cling to it "by pointing out contingent features of liberal society that make it the best available set of arrangements we can get under the circumstances, at least

---

21. Michael Walzer, *Thick and Thin: Moral Arguments at Home and Abroad* (Notre Dame, IN: University of Notre Dame Press, 1994), 12f.

22. Cf. Stanley Fish, "Why We Can't All Just Get Along," *First Things* 60, no. 2 (1996): 18–26.

23. Chantal Mouffe, "Das Paradoxon des politischen Liberalismus," *Die Gegenwart der Gerechtigkeit: Diskurse zwischen Recht, praktischer Philosophie und Politik*, ed. Christoph Demmerling and Thomas Rentsch (Berlin: Akademie, 1995), 183.

24. Ibid., 186.

25. Charles Taylor, "The Politics of Recognition," *Multiculturalism: Examining the Politics of Recognition*, ed. Amy Gutmann (Princeton: Princeton University Press, 1994), 57; cf. Charles Taylor, "Justice After Virtue," *After MacIntyre. Critical Perspectives on the Work of Alasdair MacIntyre*, ed. John Horton and Susan Mendus (Notre Dame, IN: University of Notre Dame Press, 1994). In *Liberalism and the Limits of Justice* (Cambridge: Cambridge University Press, 1982) Michael Sandel argued that the liberal notion of justice requires one to postulate a "self" that is "barren of essential aims and attachments" and that inhabits a world of selves who are "capable of constituting meaning on their own—as agents of *construction* in the case of the right, and as agents of *choice* in the case of good" (175f.).

26. Rawls, *Political Liberalism*, xviii.

by our lights."[27] If correct, the objection does, however, underline that liberal justice is but one particular account of justice, competing with alternative accounts, rather than a universal account of justice capable of judging justly between them.

Justice has not quite succeeded in shaking away the particularity of difference. Reason cannot help justice overcome the particularity because, unable to survive suspended in mid-air, it always situates justice within a particular vision of the good life. God's perspective on justice cannot help because even when God speaks we cannot avoid inserting a few lines of our own into the speech—at least not yet. Since we are inescapably particular our account of justice cannot be universal. Unable to transcend particularities, justice must continue to struggle against justice. For how long? Until the trumpet sounds and the dead are raised imperishable? Postmodern thinkers believe that the struggle of justice against justice can end sooner—provided we are willing to risk giving up the impossible search for the one and only justice.

Many Names, Many Justices

To the eye of a cynic, the recipe for getting "universal justice" may look like this: Take a particular perspective on justice, deny to yourself and others that it is particular, insist that anybody who has any piety or smarts will agree with you, and the job is done—if you can get away with it. It has become increasingly difficult to get away with it, however. Together with a heightened awareness of cultural plurality it was above all the postmodern modes of thought that have made us distrust things "universal," including the universality of justice.

The argument of postmodern thinkers is not so much that every account of justice is particular, but that every account of justice that purports to be universal is inherently oppressive. In order to have a single justice you must understand justice as a law that applies to all cases. Justice is blind; differences between people are irrelevant to its demands. But precisely because it seeks to be blind to differences between persons, the law of justice, argues John Caputo in *Against Ethics*, "inevitably, structurally, falls short of individuals."[28] As a consequence, "laws always silence, coerce,

27. Jeffrey Stout, *Ethics After Babel. The Language of Morals and Their Discontents* (Boston: Beacon, 1988), 227.

28. John D. Caputo, *Against Ethics. Contributions to a Poetics of Obligation with Constant Reference to Deconstruction* (Bloomington: Indiana University Press, 1993), 87.

squeeze, or level someone, somewhere, however small."[29] Understood as equal treatment, justice can flourish only under the shadow of injustice. No wonder, then, that "the worst injustice, the most bloody and unjustifiable transgressions of justice, are…committed daily in the name of justice, under the protection of the name 'justice.'"[30] The grander and more sweeping justice is, the more injustice it can wreak.

It can be persuasively argued that the postmodern critique of justice, like the postmodern critique of rationality, draws its pathos from the self-stultifying tendency to generate false expectations and then harbor disappointments when they fail to be fulfilled.[31] It places impossible demands on a notion of justice, despairs over them not being met, and then declares all general notions of justice impossible and undesirable. Take the charge that justice is blind to differences. The postmodern critique of systematic blindness is more or less on target when directed against the homogenizing tendencies of a typically modern understanding of justice. But does it therefore undermine all notions of universal justice? The best traditions of thinking about justice sought not to abstract from differences but to give them their due.[32] Before we dismiss the postmodern critique as misplaced, however, we should learn from it not to overlook the strong propensity of many "seekers of justice" to abstract from differences and place on justice false expectations of blind legality. Moreover, no adequate notion of justice may disregard two Nietzschean moves that the postmodern critique makes: the insight that "all judgments" are "incomplete," "premature," "impure," and therefore "unfair,"[33] and the protest against the "vindictive characters" who, "disguised as judges," carry "the word *justice* in their mouths like a poisonous spittle."[34]

What is the postmodern alternative to unjust universal justice?

Consider the following statement by Jacques Derrida from a more recent text, which signals a tentative "ethical turn" in his thought: "Justice in itself, if such a thing exists, outside or beyond law, is not deconstructible. No more than deconstruction, if such a thing exists. *Deconstruction is*

---

29. Ibid.
30. Ibid., 86.
31. Taylor, "Justice After Virtue," 36.
32. See Aristotle, *Nicomachean Ethics*.
33. Friedrich Nietzsche, *Human, All Too Human. A Book for Free Spirits*, transl. Marion Faber (Lincoln: University of Nebraska Press, 1996), 35.
34. Friedrich Nietzsche, *The Birth of Tragedy and The Genealogy of Morals*, transl. Francis Golffing (Garden City: Doubleday, 1956), 259.

justice.[35] How can deconstruction be justice?[36] Caputo, who picks up Derrida's lead, explains. Deconstruction is justice because it tears down "the large, honorable, hoary inscriptions of the law" that oppress in the name of justice, and it establishes the honor of the "little proper names."[37] Justice worthy of its name listens to the voice of the individual who protests against the law saying: "But this case is different!" No disinterested impartiality here. No cultivation of systematic blindness. Everything depends on keeping your eyes wide open, on noting and respecting all the small and big differences. A proper Book of Justice, Caputo explains, "would have to mention everybody by name...it would be like a map so perfect that it would match in size the region of which it is the map."[38] To be just, justice must be as specific as each case. Hence justice itself is "not one thing, not one name, but an uncontrollable plurality of names."[39] The gain of giving so many names to justice is "maximization of difference...letting many flowers bloom."[40]

The *loss* of giving so many names to justice becomes apparent, however, as soon as we observe that next to many flowers grow many weeds. If the goal is to maximize difference, why not let the weeds grow too, why not let *everything* bloom? Caputo is *tempted* by this line of thought. Life would then be "innocent...the way the waves that beat against the ship or the shore are innocent, however much destruction they do.... The justification is to see that there is no injustice, that nothing really is 'unjust.'"[41] He rightly refuses, however, to succumb to the "no injustice" solution to the problem of oppression—a solution that would parallel Nietzsche's "glad tidings" in *The Anti-Christ* that there are "no more opposites."[42] Instead, in addition to maximizing difference, Caputo maintains that justice demands minimizing suffering.[43] Why minimize suffering? Why not

---

35.   Jacques Derrida, "Force of Law: The Mystical Foundation of Authority," *Cardoza Law Review* 11 (1990): 945, italics mine.

36.   See Cristoph Demmerling, "Differenz und Gleichheit. Zur Anatomie eines Argumentes," *Die Gegenwart der Gerechtigkeit: Diskurse zwischen Recht, praktischer Philosophie und Politik*, ed. Christoph Demmerling and Thomas Rentsch (Berlin: Akademie, 1995), 124–26.

37.   Caputo, *Against Ethics*, 87; cf. Jean-François Lyotard, *The Postmodern Condition: A Report on Knowledge*, transl. Geoff Bennington and Brian Massumi (Minneapolis: University of Minnesota Press, 1984), 82.

38.   Ibid., 88.

39.   Ibid., 89.

40.   Ibid., 92.

41.   Ibid., 138.

42.   Nietzsche, *Human, All Too Human*, 156.

43.   Caputo, *Against Ethics*, 92.

simply forgive insult and forget the crime? After all, Caputo's forgiveness is the flip side of his justice. Like justice, forgiveness "dismisses the law, suspends it, lifts it, lets it hang in midair, in order to answer the call that wells up from the abyss of the Other."[44] So why not answer the call that wells up from the abyss of the weeds? Lack of feeling for weeds?[45] Yes, but not quite. Weeds are killers; they *minimize difference* instead of maximizing it. To maximize difference we need to affirm respect for others, and respect for others requires that we not respect "people who do not respect others," argues Caputo.[46]

This line of thought seems persuasive—though the weeds would, no doubt, object that it is heavily weighted in favor of the plants humans like to call flowers. If you respect those who do not respect others, then disrespect reigns. Notice, however, that we have come almost full circle, close to the liberal principle of justice: all should respect all; none should respect those who do not respect all. A postmodern thinker goes on his or her way to dismantle the liberal notion of universal justice but by the time such a thinker is done with the task he or she has surreptitiously reassembled much of what he or she had taken down. Out of nowhere the song celebrating *universal freedom* from domination reaches our ears.[47] All radical difference notwithstanding, there sits within most postmodern thinkers an undeconstructed liberal with universal commitments quietly subverting the work of his or her master. What gets dismantled in the end is justice as deconstruction.

The inconsistency in the postmodern understanding of justice is coupled with a difficulty in *fighting* injustice. Over against general laws, postmodern thought celebrates specific names. It would seem that the stress on "names" would secure both the agents in the struggle for justice and subjects in need of protection against injustice. In the postmodern view, however, a "name" is not a "person" in the sense of an agent with a stable identity. As a bearer of a proper name, an individual is "itself also a complex configuration of still further events, multiplicity or constellation unto itself.... The individual is a perspective, the perspective of the here, now,

---

44. Ibid., 112.

45. Obligation arises, Caputo argues, from the "feeling that comes over us when others need our help, when they call out for help, or support, or freedom, or whatever they need, a feeling that grows in strength directly in proportion to the desperateness of the situation of the other. The power of obligation varies directly with the powerlessness of the one who calls for help, which is the power of powerlessness" (Caputo, *Against Ethics*, 5).

46. Ibid., 119.

47. See Charles Taylor, *Sources of the Self: The Making of the Modern Identity* (Cambridge: Harvard University Press, 1989), 504.

at this point."[48] The notion of a "person" or a "subject" is too uniform and stable, we are told; it must be subverted. The unfortunate side-effect of giving up on the notion of "subject" is that without some sense of the stable identity of a social agent, the struggle against injustice becomes difficult (see Chapters II, VI, VII). Who will do the struggling? On behalf of whom should the struggle go on? A "complex configuration of events"? As Henry Louis Gates Jr. observes in *Loose Canons*, the irony of the radical postmodern construal of the self is that "precisely when we (and other Third World peoples) obtain the complex wherewithal to define our black subjectivity...our theoretical colleagues declare that there ain't no such a thing as a subject, so why should we be bothered with that."[49]

What is the outcome of the crusade of difference against universal justice, of the plea for radical difference as the only proper justice? Justice will not be subverted by difference. Postmodern thinkers have difficulty in thinking about justice without entangling themselves in self-contradictions, and they are hard put to explain how, on their understanding of human beings, struggle against injustice is possible. Are we then left without a viable alternative to the unacceptable construals of a universal justice? There is another way of connecting particularity and difference with justice, proposed by a philosophy that sees itself as the alternative to both modern and postmodern thought. A *coherent tradition* is very much something particular, and justice can be seen as dependent on such a tradition. Will this way of proceeding resolve the problem posed by the struggle of justice against justice?

Justice Within Tradition

Consider the difficulties of pluralistic societies when they are debating issues of justice. In *Whose Justice? Which Rationality?* Alasdair MacIntyre, the main proponent of the view that theories of justice are aspects of given traditions, puts the problem this way: since contending social groups are unable to "arrive at agreed rationally justifiable conclusions on the nature of justice," they appeal simply to their rival convictions without even attempting to justify them rationally.

---

48. Caputo, *Against Ethics*, 95.

49. Henry L. Gates, *Loose Canons: Notes on the Culture Wars* (New York: Oxford University Press, 1992), 36.

Disputed questions concerning justice and practical rationality are...treated in the public realm, not as matters for rational inquiry, but rather for the assertion and counter-assertion of alternative and incompatible sets of premises.[50]

As a result, in modern democracies the assertions of those with more political power win. In the famous words from the end of his *After Virtue*, "modern politics is civil war carried on by other means."[51] We are back to generals or, more precisely, to their democratic equivalents.

To put an end to the war, MacIntyre calls for the retrieval of what he terms "tradition."[52] Every account of justice is situated in a given tradition. He explains:

Theories of justice and practical rationality confront us as aspects of traditions, allegiance to which requires the living out of some more or less systematically embodied form of human life, each with its own specific modes of social relationship, each with its own canons of interpretations and explanation in respect of the behavior of others, each with its own evaluative practices.[53]

One might object that this is simply to restate the problem, not to solve it. Do not rival traditions and rival communities of discourse *give rise* to rival justices? They do. MacIntyre believes, however, that traditions also provide resources for settling the disputes. Genuine intellectual encounter cannot take place in some generalized way among people who stand nowhere, as the Enlightenment thinkers assumed and much of modern culture takes for granted. For rational discussion to replace the sterile exchange of assertions and counter-assertions people must inhabit traditions.[54] From within a tradition, they can then carry on rational debates not only with the fellow members of the same tradition but also with those who inhabit rival traditions.[55]

---

50. MacIntyre, *Whose Justice? Which Rationality?*, 5f.

51. Alasdair MacIntyre, *After Virtue: A Study in Moral Theory*, 2nd ed. (Notre Dame, IN: University of Notre Dame Press, 1984), 253.

52. Ibid., 221ff.

53. MacIntyre, *Whose Justice? Which Rationality?*, 391.

54. Cf. Michael Walzer, *Interpretation and Social Criticism* (Cambridge: Harvard University Press, 1987), 8–18.

55. MacIntyre, *Whose Justice? Which Rationality?*, 349–69; cf. MacIntyre, *After Virtue*, 146.

There is no need to discuss here the persuasiveness of MacIntyre's criteria for judging the relative adequacy of traditions.[56] I will grant here that, in principle, conflicts between traditions can be rationally resolved in the way he suggests. But what are the odds that they *will* be resolved? MacIntyre ends the introduction to *Three Rival Versions of Moral Enquiry* with a gloomy forecast about his own proposal: "The most that one can hope for is to render our disagreements more constructive."[57] Such hope might be good enough for some thinkers (though not of the kind MacIntyre wants to be). To earn one's bread by fine-tuning one's own tradition in constructive disagreement with other traditions is not the worst thing that can happen to you. But what do such fine-tuned, intelligent disagreements mean for warring people and the excluded needy? They may even make the ideological weapons of their destruction deadlier and thereby seal their miserable fate more firmly.

Perhaps MacIntyre achieves so little because he sets out to achieve so much. He argues that to resolve conflicts about particular issues, we need to *resolve conflicts between larger traditions*, which provide the framework for particular issues.[58] He conceives of these larger traditions, moreover, as systems, so that "the distinctive conceptions of justice and practical rationality...are understood as parts of that whole."[59] What then happens at the interface of rivaling coherent and encompassing systems? Their advocates can either internally fine-tune the traditions to which they belong, or switch traditions.[60] Leaving aside the option open only to geniuses (such as Thomas Aquinas), who are able to start a fresh tradition by creatively merging previously existing ones, the conflict between traditions on particular issues can be resolved only through the *victory* of one tradition over another. This agonistic relation results, I believe, from MacIntyre's *excessive interest in coherence and comprehensiveness*.[61] The more integrated traditions are, the more their relations will be

---

56. See John Milbank, *Theology and Social Theory: Beyond Secular Reason* (Oxford: Blackwell, 1990), 345ff.

57. Alasdair MacIntyre, *Three Rival Versions of Moral Enquiry: Encyclopaedia, Genealogy, and Tradition* (Notre Dame, IN: University of Notre Dame Press, 1990), 8.

58. Alasdair MacIntyre, "Are Philosophical Problems Insoluble? The Relevance of Systems and History," *Philosophical Imagination and Cultural Memory: Appropriating Historical Traditions*, ed. Patricia Cook (Durham: Duke University Press, 1993).

59. MacIntyre, *Whose Justice? Which Rationality?*, 390.

60. Ibid., 166f.

61. Stout, *Ethics After Babel*, 218f.; Jeffrey Stout, "Homeward Bound: MacIntyre on Liberal Society and the History of Ethics," *Journal of Religion* 69 (1989): 230ff.

agonistic.[62] One tradition struggles against another, its justice against the justice of another tradition, until one defeats the other by proving itself rationally superior. As MacIntyre himself admits, the prospects that one tradition will win are slim.

I suggest that we lower our sights in conflicts over the issues of justice. Instead of seeking overall victory, we should look for piecemeal convergences and agreements. For this more modest endeavor MacIntyre's tradition-based conception of justice can be of help, provided we resist the temptation to press traditions into coherent and well-integrated systems. But should we resist this temptation?

Overlapping Territories, Basic Commitments

Let me start my alternative proposal with two simple propositions. One: "Nobody stands 'nowhere.'" Two: "Most of us stand in more than one place." In recent years, the first proposition has acquired the status of a truism. We do not argue about justice (or anything else, for that matter) as disembodied and asocial "selves" suspended by some sky hook above the hustle and bustle of social conflicts. Social location profoundly shapes our beliefs and practices. We think and act as "encumbered selves."[63] "Traditions" are inescapable. Even "the history of liberalism, which began as an appeal to alleged principles of shared rationality against what was felt to be the tyranny of tradition, has itself been transformed into a tradition," as MacIntyre has pointed out.[64] To leave all tradition behind is not a requirement of rationality but a recipe for insanity.

Those who profess Christian faith should feel no urge to abide in the asylum of minds stripped of all tradition. To be a Christian means to be attached to a community and to be shaped by its beliefs and practices. To learn what justice is, a Christian theologian will not seek to join Descartes and spend "the whole day shut up in a room heated by an enclosed stove" meditating on his or her "own thoughts."[65] Instead, the place where the Christian theologian will learn about justice is the community called the

---

62. The agonistic side of MacIntyre's thought has been critiqued by John Milbank. Unlike Milbank, I do not want simply to replace the dialectical struggle with rhetorical attraction, but to make sure that the struggle is not set up in such a way so that it results, as a rule, in the death of one contending party (*Theology and Social Theory*, 326ff.).

63. Sandel, *Liberalism and the Limits of Justice*, 179–83.

64. MacIntyre, *Whose Justice? Which Rationality?*, 335.

65. René Descartes, *Discourse on Method and the Meditations*, transl. F. E. Sutcliffe (Harmondsworth: Penguin, 1968), 35.

church. The object of her meditation will be the biblical traditions and the beliefs and practices of saints and sinners. Christian thought on justice is rooted in the fiery protests of prophets and in the engaged reflection of apostles. It derives from the whole narrative of God's dealing with humanity, a narrative that is particularly dense at the point where Jesus Christ enters that small country under Roman occupation, proclaims and enacts the coming reign of God, is crucified by the Romans, and is resurrected by God.

Christians do stand somewhere. Much needs to be said about *how* they should stand where they stand and how they should insert their particular vision into the larger public debate. I leave all of this aside here.[66] Crucial for my purposes is whether Christians stand in one place or many, and whether they inhabit a "coherent tradition." I have argued earlier (Chapter II) for both distance and belonging. Christians inescapably inhabit two worlds—they are "in God" and "in the world"—the world of the biblical traditions and the world of their own culture. Consequently, Christian "tradition" *is never pure*; it always represents a merging of streams coming from the scriptures and from given cultures that a particular church inhabits.[67] Here I want to make the matter a bit more complicated.

Consider the first world Christians inhabit, the *world of the scriptures*. Is this world best thought of as a "coherent tradition," in the sense in which Thomism, for instance, represents a coherent tradition?[68] I do not think so. The biblical texts are a canonical bundle of overlapping testimonies from radically different contexts to the one history of God with humanity that culminates in Christ's death and resurrection. The scriptures come to us in the form of plural traditions. The texts and the underlying "story of the history" that unites them (see Chapter I) do not offer a coherent tradition. Instead, they demand a series of interrelated basic commitments—beliefs and practices. These commitments *can be developed* into traditions. But such traditions are always secondary phenomena in need of being interrogated and reshaped in the light of both basic commitments and changing cultural contexts. Christian theologians have their own good reasons to suspect that there is some truth to

---

66. See Mouw and Griffioen, *Pluralism and Horizons*, 158ff.

67. Miroslav Volf, "Theology, Meaning, and Power," *The Future of Theology: Essays in Honor of Jürgen Moltmann*, ed. Miroslav Volf et al. (Grand Rapids: Eerdmans, 1996), 99ff.

68. MacIntyre, *Three Rival Versions of Moral Enquiry*.

Nietzsche's aphorism in *Twilight of the Idols*, which states that "the will to a system is a lack of integrity."[69]

Consider, second, the world of culture that Christians inhabit. In a significant sense, that world is also not a single world. From the very beginning, the world Christians inhabited was plural—Hellenism and Judaism were mixed in Palestine,[70] and the *pax romana* extended over a multicultural empire. Similarly, today we live in a world in which multiple streams of social traditions and practices converge upon one another. We can easily agree with MacIntyre that our contemporaries in the West "tend to live betwixt and between."[71] But should we agree with his assessment of the situation? Should we endorse the solution he proposed? For him being "betwixt and between" presents an inconsistent and unstable state. The person living "betwixt and between" is neither a "citizen of nowhere,"[72] as a good liberal should be, nor "at home" in a tradition, which is where any wise person would want to be. But should we work to create such homes? If my argument about the nature of the world of the biblical traditions is plausible, then nothing in the natures of Christian beliefs themselves compels us to build a "coherent tradition" out of basic Christian commitments. What matters are these commitments. And what matters is that they be brought to bear on social realities.

Granted, it is not necessary to develop a coherent tradition, but would it not be *desirable* to do so? This is a rather complex question, and I will address here only the issue of the *social* desirability of such traditions. Would the social world we inhabit be helped if we offered our contemporaries an all-encompassing home in a coherent tradition built on the basis of basic Christian commitments? I think not. In fact, I believe that *no such home is imaginable* in contemporary societies. As Zygmunt Bauman observes in *Postmodern Ethics*,

> a community truly able to "situate" its members with any degree of lasting consequence appears to be more a methodological postulate than a fact of life. Whenever one descends from the relatively secure realm of concepts to the description of any concrete object the concepts are

69. Friedrich Nietzsche, *Twilight of the Idols and The Anti-Christ*, transl. R. J. Hollingdale (London: Penguin, 1990), 35.

70. Martin Hengel, *Judaism and Hellenism: Studies in Their Encounter in Palestine During the Early Hellenistic Period*, transl. John Bowden (London: SCM, 1974).

71. MacIntyre, *Whose Justice? Which Rationality?*, 397.

72. Ibid., 388.

supposed to stand for—one finds merely a fluid collection of men and women....[73]

Cultures and traditions are not integrated wholes and cannot be made to be such in contemporary societies. The belief that they can, argues Steven Lukes, is a "clear example of the complexity reduction with the help of mythical thinking."[74] We cannot help but live "betwixt and between" and keep using "a variety of tradition-generated resources of thought and action"[75] precisely because we cannot avoid living in *overlapping and rapidly changing social spaces.* In contemporary societies it is impossible to pursue a coherent system of goods. Instead, we must rest satisfied with holding on to basic commitments. The early Christians lived and thrived without the secure closure of a system; there is no reason why we cannot do the same.

Overlapping and changing social spaces account for a good deal of fragmentation in contemporary societies: we tolerate different rationalities in different milieus and live with partly inconsistent moral principles. But consider the consequence of eliminating fragmentation and incoherence. It would involve purging extraneous elements from traditions so as to make them pure, coherent. As MacIntyre well knows, this cannot happen simply through a change of beliefs. "Philosophical theories," he writes, "give organized expression to concepts and theories *already embodied in forms of practice and types of community.*"[76] Hence, to inhabit a single coherent tradition you must belong to a single unified community. To escape fragmentations, what needs to change is not simply the way we as individuals think but also the way we as societies live. Nothing short of an antimodern and anti-pluralistic social revolution will do. Would some new monism of beliefs and social practices be desirable, however? Would a revolution pay off? Certainly not. This may be why MacIntyre prefers retreating into "local forms of community within which civility and the intellectual and moral life can be sustained through the new dark ages which are already upon us."[77] I have strong doubts that such a "sectarian" option is either viable or desirable. I think

---

73. Zygmunt Bauman, *Postmodern Ethics* (Oxford: Blackwell, 1993), 44.
74. Steven Lukes, *The Curious Enlightenment of Professor Caritat: A Comedy of Ideas* (London: Verso, 1995), 108.
75. MacIntyre, *Whose Justice? Which Rationality?*, 397.
76. Ibid., 390, italics added.
77. MacIntyre, *After Virtue*, 263.

it is better to give up on "coherent traditions" and, armed with basic Christian commitments, enter boldly the ever-changing world of modern cultures.

The curse of inhabiting overlapping cultural territories is that we not only disagree but also that our disagreements both reflect and lead to painful social conflicts. MacIntyre is right about that. A blessing accompanies the curse, however. As we share each other's social territories, we partly inhabit each other's "traditions"; we share each other's commitments. The very cause of the fragmentation—the hybridity of our views—makes our beliefs and practices fluid, and open to change, to enrichment, and to partial agreement on such important matters as justice. Sustained by our intersecting lives and our underlying agreements, disagreements persist, however. And they are profound. We need to look for ways of resolving them without recourse to either the power of guns or the brute strength of the democratic masses.

Justice, Commitments, Differences

With MacIntyre and against typically modern thinkers I have argued that none of us stand "nowhere" and that we all stand within a "tradition." I have then affirmed what neither modern thinkers, nor postmodern thinkers, nor MacIntyre denies, namely, that most of us stand in more places than one, that our traditions are hybrid. Against MacIntyre, however, I have argued that a Christian theologian will not necessarily want to get rid of the "hybridity"—he or she will be much more interested in affirming *basic Christian commitments in culturally situated ways* than in forging coherent traditions and he or she will suspect that hybrid traditions will be more open than coherent traditions, not only to be shaped by these commitments but also to be enriched by each other. But how should this process of enrichment take place? I will work my way to a suggestion by briefly discussing the work of Edward Said and Seyla Benhabib, though the suggestion will rest on theological grounds.

For the interpretation of literature Edward Said has suggested in *Culture and Imperialism* what he calls a *contrapuntal* reading. We must be able, he writes,

> to think through and interpret together experiences that are discrepant, each with its particular agenda and pace of development, its own inter-

196

nal formations, its coherence and system of external relationships, all of them coexisting and interacting with others.[78]

In this one dense sentence, Said paints a complex picture. Put simply, his concern is to open for one another discordant worlds that all project multiple voices into the same space. How can this be done? We need to juxtapose those worlds, he proposes, and let them play off each other in order "to make concurrent those views and experiences that are ideologically and culturally closed to each other and that attempt to distance or suppress other views and experiences."[79]

So far so good. Concurrence—in the sense of "coming up against each other"—is essential if there is to be enrichment. But will it suffice? Possibly in the world of literature for which Said is making his proposal. In the world of actual social interchange, however, "concurrence of ideologically and culturally closed views" often reinforces the mutual exclusion of conflicting views, rather than enriching them. In addition to concurrence, it is essential to *open* these actual concurrent and conflicting social worlds *to one another*. If juxtaposing will not accomplish that, what will?

Conflicting parties need to practice what Hannah Arendt calls an "enlarged way of thinking." Moral judgment, she insists, "cannot function in strict isolation or solitude; it needs the presence of others 'in whose place' it must think, whose perspective it must take into consideration."[80] In *Situating the Self* Seyla Benhabib takes up this lead from Hannah Arendt and suggests a model of moral conversation "in which the capacity to reverse perspectives, that is, willingness to reason from the others' point of view, and the sensitivity to hear their voice is paramount."[81] By listening to others as they speak in their own right we can hope to reach "some reasonable agreement in an open-ended moral conversation."[82]

"Enlarged thinking" will be helpful in reflecting on the problem of justice, if we do not expect too much of it, as I think Benhabib does. For her it serves to *justify* moral beliefs and give them *validity*. She would like to make "enlarged thinking" the cornerstone of a communicative ethics whose core idea is "the processual generation of reasonable agreement

78. Edward Said, *Culture and Imperialism* (New York: Alfred A. Knopf, 1993), 32.
79. Ibid., 33.
80. Hannah Arendt, *Between Past and Future: Eight Exercises in Political Thought* (New York: Viking, 1968), 221.
81. Seyla Benhabib, *Situating the Self: Gender, Community, and Postmodernism in Contemporary Ethics* (New York: Routledge, 1992), 8.
82. Ibid., 9.

about moral principles via an open-ended moral conversation."[83] But how can one generate *moral validity* by "reasonable agreement"? If "morally valid" equals "what we agree on" through "procedures which are radically open and fair to all,"[84] what will distinguish moral validity from mere agreement? It will not do to appeal to "reasonable and fair process."[85] As she herself rightly notes, "reasonable and fair process" *presupposes* a "utopian way of life"[86] as a moral ideal. Since such a way of life is itself "a moral intuition," a reasonable and fair process that rests on it cannot serve as an adequate "substantive test" for moral intuitions, as she proposes.

We can, however, avoid reducing moral validity to agreement and still practice enlarged thinking if we carefully distinguish between the *justification* of moral beliefs and their *correction*. Consider, first, the issue of justification. If we were to ask, "How do we justify our moral convictions about what is just?" then the answer would not be: "By reaching 'some reasonable agreement in an open-ended moral conversation.'"[87] Instead, the answer would be, "By appealing to our (multifaceted) respective traditions and the resources they provide." For Christians, this would mean that we learn what justice is by observing justice as it is revealed in the biblical traditions—by hearing, say, the story of Nathan confronting David on behalf of Uriah, by listening to the judgments of court prophets like Isaiah or of outsiders like Amos, and, ultimately, by exploring the whole history of the triune God with the creation. This is what justice is for us, and we believe that this is what justice should be for everyone. Why? Because this is the justice of the one God of all peoples.[88] There is no other way to justify our notion of justice than by pointing to God's justice (though there is a way to *argue* for this way of justifying our notion of justice).

Though "enlarged thinking" cannot serve to justify our notion of justice, it is essential for *enrichment and correction* both of our notion of justice and our perception of what is just or unjust. Our understanding of God's justice is imperfect and we often pervert justice even as we seek to do it. How would the process of enrichment and correction work? In Chapter VI, I will give a detailed analysis of the art of "enlarged thinking"

83. Ibid., 37.
84. Ibid., 9.
85. Ibid., 37.
86. Ibid., 38.
87. Ibid., 9.
88. Dietrich Ritschl, *Zur Logik der Theologie. Kurze Darstellung der Zusammenhänge theologischer Grundgedanken* (München: Christian Kaiser, 1984), 284ff.

or, as I will call it, "double vision." Let it suffice here to note only that we enlarge our thinking by letting the voices and perspectives of others, especially those with whom we may be in conflict, resonate within ourselves, by allowing them to help us see them, as well as ourselves, from *their* perspective, and if needed, readjust our perspectives as we take into account their perspectives.[89] Nothing can guarantee in advance that the perspectives will ultimately merge and agreement be reached. We may find that we must reject the perspective of the other. Yet we should seek to see things from the other's perspective in the hope that competing justices may become converging justices and eventually issue in agreement.

Reversing perspectives may lead us not only to learn something from the other, but also to look afresh at our own traditions and rediscover their neglected or even forgotten resources. Consider the role the encounter with socialist tradition and its appropriation in liberation theology has played in the larger Christian debate about justice. It has forced us to readjust our reading of the biblical message: to know God means to do justice (whatever else knowing God might mean); justice is justice for the poor; God's justice includes God's compassion on those who suffer.[90] We see what we have not seen before because, in the encounter with the other, we have made space within ourselves not only for the perspective of the other but with the help of the other also for silenced voices from our own tradition.

The idea of "double vision" may strike us as reasonable, but are there good *theological grounds* for endorsing it? Are there biblical examples? Jesus himself may offer the best biblical example for the practice of "double vision," of seeing with the eyes of the others, accepting their perspective, and discovering the new significance of one's own basic commitments. Consider his encounter with the Syrophoenician woman—a text from which sometimes too hasty Christological conclusions are drawn.[91] Jesus refuses to heal the daughter of this Gentile woman from a region that exploited Galilean farmers[92] because he was sent "only to the lost sheep of the house of Israel" (Matt 15:24). Judith Gundry-Volf has argued that

---

89. The practice of "double vision," as I advocate it here, presupposes that we can both *stand within a given tradition* and *learn from other traditions* (see Nicholas Wolterstorff, *What New Haven and Grand Rapids Have to Say to Each Other* [Grand Rapids: Calvin College, 1993]).

90. Karen Lebacqz, *Six Theories of Justice. Perspectives from Philosophical and Theological Ethics* (Minneapolis: Augsburg, 1986), 103ff.

91. Rita Nakashima Brock, *Journeys by Heart: A Christology of Erotic Power* (New York: Crossroad, 1988), 50ff.

92. Gerd Theissen, *Lokalkolorit und Zeitgeschichte in den Evangelien: Ein Beitrag zur Geschichte der synoptischen Tradition* (Göttingen: Vandenhoeck & Ruprecht, 1989), 63–84.

199

the woman challenges "Jesus' duty-bound reluctance to work a miracle for a Gentile" with the principle of "mercy...by which a woman runs her household." Just as a woman cares for her whole household, so also divine mercy "knows no ethnic bias."[93] This is her "faith," so highly praised by Jesus. And in the Gospel narrative this faith moved Jesus not only to heal the daughter but also to expand his mission to the Gentiles, broadly speaking. Gundry-Volf writes:

> [The Syrophoenician woman] believes that divine mercy knows no bias. And she believes that Jesus will show this kind of mercy. As she expresses this faith in him, he also begins to believe. He, the one sent to the lost sheep of the house of Israel, can also do a miracle for a Gentile woman. He can extend help even to a Syrophoenician Hellenist, who belonged to his and his people's oppressors. For mercy is unbounded.[94]

Immediately after the encounter with the nameless woman, Jesus goes to the Sea of Galilee and attracts Gentile crowds whom he heals and feeds (Matt 15:29-39). Through the encounter, Jesus's own understanding of mission was enlarged;[95] he saw the key concept of his message—unbiased grace—in a new light.

The most important theological reason for practicing "double vision" lies not in the example of Jesus but in the inner logic of the theology of the cross. As I have argued earlier (Chapter IV), on the cross God made space in God's very self for others, godless others, and opened arms to invite them in. The practice of "double vision," I want to argue here, is the *epistemological side of faith in the Crucified.* When he was nailed to the cross, Jesus Christ was, of course, not engaged in seeing things with the eyes of those who crucified him (though, according to some manuscripts, he noted their ignorance as to what they were doing); he knew who the perpetrators were and who the victim was. Equally, by receiving the godless, God was not engaged in reversing perspectives but in exposing their godlessness in the very act of providing for its forgiveness. Does this invalidate my argument? It does not. The Lamb of God *was* innocent, but *we* are not, or at least cannot presume to be; he could recognize unfailingly the godlessness of the godless, but *we* cannot. Indeed, one of the most basic tenets of the Christian faith is that *we* are the perpetrators who crucified

---

93. Judith M. Gundry-Volf, "Spirit, Mercy, and the Other," *Theology Today* 52, no. 1 (1995): 519.
94. Ibid.
95. Ibid., 521.

Christ, *we* are the godless whose godlessness God exposed. For us sinful and limited human beings, following in the footsteps of the Crucified means not only creating space in ourselves for others but in creating space for them making also space for their perspective on us and on them—at least for a while so we can form discerning judgments.

If we believe rightly in Jesus Christ who unconditionally embraced us, the godless perpetrators, our hearts will be open to receive others, even enemies, and our eyes will be open to see from their perspective. In *Letters and Papers from Prison,* Dietrich Bonhoeffer suggested that faith enables us to take "distance" from our own immediacy and take into ourselves the tension-filled polyphony of life, instead of pressing life to "a single dimension." Through faith, he claimed, "we take in a sense God and the whole world into ourselves."[96] Bonhoeffer had in mind mainly the resources faith provides for living in extreme situations, such as the prison from which he wrote, in which people tend to be ruled by the immediacy of the pressing needs or scarce occasions for joy. But the ability to take God and the world into ourselves generated by faith is equally significant in situations of conflict. They too tend to enslave people in the exclusive commitment to "our cause." The faith in Jesus Christ, who made our cause his cause, frees us from pursuing our interests only, and creates in us the space for the interests of others. We are ready to perceive justice where we previously saw only injustice—if indeed the cause of the others is just.

Seeking Justice, Fighting Injustice

Three major objections militate against the practice of "double vision" as a way of countering injustice generated by the struggle of justice against justice. As I attend to them, I will provide positive reasons why the practice is indispensable.

First, one can object that the proposal is an exercise in wishful thinking. It will not work when we need it most. When we are looking at each other through the sights of our guns we see only the rightness of our own cause. We think more about how to enlarge our power than to enlarge our thinking; we strive to eliminate others from our world, not to grant them space in ourselves. Does our resistance to "double vision" in situations of conflict invalidate the notion? I do not think so. It does underline,

---

96. Dietrich Bonhoeffer, *Widerstand und Ergebung, Briefe und Aufzeichnungen aus der Haft* (München: Christian Kaiser, 1966), 209.

however, that *the will to embrace the unjust precedes agreement on justice.* I have argued earlier (Chapter IV) that the will to embrace is unconditional and indiscriminate. Like the sun, it should rise on the evil and on the good; like the rain, it should fall on the righteous and on the unrighteous. For validation, the will to embrace needs neither the assurance that it will in fact overcome enmity nor the inner rewards that the pleasure of loving someone unlovable may provide. This is simply what those who are the children of the "Father in heaven" and follow Christ do because this is what being God's children and following Christ means (Matt 5:45). The same holds true of "double vision," which is the epistemological side of the will to embrace.

The will to embrace—love—sheds the light of knowledge by the fire it carries with it. The eyes need the light of this fire to perceive any justice in the cause and actions of others. Granted, there may in fact be no justice to perceive there. They may prove to be as unjust as they strike us, and what they insist just may in fact be a perversion of justice. But *if* there is any justice in their cause and actions, we will need the will to embrace them to make us capable of perceiving it because it will let us see both them and ourselves with their eyes. Similarly, the will to exclude—hatred—blinds by the fire it carries with it.[97] The fire of exclusion directs its light only on the injustice of others; any justice they may have will be enveloped in darkness or branded as covert injustice—a mere contrived goodness designed to make their evil all the more deadly. Both the "clenched fist" and the "open arms" are *epistemological stances*; they are *moral conditions of moral perception*—a claim that rests on a more general Nietzschean insight that "all experiences are moral experiences, even in the realm of perception."[98] The clenched fist hinders perception of the justice of others and thereby reinforces injustice; the open arms help detect justice behind the rough front of seeming injustice and thereby reinforce justice. To agree on justice in conflict situations you must want more than justice; you must want embrace. There can be *no justice without the will to embrace.* It is, however, equally true that there can be *no genuine and lasting embrace without justice* (see Chapters VI and VII).

97. Nietzsche, *Human, All Too Human*, 244. My formulations here about the epistemological significance of the will to embrace and the will to exclusion are inspired by Nietzsche's claim in *Human, All Too Human* that "love and hate are not blind, but are blinded by the fire they themselves carry with them" (ibid.). Unlike Nietzsche here, I think that the fire of genuine love does not blind, but rather that it enlightens.

98. Friedrich Nietzsche, *The Gay Science with a Prelude in Rhymes and an Appendix of Songs*, transl. Walter Kaufmann (New York: Vintage Books, 1974), 173f.

The second objection to the notion of "double vision" concerns the struggle against injustice. Here the critical question is not whether we *can* practice "double vision" in the thick of battle but whether we *should* practice it when faced with manifest injustice. With all the pain and suffering caused by exclusion and violence, how can we afford to muse about a *possible* justice of the perpetrators? How many tears must be shed before we put an end to the spiral of reversing perspectives, that never-ending search for an agreement on justice that is so easily misused as a cover for perpetrating injustice? When shed blood cries out to heaven, is not prophetic rage called for? Must we not stop the killers rather than seek to see things from their perspective? Is not "enlarged thinking" good for the suburbs, but dangerous in the inner cities and on the killing fields? Will it not draw laughter from tyrants and sighs of despair from their victims? As we stumble toward agreement, injustice runs rampant!

The response should start with a simple but immensely significant observation: the human ability to agree on justice will never catch up with the human propensity to do injustice. We must therefore not only make judgments before agreement is reached—something we in fact inescapably do;[99] we must also *act* in accordance with these judgments. The scriptures uniformly call us not so much to reflect on justice as to *do* justice. The prophets are full of appeals to "maintain love and justice" (Hos 12:6 CEB), to "establish justice" (Amos 5:15), to "do justice" (Mic 6:8). Consider the famous words of Amos:

> But let justice roll down like waters,
> and righteousness like an everflowing stream. (5:24)

Isaiah's vision of the proper worship of God is no less activistic:

> Is not this the fast that I choose:
>> to loose the bonds of injustice,
>> to undo the thongs of the yoke
> to let the oppressed go free
>> and to break every yoke? (58:6)

---

99. Nietzsche, *Human, All Too Human*, 32.

In doing justice Israel was to imitate her God "who works vindication and justice for all who are oppressed" (Ps 103:6).[100] Doing justice, struggling against injustice, was not an optional extra of Israelite faith; it stood at the very core. To know God is to do justice.[101] Consequently, *reflection about justice must serve doing justice.* If "double vision" has a legitimate place in Christian life, then it will be not so much something we do *before* engaging in the struggle against injustice but it would be something we do *as* we engage in this struggle.

Once the primacy of the struggle against injustice over the agreement on justice is established, the problem is no longer how we can afford to go on reversing perspectives, but how we can afford *not* to do so. The principle cannot be denied: the fiercer the struggle against the injustice you suffer, the blinder you will be to the injustice you inflict. We tend to translate the presumed wrongness of our enemies into an unfaltering conviction of our own rightness. In seeking to do justice we pervert justice, turn it into "poison" (Amos 6:12).

How do we prevent perpetrating injustice in the very struggle against injustice? Unlike Mark Taylor in *Remembering Esperanza*, I do not think the key is "to affirm plurality within that struggle."[102] Though sensitivity to plurality is essential, the *affirmation* of plurality is spurious. The only way to decide among many options, all with their "different visions of 'the just,'"[103] is by appealing to our own conception of justice. Instead of simply affirming plurality we must nurture an awareness of our own *fallibility.*[104] Since there is "no impartial perspective," all constructions of what is just or unjust, indeed all judgments, are unfair and entail committing injustice;[105] since there is no morally pure struggle, every engagement for justice, indeed "every for and against," is implicated in perpetrating injustice.[106]

---

100. Stephen Charles Mott, *Biblical Ethics and Social Change* (New York: Oxford University Press, 1982), 59ff.

101. Gustavo Gutiérrez, *A Theology of Liberation: History, Politics, and Salvation*, 2nd ed., transl. Caridad Inda and John Eagleson (Maryknoll, NY: Orbis, 1988), 194ff.

102. Mark Kline Taylor, *Remembering Esperanza: A Cultural-Political Theology for North American Praxis* (Maryknoll, NY: Orbis, 1990), 42.

103. Ibid., 41.

104. Thomas Rentsch, "Unmöglichkeit und Selbsttranszendenz der Gerechtigkeit," *Die Gegenwart der Gerechtigkeit: Diskurse zwischen Recht, praktischer Philosophie und Politik*, ed. Christoph Demmerling and Thomas Rentsch (Berlin: Akademie, 1995), 195f.

105. Reinhold Niebuhr, *The Nature and Destiny of Man* (New York: Scribner's, 1964), 2:252; Nietzsche, *Human, All Too Human*, 35.

106. Nietzsche, *Human, All Too Human*, 9.

Stricken with the sense of sinfulness, should we withdraw from making judgments and working for justice? Abdication of responsibility will be tempting to those who only know how to live in a world neatly divided into territories of pure light and of utter darkness. But no such world exists, except in the imagination of the self-righteous (see Chapter III); the construction of such a world is itself an act of injustice. In a world shot through with injustice, the struggle for justice must be carried on by people inescapably tainted by injustice. Hence the importance of "double vision." We need to see our judgments about justice and our struggle against injustice through the eyes of the other—even the manifestly "unjust other"—and be willing to readjust our understanding of what is just and repent of acts of injustice.

Let us assume that I have answered adequately the two objections; we can practice "double vision" if we are willing to embrace the other, and we ought to practice it if we want to come to an agreement on justice and avoid committing injustice as we struggle for justice. A nagging question still remains, which makes up the third objection: Can we *struggle against injustice* while engaged in reversing perspectives? The problem here is not that the process is potentially interminable and that we therefore never get around to doing justice, but that it seems to imply a certain highly problematic symmetry: one perspective seems as valid as the other. Were this true, the effect would again be the failure to do justice, now not so much because we are too busy enlarging our thinking, but because as long as each side has the chance of being right, neutrality seems appropriate. Even more than just encouraging inaction, neutrality is positively harmful. For one, it gives tacit support to the stronger party, independently of whether that party is right or wrong. Second, neutrality shields the perpetrators and frees their hands precisely by the failure to name them as perpetrators. Third, neutrality encourages the worst behavior of perpetrator and victim alike. If one party can get away with atrocities without offsetting neutrality, the other party, especially since it sees itself struggling for a just cause, will resort to atrocities too. Serbian forces in the Balkan war took UN hostages, but the United Nations continued its stance of principled neutrality. Why then would the Muslims not take hostages too, if that served their ends?

Is neutrality the proper stance, however? For those who stand in the prophetic and apostolic traditions of the scriptures, *no neutrality is in fact admissible.* These people hear the groans of the suffering, take a stance, and act. Then they reflect by engaging in "double vision," take a stance again, and act. From their perspective, the grounds on which they take their stances and their judgments as to what is just are not merely expressions of their preferences. They are at liberty neither to reject the grounds on which they make judgments nor to give these grounds merely the same validity as they give to the grounds other people have for their stances. After all, they are called to seek and struggle for *God's* justice, not their own. For them, *that* justice is not only one among many possible and equally acceptable perspectives on justice. It is *the* justice—even if they are fully aware that they grasp it only imperfectly and practice it inadequately, and even if they seek correction and enrichment from others with whom they disagree but cannot presume to be totally wrong.

There is another sense in which no neutrality is possible. For those who appeal to the biblical traditions, the presumption that one perspective is as valid as the other until proven otherwise is unacceptable. The *initial suspicion against the perspective of the powerful* is necessary. Not because the powerless are invariably right, but because the powerful have the means to impose their own perspective by argument and propaganda, and support the imposition both with the attractiveness of their "glory" and with the might of their weaponry. In part, their power lies in the ability to produce and give plausibility to ideologies that justify their power.[107] Often, the only resource of the powerless is the power of their desperate cry. The Jewish prophets—and indeed the whole of the scriptures—are biased toward the powerless. Such a preferential option for the powerless implies a privileged hearing for those whose voices are excluded,[108] the so-called "epistemological privilege of the oppressed." If justice is what we are after, then we will interrupt the powerful rhetoric of the smooth-tongued and strain our ear to hear the feeble and crackling voice of "those who cannot speak" (Prov 31:8). The stammerings of the needy are often an eloquent testimony to their violated rights; the spellbinding oratory of the powerful may well bespeak their bad conscience. It is above all the powerful who need to practice "double vision"—the groans of the powerless should disturb the serenity of their comforting ideologies.

---

107. Niebuhr, *The Nature and Destiny of Man*, 2:252.
108. Taylor, *Remembering Esperanza*, 64f.

Seeking Justice, Embracing the Other

"There can be no justice without the will to embrace," I remarked earlier. My point was simple: to agree on justice you need to make space in yourself for the perspective of the other, and in order to make space, you need to want to embrace the other. If you insist that others do not belong to you and you to them, that their perspective should not muddle yours, you will have your justice and they will have theirs; your justices will clash and there will be no justice *between* you. The knowledge of what is just depends on the will to embrace. The relationship between justice and embrace goes deeper, however. Embrace is part and parcel of the very *definition* of justice. I am not talking about soft mercy tampering harsh justice, but about love *shaping* the very content of justice.

The age-old principle that best expresses the spirit of justice is *suum cuique*—render to each person his or her due. But what is each person's due? How should it be determined? To be just is to be *impartial*, says the prevalent account of justice. Justice sees human beings "thinly," all worthy of equal treatment on account of their common humanity. To act justly, that same account of justice suggests, you must step outside a given relationship and—as a judge—apply the rule of justice without pursuing any other *interest*, save that of judging justly. This done, each person will receive his or her due; this done, justice will be done. Some such account of justice underlies John Rawls's *A Theory of Justice*, for instance. As I mentioned earlier, to ensure that the "judges" would be impartial and disinterested Rawls says the decisions about justice must be made behind the "veil of ignorance."[109] A social order will be just, if designed by actors who do not know when, where, and under what circumstances they will enter the world. A similar idea of justice can be read off the ancient image of *Justitia*—the angelic woman with a blindfold, sword in her right hand and scales in the left. Blindfolded, she pursues no special interest; the scales help her treat each and every person equally; with the sword she warns against disputing her judgments. Should we leave this concept of justice undisputed, however?

If *Justitia* is just, then Yahweh is patently unjust. Consider, first, God's "*interest*." There is a pattern in Israel's history that goes something like this: the Israelites suffer, they cry out to the Lord, God hears them, and God delivers—and this is called *justice* (Judg 5:11). It does not seem to matter

---

109. Rawls, *A Theory of Justice*, 136ff.

to the narrator if the Israelites suffered because they "again did what was evil in the sight of the Lord" (Judg 4:1). What matters is God's special relationship to Israel. God is interested in the good of the Israelites, and this interest is a part of God's justice. God never treats Israel as though she were not God's covenant people, never steps outside the relationship to gain a detached objectivity, never suppresses interest in her salvation. If God did that, God would, so to speak, step outside Godself and no longer be God. Hence, God's justice and God's kindness (Ps 145:17), God's righteousness and God's salvation (Isa 45:21), are intertwined. When God saves, God does justice; when God does justice, God saves—unless one refuses to be saved.

There is a profound "injustice" about the God of the biblical traditions. It is called *grace*. As I argued in Chapter IV, in the story of the prodigal son (Luke 15:11-32), it was "unjust" of the father to receive back the prodigal as a son and, on top of that, to throw a party for him after the son had just squandered half of his inheritance. But the father was not ruled by "justice." He acted in accordance with a "must" that was higher than the "must" of "justice" (15:32). It was the "must" of belonging together as a family. Put differently, the relationship defined justice; an abstract principle of justice did not define the relationship. If we want the God of the prophets and the God of Jesus Christ, we will have to put up with the "injustice" of God's grace—and rethink the concept of justice.

Consider, second, God's *partiality*. In the biblical traditions, when God looks at a widow, for instance, God does not see only "a free and rational agent" but a woman with no standing in society. When God looks at a sojourner, God does not see simply a human being but a stranger, cut off from the network of relations, subject to prejudice and scapegoating. How does the God who "executes justice for the oppressed" act toward widows and strangers? Just as God acts toward any other human being? No. God is partial to them. God "watches over the strangers" and "upholds the orphan and the widow" (Ps 146:7-9) in a way that God does not watch over and uphold the powerful.

Why is God partial to widows and strangers? In a sense, because God is partial to everyone—including the powerful, whom God resists in order to protect the widow and the stranger. God sees each human being concretely, the powerful no less than the powerless. God notes not only their common humanity but also their specific histories, their particular psychological, social, and embodied selves with their specific needs. When

God executes justice, God does not abstract but judges and acts in accordance with the specific character of each person. Do we not read, however, that God's Messiah will "not judge by what his eyes see, or decide by what his ears hear; but with righteousness he shall judge the poor, and decide with equity for the meek of the earth" (Isa 11:3-4)? But should we conclude that the deliverer's eyes will be closed when executing justice? To the contrary. He will judge truly because he will not judge by appearances and hearsay. God treats different people differently so that all will be treated justly. "Impartiality," writes Helen Oppenheimer rightly in *The Hope of Happiness,* "is not a divine virtue, but a human expedient to make up for the limits of our concern on the one hand and the corruptibility of our affections on the other."[110]

Why does God not treat all people equally but attends to each person in his or her specificity? Why does God not abstract from the relationship but instead lets the relationship shape judgments and actions? Because God is unjust? No. Because *the justice that equalizes and abstracts is an unjust justice!* Reinhold Niebuhr has argued that "no scheme of justice can do full justice to all the variable factors which the freedom of man introduces into human history"; it is impossible, he insisted, "to define absolutely what I owe to my fellow man, since nothing that he now is exhausts what he might be."[111] No justice that "calculates in fixed proportions" can therefore be just.[112] An adequate map of justice would not only have to "match in size the region of which it is the map," as Caputo suggested, but keep readjusting itself with every slightest change on the ground.[113]

Yet even such a perfect replica would be profoundly unjust. Though it would do justice to differences, it would not do justice to justice. For the unpredictable present play of differences itself rests on *past injustice.* The whole present is built on past violence and deception, and, as Nietzsche points out in *Human, All Too Human* "we, the heirs of all these conditions,

---

110.   Helen Oppenheimer, *The Hope of Happiness* (London: SCM, 1983), 131. The Apostle Paul does insist that "God shows no partiality" (Rom 2:11). Notice, however, the character of divine "impartiality." God is impartial, argues Paul, because "anguish and distress" due to "everyone who does evil" will befall "the Jew *first*" just as the "glory and honor and peace" due to "everyone who does good" will come to "the Jew *first*" (2:9-10). God's "impartiality" as Paul understands it *entails* the priority of the Jews. Formulated paradoxically, God is impartially partial!

111.   Reinhold Niebuhr, "Christian Faith and Natural Law," *Love and Justice. Selection from the Shorter Writings of Reinhold Niebuhr,* ed. D. B. Robertson (Cleveland: The World Publishing Company, 1967), 49f.

112.   Paul Tillich, *Love, Power, and Justice: Ontological Analyses and Ethical Applications* (London: Oxford University Press, 1954), 63.

113.   Caputo, *Against Ethics,* 88.

indeed the convergence of all that past, cannot decree ourselves away, and cannot want to remove one particular part."[114] The irreversible history of injustice weighs on the shoulders of the present. The burden cannot be cast away.[115] Neither revenge nor reparations can redress old injustices without creating new ones. The injustices of the dead keep recreating and reinforcing unjust asymmetries and differences among the living, and the injustices of the living offer an unjust world as a home for the yet unborn. To return to the image of the map, a perfectly matching and self-adjusting map would simply *replicate* the injustices of the past and present. Justice demands not a perfect map of the existing world, but nothing less than the undoing of the world, past and present, and the creation of a new world.

Justice is impossible in the order of calculating, equalizing, legalizing, and universalizing actions. If you want justice and nothing but justice, you will inevitably get injustice. If you want justice without injustice, you must want love. A world of perfect justice is a world of love. It is a world with no "rules," in which everyone does what he or she pleases and all are pleased by what everyone does; a world of no "rights" because there are no wrongs from which to be protected; a world of no "legitimate entitlements" because everything is given and nothing withheld; a world with no "equality" because all differences are loved in their own appropriate way; a world in which "just deserts" plays no role because all actions stem from superabundant grace. In short, a world of perfect justice would be a world of *transcended* justice, because it would be a world of *perfect freedom and love*. The blindfold would be taken from the eyes of *Justitia* and she would delight in whatever she saw; she would lay aside the scales because she would not need to weigh and compare anything; she would drop her sword because there would be nothing to police. *Justitia* would then be like the God of justice in a world of justice—the God who is nothing but perfect love (1 John 4:8).

"Anything short of love cannot be perfect justice," wrote Reinhold Niebuhr.[116] In a world of evil, however, we cannot dispense with an imperfect and therefore essentially unjust justice. The imperfect justice is the kind of necessary injustice without which people cannot be protected from violent incursions into their proper space. The weak, above all, need such protection. Hence they issue demands for justice whereas the powerful extol the justice of the order from which they benefit, as Aristotle

114. Nietzsche, *Human, All Too Human*, 216.
115. Rentsch, "Unmöglichkeit und Selbsttranszendenz der Gerechtigkeit," 193.
116. Niebuhr, "Christian Faith and Natural Law," 50.

observed.[117] Unjust justice is therefore indispensable for satisfying the demands of love in an unjust world. It must be pursued relentlessly, above all for the sake of the oppressed. But this pursuit of justice must be situated in the context of love. Gustavo Gutiérrez has argued in *On Job* that "the gratuitousness of God's love is the framework within which the requirement of practicing justice is to be located."[118] In my terminology, if you are after justice, you must be ultimately after embrace. In a world of oppression, what service does embrace do for justice?

First, the grace of embrace must help justice deal adequately with ever-changing differences among human beings. The stability and universality of justice need to be kept flexible by mercy's sensitivity to the particularities of a given situation.[119] Against this proposal, one could argue that sensitivity is a demand of *justice*, which insists that like should be treated as like,[120] and add that it is precisely the pursuit of justice—each must get his or her due—that is most likely to tell us in what way cases are alike and in what way they are different.[121] Yet persons are never "alike," and to treat them justly we need not so much to calculate differences and similarities between cases, as to assess what is appropriate to their particular situations. The assessment cannot be adequately done, I want to argue, if no love is in play. Without the will to embrace, justice is likely to be unjust.

Second, since "justice" is impotent in the face of past injustice, reconciliation is ultimately possible only through injustice being forgiven and, finally, forgotten (see Chapter IV). The act of forgiveness will name injustice as injustice and therefore demand that its causes be removed; the self-release into non-remembrance will be possible only after the threat of repeated violation has disappeared. Yet the demands of "justice" will have to remain unsatisfied. Embrace can take place only beyond "justice"—unless we reshape the concept of justice. And this is precisely what we find in the biblical traditions: the grace of embrace has become part and parcel of the idea of justice. Putting it in terms of the most general idea of justice—*suum cuique*—what is due to each person is to seek his or her good,[122] and each person's good

---

117. Aristotle, *The Politics*, 1318b.

118. Gutiérrez, *On Job: God-Talk and the Suffering of the Innocent*, transl. Matthew J. O'Connell (Maryknoll, NY: Orbis, 1987), 89.

119. Michael Welker, *God the Spirit*, transl. John F. Hoffmeyer (Minneapolis: Fortress, 1994), 120.

120. Jeffrie G. Murphy and Jean Hampton, *Forgiveness and Mercy* (Cambridge: Cambridge University Press, 1990), 169ff.

121. Nietzsche, *Human, All Too Human*, 265f.

122. Robin W. Lovin, *Reinhold Niebuhr and Christian Realism* (Cambridge: Cambridge University Press, 1996), 203.

can be ultimately found only when he or she is "reaccepted into the unity to which [he or she] belong[s]."[123] Justice will be done to each person when each person finds himself or herself reconciled with us in the embrace of the triune God. "Justice" cannot give persons their "due"—unless it is a justice that, in an act of patent injustice, justifies the unjust (Rom 3:26; 4:5). Is wrath against injustice appropriate? Yes! Must the perpetrator be restrained? Most certainly! Is the restraining, reforming, and public opinion forming punishment for the violation necessary? Likely. But all these indispensable actions against injustice must be situated in the framework of the will to embrace the unjust. For only in our mutual embrace within the embrace of the triune God can we find redemption and experience perfect justice.

Why should we not pursue strict justice and, in an imperfect world, put up with the injustice of such justice? Why should the injustice of justice not be preferable to the injustice of embrace? Why not simply calculate what ought to be done instead of listening to the wisdom of love? Why not demand retribution and redress instead of offering forgiveness? If human beings were simply "rational agents," "autonomous beings," and "unencumbered selves" then there may indeed be no good reason we should prefer justice shaped by embrace to justice left to its own devices and why we should rather suffer the injustice of embrace than put up with the injustice of "justice." But if we see human beings as children of the one God, created by God to belong all together as a community of love, then there will be good reasons to let embrace—love—define what justice is.

In her studies on moral development, Carol Gilligan suggested that the "ethics of care" should supplement the "ethics of justice." Summing up her position on the ethics of care, she writes:

As a framework for moral decision, care is grounded in the assumption that self and other are interdependent, an assumption reflected in a view of action as responsive and, therefore, as arising in relationship rather than the view of action as emanating from within the self and, therefore, "self-governed."...Within this framework, detachment, whether from self or from others, is morally problematic, since it breeds moral blindness or indifference—a failure to discern or respond to need....Justice in this context becomes understood as respect for people in their own terms.[124]

123. Tillich, *Love, Power, and Justice*, 86.
124. Carol Gilligan, "Moral Orientation and Moral Development," *Women and Moral Theory*, ed. E. E. Kittay and D. T. Meyers (Totowa: Rowman & Littlefield, 1987), 24.

There is no need to enter here the complex debate that has raged around Gilligan's work.[125] Important for my purpose is only the observation that the shift in the understanding of the identity of persons suggests a shift in the understanding of justice. If our identities are shaped in interaction with others, and if we are called ultimately to belong together, then we need to shift the concept of justice away from an exclusive stress on making detached judgments and toward sustaining relationships, away from blind impartiality and toward sensibility for differences. And if we, the communal selves, are called into eternal communion with the triune God, then *true justice will always be on the way to embrace*—to a place where we will belong together with our personal and cultural identities both preserved and transformed, but certainly enriched by the other.

Native Languages, Shared Possessions

Will justice ever reach embrace and leave itself behind, so to speak? This will happen when "the first things have passed away" and "the home of God is established among mortals" (Rev 21:3f.). That day, when God will make "all things new" (21:5), lies still ahead, however. What lies behind is the day of Pentecost, when God poured out the Spirit on "all flesh" (Acts 2:17). The word *justice* does not occur in the story of the Spirit's coming. Yet in a sense this story is all about justice, justice that has reached embrace. I say "in a sense," for after Acts 2 comes Acts 6. But first, Acts 2.

Pentecost, it is sometimes claimed, is a reversal of Babel.[126] In Genesis 11 God punished human arrogance by confusing languages and scattering the peoples. In Acts 2 God undid the punishment and restored the unity: people from every nation come to one place and all speak and understand the language of faith. The interpretation rightly connects the two texts, but does justice to neither. Consider the account of the Tower of Babel. Living on a plain in the land of Shinar, humanity, which still speaks one language, is plagued by fear of being "scattered abroad" and is driven by the desire "to make a name" for themselves (Gen 11:4). To counter the threat of disintegration and to triumph over insignificance, they build a city and a tower "with its top in the heavens" (11:4). A single "place," a

125. Benhabib, *Situating the Self,* 1992; Lawrence A. Bloom, "Gilligan and Kohlberg: Implications for Moral Theory," *Ethics* 98, no. 2 (1988): 472–91; Owen Flanagan and Kathryn Jackson, "Justice, Care, and Gender: The Kohlberg-Gilligan Debate Revisited," *Ethics* 97, no. 2 (1987): 622–37.

126. Avery Dulles, *The Catholicity of the Church* (Oxford: Oxford University Press, 1987), 173.

single "tongue," and a single "tower" will provide the pillars for a central-ized political, economic, and religious system with universal pretensions. Humanity will be securely unified and manifestly great.

From God's perspective the endeavor was doomed to failure. With a good deal of irony the narrator describes how God must "come down" to see what was meant to intrude into God's heavenly courtyard.[127] When God disapproves, it is because of the inherent violence and godlessness of all imperial projects (Jer 50–51; Rev 18), their own self-legitimizing ac-counts of justice and piety notwithstanding.[128] Imperial architects seek to unify by suppressing differences that do not fit into a single grand scheme; they strive to make their own name great by erasing the names of simple people and small nations. Hence God confused the languages and scat-tered the imperial architects abroad. God opposed the totalitarian thought that "nothing that we purpose" is impossible (11:6), and interrupted the totalitarian project to centralize, homogenize, and control. Differences are irreducible. Political, economic, and cultural centers must be plural. Unity ought not leave "scattering" behind. Without preservation of differences, without multicentrality and dispersion, violence will reign, sanctioned by a "justice" designed with no other purpose than to keep the homogeniz-ing "tower" in place. If Walter Brueggemann is right, in Genesis 11 "scat-tering" is not only a negative activity, a punishment imposed by God. Originally, "scattering" is "blessed, sanctioned, and willed by Yahweh" (cf. Gen 10:18, 32), a way to fulfill God's design for humanity (1:28).[129] A misplaced fear of disintegration nourished by the desire for false glory led to the rejection of salutary "scattering" and to the oppressive universal "gathering."

Jacques Derrida has argued that God responded to the "colonial vio-lence" of the tower's architects by imposing on humanity "the irreducible multiplicity of idioms," along with the necessary but impossible task of translation.[130] God forbade "transparency" and made "univocity" impossi-ble; God destined humanity to "incompletion, the impossibility of finish-ing, of totalizing."[131] Derrida is right insofar as Babel will forever remain

---

127. Gordon J. Wenham, *Genesis 1–15*, Word Biblical Commentary, vol. 1 (Waco: Word Books, 1987), 245.

128. William Schweiker, "Power and Agency of God," *Theology Today* 52 (1995): 216.

129. Walter Brueggemann, *Genesis*, Interpretation: A Bible Commentary for Teaching and Preaching, vol. 1, ed. James Luther Mays (Atlanta: John Knox Press, 1982), 98. For a similar reading, see Ted Hiebert, *The Beginning of Difference* (Nashville: Abingdon, 2019).

130. Derrida, "Force of Law," 8.

131. Ibid., 3.

an unfinished project, despite unceasing attempts to continue where the original builders left off. Yet the "confusion" and false "scattering" that result from it (Gen 11:7) are not God's last response to human imperial projects. The preventative and punitive divine reaction to the oppressive unity, no less than the original transgression, cries for remedy.

Babel—confusion—is not the end-state; God is not only "deconstructing"[132] false unity, but also "constructing" salutary harmony. At Pentecost, one in a long series of God's positive responses to Babel that started with the call of Abraham (Gen 12:1-3), God is bringing order into "confusion." Notice the parallels and contrasts between Babel and Pentecost. In Jerusalem the band of Jesus's disciples are "all together in one place" (Acts 2:1), like humanity in the land of Shinar. Their fear, however, is not of being scattered but of losing their lives at the hand of a center that sought either to integrate or annihilate them. They too have political dreams; they long for the restoration of the "kingdom of Israel" (1:6), but the crucified Messiah, who will bring about such restoration at the proper time, calls them not to "build a city" but first to "repent and be baptized" so that their "sins may be forgiven" (2:38). Instead of working to make a name for themselves, they proclaim "the mighty works of God" (2:11). The Babylonian ascending movement of piercing the heavens that pulls up everything into a centralized homogeneity has given way to the Pentecostal descending movement of "pouring" (2:17) from the heavens, which, like rain, enables each of the "varied living beings to burst into new life."[133] The tower at the center that outwardly controls the whole circumference is replaced by the Spirit that "fills all" by descending "upon each" (2:3).

At Pentecost an alternative to the imperial unity of Babel is created, yet without a return to a pre-Babel state. Before Babel the whole of humanity spoke *one* language; in Jerusalem the new community speaks *many* languages. As the tongues of fire are divided and rest on each of the disciples, "each one" of the Jews from "every nation under heaven" representing the global community hears them "speaking in the native language of each" (2:3-7). A theological (rather than simply historical) reading of the Pentecost account suggests that when the Spirit comes, all understand each other, not because one language is restored or a new all-encompassing meta-language is designed, but because each hears his or her own language

132. Ibid., 7.
133. Welker, *God the Spirit*, 127.

spoken. Pentecost overcomes the "confusion" and the resulting false "scattering," but it does so not by reverting to the unity of cultural uniformity but by advancing toward the harmony of cultural diversity.

Notice who speaks in other languages. The Lukan report of the event reads simply "all," meaning "all the disciples": "all of them were filled with the Holy Spirit and began to speak in other languages" (2:4). Peter's interpretation after the event fleshes it out. The miracle of transcending broken communication is the fulfillment of a prophecy by Joel, he claims:

> In the last days it will be, God declares,
> that I will pour my Spirit upon all flesh,
> and your daughters shall prophesy
> and your young men shall see visions,
> and your old men shall dream dreams.
> Even upon my slaves, both men and women,
> in those days I will pour my Spirit;
> and they shall prophesy. (vv. 17f.)

The Lukan claim that "all" spoke contains a critical edge: even those who had no voice have been given a voice. Whereas the tower seeks to make people "not see" and "not speak" and sucks the energies out of the margins in order to stabilize and aggrandize the center, the Spirit pours energies into the margins, opens the eyes of small people to see what no one has seen before, puts the creative words of prophecy into their mouths, and empowers them to be the agents of God's reign. At Pentecost all receive a voice and all are allowed to sound it in their native language. The miracle of Pentecost consists in universal intelligibility and unhindered agency in the midst of social and cultural heterogeneity.[134]

The speech of daughters and of slaves in the middle of Acts 2 prepares us for what comes at the end. Those who are able to understand each other as they speak their native languages also *share their possessions*: they "would sell their possessions and goods and distribute the proceeds to all, as any had need" (2:45). Early Christian communism? No, if "communism" means a stable scheme of distributive justice, organized top-down and administered through a center that cannot fail to be hegemonic. No regulation required all to sign over their possessions upon joining the community; no rule obliged everyone to sell and to give; no universal

---

134. Ibid., 230ff.

216

law embodying the demands of justice seemed in play. The Spirit, which rested on each and "filled" each, made each regard his or her property "as for the use of the community as a whole."[135] Early Christian communism? Yes, if "communism" means the vision of justice that informs Marx's original project.[136] Each contributed according to his or her ability—those who "owned lands or houses" would sell them and give proceeds to the community (4:34). And each benefited according to his or her need—the goods were "distributed to each as any had need" (4:35). This is "justice in ecstasy," to borrow a phrase of Paul Tillich's,[137] justice outside of itself in love, just as the community that lived it out was "in ecstasy," outside of itself in the Spirit. Here, then, is the "justice" of Pentecost that is indistinguishable from embrace: all have their needs met, and the deep desire of people to be themselves, to act in their own right and yet to be understood and affirmed, is satisfied.

Nothing in Acts 2 prepares us for what comes in Acts 6—except our suspicion that the heaven of Pentecostal "justice" cannot last long on the earth of Babylonian fears and desires. As the number of disciples swelled, behind the scenes Pentecost was being dismantled. In Acts 6 the curtain is pulled down and we witness the done deed. The Hellenists, the Greek-speaking Jews from the Diaspora, are complaining against the Hebrews, the Aramaic-speaking Jews from Palestine. A dispute had broken out about Hellenist widows whose needs were not being met. Hebrew caretakers were neglecting Hellenist widows "in the daily distribution of food" (6:1). Because injustice was perpetrated, justice had to come down from its ecstatic heights. Given limited resources, potentially unlimited desires, and biased caretakers, the question of how much each person ought to receive so that the needs of all could be satisfied fairly had to be addressed.

The injustice against Hellenist widows was only the "economic" tip of the iceberg, however. If Martin Hengel is right, under the surface two overall conceptions of Christian faith clashed.[138] There is no need

135. I. Howard Marshall, *The Acts of the Apostles. An Introduction and Commentary* (Grand Rapids: Eerdmans, 1980), 108.

136. Miroslav Volf, *Zukunft der Arbeit—Arbeit der Zukunft: Der Arbeitsbegriff bei Karl Marx und seine theologische Wertung* (München: Christian Kaiser, 1988); Miroslav Volf, *Work in the Spirit. Toward a Theology of Work* (New York: Oxford University Press, 1991).

137. Tillich, *Love, Power, and Justice*, 83.

138. Martin Hengel, *Between Jesus and Paul: Studies in the Earliest History of Christianity*, transl. John Bowden (London: SCM, 1983), 1–29, 133–56; Hengel, *Judaism and Hellenism*, (1991), 68f.; Craig C. Hill, *Hellenists and Hebrews: Reappraising Division within Earliest Christianity* (Minneapolis: Fortress, 1992).

to look into the content of the disputes. For my purposes it suffices to point out that the protagonists in the struggle were speakers of two different languages, members of two culturally distinct (though not necessarily internally monolithic) communities—Hebrews and Hellenists. At stake were their attitudes toward Judaism and hence nothing less than the very identity of the Christian community. The speakers of "native languages" understood at Pentecost were profoundly at odds with each other, and the widows bore the economic brunt of the conflict. Needs were not met; languages were not understood; Pentecost was undone.

Well, almost. For a solution was found. The apostles called the *whole* community together, which is to say that Hellenists and Hebrews still thought of themselves as belonging together. The purpose of the gathering was not to find ways of enforcing an abstract principle of justice which would let all receive their due, but for the whole community, acting together, to choose seven men "of good standing" justly "to wait on tables" (6:3). As the names of the seven indicate, they were all Hellenists. This could suggest a defeat: Hellenists should take care of Hellenists, otherwise injustice will be committed. In fact, however, it was a small victory: representatives of the injured party have been appointed to take care of *all* the widows, their own as well as those of the injuring party. Justice was to be pursued by inverting perspectives and seeing the problem through the eyes of the wronged. Moreover, the persons in charge were to be "full of the Spirit" (6:3). They were to make judgments about right and wrong in the same Spirit of embrace that at Pentecost made them understand each other's languages and share possessions. Finally, they were to be "full of wisdom" (6:3). Practical wisdom, not abstract calculation, was to connect the vision of "justice that has become love" to the concrete situation of conflict. The forces that sought to undo Pentecost were countered through the practice of "double vision" guided by the will to embrace. These were small but significant acts of resistance, inspired by the memory of Pentecost, the memory of keeping one's identity and yet being understood, of having one's need met just because it is a genuine need.

As in our own day, where culture clashes with culture and justice struggles against justice, we should seek inspiration both in Acts 2 and Acts 6. We need the grand vision of life filled with the Spirit of God. We need reminders that the impossible is possible: we can and we will communicate with one another while we speak our own languages;

218

submerged voices will prophesy boldly and closed eyes will be opened to see visions; the needs of all will be met because none of us will call our things only our own. But along with the grand visions we need stories of small successful steps of learning to live together even when we do not quite understand each other's languages, even when we suppress each other's voices, and even when we still cling too much to our own possessions and rob others of their possessions. The grand vision and the small steps will together keep us on a journey toward genuine justice among cultures. As we make space in ourselves for the perspective of the other on this journey, in a sense we have already arrived at the place where the Spirit was poured out on all flesh. And as we desire to embrace the other while we remain true to ourselves and to the crucified Messiah, in a sense we already are where we will be when the home of God is established among mortals.

CHAPTER VI

Deception and Truth

A Toast to the Past

To the past," says Winston Smith, the tragic hero of George Orwell's *Nineteen Eighty-Four*, as he raises his glass to toast his joining the struggle of the Brotherhood against the regime of Oceania. Not to the confusion of the Thought Police, not to the death of Big Brother, not even to humanity, but *to the past*! His presumed fellow conspirator, O'Brian, who turns out to be a high Party official and his future torturer, agrees gravely: "The past is more important." For "who controls the past, controls the future: who controls the present, controls the past."[1]

Some time before the encounter with O'Brian, Winston had scribbled in his secret diary a longer version of the toast:

To the future or to the past, to a time when thought is free, when men are different from one another and do not live alone—to a time when *truth exists and what is done cannot be undone.*[2]

As for the present, Winston knew that the Party "could thrust its hand into the past and say of this or that event, *it never happened.*"[3] When the hand of the Party was done with its clean-up job, the past "had not merely been altered, it had actually been destroyed." For how could you establish even the most obvious fact, he reasoned, "when there existed no record

---

1. George Orwell, *Nineteen Eighty-Four* (New York: Harcourt, Brace and Co., 1949), 177.
2. Ibid., 29, italics mine.
3. Ibid., 35.

outside your own memory."[4] The Party erased, the Party rewrote, the Party controlled—the present, the past, and the future.[5] On the surface, the toast to the past was a toast to respect for what happened, to deference for what we call "facts." At a deeper level, a toast to the past was a toast against the arbitrariness of the powerful who mask their misdeeds by denying that they took place.

The question, "What happened?" tickles our curiosity, of course. What drives our will to know, however, is not simply a disinterested desire to un-riddle "a melange of clues and codes" about the past.[6] If we don't happen to be paid to be curious, we will want less to play the fascinating game of decoding scripts and piecing things together than to attend to the much more serious business of establishing "Who did what to whom and why?" Think of the families of those who disappeared in the torture chambers of the Latin American right-wing regimes. They want to know who the perpetrators were and what they did with their many victims; they want the record set straight. Think of the citizens of the former communist nations in Central and Eastern Europe. They want to know who the informers were and what the faceless secret service agents wrote in their thick files.[7] Are they just satisfying their curiosity? Much more is at stake. By wanting to know "what happened" they are wanting to ensure that the insult of occultation is not added to the injury of oppression; they are seeking to restore and guard human dignity, protect the weak from the ruthless. The truth about what happened is here often a matter of life and death.

For the same reason that we want to know, we also want to *remember* what we have come to know. Elie Wiesel concluded his testimony at the Barbie trial in Lyon with the following words: "Though it takes place under the sign of justice, this trial must also honor memory."[8] Rehearsing some of his favorite themes, earlier in the same speech he explained why:

---

4. Ibid., 36.

5. As Milan Kundera puts it in *The Book of Laughter and Forgetting* (transl. Michael Henry Heim [New York: Penguin, 1986], 158), the world the Party created was "a world without memory" run by the "presidents of forgetting."

6. Joice Appleby, Lynn Hunt, and Margaret Jacob, *Telling the Truth About History* (New York: Norton, 1994), 259.

7. Lewis Smedes has correctly observed that, historically, "the governments that are best at concealing their truth from people are the governments that won't allow their people to have any secrets" (*Forgive and Forget: Healing the Hurts We Don't Deserve* [San Francisco: Harper & Row, 1984], 3). Holding back the truth and not wanting to respect the privacy of some truths are important strategies in the politics of brute power.

8. Elie Wiesel, *From the Kingdom of Memory: Reminiscences* (New York: Summit Books, 1990), 189.

Justice without memory is an incomplete justice, false and unjust. To forget would be an absolute injustice in the same way that Auschwitz was the absolute crime. To forget would be the enemy's final triumph.[9]

Erase memory and you wash away the blood from the perpetrator's hands, you undo the done deed by making it disappear from history. Erase memories of the atrocities and you tempt future perpetrators with immunity. Inversely, remember the misdeeds and you erect a barrier against future misdeeds. As Wiesel puts it, "the memory of death will serve as a shield against death."[10] Forgetfulness is damnation; memory is redemption. "Salvation," he writes, somewhat overstating his case, "can be found only in memory."[11] We may insist that salvation requires more than memory, even that it ultimately entails a certain kind of "forgetting," as I argued earlier (Chapter IV). But how could we dispute that without memory of the suffering inflicted and undergone no salvation of either victims or perpetrators would be possible!?

Wiesel's preoccupation with memory echoes the biblical commandment to remember. As he himself notes in the preface to *From the Kingdom of Memory*,

> Remember.... Remember that you were a slave in Egypt. Remember to sanctify the Sabbath.... Remember Amalek, who wanted to annihilate you.... No other Biblical Commandment is as persistent. Jews live and grow under the sign of memory.[12]

Christians, too, live under obligation to remember because they live under the shadow of the cross. When they celebrate the Lord's Supper they echo the words of Jesus Christ: "This is my body that is for you. Do this in *remembrance* of me.... This cup is the new covenant in my blood. Do this, as often as you drink it, in *remembrance* of me" (1 Cor 11:23ff.). The Lord's Supper is the ritual time in which we remember the broken body and the spilled blood of our Savior. As we partake of it, we remember that night in which the "Lord of glory" was betrayed, humiliated, subjected to a mock trial, and brutally murdered; we recall why Jesus Christ was crucified and what the consequences were. There can be no Christian faith without *that* memory; *everything* in Christian faith depends on it.

---

9. Ibid., 187.
10. Ibid., 239.
11. Ibid., 201.
12. Ibid., 9.

As we remember Christ's suffering, we are reminded to remember the sufferings of his brothers and sisters for whom he died. In the memory of Christ's suffering, the memory of all the pain inflicted and suffered is sanctified.[13] The Lord's Supper, that profound ritual that occupies the center of Christian faith and symbolizes the whole of salvation, is a toast to remembering. Every time we hold the cup of God's blessing, we ought to remember the pain caused by the devil's curse.

What we have come to know we must remember, and what we remember we must *tell*. "For as often as you eat this bread and drink the cup, you *proclaim* the Lord's death until he comes" (1 Cor 11:26). Just as the memory of Christ's death for our sins must be proclaimed, so also the memory of human suffering, caused and experienced, must be made public. Rosa Luxembourg is reported to have said: "The most revolutionary deed is and always will remain to say out loud what is the case." Now, all sorts of things may be the case, such as, that the proverbial cat is lying on the mat. Saying these things out loud may be trite, even a bit foolish. But in such cases the "truth" does not matter very much. When a "regime of truth" is imposed, however, when cultural mores, public opinion, or decrees of a totalitarian state codify what may or may not be said, saying out loud what is the case may indeed be revolutionary. If you say some things that you know are the case too loudly, you may lose not only a friend or a job, but even your life.[14]

In the scriptures, suffering was the basic lot of prophets. They "saw" what the powers that be told them they should not have seen; they said in the public square what others dared only to whisper in secret chambers. Consider Isaiah's reflection on what he saw and what people wanted to hear:

> For they are rebellious people,
> > lying children,
> children unwilling to hear the Lord's teaching;
> who say to the seers, "Don't foresee";
> and to the visionaries,
> > "Don't report truthful visions;
> > tell us flattering things,
> > envision deceptions" (Isaiah 30:9-10 CEB)

---

13. In various publications Johann Baptist Metz has emphasized the significance of *memoria passionis*, most recently in "The Last Universalists" (*The Future of Theology: A Festschrift for Jürgen Moltmann*, ed. Miroslav Volf [Grand Rapids: Eerdmans, 1996], 47–51).

14. Václav Havel, *Living in Truth* (London: Faber and Faber, 1986).

Why does Israel want to hear "flattering things" and "deceptions"? Because she has put her trust in "oppression and cunning" (30:12).[15] The two are inseparable: if you oppress you will seek to conceal your iniquity by deception; oppression needs deceit as a prop. In Marxian terms, exploitation seeks legitimacy in ideology. Blow the cover off deception, and oppression becomes naked, ashamed of itself. Secrecy is indispensable for the operation of power,[16] and hence saying out loud what is the case can be a dangerous act of subversion. More than anyone else, the oppressed are aware of the danger. In a climate of deceit that conceals oppression, they often choose to eschew a direct attack on deception. Instead they engage in a guerrilla warfare by employing small frauds and falsehoods as weapons against big lies and distortions. Though the strategy may succeed in subverting the oppressors' control over the truth, it will enthrone precisely the enemy it set out to fight—the power of deception. The greatness of the prophets consists in the refusal to be drawn into the war of dissimulations. Instead of offering their own "counter-truths" as weapons in a battle, they simply dared to see what was behind the veil of deception and had the courage to speak out loud the truth about the oppressors. This seeing and this speaking were the original prophetic revolution, if you please.

Every other revolution rests on this one. In Orwell's *Nineteen Eighty-Four,* Winston Smith raises his glass and says, "To the past!" I want to join him and say, "To the will to know 'what was the case'! To the power to remember it! To the courage to proclaim it out loud!"[17]

A Counter Toast

After I have finished my toast, tasted a sip of good wine, and sat down, someone who refused to take a sip from her glass may stand up and take exception: "Ladies and gentlemen, I suggest that the toast Professor Volf proposed is mistaken in two important ways. My first objection concerns *memory*. 'Salvation lies in memory,' we were told. But is all memory saving? Elie Wiesel, to whom appeal was made, was aware of a potential

15. Dale Aukerman, *Reckoning with Apocalypse: Terminal Politics and Christian Hope* (New York: Crossroad, 1993), 59f.

16. Michel Foucault, *History of Sexuality. Volume I: Introduction*, transl. Robert Hurley (New York: Random House, 1978), 86.

17. In the epilogue to *The Conquest of America* (transl. Richard Howard [New York: HarperCollins, 1984], 247) Tzvetan Todorov explains that he wrote the book because of the belief "in the necessity of 'seeking the truth' and in the obligation of making it known," which itself is grounded in the persuasion that the memory of "what can happen if we do not succeed in discovering the other" matters profoundly.

problem. In the same book in which he praised memory he asked: 'Isn't there a danger that memory may perpetuate hatred?' Listen to his answer and judge for yourselves whether it is convincing: 'No, there is no such danger. Memory and hatred are incompatible, for hatred destroys memory. The reverse is true: memory may serve as a powerful remedy against hatred.'"[18] I presume no one would dispute that hatred sometimes distorts, even destroys memory. Yet does it follow that memory and hatred are incompatible, as Wiesel claims? By no means. Even Wiesel is not quite persuaded. Though he posits incompatibility between memory and hatred, he can bring himself to say only that memory *may* serve as a remedy against hatred, not that it *will*. History is brutal enough. There is no need to fabricate injuries in order to find reasons to hate; real crimes suffice. What resources does memory have, I ask you, to dissuade me from hating those who I know inflicted suffering on me or my people? You could as well argue that memory teaches to hate, that you must strike a potential perpetrator today if you want to prevent suffering injustice tomorrow. As Amos Elan put it, "remembrance can be 'a form of vengeance.'"[19]

"You see, it is important not only *that* we remember but *how* we remember—with love or with hate, seeking reconciliation or going after revenge. Salvation, ladies and gentlemen, does not lie simply in memory; it lies also in *what we do* with our memory.[20] Memory itself must be redeemed before it can save us. If you extol the virtues of memory, do not fail to tell us what will sanctify it.

"My second objection to the toast Professor Volf has proposed is more complicated, but bear with me because I shall be brief. The objection can be stated something like this: in addition to being careful about *how* we remember, we also need to watch *what* we remember. The power of memory lies in its claim to be true, in its implicit assertion that what is remembered actually happened. You will tell me, no doubt, that false memory has immense power too. And you are right—provided people believe the false memory to be true. Strip down the pretense of truth and false memory becomes impotent. The problem of remembering the past takes us therefore to the problem of *knowing* the past.

---

18. Wiesel, *From the Kingdom of Memory*, 201.

19. Amos Elon, "The Politics of Memory," *The New York Review of Books* 40 (October 7, 1993): 5.

20. In *Genocide and the Politics of Memory: Studying Death to Preserve Life* (Chapel Hill: University of North Carolina Press, 1995), Herbert Hirsch has emphasized the importance of the right politics of memory on the grounds that "history is reconstructed memory, and states and individuals use and manipulate it to serve sometimes less than noble ends" (34).

"We were told that we must know who did what to whom and why, that we must remember it, and say it out loud. But how do we know what is worthy of being remembered? You will no doubt say: 'Remember what happened!' Fair enough. But do not pretend that you can figure out what happened as simply as adding two and two. Let me remind you, ladies and gentlemen, of the obvious: different people see and remember the same things differently. Why are there different memories of the same things? Let me answer by giving an example from the past of the country of Professor Volf's origin.

"On the surface, the dispute is about numbers—how many Serbs were killed in Croatian concentration camps during World War II. Numbers, of all things, should be easy to figure out, one would think. They are not. Serbian historians speak of seven hundred thousand victims; Croatian historians speak of 'only' thirty thousand, and add that Serbs murdered as many if not more Croatians during and immediately after the war. Croatians would tell you that Serbian historians inflate the numbers because the status of victims provides moral legitimation for past dominance and present aggression; as one of their leaders, a priest, said, 'Our power is in our graves.' Serbs would respond that, like any perpetrator, Croatians are whitewashing their crimes. And Croatians would retort that like any victor, Serbs write history the way it suits them. As each accusation meets with a counter-accusation it becomes clear that memories are selective. Lest Professor Volf, a native of Croatia, misunderstand me, my point is not that every memory is as good as any other, but that no memory tells simply 'what was the case' because every concrete remembrance is laden with individual and collective desires and interests as well as with collectively shared convictions, which themselves are shaped by what Jan Assmann calls 'cultural memory.'[21]

"You see, the dispute about the numbers is not simply about numbers. Flesh-and-blood people are not figures on a white sheet of paper; when you deal with them you never deal just with numbers. Let me take for a moment a different example from the same brutal period in European history. Many more people would be willing to say that the Nazis murdered 'x' million Jews than to say that the Allies murdered 'x' million Germans, even if there were no dispute over the numbers of people who died in the course of the war. It matters a great deal whether one is killed

21. Jan Assmann, *Das kulturelle Gedächtnis: Schrift, Erinnerung und politische Identität in frühen Hochkulturen* (München: C. H. Beck, 1992).

in self-defense or as an act of aggression and in pursuit of genocidal policies. And here, as you will no doubt agree, the questions of interpretation rush in. Who started what and when and why? There are cases in which we can give rather clear answers to these questions, as with Nazi extermination of Jews. But most cases are not so clear. Indulge me to put things somewhat philosophically and then I will conclude: a statement that this or that happened cannot be isolated from a reconstruction of history that makes sense of such a statement. Facts and events need larger narratives to be intelligible; and since larger narratives are disputed, facts and events are disputed too.[22]

"Ladies and gentlemen, here are my two objections in plain terms: first, we remember what we want to remember because we know what we choose to know. Second, we do with our memories what we want to do with them because they themselves do not dictate what ought to be done with them. If these two objections carry any weight, the toast to the will to know, to the obligation to remember, to the courage to say what was the case, though well meaning, is profoundly misguided. What toast would I propose in its place? I'll give you *two* toasts and you can choose the one that suits you better, or take them both, if you wish." She lifted her glass and, scanning the table, asserted, "To the truth of each community! To the truth of each little name!"[23]

"Nice speech," I thought to myself, "very nice! Even the toast was not all bad, provided you understand it rightly. How would I respond if I had more time than just to give a courtesy reply to the effect that our friend's objections are important and in many ways right, that she misunderstood what I said, and that I nevertheless stand behind my toast for reasons that the present social occasion does not allow me to elaborate!?" All eyes were upon me, so I stood up, gave my courtesy reply with a smile, and added: "I want to invite you to a lecture in which I will explore the questions, To what extent can we know 'what was the case'? and, How should we go about finding that out in situations of conflict? You are all welcome...." What follows is the lecture to which I thought it would be appropriate to invite my fictional opponent. I will begin with a critique and then switch in the second part to a constructive proposal. In conclusion I will sum up both constructive and deconstructive moves about deception and truth

---

22. Lionel Gossman, *Between History and Literature* (Cambridge: Harvard University Press, 1990), 290ff.

23. Cf. Bernard-Henri Lévy, *Gefährliche Reinheit*, transl. Maribel Königer (Wien: Passagen Verlag, 1995), 209f.

by examining the encounter between Jesus and Pilate and drawing some implications for the relation between truth, freedom, and violence.

Before I proceed, let me make one methodological comment. So far I have been letting the terms "memory" and "history" enter each other's semantic fields without much attention to their boundaries. In his classical work on collective memory, Maurice Halbwachs distinguished between objective and universal "history" and subjective and collective "memory."[24] Though a sharp polarity between the two cannot be sustained, the distinction between a critical reconstruction of the past ("history") and the identity shaping remembrance of the past ("memory") is necessary. Yet the boundaries are fluid. All historical reconstructions are shaped by particular identities and interests, and memories of the past must be distinguished from myths about the past. "History" is but a special case of social "memory,"[25] and, in its own way, "memory" no less than "history" must show deference before "what was the case." Though in the following I will concentrate more on "history" than on "memory," the topic of my exploration is in what sense we can know and remember what transpired between people and what the social significance and moral presuppositions of such knowledge and such memory may be.

To Say It the Way It Really Was

Once upon a not so distant time it was expected of a historian to say things the way they really were; this was the historian's main task. A classical formulation of this expectation comes from the young Leopold von Ranke's description of his own work as a historian:

> People have assigned to history the office of judging the past and instructing the present generation for the benefit of future ages: the present attempt does not aspire to such high offices: *it merely wants to show how things really were.*[26]

The word "merely" is deceptively modest, von Ranke's assurances of no aspirations to the high office of judging the past and instructing the present notwithstanding. Behind the unpretentious goal hides a rather immodest

---

24. Maurice Halbwachs, *Das Kollektive Gedächtnis* (Frankfurt: Suhrkamp, 1985), 74.

25. P. Burke, "Geschichte als soziales Gedächtnis," *Mnemosyne,* ed. A. Assmann and D. Harth (Frankfurt: Suhrkamp, 1991).

26. Leopold von Ranke, *Geschichte der romanischen und germanischen Völker, 1494–1535* (Berlin: Reimer, 1824), vii, italics added.

program: historians must reconstruct what actually transpired, neither more nor less; they must find and tell the truth, and nothing but the truth. To accomplish this goal the historical narrator had to stand "above superstition and prejudice to survey calmly and dispassionately the scenes of the past and tell a truth that would be acceptable to any other researcher who had seen the same evidence and applied the same rules."[27] This was the elevated modern ideal of historical research.

It is sometimes said that historians pursuing this ideal saw themselves as omniscient narrators: they presumed to know everything and hence could tell it the way it was. Though some lesser minds might have thought of themselves in such exalted terms, the best of historians were aware of their own fallibility and subjectivity. Von Ranke certainly knew that his knowledge was limited and his perspective relative; he never imagined that he could transcend his object of study as Zeus could float over the fighting enemies of Troy. Yet most typically modern historians had two things in common: they aspired to objectivity and truth and they believed that a single correct method would curtail relativism and let the light of truth shine brightly. There is only one correct view about any given matter and only one correct way to attain it, they maintained. Follow the method, and you will be able to show how things really were—more or less, sooner or later. What characterized modern historians was not presumed omniscience but belief in objectivity, not the claim to infallibility but to a method designed to counter fallibility. Historians, of course, shared this belief with other followers of the "rational" method, who assumed that they could eventually melt down different points of view to a common currency of a single truth.[28]

It has long been believed that the modern approach to history and knowledge in general was concocted by idle philosophers removed from the brutal realities of human life, disinterested thinkers who followed rigorously where their pure thought led them and discovered an indubitable foundation of knowledge and an inerrant method of achieving it. As a child of protracted solitude, rational method emerged in the minds of free spirits and replaced the medieval reliance on tradition and superstition. This traditional account of the emergence of the modern rational method corresponds to the method's character: a certain sense of propriety

27. Appleby et al., *Telling the Truth About History*, 73.

28. Michael Luntley, *Reason, Truth and Self: The Postmodern Reconditioned* (London: Routledge, 1995), 33.

(though not the strict logic) demanded that the discovery of a purely objective method not depend on the accidents of history. Well, it did.

In *Cosmopolis* Stephen Toulmin has argued for a need to revise the traditional account of the rational method's emergence. Rather than having been born out of tranquil decontextualized reflection, it was formulated in response to a given historical situation—to the ravages of the Thirty Years' War fought in the name of differing religious persuasions. Toulmin writes:

> If uncertainty, ambiguity, and the acceptance of pluralism led, in practice, only to an intensification of the religious war, the time had come to discover some *rational method* for demonstrating the essential correctness or incorrectness of philosophical, scientific, or theological doctrines.[29]

Enter Descartes. In *Discourse on Method* he proposed the one correct method to acquire absolutely certain knowledge. The Thirty Years' War might have had more to do with this proposal than did the day he spent "shut up in a room heated by an enclosed stove" where he had, as he writes, "complete leisure to meditate on my own thoughts."[30]

Ever since Descartes, modernity has been dominated by "the charms of certainty and uniqueness"[31] and has continued to dream of a purely rational method and a unified science that would provide a single right answer to any given question. Without a rational method we will end up disagreeing, and without agreement, we will end up fighting. The desire for peace gave birth to the belief that we can tell the one single truth about our societies and their history, and indeed about the makeup of the whole world. If there were no such truth, war seemed inescapable.

The argument that there is a single truth about some important matters and that one should strive to find it should be plausible to Christians. After all, do we not believe that the day will come when the secrets of the hearts will be revealed and when God will say out loud the way things really were—who did what to whom and by what means? No doubt, there is more to divine judgment than setting the records straight; the One who judges at the end of history is the same One who "justifies sinners" in the middle of history. But can divine judgment be anything less

---

29. Stephen Toulmin, *Cosmopolis: The Hidden Agenda of Modernity* (New York: Free Press, 1990), 53.

30. René Descartes, *Discourse on Method and the Meditations*, transl. F. E. Sutcliffe (Harmondsworth: Penguin, 1968), 35.

31. Toulmin, *Cosmopolis*, 75.

than setting the records straight? Anyone who holds to the classical Christian doctrine of God will be compelled to search in some sense for "the way things really were." As Richard J. Mouw and Sander Griffioen argue, if there is an all-wise and all-knowing divine Person whose perspective on what happens matters, then it is difficult to see how Christians could deny that there is "objective" truth about history and that it is important to try to find it out.[32]

Trying is not the same as succeeding, however. Though God knows the way things were and will one day say it out aloud, human beings know only partially and can say it only inadequately. There is no way to climb up to God's judgment seat to make infallible pronouncements, so to speak, in God's stead as God's vicars on earth. Christians know God, but they do not know all that God knows—at least not yet, though Thomas Aquinas believed that one day they will.[33] We know only something of what God knows—as much and as little as God has revealed. It so happens that God tells us much about what God's purposes with humanity and the world are and how they are to be achieved, but nothing about Native American history after the arrival of Europeans or about what transpired between Tamils and Sengalese in Sri Lanka over past decades. Our belief in an all-knowing God notwithstanding, we are left on our own to search for "what was the case," sustained by the persuasion that there is an eternal truth, one not skewed by particular standpoints because there is an everlasting and universal God.

The belief in an all-knowing God should inspire the search for truth; the awareness of our human limitations should make us modest about the claims that we have found it, however. We "know in part" (1 Cor 13:12) first because we are finite beings. As Thomas Nagel put it, "even if each of us possesses a large dormant capacity for objective self-transcendence, our knowledge of the world will always be fragmentary, however much we extend it."[34] We "know in part," second, because our limited knowledge is shaped by the interests we pursue and filtered through the cultures and traditions we inhabit. As Alasdair MacIntyre has argued in *Three Rival Versions of Moral Enquiry,*

---

32. Richard Mouw and Sander Griffioen, *Pluralism and Horizons: An Essay in Christian Public Philosophy* (Grand Rapids: Eerdmans, 1993), 101ff.

33. Thomas Aquinas, *Summa Contra Gentiles* (Notre Dame, IN: University of Notre Dame Press, 1975), 3/1, 196f.

34. Thomas Nagel, *The View from Nowhere* (New York: Oxford University Press, 1986), 86.

the notion of a single neutral nonpartisan history is one more illusion engendered by the academic standpoint of the encyclopaedist; it is the illusion that there is the past waiting to be discovered, *wie es eigentlich gewesen*, independent of characterization from some particular standpoint.[35]

The agenda of modernity has overreached itself. Its optimism about human capacities is misplaced and its assumption that there is a neutral standpoint wrong. There can be no indubitable foundation of knowledge, no uninterpreted experience, no completely transparent reading of the world. A cosmic or a divine language to express "what was the case" is not available to us; all our languages are human languages, plural dialects growing on the soil of diverse cultural traditions and social conditions.[36] We have no access to "pure facts" and we are incapable of reconstructing strictly objective narratives of what actually transpired. The lure of "mimetic realism"—the belief that our statements can correspond exactly to reality—must be resisted; the notion that we can hold a mirror to the past and behold in it "pure facts" must be rejected. What we will see in the mirror of our reconstructions is the past mixed with some present, we will behold the other upon whom we ourselves are dimly superimposed. As a consequence, we must "balance the hope for certainty and clarity in theory with the impossibility of avoiding uncertainty and ambiguity in practice."[37]

To reconstruct the past as it actually happened, independent from a particular standpoint, is impossible. To presume otherwise is not only naively mistaken but positively dangerous. For the claim to universal truth often serves to give legitimacy to very particular interests. These interests can be noble, like the desire for universal peace in a world torn by war, but they can also be nasty, like the desire to preserve one's own privileged position of power. Think of the "objective" truths about the nature of women or of blacks, which were nothing but the cognitive obverse of male and white oppression! Similarly, the communist claim to be the final resolution of the "riddle of history" served only to bolster the oppressive power of the Party over all domains of people's lives. Such objective truths are

---

35. Alasdair MacIntyre, *Three Rival Versions of Moral Enquiry: Encyclopaedia, Genealogy, and Tradition* (Notre Dame, IN: University of Notre Dame Press, 1990), 151.
36. Luntley, *Reason, Truth and Self,* 15–17, 137–44.
37. Toulmin, *Cosmopolis,* 75.

terrible weapons, effective because they generate the illusion of their own inescapability, deadly because they exude innocence.

This brings me to the contemporary, postmodern suspicion about truth.

Regimes of Truth

In recent decades the desire to speak truth about what was (or what is) the case has fallen into serious disrepute. If some hundred years ago a "nothing is true" theory was the prerogative of an elite, today it has become "a platitudinous clincher, casually adopted and indiscriminately used."[38] When justifying the "nothing is true" theory, its contemporary proponents tell us there is something both perverse and malicious about the desire for truth—perverse because it can never be satisfied, malicious because speaking "truth" is just another punch in a struggle for power. Let me explicate this rather cynical perspective on truth by looking at some aspects of Michel Foucault's thought.

Foucault learned to distrust truth from Friedrich Nietzsche, the first critic of "the will to truth."[39] The pupil's sophisticated and profound polemic against "the regimes of truth" is today, however, much more influential than the master's critique of "the will to truth." Consider Foucault's following brief statement on the issue from *Power/Knowledge*:

> Truth is a thing of this world: it is produced only by virtue of multiple forms of constraint. And it induces regular effects of power. Each society has its regime of truth, its "general politics" of truth: that is, the types of discourse which it accepts and makes function as true; the mechanism and instances which enable one to distinguish true and false statements, the means by which each is sanctioned; the techniques and procedures accorded value in the acquisition of truth; the status of those who are charged with saying what counts as true.[40]

In the above text an unsuspecting reader will stumble immediately over the strange association between truth and *production*. A venerable theological and philosophical tradition has taught that truth is either

---

38. Johan Goudsblom, *Nihilism and Culture* (Oxford: Blackwell, 1980), 190.

39. Friedrich Nietzsche, *The Birth of Tragedy and The Genealogy of Morals*, transl. Francis Golffing (Garden City: Doubleday, 1956), 286ff.

40. Michel Foucault, *Power/Knowledge: Selected Interviews and Other Writings 1972–1977*, transl. Colin Gordon et al. (New York: Pantheon Books, 1980), 131.

disclosed or discovered; Foucault insists that it is "produced." Statements are not true or false in and of themselves; they are "made to function" *as true* or *as false*. What is he after? Is he simply stating the obvious, namely that patent falsehoods are often peddled as manifest verities by deluded or unscrupulous people, that demagogues paint "false consciousness" as liberating truth? Is he griping about lies and ideologies? No, for both lies and ideologies presuppose that there *is* truth out there that must be told and may not be masked. For Foucault, who wishes to set himself apart as much from the commonsense disapproval of lies as from the Marxist demasking of ideologies, there is no such truth—or at least he is not interested in it, if there is. He writes,

> the problem does not consist in drawing the line between that in a discourse which falls under the category of scientificity or truth, and that which comes under some other category, but in seeing historically how *effects of truth* are produced within discourses which in themselves are neither true nor false.[41]

If truth is produced, then what matters are the mechanisms by which the true and the false are separated within a given social order and the authorities endowed with the power to pronounce something as true or false. The significant question is not so much *what* is the case, but *why* and *how* is something proclaimed and believed to be the case. Why is it, for instance, that in the nineteenth century medical science claimed that "the male body expresses positive strength, sharpening male understanding and independence, and equipping men for life in the State, in the arts and sciences," whereas "the roomy pelvis determines women for motherhood" and their "weak, soft members and delicate skin are witness of woman's narrower sphere of activity, of home-bodiness and peaceful family life"?[42] Why is it that today's medical science tells us nothing of the kind? Why is it that our nineteenth-century predecessors believed their science as much as we believe ours? Foucault's answer: there is a "regime" of truth in which certain statements can *pass as* true and others as false.

Notice, second, the association between *truth and power*, suggested in the phrase "regime of truth." To produce truth and sustain it you need "multiple forms of constraint,"[43] and to have constraint you need social

---

41. Ibid., 118, italics added.
42. Barry Allen, *Truth in Philosophy* (Cambridge: Harvard University Press, 1993), 172f.
43. Foucault, *Power/Knowledge*, 131.

power—whether that power is concentrated in the person of a sovereign or diffused in a given social system as a whole. First comes power, then comes truth; no power, no truth. The relation between power and truth is not a one-way street, however: power only producing truth. Truth itself is not powerless; it holds sway over people or, as Foucault states, it "induces regular effects of power."[44] "Truth" therefore gives even more power to the powerful. Truth is produced by a power in order to wield power. It is a weapon in social struggle.

Apply to historical sciences the idea of truth as a weapon and you get the following picture:

> In appearance, or rather, according to the mask it bears, historical consciousness is neutral, devoid of passions and committed solely to truth. But if it examines itself and if, more generally, it interrogates the various forms of scientific consciousness in its history, it finds that all these forms and transformations are aspects of the will to knowledge: instinct, passion, the inquisitor's devotion, cruel subtlety and malice.[45]

Malice? Cruelty? Inquisitor's devotion? In the job of a historian? Yes, answers Foucault. As historians strive to be neutral and comprehensive, they silence voices that do not fit, exclude differences; as they grasp for universals, they distort particulars.[46] In their search for "total knowledge" they trample the fine-textured and differentiated social life with their oversized generalizing boots. Much like the quest for any other knowledge, the quest for historical knowledge does violence to its object. Why? Because "the prediscursive realm from which discourse is formed never can be drawn fully into discourse," or put more simply, because "there is more to life than knowing."[47] Foucault states it this way:

> We must not imagine that the world turns toward us a legible face which we would have only to decipher; the world is not the accomplice of our

---

44. Ibid.

45. Michel Foucault, *Language, Counter-Memory, Practice: Selected Essays and Interviews*, transl. Donald E. Bouchard and Sherry Simon (Ithaca, NY: Cornell University Press, 1977), 162.

46. Jürgen Habermas has suggested that from one perspective Foucault's critique can be seen as presupposing his own self-perception as "a historian in distilled state," who wants nothing else but stoically to say the way things really were (*Der Philosophische Diskurs der Moderne: Zwölf Vorlesungen* [Frankfurt: Suhrkamp, 1985], 324). Yet this would either exempt Foucault's own knowledge from immersion in power or demand that he postulate a correlation between "true knowledge" and the "proper exercise of power." In any case, from this perspective Foucault would appear as a critic of ideologies, a description he explicitly rejects.

47. William Connolly, "I. Taylor, Foucault, and Otherness," *Political Theory* 13, no. 3 (1985): 367.

knowledge; there is no prediscursive providence which predisposes the world in our favor. We must conceive discourse as a violence which we do to things, or, in any case as a practice which we impose on them.[48]

Knowledge is violence, truth an imposition! How different this is from the way we commonly think of knowledge and truth. Knowledge is supposed to represent reality; if it does, it is true, if it does not, it is false. Instinctively we think that Foucault must be profoundly mistaken. Yet even the most innocent sense that he might be onto something important. In the convoluted world of social intercourse, we all know how extremely difficult it is to agree on what transpired at a given time between individual people, let alone between people groups. Our desires and interests, the desires and interests of our communities, a common history of aggression and suffering, make us see what we suspect we will find and believe what we want to believe (as my opponent from the beginning of the chapter pointed out).

In his famous comment on pride and memory, Nietzsche expresses the thought unforgettably: "'I have done that,' says my memory. 'I cannot have done that,' says my pride, and remains inexorable. Eventually memory yields."[49] What is at stake in the question about truth is not just our pride, however, but our power. In recounting the past we are jockeying for a position. The fiercer the struggle the less willing we will be to accept any statement that calls into question our power. It is not only that our human knowledge is inescapably limited because we are finite beings or that what we know is culturally tinted. The little knowledge we have is skewed because we suppress truth through desire to overcome others and protect ourselves. As we seek to know we are caught in the field of powers that distort our vision. Michel Foucault was right to remind us of this. And Richard Rorty was right to tell us to be neither incredulous nor horrified by Foucault's reminder but to recognize "that it was only the false lead which Descartes gave us (and the resulting over-valuation of scientific theory which, in Kant, produced 'the philosophy of subjectivity') that made us think truth and power *were* separable."[50] The insight into the involvement of knowledge in power and power in knowledge, of the

48. Michel Foucault, *The Order of Things* (London: Travistock Publications, 1970), 316.
49. Friedrich Nietzsche, *Jenseits von Gut und Bose*, vol. 6/2, Nietzsche Werke, ed. G. Colli and M. Montinari (Berlin: Walter de Gruyter, 1968), 68.
50. Richard Rorty, "Habermas and Lyotard on Post-modernity," *Praxis International* 4, no. 1 (1984): 42.

impossibility that "the games of truth could circulate freely," should not be given up.[51]

Foucault, however, wants to say more than simply, "strategies of power are immanent in (the) will to knowledge"[52]—much more. What seems to bother him is not just the immodesty of all claims to possess pure truth nor simply the multiple forms of "rationalities of terror,"[53] but the traditional notion of truth itself. Truth, he claims, is produced, constructed, imposed; true is what *passes for true*.[54] Notice one extremely unfortunate consequence of such a view. As Charles Taylor has put it, "if all truth is imposition, no change can be a gain"[55]—at least not a gain in knowledge. All cultural systems must then be equally true, and (apparently) all truth-claims equally valid—the truths of the victims and the truths of the perpetrators. At least, as Bernhard-Henri Lévy puts it, this is the risk of such a position.[56]

Though his rhetoric pushes him toward a complacent relativism,[57] Foucault is no self-confessed or even just inconsistent practicing relativist. Kyle Pasewark has argued that in the last phase of Foucault's work "aesthetic freedom, through which each person forms his or her own subjectivity," emerges as the grounds of Foucault's critique of domination and exclusion.[58] The price Foucault pays for offering such grounds, however, is giving up at least some of his most distinctive and most significant insight, namely the involvement of knowledge in power. The knowledge of the self and of the self's freedom, that underpins Foucault's critique is not problematized but implicitly asserted as pure, unburdened by the weight of power.[59]

---

51. Michel Foucault, "The Ethic of Care of the Self as a Practice of Freedom," *The Final Foucault*, ed. James Bernauer and David Rasmussen (Cambridge: MIT Press, 1988), 18.

52. Foucault, *History of Sexuality*, 73.

53. Maurice Blanchot, *Michel Foucault*, transl. Barbara Wahlster (Tübingen: Edition Diskord, 1987), 31.

54. Allen, *Truth in Philosophy*, 1993.

55. Charles Taylor, "Connolly, Foucault, and Truth," *Political Theory* 13, no. 3 (1985): 377–85, 383.

56. Bernard-Henri Lévy, *Gefährliche Reinheit*, transl. Maribel Königer (Wien: Passagen Verlag, 1995), 210. A consequence of this view is, as Alasdair MacIntyre has noted in *Three Rival Versions of Moral Enquiry*, that a genealogist such as Foucault cannot, "first in characterizing and explaining his project, to him or herself as much as to others, and later in evaluating his or her success or failure in the genealogist's own terms, avoid falling back into a nongenealogical, academic mode, difficult to discriminate from that encyclopaedist's or professorial academic mode in the repudiation of which the genealogical project had its genesis and its rationale" (MacIntyre, *Three Rival Versions of Moral Inquiry*, 53).

57. Habermas, *Der Philosophische Diskurs der Moderne*, 327.

58. Kyle A. Pasewark, *A Theology of Power: Being Beyond Domination* (Minneapolis: Fortress, 1993), 38.

59. Ibid., 39–51. Foucault's inability to justify rationally his struggle against domination has been noted by many thinkers. Nancy Fraser, for instance, underscores that he is unable to give grounds to himself or anybody else why freedom is better than domination and struggle better than submission ("Fou-

If truth is imposed, there can be no gain in knowledge, but there can be gain in power. Consider how Foucault understands his own task as philosopher and historian. Traditionally, philosophers have battled "on behalf" of truth; they sought to remove ignorance, expose lies, or unmask ideologies. Foucault will have none of this because he is not interested in "truth" but in what passes for truth, in what he calls "truth-effects." As a philosopher he must therefore enter the arena in which "truth-effects" wage war against each other. He writes, "The problem is not changing people's consciousness—or what's in their heads—but the political, economic, institutional regime of the production of truth."[60] How do you change the regime of truth if you are a philosopher? You exert the kind of power you have, the power of a well-crafted argument expressing an attractive vision of life. If you have a smoother tongue or a louder voice than your opponent, you win—until someone stronger comes along who does not respect the power of the word. Intellectual efforts being only tactical moves in a warfare, however, it is not clear why it would be unacceptable to subdue the power of the word by the power of the gun; and therefore it is also not clear why one would bother much with intellectual life, which is not the fastest and the surest way to power.[61]

Foucault's solution is as alluring as it is wrongheaded. We swim in an ocean of distortions and deceptions, and the truth seems impotent to sustain us. You trust the power of truth but the "truth" of power proves stronger—that iron fist in a velvet glove of statistics, research results, pronouncements by undisputed authorities, of appeals to tradition or common sense. The only sensible thing seems to return in kind, to define your own truth and assert it in the face of your opponents with the help of intimidation, propaganda, and manipulation. When opinions clash, weapons must ultimately decide because arguments are impotent. The logic of violence is enticing, but can we afford to concede to it? The answer is easy: we cannot

cault on Modern Power: Empirical Insights and Normative Confusions," *Praxis International* 1 [1981]: 272–87). Hubert L. Dreyfus and Paul Rabinow ask pointedly: on Foucault's premises, "what is wrong with carceral society? Genealogy undermines a stance which opposes it on the grounds of natural law or human dignity, both of which presuppose the assumptions of traditional philosophy. Genealogy also undermines opposing carceral society on the basis of subjective preferences and intuitions (or posing certain groups as carriers of human values capable of opposing carceral society). What are the resources which enable us to sustain a critical stance?" (*Michel Foucault: Beyond Structuralism and Hermeneutics*, 2nd ed. [Chicago: University of Chicago Press, 1983], 206).

60. Foucault, *Power/Knowledge*, 133.

61. Amy Gutmann, "Introduction," *Multiculturalism: Examining the Politics of Recognition*, ed. Amy Gutmann (Princeton: Princeton University Press, 1994), 18f.

because violence must not have the last word. But a more difficult question remains: What resources will help us resist the temptation of violence?

An alternative to Foucault's account of the relation between knowledge and power that avoids the problems that beset the idea of "produced" and "imposed" truth, while preserving the insight of the involvement of power in knowledge, would be to suggest that, at least in the realm of human affairs, *in order to know truly we need to want to exercise power rightly.* This is what I will try to argue for in the remainder of the chapter. In the nature of the case, such argument cannot be made from a neutral standpoint located in a power-free zone. I will make it from within a commitment to a particular strand of Christian tradition and its practices. There are no *a priori* reasons, however, why those who do not belong to this tradition would find the argument unacceptable.

Double Vision

From our discussion so far emerges a marked contrast between two accounts of the nature and importance of truth, neither of which is entirely satisfactory. The aim of our modern predecessors was, as Lionel Gossman puts it in *Between History and Literature*, "to disengage knowledge from power struggles and to disarm the violence of confrontation by establishing a truth of fact that would dissipate the aggressiveness of the pronouncements brandished by the parties in conflict." As the example of Foucault shows, the aim of many of our postmodern contemporaries is "to expose the manifestations of power and the confrontation of competing forces behind the notions of law, meaning, and truth."[62] Against the modern approach I have argued that the "truth of fact" cannot be established because, try as we might, we cannot discard our own standpoint and perspective. Against the postmodern approach I have objected that exposing the "manifestations of power" behind the very notion of truth in fact enthrones violence. If neither the "truth of fact" nor the "truth of power" can save us from the reign of terror, what can?

In *The View from Nowhere* Thomas Nagel suggests that in order to know the world adequately we must "step outside of ourselves" and ask "what the world must be like from no point of view."[63] When we distance ourselves from ourselves "each of us...in addition to being an ordinary

---

62. Gossman, *Between History and Literature*, 323.
63. Nagel, *The View from Nowhere*, 62.

person, is a particular objective self, the subject of a perspectiveless conception of reality."[64] Nagel is aware that we can never quite succeed in leaving the "ordinary person" behind: "However often we may try to step outside of ourselves, something will have to stay behind the lens, something in us will determine the resulting picture."[65] Indeed, he suggests that a *purely* perspectiveless view—a view *only* from nowhere—would not even be desirable. For my own life can never be for me "merely one of myriad sentient flickers" in a world that my objective self observes from outside.[66] Nagel concludes: "One must arrange somehow to see the world from nowhere and from here, and to live accordingly."[67] This seeing "from nowhere" and "from here" he calls "double vision."

I suggest that we keep the double vision, but that, at least when it comes to knowing the social world, we replace "the view from *nowhere*" with "the view from *there*." We should try to see the world "from *there*" and "from *here*."[68] To view others "from nowhere" would mean to neutralize both our perspective and their perspective. This, as I have argued earlier (and as Nagel agrees), cannot be done. Moreover, even if it could be done, it *should not* be done; we can never adequately understand human beings from a purely objective standpoint. Instead of seeing the self and the other or the two cultures and their common history from no perspective we should try to see them *from both* perspectives, both "from here" and "from there."

Ideally, of course, we should see things *from everywhere* (which is what Nagel may have at least partly in mind when he talks about "the perspectiveless subject that constructs a centerless conception of the world by casting *all perspectives into the content of that world.*"[69] For what happens "here" and "there" are not isolated events, but are a part of a larger stream of social events. "From everywhere" is how God sees human beings, I would argue. God sees not simply from outside but also from within, not abstracting from peculiarities of individual histories but concretely, not disinterestedly but seeking the good of all creation.[70] God's truth is

---

64. Ibid., 63f.
65. Ibid., 68.
66. Ibid., 86.
67. Ibid.
68. See Charles Taylor, *Philosophy and the Human Sciences*, Philosophical Papers, vol. 2 (Cambridge: Cambridge University Press, 1985), 116–33.
69. Nagel, *The View From Nowhere*, 62, italics added.
70. Marjorie Hewitt Suchocki, *The Fall to Violence: Original Sin in Relational Theology* (New York: Continuum, 1995), 50f., 59.

eternal, but it is emphatically not "nonlocal," as Nagel suggests the truth of philosophy should be—both eternal and nonlocal.[71] God's eternal truth is *panlocal*, to follow Nagel's idiom. This is why God's truth is not simply one among many perspectives, but *the truth* about each and all perspectives.

In a creaturely way we should try to emulate God's way of knowing. Not that we can crawl inside the mind of God and see things from God's panlocal perspective. But we can try to see the other concretely rather than abstractly, from within rather than simply from without. What human way of seeing corresponds to God's seeing "from everywhere"? Seeing both "from here" and "from there." Only such double vision will ensure that we do not domesticate the otherness of others but allow them to stand on their own.[72]

Seeing "from here" comes naturally. That is how we normally see, from our own perspective, guided by our own values and interests that are shaped by the overlapping cultures and traditions we inhabit. But what does it take to see "from there," from the perspective of others? First, we *step outside ourselves*—a move that in no way entails a denial of human creatureliness and situatedness in the name of an illusory absolute self-transcendence, but is "a constitutive part of that specific mode of insertion into a world which we call human."[73] We examine what we consider to be plain verities about others, willing to entertain the idea that these "verities" may be but so many ugly prejudices, bitter fruits of our imaginary fears, or our sinister desires to dominate or exclude. We also observe our own images of ourselves, willing to detect layers of self-deceit that tell us exalted stories about ourselves and our history. To step outside means to distance ourselves for a moment from what is inside, ready for a surprise.

"For a moment" qualifies the distancing, because after we have taken a step outside ourselves we will have to return, as we will see shortly. It is important also to keep in mind that when we distance ourselves from ourselves, we cannot step completely outside ourselves, not even for a moment. Not that we would have no place to go so that if we stepped outside ourselves an abyss would swallow us. After all, there is the world of the other out there; there might also be the tenuous "liminal world"

---

71. Nagel, *The View From Nowhere*, 10.

72. Charles Taylor, "Comparison, History, Truth," *Myth and Philosophy*, ed. Frank Reynolds and David Tracy (New York: State University of New York Press, 1990), 40ff.

73. Terry Eagleton, "The Death of Self-Criticism," *Times Literary Supplement* (November 24, 1995): 6.

that is born in the prolonged encounter between us and the other, as Mark Taylor has argued.[74] It is not for the lack of space to go that we cannot completely step outside ourselves. It is rather that the split between a "situated" and a "distancing" self can never be complete; every place we go in our "distancing" self *we must take ourselves with us.* We can step outside ourselves, so to speak, only with one foot; the other always remains inside.

Second, we *cross a social boundary and move into the world of the other* to inhabit it temporarily.[75] We open our ears to hear how others perceive themselves as well as how they perceive us. We use imagination to see why their perspective about themselves, about us, and about our common history, can be so plausible to them whereas it is implausible, profoundly strange, or even offensive to us. To move inside means to seek to come as close to others as they are to themselves, to get into an "inner correspondence of spirit" with them, put oneself into their skin, as Clifford Geertz says of the anthropologist's work.[76]

Third, we *take the other into our own world.* We compare and contrast the view "from there" and the view "from here." Not that we will necessarily reject the view "from here" and embrace the view "from there"; nor even that we will find some compromise between the two. These are two possible outcomes of the comparison, but other outcomes are possible too. We could decide that we have to reject the view "from there." The only thing we must do as we take others into our world is let their perspective stand next to ours and reflect on whether one or the other is right, or whether both are partly right and partly wrong.

Fourth, we *repeat the process.* Before the movement away from the self to the other and back starts, we inevitably possess explicit or implicit judgments about the rightness or wrongness of the view "from here" and the view "from there"; it would be both impossible and undesirable to suppress these judgments. But no judgment should be final, bringing the movement to a halt. We can never presume that we have freed ourselves completely from distortions of others and deceptions about ourselves, that we possess "the truth." Every understanding that we reach is forged

74. Mark Kline Taylor, "Religion, Cultural Plurality, and Liberating Praxis: In Conversation with the Work of Langdon Gilkey," *The Journal of Religion* 72, no. 2 (1991): 152ff.

75. Alasdair MacIntyre, "Are Philosophical Problems Insoluble? The Relevance of Systems and History," *Philosophical Imagination and Cultural Memory: Appropriating Historical Traditions*, ed. Patricia Cook (Durham: Duke University Press, 1993), 78.

76. Clifford Geertz, "'From the Native's Point of View': On the Nature of Anthropological Understanding," *Local Knowledge: Further Essays in Interpretative Anthropology* (New York: Basic Books, 1983), 58.

from a limited perspective: it is *a view "From here"* about how things look "from here" and "from there." The modest goal we *can* reach, however, is to acquire "a common language, common human understanding, which would allow both us and them undistortively to be"[77]—an understanding that will, we hope, in some way approximate the way the all-knowing God, who views things from everywhere, sees both us and them.

What happens *before* we have acquired "a common language," however? Do we just keep going from step one to two to three and then back to one? A privileged few who are paid to reflect can have the luxury of letting the double movement toward the other and back to the self go on until a complete agreement is reached. Those caught in the midst of personal and social struggles cannot. They must act. As Langdon Gilkey observes,

> Praxis brings with it *forced* option, one that cannot be avoided. When praxis is called for, puzzled immobility before contradiction or indifferent acceptance of plurality of options must both cease—for to exist humanly we must wager, and must enact our wager.[78]

As we must act *before* we have resolved a contradiction and sorted out between multiple opinions, so too we must act before we have come to a "common human understanding, which would allow both us and them undistortively to be." But before and after we act we can and must see ourselves and others with a "double vision." Elsewhere I have explored why "double vision" is necessary when we are engaged in conflicts and how we should practice it in such situations (Chapter V). Here I want to discuss what it takes to start and keep alive the movement from the self to the other in search for truth between people.

Truthfulness and Embrace

Why be committed to seeing things both "from here" and "from there," as I argued? Why care how things look from God's perspective? Why bother with truth at all? If "truth" is for us, we'll use truth's help. If "truth" is against us, why should we be for truth? Why should we want to part with our self-deceit and prejudice if they give us power and privilege?

77. Taylor, "Comparison, History, and Truth," 42.

78. Langdon Gilkey, "Plurality and Its Theological Implications," *The Myth of Christian Uniqueness: Toward a Pluralistic Theology of Religions*, ed. John Hick and Paul Knitter (Mary-knoll, NY: Orbis, 1987), 46.

Because the "truth will make us free" (John 8:32)? But why should we not prefer "captivity" with power and privilege to "freedom" with weakness and suffering? Why not treat "truth" and "untruth" simply as political words, "weapons in competition for power"?[79] Answers to these questions will differ. The exploration of various answers, sorting out which might be closer to being right, and of how to convince those who disagree with us, can be left aside here. My purpose in raising the questions is to make a simple but frequently overlooked point: *before you can search for truth you must be interested in finding it.*

Consider the following statement of the prophet Ezekiel: "Human one, you live in a household of rebels. They have eyes to see but they don't see, ears to hear but they don't hear, because they are a household of rebels" (Ezek 12:2 CEB; cf. Rev 2:7). One can read the text as posing the fundamental epistemological question about the adequacy of sense perception: What does it take for eyes to see and ears to hear? A part of the answer, suggested between the lines, is that the organs of perception must function properly if, helped by the interpretative activity of the mind, they are to connect adequately the knower with the known. The text presumes, however, that this condition of knowing has been met—that said people do "have eyes to see" and "ears to hear." I can leave aside here the question of whether such an assumption naively circumvents the problem of the reliability of sense perception[80] or rightly suggests that too much talk about the reliability of sense perception diverts attention from other kinds of conditions of knowing that are at the core of the reason why different people perceive the same things differently, especially in conflict situations. In either case, the text underscores that knowing can fail even if we assume that "the mechanism of perception" functions adequately. The fundamental epistemological problem as the prophet understands it is that *with eyes capable of seeing people do not see and with ears capable of hearing people do not hear.* The reason, he claims, is that they are "a rebellious house" (NRSV). Blinded by mutually reinforcing patterns of private and collective "rebellions" they are unable to see the truth with which they are confronted and instead produce their own "truths" that correspond to their rebellions. To employ the vocabulary of Thomas Aquinas, the will and the intellect, which each moves the other,[81] are caught in a downward

79. E. G. Bailey, *The Prevalence of Deceit* (Ithaca, NY: Cornell University Press, 1991), 128.

80. William P. Alston, *The Reliability of Sense Perception* (Ithaca, NY: Cornell University Press, 1996).

81. See Thomas Aquinas, *Summa Theologica*, transl. Fathers of the English Dominican Province (New York: Benzinger, 1948), Ia, 83, 3–4.

spiral in which each corrupts the other; a misdirection of the will prepares the way for the failure of the intellect and a failure of the intellect reinforces the misdirection of the will. In terms of the search for truth in interhuman exchanges, the most consequential distinction is not between those who are "technically" equipped to perceive the truth and those who are not; it is between those "who want to want the truth," and those "who turn away from the truth" because their will does not want to strive after truth.[82] Knowing adequately is not just a matter of what eyes, ears, and minds do, but also of what "hearts" do, not just a matter of perception but also of habits and practices.

The will to truth was never easy to sustain. Nietzsche knew this well and therefore lashed out with equal force at the intellectual dishonesty that so often hides behind "the will to truth" as he did "the will to truth" itself.[83] Truth is a stern mistress; "the service to truth is the hardest service."[84] Hence even philosophers, says Nietzsche, would rather take "flight in the face of reality"[85] and peddle "people's superstitions" as elevated verities[86] than submit to the rigors of truth's service. There are, of course, trivial truths that demand only a change of opinion, like the truth about what you ate for dinner on your tenth wedding anniversary or what color of suit Martin Luther King Jr. wore when he was shot. Other truths are all but trivial and demand a radical change of behavior, like the truth about whether you forgot your wedding anniversary five years in a row, or the truth about the reasons why Martin Luther King Jr. was assassinated. Such truths lay claim on much more than one's mind and therefore require that "one be stern towards one's heart."[87] To accept them, much more to actively pursue them, we must be willing to part with ego-boosting self-deceit and power-maintaining ideologies, be ready to rewrite the story of our identities, and be ready to reform our practices. If we refuse to be unsettled and transformed, we will shy away from truth and stick to our

82. Lévy, *Gefährliche Reinheit*, 211. Lévy himself rejects the "transcendence of truth." He insists rightly, however, that "even if the truth did exist" (which, in his opinion, it does not), the will would have the primacy over technical epistemological competence.

83. Friedrich Nietzsche, *Twilight of the Idols and The Anti-Christ*, transl. R. J. Hollingdale (London: Penguin, 1990), 179.

84. Ibid.

85. Friedrich Nietzsche, *Ecce Homo: How One Becomes What One Is*, transl. R. J. Hollingdale (London: Penguin, 1979), 98.

86. Friedrich Nietzsche, *Thus Spoke Zarathustra: A Book for Everyone and No One*, transl. R. J. Hollingdale (London: Penguin, 1969), 126.

87. Nietzsche, *Twilight of the Idols and The Anti-Christ*, 179.

preferred beliefs, which make us "blessed" precisely because they tell us lies. The will to truth cannot be sustained without the *will to obey* the truth.

Where does the will to obey the truth stem from, however? It is a fruit of a truthful character. As Stanley Hauerwas has argued, truth requires a *truthful life*. "Our ability to 'step back' from our deceptions is dependent on the dominant story, the master image, that we have embodied in our character," he writes.[88] Hauerwas tells the story of Albert Speer, Hitler's architect and later Minister of Armaments, to illustrate the point. How could an intelligent man like Speer go along with Hitler? Speer explains to his daughter:

> You must realize that at the age of thirty-two, in my capacity as archi-tect, I had the most splendid assignments of which I could dream. Hit-ler said to your mother one day that her husband could design buildings the like of which had not been seen for two thousand years. One would have had to be morally very stoical to reject the proposal. *But I was not at all like that.*[89]

Speer was "above all an architect" and out of "fear of discovering something which might have made me turn from my course" he chose not to know. "I had closed my eyes," he writes. With his eyes shut, he was oblivious to the crimes of the system he served, unable even to "see any moral ground outside the system where I should have taken my stand."[90] Speer suppressed the truth in order not to have to "turn from his course." His character was shaped by ambition, not by truth. The story of Speer illustrates that, as James McClendon puts it, our common task is not so much discovering a truth hiding among contrary viewpoints as it is com-ing to possess a selfhood that no longer evades and eludes the truth with which it is importunately confronted.[91]

The New Testament writers put it this way: before you can search for and accept the truth, before you can unmask deceptions and ideologies, the truth must be "in you" (see John 8:45; 2 Cor 11:10). In a well-known passage in Ephesians, readers are warned not to be "tossed to and fro and

---

88. Stanley Hauerwas, Richard Bondi, and David B. Burrell, *Truthfulness and Tragedy: Further Inves-tigations in Christian Ethics* (Notre Dame, IN: University of Notre Dame Press, 1977), 95.
89. Ibid., 91.
90. Ibid., 90.
91. James Wm. McClendon Jr., *Ethics: Systematic Theology*, vol. I (Nashville: Abingdon, 1986), 352.

blown about" by "people's trickery, by their craftiness in deceitful scheming" (4:14). What anchor will keep them from being carried away by distortions of truth? They should *alētheuein en agapē*, says the writer (4:15). Commentators usually render this term "speaking the truth in love." But the verb used in the original is not "to speak" but "to truth," which in addition to speaking the truth may mean cherishing, maintaining, doing, or living the truth (see John 3:21). Since the notion of "deceitful scheming," which functions as a contrast, denotes more than just speaking falsehood, *alētheuein* includes here both telling and living the truth.[92] Speaking is only part of what we do with truth as we struggle against its distortions; living the truth is certainly equally important. Untruth holds captive both minds and lives and therefore cannot be overcome only with right thoughts and right words. It takes a *truthful life* to want to seek after the truth, to see the truth when confronted by it, and to say the truth out loud without fear.

Notice that Ephesians qualifies the injunction "to live the truth" with the phrase "in love" (4:15). If the search for truth were only a private affair between the knowing subject and its object, the virtue of truthfulness would suffice; when we encountered "the truth" we would submit to it, willing to go wherever it takes us and do whatever it demands of us. If we are after the "unity of knowledge" *between people* (see 4:13), however, the virtue of truthfulness will not suffice; love for the other must be added. For there is a perverse kind of obedience to the stern mistress that makes use of her powers to subdue and destroy the other. In *The Conquest of America*, Tzvetan Todorov speaks of "the understanding-that-kills," sustained by "an entirely negative value judgment of the Other"[93] and grounded in the will to dominate. To serve life rather than death, the will to truth needs to be accompanied by the *will to embrace the other, by the will to community*.

I have argued earlier that the search for truth among individuals and cultural groups takes place through the movement from the self to the other and back; it involves a "double vision," viewing things "from here" as well as "from there." But when war is raging—a war with words or with weapons—why should we *want* to make a movement from the self to the other? When nothing in our perspective suggests that they may be right why would we still want to see things from their perspective? Why allow

---

92. F. F. Bruce, *The Epistles to the Colossians, to Philemon, and to the Ephesians*, NICNT (Grand Rapids: Eerdmans, 1984), 352.

93. Todorov, *The Conquest of America*, 127.

their perspective to confront and challenge ours? What will make us submit to truth about our enemies, especially if it undermines prejudices that sustain our enmity? Nothing will. Nothing, that is, unless in the midst of enmity we refuse to project dehumanizing images on them and are striving to embrace them as friends.

In the essay "Theonomy and/or Autonomy," Paul Ricoeur made a similar kind of argument against the communicative ethics of Jürgen Habermas. A sharp way to put the fundamental social option as Habermas sees it, is in the form of an alternative: either rational discourse or irrational violence. The alternative was formulated so as to make the choice obvious: we are for discourse and against violence. Yet in conflict situations the question is precisely *why* make this most fundamental choice for discourse instead of violence, a question that cannot be answered through discourse itself precisely because the choice for or against discourse is a choice for or against "the utopian way of life in which respect and reciprocity reign."[94] Once the protagonists opt for discourse—once they "decide to have no recourse in their conflicts but to the argument of the better argument"[95]— the conflict is half resolved. But what will make them want to listen to better arguments instead of firing the most powerful guns? Ricoeur rightly points out that "loving obedience" grounded in the Lover's love must undergird "discursive will formation."

The will to truth and communion rests on a goodness that is the exact opposite of the goodness of "the good," of whom Nietzsche says that they "never tell the truth" because they are "least of all" capable of being "truthful."[96] Though the "goodness" that consists either in blind obedience or narcissistic self-righteousness thwarts the search for truth, the goodness that creates space in the self for the other facilitates the search for truth. Indeed, without *such* goodness no movement from the self to the other and back will commence, no agreement will be reached. Each party will remain alone with its own truth, persuaded equally of the wrongness of those who disagree as of its own rightness. And when parties clash, their "truths" will turn into "understandings-that-kill"; the more true they are held to be the more deadly they will be. Without the will to embrace

---

94. Seyla Benhabib, *Situating the Self: Gender, Community, and Postmodernism in Contemporary Ethics* (New York: Routledge, 1992), 38; Michael Walzer, *Thick and Thin: Moral Arguments at Home and Abroad* (Notre Dame, IN: University of Notre Dame Press, 1994), 12f.

95. Paul Ricoeur, "Theonomy and/or Autonomy," *The Future of Theology: Essays in Honor of Jürgen Moltmann*, ed. Miroslav Volf (Grand Rapids: Eerdmans, 1996), 298.

96. Nietzsche, *Thus Spoke Zarathustra*, 218.

the other there will be no truth *among people*, and without truth among people there will be no peace.

With the emphasis on the singular importance of the will to truth and communion are we in the last analysis left with a clash of competing wills? Partly on the basis of similar reasons that I have used in this section, Stanley Fish has argued that "behind any dispute that occurs will be a conflict of conviction that cannot be rationally settled because it is also and necessarily a conflict of rationalities, and when there is a conflict of rationalities, your only recourse is, well, to conflict since there is no common ground in relation to which dialogue might proceed."[97] Fish both exaggerates and misconstrues the problem. The kind of strong incommensurability—the belief that there is *no* common ground whatsoever—that Fish assumes, strikes me as patently false. My earlier proposal of pursuing a "double vision" was meant precisely as an alternative to this belief. In some (not all) disputes the only option is "to conflict." When such irrational conflict is unavoidable, however, it is not so much because there is a clash of rationalities (basic rules of evidence and argument), but because the will to truth and to communion is absent. Supply such will, and rational communication will commence and replace irrational conflict.

Truth and Community

There can be no truth among people without the will to embrace the other, I have just argued. Inversely, the will to embrace cannot be sustained and will not result in an actual embrace if truth does not reign. If truth cannot do without the will to embrace, neither can embrace do without the will to truth. Here I want to examine this other side of the relationship between embrace and truth: the need of embrace for truth.

The idea that truth sustains community while deception destroys it is woven into the very notion of truth that we encounter in the biblical traditions. Along with the majority of scholars, A. Jepsen has argued that in the Hebrew Bible truth "was used of things that had proved to be reliable.... 'Reliability' would be the best comprehensive word in English to convey the idea. Truth is that on which others can rely."[98] Especially when used of God, truth denotes faithfulness. As Thomas F. Torrance puts it, truth is "God's being true to Himself, his faithfulness or consistency.

---

97. Stanley Fish, "Why We Can't All Just Get Along," *First Things* 60, no. 2 (1996): 18–26, 23.

98. Alfred Jepsen, "Aman," *Theological Dictionary of the Old Testament*, ed. G. J. Botterweck and H. Ringgren (Grand Rapids: Eerdmans, 1974), 313.

God's Truth means, therefore, that he keeps truth or faith with his people and requires them to keep truth or faith with him."[99] Faithfulness and reliability are personal and social terms. They describe the character of a person both as he or she is in himself or herself and as he or she is toward others. Just as "God is who God is" for others—this is what God's name "Yahweh" means (Exod 3:13ff.)—so humans should be who they are for others, transparent and dependable. Truth is an arm extended toward others; deceit is a sword that keeps them at a distance and cuts into their flesh. Without truthfulness built into the very foundations of the community its pillars will crack and erode.[100]

It is unfortunate that theologians who stress "truth as faithfulness" sometimes think they need to discard "truth as accordance with 'reality'"; the one is Hebrew and good, the other Greek and bad, they tell us. As a careful study of the biblical texts demonstrates,[101] this is surely a false alternative, just as the alternative between "lie as an offense against trust" and "lie as an offense against truth" is a false one.[102] In biblical texts the notions of "reliability" and of "truthful speech" frequently appear together and are inextricably intertwined, though neither can be reduced to the other. Consider the following two passages. The first is from Jeremiah:

> Beware of your neighbors,
>> and put no trust in any of your kin;
> for all your kin are supplanters,
>> and every neighbor goes around like a slanderer.
> They all deceive their neighbors,

---

99. Thomas F. Torrance, "One Aspect of the Biblical Conception of Faith," *Expository Times* 67, no. 4 (1957): 112.

100. Truthfulness is not the only thing that keeps communities together, of course. This explains why the social fabric can stand a good deal of lying. Harry Frankfurt has remarked that "the actual quantity of lying is enormous after all, and yet social life goes on. That people often lie hardly renders it impossible to benefit from being with them. It only means that we need to be careful" ("The Faintest Passion," *Proceedings and Addresses of the A. P. A.* 66, no. 3 [1992]: 6). It is the *quality* of social life, not the social life itself, that the practice of lying and truth-telling either sustains or destroys. MacIntyre has, for instance, argued that "the evil of lying" consists "in its capacity for corrupting and destroying the integrity of rational relationships" (Alasdair MacIntyre, "Truthfulness, Lies, and Moral Philosophers: What Can We Learn from Mill and Kant?" *The Tanner Lectures on Human Nature*, ed. Grete B. Peterson [Salt Lake City: University of Utah Press, 1995], 355).

101. James Barr, *The Semantics of Biblical Language* (Oxford: Oxford University Press, 1961), 161–205; Anthony C. Thiselton, "Truth," *The New International Dictionary of New Testament Theology*, ed. Colin Brown (Grand Rapids: Zondervan, 1986), 3:874–902.

102. MacIntyre, "Truthfulness, Lies, and Moral Philosophers."

and no one speaks the truth;
> they have taught their tongues to speak lies;
>> they commit iniquity and are too weary to repent.
> Oppression upon oppression,
>> deceit upon deceit!
> They refuse to know me, says the Lord. (9:4-6)

One should put no trust in persons who have taught their tongue to speak lies, insists Jeremiah. The Apostle Paul underscores the obverse of the same idea by zeroing in on the relation between trust and truthful speech rather than between distrust and deceit: "We have renounced the shameful things that one hides; we refuse to practice cunning or to falsify God's word; but by the open statement of the truth we commend ourselves to the conscience of everyone in the sight of God" (2 Cor 4:2).

The concreteness of Jeremiah's and Paul's narratives of truth-telling and deception as they relate to community stands in contrast to a certain abstractness in the typically modern epistemological reflection. Notice, first, the obvious. In both texts "true" refers to what in some sense *accords with reality*. Jeremiah contrasts "truthful speech" with "speaking lies," "slandering," and "deceiving." Paul contrasts "openness" with "hiding," and "stating truth" with "falsifying." For both, things ought to be said the way they are, rather than distorted or disguised; words ought to correspond in some unspecified (and maybe unspecifiable) sense to reality.

Second, neither Jeremiah nor Paul speaks abstractly of the relation between "minds" and "facts," as the Western philosophical tradition liked to state the relation between the knower and the object of knowledge. In a sense, for them there are no such things as "minds" and "facts." Instead of forging abstract categories of "facts" and "minds," they narrate the *things people do to each other*. In Jeremiah, neighbors commit iniquity and pile oppression upon oppression. Paul's enemies do shameful things and practice cunning while he claims to do exactly the opposite. One can label evil, oppressive, shameful, or cunning actions as "facts," but one should then not forget that such "facts" exist only within a complex field of forces that human interaction always represents. Similarly, instead of "minds," in Jeremiah one encounters a community of "neighbors"—"all," says the prophet!—engaged in a project of teaching their tongues to tell lies and outdoing one another in deception. Similarly, Paul, who is afflicted by hardships and slandered by enemies, and who is trying to speak in Christ's name to Christ's church, is not a pure "mind." Of course all these people *have* "minds," but these are embodied minds, pulled in various directions by various desires, interests, and conflicts, and shaped by cultural and religious convictions and practices.

For Jeremiah and Paul, the point of speaking the truth, as opposed to deceiving, is not to win the contest in whose "mind" can better correspond to the actual "facts," but to *name adequately what transpires among people*. Recent epistemological discussion suggests that no more than that seems possible because all experience relies on prior interpretation and all interpretations are offered in particular languages and guided by particular interests. Yet it would be a mistake to think that "truth" must be irretrievably lost underneath the heap of particular interests, languages, and interpretations. There is such a thing as a simple, human, and situated truth that, in a creaturely way, corresponds to the divine truth. It is acknowledged in the observation that "when we make a judgment, there is a notion of whether or not what we have said is correct independently of what we happen to think."[103] Though we may have philosophical difficulties defending even such a humble notion of a "simple" truth, most of us can tell the difference between the truth and a lie when we see one—if we are truthful, if our relationship with others matters to us, and if we want to make a movement away from the self toward the other and back. Most of us also know that nothing will make people see and respect the truth who, for whatever reason, insist on deceiving themselves or misleading others.

Third, in both texts *truth sustains community and lies destroy it*. By "the open statement of truth" Paul is trying to commend himself to the Corinthians, who accuse him of saying "'Yes, Yes' and 'No, No' at the same time" (2 Cor 1:17). Inversely, when everyone tells lies and slanders, people have to "beware" of their neighbors (Jer 9:4). One can "put no trust" (9:4) in those who do not speak the truth (9:5), for those who pile "deceit upon deceit" pile also "oppression upon oppression" (9:6). Truth sustains trust, deceit destroys it. If truth does not reign, we will not trust others and we ourselves will not be trustworthy.

Merely *telling* the truth will not suffice, however. One must *do* truth. Consider the profoundly disturbing case of Ananias and Sapphira in the Acts of the Apostles. When Ananias came with a gift to the Apostle, Peter saw through the deception and asked: "Ananias, why has Satan filled your heart to lie to the Holy Spirit and to keep back some of the proceeds of

---

103. Luntley, *Reason, Truth, and Self*, 108.

the land? While it remained unsold, did it not remain your own? And after it was sold, were not the proceeds at your disposal?" (Acts 5:3-4). Ananias deceived without telling a lie. He "kept back" something while pretending to give all. The lived-out lie undermined trust: Ananias and Sapphira wanted to receive sustenance from the community and yet withhold their own possessions from it. After being exposed, they were struck dead, and we are at a loss as to the reasons for the severity of the punishment. Though many uncomfortable questions remain, one thing is clear: when they fell dead and were "carried out" (5:6, 10) they were physically separated from the community from which they cut themselves off by *doing* deception. In an important sense deception *is* death because isolation is death, and truth is life because community is life.

Taken together, the previous three comments suggest that the concern for truth and the concern for trust are complementary. In the essay "Truthfulness, Lies, and Moral Philosophers," Alasdair MacIntyre argued that such complementarity makes sense if we "understand the rules prescribing unqualified truthfulness as governing relationships, rather than individuals apart from their relationships."[104] Telling what one believes to be true is a way of being loyal to a relationship; telling what one believes not to be true is a way of defecting from a relationship. As a consequence, "the virtues of integrity and fidelity are understood to be at stake in all those situations in which the virtue of truthfulness is at stake."[105] We speak truth because community matters to us, and we sustain community that matters to us by speaking truth.[106] The same idea is underscored by the way in which both Jeremiah and Paul bring God to bear on the question of truth-telling and community. In pleading for truth-telling both Paul and Jeremiah appeal to the *character of God*. When Paul speaks the truth, he does so not just before "everyone" but also "in the sight of God" (2 Cor 4:2). Earlier in the same letter he sets up God's faithfulness as a model for his own truthfulness: "As surely as God is faithful, our word to you has not been 'Yes and No'" (2 Cor 1:18). Similarly, for Jeremiah, deceit, along with oppression, is a form of refusal to know God (9:6).

---

104. MacIntyre, "Truthfulness, Lies, and Moral Philosophers," 359.

105. Ibid.

106. In Ephesians, both aspects of the relation between the truth and community are mentioned in the same context. On the one hand, the injunction to "speak the truth to our neighbors" is supported by the claim that "we are members of one another" (4:25). On the other hand, the growth of the body in unity takes place in part through "speaking the truth in love" (4:15).

How do such appeals to God function, however? One could read Paul's comment in 2 Corinthians to imply that the universality of truth ("everyone") requires transcendental underpinnings ("in the sight of God"). As I argued earlier, for Christian theology God does offer transcendental grounds for the notion of truth and the obligation to truthtelling. This is, however, not the primary thrust of the biblical texts about God and truth-telling. There are good reasons for this, I believe. It may be that the will to truth cannot be *justified* without recourse to God, so that without God the only intellectually compelling principles would be "nothing is true" and "everything is permitted."[107] It is undeniable, however, that the will to truth can be *practiced* with no conscious recourse to God whatsoever. In the midst of quite impressive amounts of lying people do continue to engage in even more impressive amounts of truth-telling, if for no other reason than that lying is possible only against the backdrop of truth-telling.[108] Most of this truth-telling takes place without a single thought given to its philosophical justification and most of the lying would continue even if everyone thought the obligation to truth-telling is rooted in the existence of God. It is more important to see God as *a warrior engaged in the struggle for truth,* as the prophets and the apostles do, than as the transcendental condition for the possibility of truthful speech.

Take Isaiah's prophecy against "scoffers," who rule in Jerusalem:

> Because you have said, "…we have made lies our refuge
> > and in falsehood have taken shelter";
> > therefore thus says the Lord God,
> See, I am laying in Zion a foundation stone, a tested stone,
> > a precious cornerstone, a sure foundation:
> > "One who trusts will not panic."
> And I will make justice the line,
> > and righteousness the plummet;
> > hail will sweep away the refuge of lies,
> > and waters will overwhelm the shelter. (28:15-17)

The passage is thoroughly agonistic. Lies and falsehood are the refuge and shelter of corrupt rulers; they fear for their power, indeed for their very lives

---

107. Nietzsche, *The Birth of Tragedy and The Genealogy of Morals*, 287.
108. MacIntyre, "Truthfulness, Lies, and Moral Philosophers," 311ff.

because they oppress those whom they should serve. Yet the rulers know that they will withstand the assaults as long as they can pass off as truth what is in fact a lie. The battle for power is a battle for control over truth. This is where God comes in for Isaiah. God is on the side of those who are too weak to resist the "regimes of truth." Lies and falsehoods cannot protect the rulers from God. Like a mighty flood, God will sweep their refuge away and overwhelm their shelter. God will expose the power game the rulers play and bring to light their injustice; God will pull them down from their thrones and crown in Zion a ruler. "A tested stone," he will be "a sure foundation" of a new community of justice and peace because he will not deceive those who trust in him. Community depends on truth and the truth depends not so much on the plausibility of the transcendental conditions of its possibility, but on the struggle of the truthful warriors on behalf of the truth.

The early church saw this passage from Isaiah as a messianic prophecy, fulfilled in the coming of Jesus Christ (see Rom 9:33; 1 Pet 2:6). In the following, I will pull together aspects of what I have been saying about truth as well as take the discussion a step farther by reflecting on a segment from the narrative about Jesus Christ: his encounter with a representative of the strongest political and military power of the time who sentenced him to death on the cross.

Jesus Before Pilate: Truth Against Power

Some of the most profound New Testament comments about truth are found in John's Gospel, especially in the drama of Jesus's arrest, trial, and execution (John 18–19). I will highlight the social aspects of the narrative, concentrating on the relation between power and truth. This is not the only possible, not even the only important, reading of the text. John's primary intent, at any rate, is to engender belief in Jesus Christ, who is the Truth (see John 20:30f.). The soteriological perspective on truth has, however, important sociological and epistemological dimensions. The narrative itself invites us to draw them out since it moves both on theological and social planes at the same time: in deciding on the truth of the allegations against Jesus and his place within his social world, one decides for or against "the Truth."[109]

---

109. For my purposes it is not necessary to sift out "historical" from "nonhistorical" materials in the narrative. I am reading the text as a *story* about the nature and significance of the commitment to truthfulness. My argument for the importance of telling "what was the case" (in a carefully qualified sense) in no way implies either that we cannot keep telling narratives whose point is not to tell "what was historically

During the trial Jesus is caught in the field of social forces with religious, ethnic, and political bases, all interested in maintaining and bolstering their power. The main protagonists are the Jewish leaders and Pilate. The Jewish leaders, who brought Jesus to Pilate, are afraid of his popularity.[110] If he continues his ministry "everyone will believe in him," they reason, and "the Romans will come and take away from us both our holy place and our nation" (John 11:48).[111] To prevent their own deposition as protectors of a nation and its religion, they plot Jesus's death and, as rulers often do, couch the desire for power in concern for the well-being of the people (11:50). The rhetoric of benevolence does not succeed in fully hiding their motivation, however: it is better for *them* ("for you," says the high priest, Caiaphas) "to have one man die for the people than to have the whole nation destroyed" (11:50). Between a whole nation with its venerable religious tradition (including its wise leaders) and a single man, the choice is easy.

Pilate represents Roman power. Most commentators portray him as a fair but inexplicably impotent judge who tries unsuccessfully to release Jesus. As Raymond Brown puts it, Pilate is "the person-in-between who does not wish to make a decision and so vainly tries to reconcile the opposing forces."[112] David Rensberger has argued, on the other hand, that we should see him as a cunning representative of Roman power who ridicules Jewish "national hopes by means of Jesus."[113] Though I think Rensberger is right, we do not need to decide here between the two interpretations. In either case, Pilate's goal was to preserve his own power—his hold over a province, his right to decide over life and death (19:10)—and the power of Caesar. If during the trial Pilate acted as a cunning Procurator,

the case," or that we cannot learn about the importance of telling "what was the case" from the narratives that do not intend to tell "what was historically the case."

110. In analyzing the relation between truth and power by using the encounter between Jesus, the Jewish religious leaders, and Pilate, I by no means wish to perpetuate the anti-Jewish attitudes and actions that have characterized so much the Christian church's history and drawn their inspiration in part from John's Gospel. Since Jesus was himself a Jew, "Jewish religious leaders" in my reading of the text do not stand for a general category of "the Jews." The story of the encounter between Jesus and Pilate invites us to emulate *Jesus the Jew* by renouncing violence in the name of the commitment to truth rather than scapegoating the Jewish people under the pretense of "avenging" the death of a wrongly de-judaised Jesus.

111. Following George R. Beasley-Murray (*John*, Word Biblical Commentary, vol. 36 [Waco: Word, 1987], 196) I prefer the above reading to the alternative one ("the Romans will come and *destroy* both our holy place and our nation").

112. Raymond E. Brown, *The Death of the Messiah: From Gethsemane to the Grave: A Commentary on the Passion Narrative in the Four Gospels*, vol. 1 (New York: Doubleday, 1994), 744.

113. David Rensberger, "The Politics of John: The Trial of Jesus in the Fourth Gospel," *JBL* 103, no. 3 (1984): 402.

then what mattered to him was not whether Jesus in fact had aspirations to a Jewish throne, but whether *people believed* him to be the king; in the world of politics, perceived power is real power and ought to be held in check. If, on the other hand, Pilate was a weak go-between, what mattered to him was to maintain his tenuous grip on power; truth and justice had to be subordinated to that goal. "One man must be sacrificed for the sake of my power and the glory of Caesar," thought Pilate. "One man should not stand in the way of our rule for the good of our nation and the survival of our religion," argued Caiaphas.

Notice the nature of exchange between the religious leaders and Pilate in the course of the trial. It is a discourse of power. They bring Jesus to Pilate and want him sentenced because they have already decided that he deserves death. They give no arguments; they issue *demands*. When Pilate hesitates on account of Jesus's innocence, they *shout* "Crucify him! Crucify him!" (19:6). When Pilate makes an effort to release Jesus, they employ intimidation tactics: "If you release this man you are no friend of the emperor" (19:12). They do not even bother to provide "reasons" for their desire to see Jesus dead. The exchange of reason and counter-reason, appropriate for the court setting, has been replaced by the rhetoric of pressure. That is the picture painted if we see Pilate as a mere "person-in-between." If he was a cruel advocate of Caesar's rule, as Rensberger argues, then he wins by shrewd deceit: he manages to have a popular preacher and potential trouble-maker hanged and the Jewish leaders held responsible for the act; he succeeds both in having the Jewish religious leaders express publicly their allegiance to Caesar as their only king (19:15) and in making Jesus's fate a showcase to any pretenders to the title of Jewish king (19:21). The religious leaders seek to twist Pilate's arm, but he makes them executioners of his own hidden purposes. In both cases—religious leaders' pressure or Pilate's cunning—communication is a tool of violence, not an instrument of reasonable exchange.

Trials are supposed to be about finding out what happened and meting out justice. In Jesus's trial, neither the accusers nor the judge cared for the truth. The accusers want condemnation; they are even insulted at the judge's request that they name the crime: "If this man were not a criminal, we would not have handed him over to you" (18:30). The judge scorns the very notion of truth: "What is truth?" he asks, and, uninterested in any answer, he leaves the scene of dialogue with the accused to return to the arena in which the play of clashing forces determines the outcome. For both the accusers and the judge, the truth is irrelevant because it works at cross-purposes to their hold on power. The only truth they will recognize is "the truth of power." It was the accused who raised the issue of truth by subtly reminding the judge of his highest obligation—find out the truth. And significantly enough, he, the innocent and powerless one, remained alone in his interest in truth. As an innocent victim in search for truth, Jesus is the judge of his judge. In the Johannine narrative we sense a counter trial taking place, in which the judgment will be passed on Pilate.[114]

In the exchange with Pilate, Jesus argues against "the truth of power" and for "the power of truth." "Are you the King of the Jews?" asks Pilate. He means, "Are you a bearer of a power that competes with the power of the religious leaders, with my own power, and with the power of Caesar?" Jesus does not refuse the title "king" but alters its content. His kingship is not "from here," not "from this world" (18:36). The point of these denials is not that Jesus's kingship is not a force defining social reality. After all he "came into the world" (18:37) and his disciples are "in the world" (17:11), inserted in the play of social forces. As a "king," however, he does not stand in the same arena with other contenders to power, fighting the same battle for dominance. His is not an alternative power of the same kind as the powers of Caiaphas, Pilate, and Caesar. If it were, his followers would "be fighting" to keep him from "being handed over" to his accusers who in turn handed him to Pilate (18:36). His kingship does not rest on "fighting" and therefore does not issue in "handing over" people to other powers. The violence of eliminating other contenders for power or holding them in check by treating them as things is not a part of his rule. In a profound sense the kind of rule Jesus advocates cannot be fought for and taken hold of by violence. It is a rule that must be given, conferred (19:11), and that will continue only as long as one does not try to seize it.

By renouncing the power of violence, Jesus advocated *the power of truth.* "For this I was born, and for this I came into the world, to testify to the truth" (18:37), he tells Pilate. To be a witness to truth does not mean to renounce all power. For truth itself is so much a power that witnessing to it can be described as *kingship.*[115] As the one who gives the testimony to the truth, Jesus *is* a king. Is he therefore a threat to Caesar? Not directly, because he is unwilling to engage Caesar with Caesar's weapons. As Rensberger points out, for Jesus, "both the continued expectation of a

---

114. Thomas Söding, "Die Macht der Wahrheit und das Reich der Freiheit: Zur Johanneischen Deutung des Pilatus-Prozesses (John 18,28—19,6)," *Zeitschrift für Theologie und Kirche* 93 (1996): 40.

115. Paul Anderson, "Was the Fourth Evangelist a Quaker?" *Quaker Religious Thought* 76, no. 2 (1991): 41.

revolutionary Messiah and the accommodation of the emerging Pharisaic leadership to the kingship of Caesar" were unacceptable.[116] But precisely in refusing the sword, Jesus calls Caesar's power most radically into question. "Caesar is king" and "Jesus is king" are therefore two competing and ultimately incompatible claims. They are competing claims, because Jesus's *reign* lays claim to the same loyalties and investments of the self as Caesar's; they are incompatible, because Jesus's *rule* is of an entirely different nature.

The power of truth is a power different from the power of Caesar. In a profound sense, truth is *not* "a thing of this world," as Foucault would have it. Rather, truth is a power from a *different* world. The instrument of this power is not "violence" but "witness." What is the task of a witness? To tell what he or she has seen or heard; the obligation is to tell it the way it was, to point to the truth, not to produce the truth. Much like the language as a system of signs in Foucault's account of the classical tradition, the witness "exists only to be transparent."[117] Speaking of himself Jesus claims, we "testify to what we have seen" (John 3:11); he spoke "the truth" that he had "*heard* from God" (8:40). A witness, unseduced by the lure of power, strives not to bring anything of his or her own to his or her speech; not seeking his or her "own glory" (7:18), the witness strives to point precisely to what is *not* his or her own. There is no better summary of Jesus's mission as a witness than his statement, "My teaching is not mine but his who sent me" (7:16; cf. 12:49; 14:24).

To be a witness means to strive to do the self-effacing and noncreative work of telling the truth. That does not mean that a witness will have to situate himself or herself "nowhere" and in sublime disinterestedness make perspectiveless pronouncements about what everyone and anyone must have seen or heard. No, standing at one place or another a witness will tell in his or her own words what the witness has seen or heard. But though a good witness cannot, and need not, abstract from his or her particular situatedness, a witness will seek to renounce the clandestine imperialism of his or her own self-enclosed self, which refuses to make space for the other *as* other in its cognition. That a witness will rarely fully succeed and sometimes not even try, goes without saying. Hence we keep suspicion close at hand even when listening to those whom we take to be good witnesses. But neither our suspicion nor witnesses' frequent failure alters the

---

116. Rensberger, "The Politics of John," 407.
117. Foucault, *The Order of Things*, 376.

obligation and the ability of the witness to respect the otherness of the other—by *seeking* to tell the truth.

To insert "something of one's own" in the act of witnessing is always a covert act of violence, maybe small and insignificant, but nevertheless a real one. Jesus renounces such violence because to accept it would be to give in to those who define social interaction as a power game. He would rather die witnessing to the truth than live manipulating others by making his own agenda pass as truth. He would rather have the truth carry a victory while he himself suffers a defeat than trample truth underfoot and emerge a "hero." Why? Because the whole purpose of his existence is to witness to the truth. Indeed, truth defines his very being. "I *am*...the truth," said Jesus, adding that he also *is* "the life" (14:6). The defeat of truth is the defeat of life; the victory of truth is the victory of life. A man dressed in a purple robe with a crown of thorns on his head, a man stripped naked hanging on the cross, represents the victory of truth and life, not their defeat. Should we be surprised that John considers crucifixion an act of *glorification* (13:31-32)!?

"This is naive," somebody could protest. "You make the Johannine Jesus advocate the kind of objectivity that is both philosophically and socially implausible! Do we not always insert our own interests into what we see and hear, let alone into the act of witnessing? Is it not true that social struggle, of which we are inescapably part, unavoidably colors our perspectives?" We do, and it is true (though the case of Jesus, the Word become flesh, is unique). Still, the objection is misplaced. I have already stated that abstract "objectivity" is not essential for witnessing. Notice, furthermore, that the Johannine Jesus underscores that the witness, even when telling the truth, cannot count on persuading the hearers; no rules governing the exchange between the witness and the hearers can be designed to guarantee adequate transmission of "true knowledge." This, I think, is implied when, after stating that he came to witness to the truth, Jesus added cryptically: "Everyone who belongs to the truth listens to my voice" (18:37).

What does the talk about "belonging to the truth," or literally "being of the truth," mean? That the witness is *addressed* to a chosen few? That access to the truth is restricted to the elect? During his interrogation before the high priest Jesus insists that he has "spoken openly to the world" and that he said "nothing in secret" (18:20; cf. 10:24ff.). How else could the one speak whose very purpose of coming into the world was to witness to the truth? He spoke in public places—in synagogues and in the temple—"where *all*...come together" (18:20). His testimony was public, open to all.[118] His truth-claims were universally accessible, inviting assent and exposing themselves to rejection of all. The truth to which he came to witness was not restricted to his own community. How else would he be able to declare both his accusers and the judge guilty of misreading and misjudging his actions? "The one who handed me over to you is guilty of a greater sin" (19:11) he says to Pilate, implying that Pilate too was guilty.

Yet even if all could hear, not all did agree. In fact, Jesus implies that all *could not have agreed*. Why? In addition to hearing the witness to the truth, acceptance of the truth requires that the hearer be "of the truth," Jesus said. In John 8—a passage whose anti-Jewish reverberations we must carefully avoid—Jesus contrasts those who are "of the truth" and ultimately "of God" with those who are of the devil and are liars. In marked contrast to himself who is the truth and the life, the devil is "a murderer from the beginning" and therefore "a liar and the father of lies"; when he speaks lies "he speaks according to his own nature" (8:44). Those who are from the devil want to do the desires of the devil.

Hence they do not understand and cannot accept the truth. Conversely, to be able to accept the witness to truth one must "stand in truth" and truth must be "in" one (8:44). The willingness to listen to truth depends on the way one lives: just as "all who do evil hate the light and do not come to light" so also "those who do what is true come to the light" (3:20). Hence Jesus can say to his opponents that they do not believe him, not *although* he is telling them the truth but *because* he is telling them the truth (see 8:45).

The ability to know the truth is not just a matter of what your mind does—whether it adjusts itself adequately to reality or thinks coherently—but is also a matter of what your character is. You must have an affinity with the truth by being "sanctified" in truth (17:17). In the terminology of Michel Foucault, because knowledge of truth is never "pure"—at least it is not pure when it comes to the kinds of knowing that are more significant than knowing the phone number of your grandfather—but always already immersed in the multiple relations of power that shape the self,[119] the self must become truthful before it can know and accept the truth. Since the self cannot be taken into a power-free space in which its

---

118. Söding, "Die Macht der Wahrheit und das Reich der Freiheit," 37.
119. Foucault, *History of Sexuality*, 73.

cognition could function undisturbed by power relations, the self must be reshaped within the power relations so as to be willing and capable of pursuing and accepting the truth. In this sense, the truthfulness of being is a pre-condition of adequate knowing.

What about those—indeed, all of *us*—who are not truthful? Have I split humanity into a handful of the truthful ones and the remainder that is enslaved in untruthfulness? Are the untruthful ones destined forever to walk in darkness because they cannot find what their eyes cannot see? In a profound sense, in order to know the truth we must be led "into the truth" by the "Spirit of truth" (16:13). Should we then say that the comprehension of truth is "not a free act of existence" but is grounded in "the determination of existence by divine reality," as Rudolph Bultmann did?[120] The opposition between the two is false—at least it is false at the social level at which I am here reading John's Gospel. All of us are always nudged by the Spirit of truth, yet only some remain in the truth. Those who do remain, says John, will "know the truth" and "the truth will make them free" (8:32).

Better than most people, Nietzsche knew what was at stake with the question of truth. Contesting the Johannine correlation between truth and freedom, he insisted in *The Genealogy of Morals* that as long as human beings "still believe in truth," they are "a long way from being *free* spirits." The "real freedom" can be had only where "the notion of truth itself has been disposed of."[121] Hence in *The Anti-Christ* Pilate is the sole New Testament figure who commands Nietzsche's respect. The "noble scorn" of this Roman governor "before whom an imprudent misuse of the word 'truth' was carried on," writes Nietzsche, "has enriched the New Testament with the only expression which possesses value—which is its criticism, its *annihilation* even: 'What is truth?' "[122] Whether the scorn for truth represents the annihilation of Christianity or an unwitting suicide of Nietzsche's own thought, however, will be decided partly on what we do with another kind of scorn, which is the flip side of the scorn for truth, the scorn for human life. Nietzsche knew that by not taking truth seriously Pilate was deciding not to take "a Jewish affair" seriously. And he shared Pilate's scorn for the "little Jew" from Galilee: "One Jew more or less—what does it matter?"[123]

120. Rudolph Bultmann, "*Alētheia*," *Theological Dictionary of the New Testament*, ed. G. Kittel (Grand Rapids: Eerdmans, 1964), I:246.
121. Nietzsche, *The Birth of Tragedy and The Genealogy of Morals*, 287.
122. Nietzsche, *Twilight of the Idols and The Anti-Christ*, 174.
123. Ibid., 174.

Unlike Pilate and Nietzsche, however, the followers of the crucified Messiah must have passion for the freedom of "every little Jew." Hence they will seek both to speak truth and to be truthful people.

Truth, Freedom, Violence

In a postmodern, post-Nietzschean context, probably the two most troubling aspects of what the Johannine Jesus says about the "truth" is the double claim that one can "know the truth" and that "the truth makes free." What audacity to insist that one knows *the* truth! What naiveté (or is it malice?) to maintain that *the* truth will make people free! No, *the* truth does not liberate, our postmodern sensibilities tell us; it enslaves. The one big Truth is but the one big Lie made to pass as truth in order to garb the evil holders of the oppressive power with the vestments of the holy guardians of liberating Truth. To make people free we must disperse the one big Truth into many little truths. Deeply suspicious of any claim to the knowledge of *the* truth, we are comfortable only with the play of multiple perspectives. What can we postmoderns learn from that premodern interface between "truth" and "power," as played out in the encounter between Jesus, Caiaphas, and Pilate?

In conclusion, let me draw two implications of this interface for the question of competing truth claims in the struggle for individual and communal recognition. The implications concern the stances we should take in search for truth. I need to preface what I am about to say by making a protective disclaimer to guard against false inferences. The first thing we need to remember as we seek to learn anything from Jesus Christ is that *we are not Jesus Christ*. Applied to the question of truth this means that, unlike Jesus Christ, we are *not* the truth and we are *not* self-effacing witnesses to the truth. This is why we believe in Jesus Christ—to help us see that we are not what we ought to be and to help us become what we ought to be. Our commitment to Jesus Christ who is the truth does not therefore translate into the claim that we possess the absolute truth. If we know the truth, we know it in our own human and corrupted way; as the Apostle Paul puts it, we "know in part," we see "in a mirror, dimly" (1 Cor 13:12f.). There is an irremovable opaqueness to our knowledge of things divine. Equally, there is an irremovable opaqueness to our knowledge of things human.

The first implication of the encounter between Jesus, Caiaphas, and Pilate is a disturbing insight that in an important sense *the truth matters more than my own self.* Jesus Christ was crucified as witness to the truth. Sandwiched between the powers of Caiaphas and Pilate this "marginal Jew" refused to place his own self above the truth—and became the Messiah of the world. Why this self-denying refusal in the face of powers that threatened to crush both him and his project? Because when we put ourselves above the truth we open the floodgates of violence whose torrents are most deadly to the weak. If the truth ceases to matter more than our individual or communal interests, violence will reign and those with stammering tongues and feeble hands will fall prey to those with smooth words and sharp swords.[124]

But what about those who in the name of truth oppress the weak? This brings me to the second implication of the encounter between Jesus, Caiaphas, and Pilate, which must always complement the first: *the self of the other matters more than my truth.* Though I must be ready to deny myself for the sake of *the* truth, I may not sacrifice the other at the altar of *my* truth. Jesus, who claimed to be the Truth, refused to use violence to "persuade" those who did not recognize his truth. The kingdom of truth, he came to proclaim, was the kingdom of freedom and therefore cannot rest on pillars of violence. Commitment to nonviolence must accompany commitment to truth; otherwise commitment to truth will generate violence. The truth is a shield against the violence of the strong against the weak, I argued earlier. If the shield is not to turn into a deadly weapon, it must be held in a hand that refuses to do violence, I want to add here.

Our postmodern sensibilities tell us that to engage in the quest for truth is covertly to sanction violence; for the sake of freedom we shy away from the pursuit of truth. Yet this pursuit may be less of a culprit than we think. It could be that we feel compelled to abandon talk about the truth *because we are afraid to renounce violence.* But if we do not relinquish violence the many little truths that we like to enthrone in place of the one big Truth will lead to as many little wars—wars that are as deadly as any war waged in the name of the one big Truth. The lesson we should learn from the encounter between Jesus, Caiaphas, and Pilate is that authentic freedom is the fruit of a double commitment to truth and to nonviolence.

---

124. Stanley Hauerwas has argued that to lose the hold on truth is to "submit to the order of violence" ("In Praise of Centesimus Annus," *Theology* 95 [1992]: 416–32).

"The truth will make you free," said Jesus. Free for what? In the light of my larger argument in this chapter, I will put it this way: free to make journeys from the self to the other and back, and to see our common history from the other's perspective as well as ours, rather than closing ourselves off and insisting on the absolute truth of our own perspective; free to live a truthful life and hence be a self-effacing witness to truth rather than fabricating our own "truths" and imposing them on others; free to embrace others in truth rather than engage in open or clandestine acts of deceitful violence against them. For the sake of *this* freedom I raise my glass and repeat the toast to the truth with some hope that my imaginary interlocutor from the introduction of this chapter will be able to join me because her misperception of my position has been removed and her objections answered—to the will to know "what was the case," to the power to remember it, to the courage to proclaim it out loud.

CHAPTER VII
Violence and Peace

Crucified Messiah, Rider on the White Horse

"And will the kingdom of truth come?" inquired Pilate of Jesus in Mikhail Bulgakov's *The Master and Margarita*. "'It will, hegemon,' replied Yeshua with conviction. 'It will never come!' Pilate suddenly shouted in a voice so terrible that Yeshua staggered back." Many years earlier, writes Bulgakov, during the fierce battle in the Valley of the Virgins at which Pilate's giant bodyguard, Muribellum, was wounded, "Pilate had shouted in that same voice to his horsemen: 'Cut them down! Cut them down!'"[1] Now as a judge, he sealed the fate of the accused with the same deadly rage. "Criminal, Criminal, Criminal," he shouted, and confirmed the sentence of death.

Just a few moments earlier, Bulgakov's Pilate had intended to clear Jesus of all criminal charges. The accusation that he had incited the people to destroy the temple in Jerusalem seemed absurd. For Pilate, Jesus was mentally ill, not a criminal. But there was one more accusation on the parchment in the scribe's hand. When he read it, blood flushed into his neck and face. "Have you ever said anything about the great Caesar? Answer! Did you say anything of the sort?" he yelled at the accused. Jesus replied,

> Among other things I said that all power is a form of violence exercised over people, and that the time will come when there will be no rule by

---

1. Mikhail Bulgakov, *The Master and Margarita*, transl. Michael Glenny (Ontario: Signet, 1967), 33.

Caesar nor any other form of rule. Man will pass into the kingdom of truth and justice where no sort of power will be needed.[2]

Now Pilate understood why "a tramp like Jesus upset the crowd in the bazaar by talking about truth."[3] In Pilate's world, truth and justice were *fruits* of Caesar's sword. In Jesus's kingdom, truth and justice were *alternatives* to Caesar's sword. It dawned on Pilate that in talking about truth and justice Jesus was after the pillar of Caesar's rule, the foundation of his truth and justice. Demented or not, Jesus was the ultimate criminal; he challenged Caesar's rule not at one or the other location, but in principle. He had to die. "Do you imagine, you miserable creature," Pilate said to Jesus after Jesus pleaded with him to let him go, "that a Roman Procurator could release a man who has said what you have said to me? Oh gods, oh gods! Or do you think I'm prepared to take your place? I don't believe in your ideas!"[4]

Bulgakov's Pilate deserves our sympathies, not because he was a good though tragically mistaken man, but because we are not much better. We may believe in Jesus, but we do not believe in his ideas, at least not in his ideas about violence, truth, and justice. Do we not live in a world of barbarians who ambushed Muribellum and threw themselves upon him like dogs at a bear, in a world of Pilate who shouted at his horsemen, "Cut them down! Cut them down! They have caught the giant Muribellum," in a world of the giant Muribellum whose whip taught Yeshua no longer to call the self-confessed "raving monster," Pilate, "a good man" but "hegemon"? How can we then truly believe that whenever one strikes us on the right cheek, we should turn the left also (Matt 6:39)? We are not quite prepared to take up our cross and follow the nonviolent Jesus. Like Matthew the Levite in Bulgakov's rendering of the story of the crucifixion, we might be fascinated enough with Jesus to steal a knife in order to cut the ropes that tied him to the cross, but, again like Bulgakov's Matthew, we will follow him only from a safe distance, afraid of sharing in his terrible fate.

In a world whose order rests on violence we instinctively grasp for the *resurrected* Messiah who was given all power in heaven and on earth (Matt 28:20). Not that we find no use for the crucified one. We only insist on a

---

2. Ibid., 32.
3. Ibid., 26.
4. Ibid., 33.

clear division of labor between the crucified one and the resurrected one. The crucified Messiah is good for the inner world of our souls tormented by guilt and abandonment. He is the Savior who dies in our place to take away our sins and liberate our conscience; he is the fellow sufferer who holds our hands as we walk through the valley of tears. But for the outer world of our embodied selves, where interests clash with interests and power crosses sword with power, we feel we need a different kind of Messiah—"the King of Kings and the Lord of Lords," who will make our wills unbending, our arms strong, our swords sharp. Superimposed on the image of the helpless Messiah hanging on the cross is the image of the victorious Rider on the white horse, his eyes "like a flame of fire" and his "robe dipped in blood," coming "to tread the wine press of the fury of the wrath of God the Almighty" (Rev 19:11-17). We will believe in the Crucified, but we want to march with the Rider.

There are many reasons why we would rather be the army of the Rider than the disciples of the Crucified. We all recoil from suffering, and many of us secretly enjoy doing violence. Yet we would be both less desirous of inflicting violence and more willing to suffer it if we lived in a world in which justice were done and truth respected. We do not, however. Without Caesar's sword, we feel, truth and justice will not reign. Thomas Hobbes might not have gotten *everything* wrong when in *Leviathan* he sought to protect humans from the chaos of mutual extermination through the power of an absolute state.[5] But as we long for Caesar's sword, we should not forget to ask whether truth and justice will reign *with* Caesar's sword. How can truth and justice be anything but deception and oppression to those who have been brought to insight by violence? Will they not reach for the sword themselves to establish *their* truth and *their* justice? The sword intended to root out violence ends up fostering it. The fear of the "chaos from below" elicits "chaos from above," which in turn perpetuates "the chaos from below."[6] We are caught in a vicious cycle: competing truths and justices call forth violence, and violence enthrones the truths and justices of its perpetrators. To avoid this cycle, must we not embrace the thought that brought Bulgakov's Jesus to the cross? If we hope for the reign of truth and justice, must we not hope for the day when the power of Caesar will be no more, when swords will be beaten into plowshares?

---

5. Thomas Hobbes, *Leviathan*, The Library of Liberal Arts, ed. Oskar Piest (Indianapolis: Bobbs Merrill, 1967).

6. Cf. Aleida Assmann and Jan Assmann, "Aspekte einer Theorie des unkommunikativen Handelns," *Kultur und Konflikt*, ed. Jan Assmann and Dietrich Harth (Frankfurt: Suhrkamp, 1990), 20.

Yes, we must *hope*. But in the meantime, we continue to live in a world that would rather stockpile swords than make enough plowshares, in which every minute the nations of the world spend 3.46 million dollars on military armaments as every hour 353 children die of hunger, according to 2018 data. Rapid population growth, ecological degradation, gross economic inequality, lack of education, migration to shanty towns, and millions of refugees are steadily increasing pressure along the many social fault lines of our globe, creating ripe conditions for more Rwandas and Bosnias in the future.[7] As violence erupts, oppression and deception will hold sway, new imbalances of power will be generated, and profound disagreements over truth and justice perpetuated. And this all will be done by big and little Caesars wielding their large and small swords. In such a world, our question cannot be whether the reign of truth and justice—the reign of God—should replace the rule of Caesar. It should—the sooner the better. Our question must be *how to live under the rule of Caesar in the absence of the reign of truth and justice.* Does the crucified Messiah have any bearing on our lives in a world of half-truths and skewed justice?

Or should we lock him up in the inner chambers of our hearts and churches, and seek in the image of the Rider on the white horse inspiration for our action in the world? Should we give up on both, abandon religion altogether, and seek resources for peace elsewhere?

Starting with some of our Enlightenment forebears who decided in favor of this last option (abandoning religion), I will first critically engage some major proposals for countering violence—universal reason as an alternative to conflict-generating particular loyalties, dialogue between religions as a supplement to reason, and debunking of both reason and religion as promoters of the "system of terror" in the name of a decentered and nonjudgmental self. In the second part I will argue that the crucified Messiah (the theology of the cross) and the Rider on the white horse (the theology of judgment) do not underwrite violence but offer important resources for living peacefully in a violent world.

Reason Against Violence

What was the dark night into which Enlightenment thinkers sought to bring their bright light? The traditional account is that the protagonists

---

7. See Paul Kennedy, *Preparing for the Twenty-First Century* (New York: Vintage Books, 1994).

of modernity dispelled the darkness of tradition and superstition with the light of scientific and philosophical reason; modern, rationally self-justifying method replaced medieval reliance on tradition. After the twentieth century, we are much less ready to associate tradition with darkness than our Enlightenment forbears were. At the same time, we have come to recognize a truly sinister darkness that served as a backdrop for the development of the modern rational method. As Stephen Toulmin argued in *Cosmopolis*, Descartes "discovered" the one correct method to acquire knowledge in a time when "over much of the continent…people had a fair chance of having their throats cut and their houses burned down by strangers who merely disliked their religion"[8] and when "Protestant and Catholic armies sought to prove theological supremacy by force of arms."[9] A new way of establishing truth "that was independent of, and neutral between, particular religious loyalties"[10] seemed an attractive alternative to war fueled by dogmatic claims. The modern trust in abstract, universal, and timeless reason was a response to social chaos created by opposing religious claims, an attempt to make an end to violence created by particular loyalties. The chaos of religious wars was, of course, not the only factor in the emergence of the Enlightenment reason. At other times and in other places religious wars had no such effects. But within the cultural matrix of the West, these wars provided a backdrop for the development of the rational method, a problem for which a solution needed to be found.

The rational method as an antidote to violence was part and parcel of the Enlightenment's optimistic vision of the civilizing process as a story of humanity emerging from pre-social barbarity into peaceful social civility. As history progresses, the argument went, all irrational and antisocial drives will be gradually suppressed and violence increasingly eliminated from social life. In the essay "What Is Enlightenment?" Immanuel Kant stated almost as a matter of incontestable fact about human nature that "men work themselves gradually out of barbarity if only intentional artifices are not made to hold them in it."[11] From this perspective, the outbursts of violence were a sign that the civilizing process had not yet been completed, a reminder that we ought to press on.

8. Stephen Toulmin, *Cosmopolis: The Hidden Agenda of Modernity* (New York: The Free Press, 1990), 17.
9. Ibid., 69.
10. Ibid., 70.
11. Immanuel Kant, *On History*, transl. Lewis White Beck et al. (Indianapolis: Bobbs-Merrill, 1963), 9.

Kant restated the same belief in the steady elimination of violence in the essay "Is the Human Race Constantly Progressing?":

> Gradually violence on the part of the powers will diminish and obedience to the laws will increase. There will arise in the body politic perhaps more charity and less strife in lawsuits, more reliability in keeping one's word, etc., partly out of love of honor, partly out of well-understood self interest. And eventually this will also extend to nations in their external relations toward one another up to the realization of the cosmopolitan society.[12]

In the conclusion to the same essay, Kant tells a story of a doctor who consoled his patients from one day to the next with hopes of a speedy recovery, "pledging to one that his pulse beat better, to another an improvement in his stool, to a third the same regarding his perspiration, etc." One day the doctor received a visit from one of his friends. "How's your illness, my friend?" was the doctor's first question. "How should it be? I'm dying of improvement, pure and simple."[13] After telling the story, Kant brushed it aside as a parable of how humanity's modern doctors treat their patients. Instead, he suggested that the painful consequence of wars should "compel the political prophet to confess a very imminent turn of humanity toward the better."[14] Today, two centuries later and two world wars, the Holocaust, and many other atrocities wiser, we wish Kant had told the story at the beginning of his essay, and proceeded to tell us how we should live so as to avoid dying of improvement.

In *The Civilizing Process*, written at the eve of World War II, Norbert Elias argued that the modern organization of society entails a taming of instincts and hence reduction of aggressiveness and violence.[15] His thesis was simple: the more people are interdependent, the less spontaneous they can be, and the less spontaneous they are, the less aggressive they will be because their behavior will be regulated by a plethora of rules and regulations. The state now has a monopoly on the violence with which people previously fought for their position in society. A "continuous, uniform pressure is exerted on individual life by the physical violence stored

---

12. Ibid., 151.
13. Ibid., 153.
14. Ibid., 154.
15. Norbert Elias, *The Civilizing Process: The History of Manners and State Formation and Civilization*, transl. Edmund Jephcott (Oxford: Blackwell, 1994).

behind the scenes of everyday life,"[16] which diminishes unpredictable physical violence. As a result, he argued, modern societies are more peaceful and therefore more civilized than premodern ones.

Elias offered a sociological explanation of the Enlightenment pledges that, symptoms notwithstanding, humanity is in fact gradually emerging from presocial barbarity to peaceful coexistence. The notion that the "civilizing process" entails reduction in violence has proven a naive myth, however. Notice the obvious: the state monopoly on violence does not necessarily entail the *reduction* of violence as such, but the reduction of *irregular* violence. Anthony Giddens has argued that whatever "internal pacification" exists in modern nation states, it has been intimately associated with a thoroughgoing militarization of intersocietal exchange and the inner-societal production of order.[17] One may have good reasons to prefer the "civilized" violence of nation states to the "uncivilized" violence of "tribal" wars with its massacres and the rule of terror, but one should not mistake it for nonviolence. Moreover, it is not clear at all that in the societies that have been "pacified" by the state's monopoly on power violence has diminished.[18] Hans Peter Duerr's *Obszönität und Gewalt* (Obscenity and Violence)—one in a series of volumes under the title "The Myth of the Civilizing Process"—represents one massive argument that aggression and cruelty, and the enjoyment of those, have not decreased in modern societies.[19]

It is ironic that Elias formulated his vison of the "civilizing process" at the same time that the horrors of the Holocaust were being concocted (1939). Granted, against the unwavering belief in the progressive elimination of violence, the Holocaust could appear as "an irrational outflow of the not-yet-fully-eradicated residues of premodern barbarity," as Zygmunt Bauman, a critic, puts it.[20] The appearance proves illusory as soon as we invert the interpretative relation between modernity and the Holocaust. Instead of trying to fit the Holocaust into our preconceived notions about progress, we need to ask how the Holocaust should impact these notions. Against the brutal reality of the Holocaust, belief in the progressive

---

16. Ibid., 238.

17. Anthony Giddens, *The Nation-State and Violence* (Berkeley: University of California Press, 1985).

18. Hannah Arendt has argued that "the greater the bureaucratization of public life, the greater will be the attraction of violence" (*On Violence* [New York: Harcourt, Brace & World, 1970], 81).

19. Hans Peter Duerr, *Obszönität und Gewalt: Der Mythos vom Zivilisationsprozeß* (Frankfurt: Suhrkamp, 1993).

20. Zygmunt Bauman, *Modernity and the Holocaust* (Ithaca, NY: Cornell University Press, 1989), 17.

elimination of violence appears more as a modern superstition than as truth about progress in history.

In *Modernity and the Holocaust* Bauman himself has persuasively argued that the Holocaust is not a foreign intruder into the house of modernity, but "a legitimate resident...indeed, one who would not be at home in any other house."[21] Modernity made the Holocaust possible, argues Bauman, and it contained no effective mechanisms to prevent it from happening. In Bauman's view, the culprit was the typically modern "bureaucratic culture." Explaining his position, he writes,

> I suggest...that the bureaucratic culture, which prompts us to view society as an object of administration, as a collection of so many "problems" to be solved, as "nature" to be "controlled," "mastered," and "improved" or "remade," as a legitimate target for "social engineering," and in general a garden to be designed and kept in the planned shape by force (the gardening posture divides vegetation into "cultured plants" to be taken care of, and weeds to be exterminated), was the very atmosphere in which the idea of the Holocaust could be conceived, slowly yet consistently developed, and brought to its conclusion. I also suggest that it was the spirit of instrumental rationality, and its modern, bureaucratic form of institutionalization, which had made the Holocaust-style solutions not only possible, but eminently "reasonable"—and increased the probability of their choice. This increase in probability is more than fortuitously related to the ability of modern bureaucracy to co-ordinate the action of a great number of moral individuals in the pursuit of any, also immoral ends.[22]

Instead of evicting violence from social life, the modern "civilizing" process, Bauman claims, only redeployed it in new locations where it continued with the same destructive and murderous work. By "substituting artificial and flexible patterns of human conduct for natural drives" modernity has "made possible a scale of inhumanity and destruction which had remained inconceivable as long as natural predispositions guided human action";[23] the bureaucracy and technology of the modern state made the scale of barbarity so horrifyingly unique.

On the grounds that "moral inhibitions do not act at a distance" and that "commitment to immoral acts...becomes easier with every inch of

21. Ibid.
22. Ibid., 17f.
23. Ibid., 95.

social distance," Bauman expects improvement from letting "natural pre-dispositions" play themselves out in situations of "human proximity."[24] The expectation would seem justified insofar as killing at a distance does indeed come easier—when you "never have to look your victim in the eyes," when you "count dots on the screen, not corpses."[25] Yet even if distance kills moral responsibility, it does not follow that proximity restores it. Against Bauman, Arne Vetlesen has argued in *Perception, Empathy, and Judgment* that "there is no *necessary* correlation between human proximity and moral conduct.... Proximity interacts with a number of factors; it does not by itself bring about, does not by itself account for, moral conduct or lack of it."[26] Whether we like it or not, it is not an exception but a rule that human beings destroy what they hate, and what they hate most is a rival on their own territory.[27] Bauman's analysis of the interrelation between modernity and the Holocaust underlines correctly, however, that we should not expect peace from "civilization," certainly not from modern rational and bureaucratic civilization. Richard L. Rubenstein has correctly observed that civilization means not only "medical hygiene, elevated religious ideas, beautiful art, and exquisite music," but also "slavery, wars, exploitation, and death camps. It is an error to imagine," he concludes, "that civilization and savage cruelty are antitheses."[28] "Civilization" is a deeply ambiguous process (see Chapter III).

Warring Peoples, Bellicose Gods

Modernity has failed to deliver on the promise of peace. It has also failed to displace religion in the name of reason. This brings us back to the question of how religion is related to the unabating violence in contemporary societies. The answer depends partly on the place of religion in these societies.

In the non-Western world we have witnessed a veritable resurgence of religion as a political force. As Mark Juergensmeyer observes in *The New Cold War,*

24. Ibid., 192.
25. Zygmunt Bauman, *Life in Fragments: Essays in Postmodern Morality* (Oxford: Blackwell, 1995), 150.
26. Arne Johan Vetlesen, *Perception, Empathy, and Judgment: An Inquiry into the Preconditions of Moral Performance* (University Park: The Pennsylvania State University Press, 1994), 275.
27. Hans Magnus Enzensberger, *Aussichten auf den Bürgerkrieg* (Frankfurt: Suhrkamp, 1993), 11.
28. Richard L. Rubenstein, *The Cunning of History* (New York: Harper, 1978), 91.

The new world order that is replacing the bipolar powers of the old Cold War is characterized not only by the rise of new economic forces, a crumbling of old empires, and the discrediting of communism, but also by the resurgence of parochial identities based on ethnic and religious allegiances.[29]

In many parts of the non-Western world religion is reasserting itself in public life. Attempts are made to fuse religious and political identities, partly in order to complete the process of cultural liberation from secular Western colonialism. In situations of conflict, religion then becomes a potent force for legitimizing the use of violence for political ends. Christians may wear an oversized cross and Muslims a replica of the Koran around the neck, and by ostentatiously announcing a religious conviction they will be making an unmistakably political assertion not only about who they are but also in what name they are fighting.

Things are somewhat more complex in the so-called advanced industrial societies. As James A. Beckford has argued in *Religion and Advanced Industrial Society*, the dominant ways of understanding the relation between religion and society—religion as ideology that masks the material interests of classes, religion as a system of social integration, and religion as a provider of normative guidelines for action and of the ultimate ground of meaning—will not work for advanced industrial societies.[30] I do not need here to go into his reasons why this is the case, not even into those that I find unpersuasive. For my purposes here, more significant than his critique is his positive suggestion as to how we should think of the place of religion in modern societies.

Unlike sociologists who consign religion to the margins of the modern world, Beckford argues for its continued relevance, though less as a social institution than as a *cultural resource*. He writes,

The post-Second World War transformation of the kind of industrial society envisaged by sociologists in the early twentieth century has tended to undermine the communal, familial, and organizational bases of religion. But religious forms of sentiment, belief, and action have survived as relatively autonomous resources. They retain the capacity to symbolize, for example, ultimate meaning, infinite power, supreme

---

29. Mark Juergensmeyer, *The New Cold War? Religious Nationalism Confronts the Secular State* (Berkeley: University of California Press, 1993), 1f.

30. James A. Beckford, *Religion and Advanced Industrial Society* (London: Unwin Hyman, 1989).

indignation, and sublime compassion. And they can be deployed in the service of virtually any interest group or ideal.... Religion can be combined with virtually any other set of ideas or values. And the chances that religion will be controversial are increased by the fact that it may be used by people having little or no connection with formal religious organizations. The deregulation of religion is one of the hidden ironies of secularization.[31]

One could argue about whether it is adequate to concentrate only on the social uses to which religions are put while disregarding the question of their truth content. One could also question whether every religion can be combined with any set of ideas or values. But even if Beckford has overstated his case, as I believe he has, his stress on the variety of uses to which religion can be put in modern societies is important. The loss of great religious monopolies in the West and the deregulation of religion does not necessarily imply a lesser role of religion in social conflicts. Rather, as the spread of pluralism and relativism eats away at the internal unity of societies, religious symbols can continue to be used in the conflicts between various social groups. As long as religious symbols continue to capture the imagination of people and as long as societies remain conflict-ridden, people will seek to draw religious symbols into their conflicts, to use them as weapons in their wars. How can you resist making your gods, your symbols of ultimate meaning, fight for you when the life of your family or your country is at stake!? You cannot—unless your god refuses to fight.

Religion is alive and well in today's world, and so is violence. Moreover, it would seem that both can work together today, sowing desolation as they have done throughout human history. On the double assumption that religions are an important factor in public life and that "the most fanatical, the cruelest political struggles are those that have been colored, inspired, and legitimized by religion,"[32] Hans Küng has argued over the years that peace cannot be promoted "against the religions but only with them."[33] In theological circles his slogan linking world peace to religious peace has acquired the status of a truism: "There can be no peace among nations without peace among the religions."[34] Since religious peace can be

---

31. Ibid., 171f.
32. Hans Küng et al., *Christianity and World Religions: Paths to Dialogue with Islam, Hinduism, and Buddhism*, transl. Peter Heinegg (Maryknoll, NY: Orbis, 1993), 442.
33. Hans Küng, *Global Responsibility: In Search for a New World Ethic*, transl. John Bowden (New York: Continuum, 1993), 89.
34. Ibid., 76.

established only through religious dialogue,[35] Küng believes that reconciliation between the peoples depends on the success of the inter-religious dialogue.

At one level Küng's thesis is hard to argue against. The majority of the world's population is religious, and when they are at war, their gods are invariably at war too. It would seem that if we reconciled the gods we would come closer to reconciling the peoples. The question is, however, who is fighting whose battles in those wars? Are the peoples fighting the battles of their power-hungry gods or are the gods fighting the battles of their bellicose peoples? The two are not mutually exclusive, of course. My suspicion is, however, that the gods mostly get the short end of it: they end up doing more of the dirty work for their presumed earthly servants than their servants do for them. And when the gods refuse to do the dirty work most people involved in conflicts either discard them in favor of more compliant gods or seek to reeducate them, which amounts to the same thing. The poor gods! What they have to endure at the hands of their humble devotees!

To test whether my sympathy for the abused gods is in order let us stipulate a world in which *various gods* do not fight each other. It would be a world in which various religions—various sets of beliefs and practices—exist peacefully side by side. Although each *may* make the claim that it is truer than the others, each shares the belief that all others deserve respect. One cannot wish for more with respect to reconciliation between religions—unless one is interested in reducing all religions to a single religion (by advocating either the old-style exclusivism or the new-style inclusivism), or seeing in each concrete religion a culturally conditioned manifestation of a single common religious commitment (say, by advocating a Hickian kind of pluralism)[36]—all options Küng rightly finds unpersuasive.[37] No doubt, the world of reconciled religions would be more peaceful than the one we inhabit. Religious intolerance is a factor in fomenting conflict. Would people stop fighting and become reconciled, however, if their religions were reconciled? Of course not. There are plenty of worshippers of one and the same god, adherents of one and the same religion, who fight each other to the point of extermination, each believing that his or her common god is on his or her side, fighting in his or her

---

35. Ibid., 105.

36. John Hick, *An Interpretation of Religion: Human Responses to the Transcendent* (New Haven: Yale University Press, 1989).

37. Küng, *Global Responsibility*, 78ff.

battles. People sometimes do fight because their gods fight. As a rule, however, their gods fight because people are at war with each other. Whether or not they believe in the *same* god makes little difference.

The thesis that there can be no peace in the world without peace among religions is true, but much less significant than its high-sounding character would have us believe. Peace among religions would do little to create peace among peoples—unless, of course, one understands peace among religions as peace among *people* who espouse them, in which case the thesis is trite. The only thing peace among religions would prevent is strictly religious wars. In terms of fostering peace the issue of reconciliation among religions as systems of beliefs and practices is less important than *the character of each religion*. How ready are its gods to get involved in the conflicts of their worshippers? If each religion foments violence, reconciliation among them will do little to foster peace. On the other hand, even if religious beliefs and the practices of concrete religions are at odds with each other, if each of them promotes nonviolence one will hardly be able to accuse them together of fostering war. If peace is what we are after, then a critique of the religious legitimation of violence—the critique of bellicose gods—is more urgent than reconciliation among religions.

Hans Küng has done much not only to promote dialogue among religions but also to underline that nonviolence is at the heart of many religions. A Declaration of the Parliament of the World's Religions,[38] which Küng drafted, contains as the first of its four "irrevocable directives" the "commitment to a culture of nonviolence and respect for life."[39] Notice, however, how the commitment is fleshed out: "Persons who hold political power must work within the framework of a just order and commit themselves to the most nonviolent, peaceful solutions possible."[40] Though significant, the espousal of "*the most* nonviolent solutions *possible*" is beset by precisely the kind of ambiguity that we observe in many religions (including Christianity) in relation to nonviolence. Religions advocate nonviolence in general, while at the same time finding ways to legitimate violence in specific situations; their representatives both preach against war and bless the weapons of their nation's troops. And so the deep religious wisdom about nonviolence boils down to a principle that no self-respecting warlord will deny, namely that you can be violent whenever you cannot

---

38. Hans Küng and Karl-Josef Kuschel, eds., *A Global Ethic: The Declaration of the Parliament of the World's Religions* (New York: Continuum, 1993).

39. Ibid., 24.

40. Ibid., 25.

be nonviolent, provided your goals are just (which they usually are for the simple reason that they are yours). Religious dialogue or no religious dialogue, without the principled assertion that it *is never appropriate to use religion to give moral sanction to the use of violence*, religious images and religious leaders will continue to be exploited by politicians and generals engaged in violence.

Cosmic Terror

Why is it so difficult for religious people to espouse principled non-violence even when the virtue of nonviolence is essential to their system of beliefs? Is it simply because they are not able to resist the logic of violence in a world of bloodshed and therefore renege on their beliefs when their interests demand it? Could it be that their religions themselves are violent at heart,[41] their deeper structure promoting what their surface statements seek to prevent? Do they not all speak of cosmic struggle?[42] What is to prevent ritual enactments of this struggle from underwriting political violence? Are not divine cosmic violence and human social violence correlates?

I cannot speak for all religions. My purpose is to take a brief look at the deeper structure of Christian faith and inquire about its relation to violence. I will let a sharp critic of what he calls Christian "cosmic terror" speak first. His name is Gilles Deleuze, and the immediate object of his critique is the book of Revelation. His target, though, is nothing less than the Christian faith as a whole. Both in content and strategy, moreover, his attack on the Christian faith parallels the attack that he and other postmodern thinkers level against modernity. Modernity's universal reason and Christianity's absolute God are but two manifestations, sacred and secular, of one and the same system of terror. For the sake of human freedom, they argue, we need to deconstruct both modern reason and ancient religion.

In the essay "Nietzsche and Paul, Lawrence and John of Patmos," Deleuze argues that Revelation contains a message from the heart of the poor and the weak. Following Nietzsche,[43] he contends that these people are

---

41. Maurice Bloch, *Prey into Hunter: The Politics of Religious Experience* (Cambridge: Cambridge University Press, 1992).

42. Juergensmeyer, *The New Cold War?*

43. Friedrich Nietzsche, *The Birth of Tragedy and The Genealogy of Morals*, transl. Francis Golffing (Garden City: Doubleday, 1956), 258ff.

not the humble and the unfortunate one often thinks they are. They are teeming with resentment and vindictiveness. But do they not dream of the New Jerusalem, the city of light, of truth, and of justice? Yes, and this is precisely where the problem lies. Deleuze writes:

> There is maybe a slight similarity between Hitler and Antichrist, but there is much similarity between the New Jerusalem and the future promised to us not only in science-fiction but even more in the military-industrial planning of the absolute world-government. The Apocalypse is not the concentration camp (Antichrist); it is the big military, police, and civil security of the new state (heavenly Jerusalem). The modernity of the Apocalypse does not lie in the catastrophes that it announces, but in the programmed self-glorification, in the glorious establishment of the new Jerusalem, in the mad construction of a final juridical and moral rule....Without intending to do so, the Apocalypse is persuading us that the worst thing is not the Antichrist, but that new city that is coming down from heaven, the holy city.... Every half witted reader of the Apocalypse feels that he is already in the lake of sulfur.[44]

Why does Deleuze think that walking the golden streets of the city of light is no better than the torture in the fiery lake of burning sulfur? Why does he insist that the company of the beast and the false prophet is no worse than fellowship with God and the Lamb?

Deleuze gives two interrelated reasons. Put simply, the first is that the New Jerusalem is totalitarian; it stands for an absolute juridical and moral rule. The totalitarianism of the New Jerusalem is more sinister than the open dictatorship characterized by a thoroughgoing monism and the all-encompassing control of society by the state. Its subjects are ruled *from inside* by a power that seeks to permeate all pores of reality, to enter every corner and every dark niche until it has filled the whole universe. Moreover, one can make no appeal to higher gods; the one God is the final judge over all other powers.[45] In the New Jerusalem there is no place to hide and no higher court to which to appeal; God sees and judges everything. People immersed "in a field of total visibility" and forced to interiorize the judgments of the final absolute arbiter! If you call this heaven, how will you distinguish it from hell? A close friend of

---

44. Gilles Deleuze, *Kleine Schriften*, transl. K. D. Schacht (Berlin: Minerva, 1980), 114. Deleuze's reflections on Revelation are given in the context of an analysis of D. H. Lawrence's commentary on the Apocalypse. I treat the text simply as an expression of Deleuze's views.

45. Ibid., 102.

Deleuze, Michel Foucault, describes precisely in these terms the ultimate prison, Bentham's "panoptikon."[46]

The second reason for Deleuze's rebellion against the holy city is that the bright light of the New Jerusalem can shine only after the whole universe has been enveloped in the darkness of death. Echoing Nietzsche's claim that early Christians, those "holy anarchists," made it "an 'act of piety' to destroy 'the world,'"[47] Deleuze interprets the vision of the heavenly New Jerusalem as the flip side of the cosmic terror about which the poor and the weak so readily dream. They will damn the whole world to destruction in order to get revenge against their enemies. And then on top of it all they will insist on calling this deadly will "justice" and "holiness"![48] To put Deleuze's two objections against the New Jerusalem together, the Christian heaven is not only indistinguishable from hell but emerges from the cosmic terror that masks itself as the execution of final truth and justice.

Strangely enough, the executor of the cosmic terror that destroys the world and recreates it according to its own will is *the Lamb*. But then, it is a strange Lamb that we encounter in Revelation—"a lamb with horns that roars like a lion,"[49] "a carnivorous lamb."[50] Never mind that it looks "slain." It only wears the mask of a victim to hide the hangman's face so as to free his death-dealing hand. In the final chapters of Revelation, the mask comes down and the innocent Lamb emerges as the Rider on a white horse who will "trample the winepress of the Almighty God's passionate anger" and wears "a robe dyed with blood" (Rev 19:13, 15 CEB). True, the Lamb is said to execute righteous judgment. But what is the content of this judgment? Deleuze answers, nothing but "will to destroy, will to crawl into every corner, the will always to have the last word: the threefold will that is only a single will, Father, Son, and Holy Spirit."[51] And so the poor, their Lamb, and their God are all best portrayed with the image of a "man with the sword between his teeth."[52]

---

46. Michel Foucault, *Power/Knowledge: Selected Interviews and Other Writings 1972–1977*, transl. Colin Gordon et al. (New York: Pantheon Books, 1980), 153ff.

47. Friedrich Nietzsche, *Twilight of the Idols and The Anti-Christ*, transl. R. J. Hollingdale (London: Penguin, 1990), 192.

48. Deleuze, *Kleine Schriften*, 113.

49. Ibid., 101.

50. Ibid., 102.

51. Ibid., 103.

52. Ibid., 121.

Do not the Gospels paint a different picture, however? At first sight, John of Patmos and Jesus of Nazareth seem indeed like irreconcilable contrasts. According to Deleuze, Jesus is full of love and his message is directed to the individual; John dreams of cosmic terror and addresses the collective soul of the masses. The religion of personal love stands over against the religion of collective violence. The contrast is, however, not incompatibility. As opposites, the Christ of the Gospels and the Christ of the Apocalypse belong to each other "more than if they were one and the same person."[53] They are two sides of the same coin. When the Christ of the Apocalypse destroys the world brutally and reconstructs a new one according to his will, he takes without wanting to give. When the Jesus of the Gospels loves selflessly, he gives without wanting to take. In Revelation, the masses get whipped out of existence; in the Gospels, Jesus of Nazareth is engaged in a suicidal mission. In both, violence and death reign. The apocalyptic destruction of the world grows in soil prepared by the evangelical sacrifice of the self. As Michel Foucault observed, genocide and total self-sacrifice are never far apart.[54]

According to Deleuze, the "I," the "subject," is the bloodthirsty culprit that does the sacrificing both of the self and the other. A stable self sows death wherever it turns. Why? Deleuze gives two answers. First, a stable subject (an "I") invariably makes judgments by using codes of symbolic representation. Every time a physical relationship is translated into a logical relationship, a stream has been cut into segments, a living thing has been killed.[55] Thinking and setting goals are by their very nature repressive. Deleuze therefore recommends to "stop thinking of oneself as an 'I' in order to live as a current, as a bundle of currents in relation to other currents inside and outside of oneself."[56] Second, the unity of the rational self corresponds to the unity of the world, and the unity of the world can be achieved only by suppression of multiplicity. Deleuze therefore insists that we should give primacy to the multiplicity; unity is nothing but an unacceptable reduction in multiplicity.

Deleuze's solution to the problem of cosmic terror seeks to make three elegant steps: no subject—no setting of boundaries by making judgments—no terror. It trips, however, before it has come to the second. One

53. Ibid., 121.
54. Michel Foucault, *History of Sexuality. Volume I: Introduction*, transl. Robert Hurley (New York: Random House, 1978), 149f.
55. Deleuze, *Kleine Schriften*, 125.
56. Ibid., 124.

cannot negate the "I"—one's own "I"—without in the same act affirming it. Who would be doing the job of negating? To put it slightly differently, Deleuze "cannot include the self out of which he speaks in explaining himself" within his own philosophical narrative, as Alasdair MacIntyre has argued.[57] Even if Deleuze managed to make the first step, he would trip in making the second. As I argued earlier (Chapter III), without boundaries we would have chaos; there would be no streams but an undifferentiated ocean flowing in all directions, which is to say not flowing at all.[58] If we seek to avoid all judgments, how do we avoid reaching the "deadly point" at which, as Deleuze himself puts it, "everything mixes with everything else without any measure"?[59]

For the sake of argument let us grant, however, that Deleuze was successful in making the first two steps. Would these two steps place us in a position from which we could make the decisive third step? Does freedom from terror follow? By no means. Without use of symbolic codes, without judgments, all we would have is the wild flow of desire. One should not mistake this unreflexive immediacy for absence of violence. To the contrary. As Jean Paul Sartre argued, the option for immediacy and the absence of communication is the source of violence.[60] If one *thinks* one has negated the "I," one will eschew judgment, but terror will remain. The one thing worse than terror resulting from the system of judgment is terror without any judgment: heads roll, but you can tell neither when, nor where, nor why. Moreover, without a system of judgment we would have no way of struggling against oppression and deception because we could not distinguish between the Butcher of Lyon and Mother Teresa. Whoever wants to replace the "subject" of critical reflection with "streams" of desire must affirm the world the way he or she finds it, with all its gruesome violence. The attempt to transcend judgment—whether it be judgment of reason or of religion—does not eliminate but enthrones violence. The escape from the castle of (judging) conscience lands one in the castle of murders.[61]

---

57. Alasdair MacIntyre, *Three Rival Versions of Moral Enquiry: Encyclopaedia, Genealogy, and Tradition* (Notre Dame, IN: University of Notre Dame Press, 1990), 210.

58. Manfred Frank, *Was ist Neostrukturalismus?* (Frankfurt: Suhrkamp, 1984), 431.

59. Deleuze, *Kleine Schriften*, 117.

60. Cf. Frank, *Was ist Neostrukturalismus?*, 412.

61. James E. Miller, *Passion of Michel Foucault* (New York: Simon & Shuster, 1993), 115. In *Life in Fragments* Zygmunt Bauman has argued that on account of "disengagement and commitment-avoidance" of typically postmodern (in sociological sense) "sensation-gathering consumers," violence "may return to the sites from which the 'civilizing process' promised to evict it forever: to the neighborhood, to the

It may be relatively easy to show that Deleuze's solution to the problem of violence is wrongheaded, that his alternative is worse than what he rejects. But when we are done deconstructing Deleuze, we have not yet defended the Christian faith from the devastating critique he leveled against it. Is Christian faith implicated in promoting violence not simply at the level of isolated and accidental beliefs but at its very core? Are not its images of God's new world profoundly oppressive? Does that world not come about through an act of unprecedented violence? The serious challenge that Deleuze poses is *whether one can have ultimate judgment against terror without the terror of judgment.* Can Christian faith affirm judgment about truth and justice and deny violence? As you will recall, this is precisely what the Jesus of Bulgakov's *The Master and Margarita* does. He *contrasts* the kingdom of truth and justice with the kingdom of violence. Will a closer look at Revelation and at the Gospels bear Bulgakov's interpretation out?

Breaking the Cycle of Violence

Though not its dominant theme, violence provides a backdrop for much of the New Testament narrative. The drama of salvation starts and ends with violence, and without violence its central act is unthinkable. On the first pages of the New Testament, when Jesus Christ enters the stage of history, King Herod, fearing for his throne, slaughters the innocents to eliminate a potential rival (Matt 2); on its last pages, when history finally comes to an end, a great war takes place in which Jesus Christ casts the beast and the false prophet into the fiery lake and kills their followers with the sword of his mouth (Rev 19). And in the central act of the New Testament drama, the rulers of this age plan and execute the brutal murder of Jesus Christ using a mock trial to give it political legitimacy.

A Christian perspective on violence must be won by reflecting on attitudes to violence in this whole drama of Jesus Christ's coming into the world, living in it, and judging it. It will not do simply to pick out Jesus's individual statements about how his disciples should take a sword (Luke 22:36) but not use it (Matt 26:52), to look at Paul's instruction about how a sword-bearing state is a servant of God (Rom 13:1-5) although Christians are "never to avenge themselves, but leave room for the wrath

---

family, to the couple partnerships—the traditional sites of moral proximity and face-to-face encounter" (124, 156).

of God" (Rom 12:19), or to reflect on the failure of John the Baptist to tell the soldiers that they should give up their jobs (Luke 3:14). Each of these texts is significant in its own right, but none of them compare in importance to what is inscribed in the key junctures in the drama of Jesus Christ, notably the cross and the second coming. I will briefly reflect on the violence that Jesus Christ as the crucified Messiah suffered and the violence that he as the triumphant Rider on the white horse is said to inflict.

According to Deleuze, it will be remembered, the selfless love of the earthly Jesus prepares the way for the terror of the heavenly Lord because the denial of the self is the first step in the erasure of the self, both one's own self and that of another. Does Deleuze's reading of the story make sense, however? It does not. The cross was not a tragic result of the kind of self-denial that underwrites violence, but a likely end to a life of a self engaged in the struggle for God's peace in a world of violence. Consider the following four ways in which the crucified Messiah challenges violence.

First, the cross *breaks the cycle of violence.* Hanging on the cross, Jesus provided the ultimate example of his command to replace the principle of retaliation ("an eye for an eye and a tooth for a tooth") with the principle of nonresistance ("if anyone strikes you on the right cheek, turn the other also" (Matt 5:39). By suffering violence as an innocent victim, he took upon himself the aggression of the persecutors. He broke the vicious cycle of violence by absorbing it, taking it upon himself.[62] He refused to be sucked into the automatism of revenge, but sought to overcome evil by doing good—even at the cost of his life. Jesus's kind of option for nonviolence had nothing to do with the self-abnegation in which I completely place myself at the disposal of others to do with me as they please; it had much to do with the kind of self-assertion in which I refuse to be ensnared in the dumb redoubling of my enemies' violent gestures and be reshaped into their mirror image. No, the crucified Messiah is not a concealed legitimation of the system of terror, but its radical critique. Far from enthroning violence, the sacralization of him as victim subverts violence.

Second, the cross *lays bare the mechanism of scapegoating.* All the accounts of Jesus's death agree that he suffered *unjust* violence. His persecutors believed in the excellence of their cause, but in reality hated without a cause. Jesus was a scapegoat. To say, however, that Jesus was hated without a cause—that he was an innocent victim—is not to say that he was an

---

62. See Michael Welker's discussion of the powerlessness as a political stance (*God the Spirit*, transl. John F. Hoffmeyer [Minneapolis: Fortress, 1994], 128ff.).

arbitrarily chosen victim, as René Girard, who proposed the theory of scapegoating, claims.[63] In a world of deception and oppression, his innocence—his truthfulness and his justice—was reason enough for hatred. Jesus *was* a threat, and precisely because of his threatening innocence, he was chosen also as a scapegoat. In *The Scapegoat* Girard has rightly emphasized, however, that one of the functions of the Gospel accounts is to demask the mechanism of scapegoating.[64] Instead of taking the perspective of the persecutors, the Gospels take the perspective of the victim; they "constantly reveal what the texts of historical persecutors, and especially mythological persecutors, hide from us: the knowledge that their victim is a scapegoat."[65]

For Girard the identification of a victim as a scapegoat has the significance of a revelation:

> Once understood, the mechanisms can no longer operate; we believe less and less in the culpability of the victims they demand. Deprived of the food that sustains them, the institutions derived from these mechanisms collapse one after the other about us. Whether we know it or not, the Gospels are responsible for this collapse.[66]

Though demasking the scapegoating mechanism is significant enough, Girard expects too much from it. Even if we grant the questionable assumption that the misrecognition of the scapegoating mechanism is essential for its functioning,[67] Girard takes too lightly people's tendency to remask what has been demasked when it fits their interests. Moreover, though Jesus was innocent, not all who suffer violence are innocent. The tendency of persecutors to blame victims is reinforced by the actual guilt of victims, even if the guilt is minimal and they incur it in reaction to the original violence committed against them. Demasking the scapegoating mechanism will not suffice.

Are the strategies of "absorbing" and "demasking" the only ways Jesus fought violence? Is the suffering of violence, paradoxically, the only cure

---

63. Paul Dumouchel, "Introduction," *Violence and Truth: On the Work of René Girard*, ed. Paul Dumouchel (Stanford: Stanford University Press, 1988), 13f.

64. René Girard, *The Scapegoat*, transl. Yvonne Freccero (Baltimore: The Johns Hopkins University Press, 1986), 100ff.

65. Ibid., 117.

66. Ibid., 101.

67. Henri Atlan, "Founding Violence and Divine Referent," *Violence and Truth: On the Work of René Girard*, ed. Paul Dumouchel (Stanford: Stanford University Press, 1988).

against it? Certainly not. The cross is, third, part of Jesus's *struggle* for God's truth and justice. Jesus's mission certainly did not consist merely in passively receiving violence. The cry of anguish to an absent God was not Jesus's only utterance; falling under the weight of the cross on the road to execution was not his only accomplishment. If Jesus had done nothing but suffer violence, we would have forgotten him as we have forgotten so many other innocent victims. The mechanism of scapegoating would not have been demasked by his suffering, and violence not diminished by his nonresistance. The pure negativity of nonviolence is barren because it shies away from "transgressing" into the territory of the system of terror. At best, oppressors can safely disregard it; at worst, they can see themselves indirectly justified by it. To be significant, nonviolence must be part of a larger strategy of combating the system of terror.

Is not the language of "struggle" and "combat" inappropriate, however? Does it not run at cross-purposes with nonviolence? Consider the fact that Jesus's public ministry—his proclamation and enactment of the reign of God as the reign of God's truth and God's justice—was not a drama played out on an empty stage, vacated by other voices and actors. An empty stage was unavailable to him, as it is unavailable to us. It was there only in the beginning, before the dawn of creation. On the empty stage of nonexistence, God enacted the drama of creation—and the world came into being. Every subsequent drama is performed on an occupied stage; all spectators are performers. Especially in a creation infested with sin, the proclamation and enactment of the kingdom of truth and justice is never an act of pure positing, but always already a transgression into spaces occupied by others. Active opposition to the kingdom of Satan, the kingdom of deception and oppression, is therefore inseparable from the proclamation of the kingdom of God. It is this opposition that brought Jesus Christ to the cross; and it is this opposition that gave meaning to his nonviolence. It takes the struggle against deception and oppression to transform nonviolence from barren negativity into a creative possibility, from quicksand into the foundation of a new world.

Fourth, the cross is a *divine embrace of the deceitful and the unjust*. One way to embrace the evildoers would be simply "to act as if their sin was not there," as John Milbank has suggested in *Theology and Social Theory*.[68] Jesus on the cross would then be our model. Like him we would say of

---

68. John Milbank, *Theology and Social Theory: Beyond Secular Reason* (Oxford: Blackwell, 1990), 411.

Violence and Peace

the perpetrators, "Father, forgive them; for they do not know what they are doing" (Luke 23:34). In an act of sheer grace, justice and truth would be suspended, and a reconciling embrace take place. We seriously misconstrue forgiveness, however, if we understand it as acting "as if the sin was not there" (see Chapter IV).[69] More significantly, whereas the suspension of truth and justice in an act of forgiveness is meant to help create a new world, such suspension in fact *presupposes* a new world, a *world without deception and injustice.* Suspend justice and truth, and you cannot redeem the world; you must leave it as it is. Acting "as if not" in the face of sin might indeed anticipate heaven in which there will be no sin, as Milbank argues. However, the price of such anticipation is abandonment of the world to the darkness of hell; the world will remain forever awry, the blood of the innocent will eternally cry out to heaven. There can be no redemption unless the truth about the world is told and justice is done. To treat sin as if it were not there, when in fact it is there, amounts to living as if the world were redeemed when in fact it is not. The claim to redemption has degenerated into an empty ideology, and a dangerous one at that.[70]

There is a profound wisdom about the nature of our world in the simple credo of the early church "that Christ died for our sins" (1 Cor 15:3). At the core of Christian faith lies the claim that God entered history and died on the cross in the person of Jesus Christ for an unjust and deceitful world. In taking upon himself the sin of the world, God told the truth about the deceitful world and enthroned justice in an unjust world. When God was made sin in Christ (2 Cor 5:21), the world of deceit and injustice was set aright. Sins were atoned for. The cry of the innocent blood was attended to. Since the new world has become reality in the crucified and resurrected Christ (2 Cor 5:17), it is possible to live the new world in the midst of the old in an act of gratuitous forgiveness without giving up the struggle for truth and justice. One can embrace perpetrators in forgiveness because God has embraced them through atonement. In the wake of Girard's theory of scapegoating, James G. Williams has argued in *The Bible, Violence, and the Sacred* that in the biblical texts "sacrificial language is

---

69. In *Embodying Forgiveness: A Theological Analysis* (Grand Rapids: Eerdmans, 1995), Gregory Jones has rightly argued against Milbank that we can genuinely achieve reconciliation only "by acknowledging that their sin is there, but dealing with it through a judgment of grace" (146 n4).

70. Acting "as if not" in the face of sin—one might call this "redemption through disregard"—is too close for comfort to Nietzsche's reconstruction of the "psychology of the redeemer" in *The Anti-Christ.* There too, one lives "in order to feel oneself 'in Heaven'"; there is no struggle, but not because the evil has been overcome, but because "the concept of sin" has been abolished; the 'glad tidings' are precisely that there are no more opposites" (*Twilight of the Idols and The Anti-Christ,* 152–58).

used, necessarily, in order to break out of a sacrificial view of the world."[71] I believe, instead, that the biblical texts narrate how God has necessarily *used the sacrificial mechanism* to remake the world into a place in which the need to sacrifice others could be eschewed—a new world of self-giving grace, a world of embrace.

The Enlightenment has left us with an alternative: either reason or violence. Nietzsche and his postmodern followers have demonstrated aptly that reason itself is violent,[72] adding in their honest moments the horrifying thought that violent reason can be transcended only in the violence of unreason.[73] The cross of Christ should teach us that the only alternative to violence is self-giving love, willingness to absorb violence in order to embrace the other in the knowledge that truth and justice have been, and will be, upheld by God. Does the cross teach us to abandon reason along with violence? Is its message that the immediacy of self-donation is the only antidote to the immediacy of violence? Certainly not. We cannot dispense with reason and discourse as weapons against violence. But the cross does suggest that the "responsibility of reason" can replace neither the "consciousness of sin"[74] nor the willingness to embrace the sinful other. Instead, reason and discourse themselves need to be redeemed to the extent that they are implicated in the agonistic and sinful relations of power. Only those who are willing to embrace the deceitful and unjust, as Christ has done on the cross, will be able to employ reason and discourse as instruments of peace rather than violence.

The Rider on the White Horse

What about the Rider on the white horse who seems to deploy violence without any thought of embracing the enemy? Is he not that same suffering Messiah who was all along secretly dreaming of revenge and has now finally come to take it with a fury? Does he not come to pour out "the wrath of God Almighty" (Rev 19:15)? Does not heaven rejoice at the sight of the destruction of Babylon (Rev 18:20)? Do not the saints gleefully cheer from the sides, "Give her what she has given to others. Give

---

71. James G. Williams, *The Bible, Violence, and the Sacred: Liberation from the Myth of Sanctioned Violence* (Valley Forge: Trinity Press International, 1991), 224.

72. Nietzsche, *Twilight of the Idols and The Anti-Christ*, 43.

73. Michel Foucault, "The Ethic of Care of the Self as a Practice of Freedom," *The Final Foucault*, ed. James Bernauer and David Rasmussen (Cambridge: MIT Press, 1988), 285.

74. Hans-Otto Apel, *Diskurs und Verantwortung* (Frankfurt: Suhrkamp, 1988), 17f.

her back twice as much for what she has done. In the cup that she has poured, pour her twice as much" (Rev 18:6 CEB)? Is not this veritable orgy of hatred, wrath, and vindictiveness on the part of those who like to see themselves dressed in white robes a final victory of revenge over love, of violence over nonviolence? Had John of Patmos, who saw Jesus Christ as "a Lamb standing as if it had been slaughtered" (Rev 5:6), taken a better look would he not have seen a bloodthirsty beast?

But who are those who suffer violence at the hand of the Rider? They are the people drunk with the blood of the innocent (Rev 17:6) who make war against the Lamb and those who adorned themselves with righteous deeds (Rev 19:19). Its imposing political order and economic splendor notwithstanding, the imperial power of Rome is, in the eyes of John the Seer, a system of "political tyranny and economic exploitation," founded "on conquest and maintained by violence and oppression."[75] The violence of the Rider is the judgment against this system of the one called "Faithful and True" (Rev 19:11). Without such judgment there can be no world of peace, of truth, and of justice: terror (the "beast" that devours) and propaganda (the "false prophet" that deceives) must be overcome, evil must be separated from good, and darkness from the light. These are the causes of violence, and they must be removed if a world of peace is to be established.

Why must God say the unrelenting "no" to a world of injustice, deception, and violence in such a *violent* way? Why must the "no" be symbolically coded in the images of terror breaking out and covering the world with blood and ashes? Is nonviolence impotent? One strategy of responding to these questions will not work. The attempt to exonerate the Revelation from the charge of affirming divine violence by suggesting that the Rider's victory was not "fought with literal weapons," but with the sword "which protrudes from his mouth," which is "the Word of God,"[76] is implausible. The violence of the divine word is no less lethal than the violence of the literal sword. We must either reject the Rider's violence or find ways to make sense of it; we cannot deny it. Is there a way of making sense not only of the language of divine "conquest" but of the phenomenon of divine "violence" in Revelation?

There are people who trust in the infectious power of nonviolence: sooner or later it will be crowned with success. In this belief, however, one

75. Richard Bauckam, *The Theology of the Book of Revelation*, New Testament Theology, ed. James D. G. Dunn (Cambridge: Cambridge University Press, 1993), 35.
76. William Klaassen, "Vengeance in the Apocalypse of John," *Catholic Biblical Quarterly* 28 (1966): 308.

can smell a bit too much of the sweet aroma of a suburban ideology, entertained often by people who are neither courageous nor honest enough to reflect on the implications of terror taking place right in the middle of their living rooms! The road of nonviolence in the world of violence often leads to suffering: one can sometimes break the cycle of violence only at the price of one's life, as the example of Jesus demonstrates. If history is any guide, the prospects are good that nonviolence will fail to dislodge violence.

Will not patient appeals to reason make people want to abandon the unreason of violence, however? To think that we can reason ourselves and others into making the right kinds of choices—especially the costly choices of eschewing violence—is to forget that "reason" and "freedom" are never pure, never situated in some neutral territory in which arguments are weighed judiciously and choices made without bias. Reason and freedom are always implicated in the relations of power; these relations muddle reason and misdirect choices (see Chapter VI). One has to *want* peace, in order to be persuaded to be peaceful. One has to *want* to embrace the other in order to be reasoned into embracing the other. Can we simply assume that the violent will want to be transformed so as to want the well-being of the other and therefore peace? Many may want such transformation. But will all?

Underlying the theology of judgment in the Apocalypse is the assumption that *nothing* is potent enough to change those who insist on remaining beasts and false prophets. Certainly, most of us are not beasts, though the beast can all-too-easily be awakened in us; most of us are not false prophets, though we are so easily seduced by the seeming effectiveness of deception. We should not, however, shy away from the unpleasant and deeply tragic *possibility* that there *might* be human beings, created in the image of God, who, through the practice of evil, have immunized themselves from all attempts at their redemption. Ensnared by the chaos of violence, which generates its own legitimizing "reason" and "goodness," they have become untouchable for the lure of God's truth and goodness.

This is where God's anger comes in. As Jan Assmann points out in his study of political theology in Egypt and Israel, anger over injustice is so much a political emotion that "the inability to be indignant over injustice is a sure sign of an a-political attitude."[77] Much like the God

---

77. Jan Assmann, *Politische Theologie zwischen Ägypten und Israel* (München: Carl Friedrich von Siemens Stiftung, 1992), 93.

of the whole Bible, the God of the Apocalypse is an eminently political divinity—the God not only of individuals and their families but of the kingdoms of this world (Rev 11:15). If Augustine was right that "the city of this world...aims at domination, which holds nations in enslavement" and "is itself dominated by that very lust for domination,"[78] then God *must* be angry. A nonindignant God would be an accomplice in injustice, deception, and violence.

We need not bother here much with the "mechanism" of God's anger. In *The Wrath of the Lamb*, Anthony T. Hanson rightly stressed that in Revelation God's wrath consists partly in the "working out in history of the consequences of men's sins."[79] Yet without an eschatological dimension, the talk of God's wrath degenerates into a naive and woefully inadequate ideology about the self-cancellation of evil. Outside the world of wishful thinking, evildoers all too often thrive, and when they are overthrown, the victors are not much better than the defeated. God's eschatological anger is the obverse of the impotence of God's love in the face of the self-immunization of evildoers caught in the self-generating mechanism of evil. A "nice" God is a figment of liberal imagination, a projection onto the sky of the inability to give up cherished illusions about goodness, freedom, and the rationality of social actors.

The Anabaptist tradition, consistently the most pacifist tradition in the history of the Christian church, has traditionally had no hesitation about speaking of God's wrath and judgment,[80] and with good reasons. There is no trace of this nonindignant God in the biblical texts, be it Old Testament or New Testament, be it Jesus of Nazareth or John of Patmos. The evildoers who "eat up my people as they eat bread," says the psalmist in God's name, will be put "in great terror" (Ps 14:5). Why terror? Why not simply reproach? Even better, why not reasoning together? Why not just display suffering love? Because the evildoers "are corrupt" and "they do abominable deeds" (14:1); they have "gone astray," they are "perverse" (14:3). God will judge, not because God gives people what they deserve, but because some people refuse to receive what no one deserves; if evildoers experience God's terror, it will not be because they have done

---

78. Augustine, *Concerning the City of God Against the Pagans*, transl. Henry Bettenson (Harmondsworth: Penguin, 1976), I, Preface.

79. Anthony Tyrrel Hanson, *The Wrath of the Lamb* (London: SPCK, 1957), 160.

80. Walter Klaassen, ed., *Anabaptism in Outline* (Scottdale: Herald Press, 1981), 316–44.

evil, but because they have resisted to the end the powerful lure of the open arms of the crucified Messiah.

If we accept the stubborn irredeemability of some people, do we not end up with an irreconcilable contradiction at the heart of Christian faith? Here the "crucified Messiah" with arms outstretched embracing the "vilest sinner," there the Rider on the white horse with a sharp sword coming from his mouth to strike down the hopelessly wicked? The patient love of God over against the fury of God's wrath? Why this polarity? Not because the God of the cross is different from the God of the second coming. After all, the cross is not forgiveness pure and simple, but God's *setting aright the world of injustice and deception.* The polarity is there because some human beings refuse to be "set aright." Those who take divine suffering (the cross) as a display of divine weakness that condones violence—instead of divine grace that restores the violator—draw upon themselves divine anger (the sword) that makes an end to their violence.[81] The violence of the Rider on the white horse, I suggest, is the *symbolic portrayal of the final exclusion of everything that refuses to be redeemed by God's suffering love.* For the sake of the peace of God's good creation, we can and must affirm *this* divine anger and *this* divine violence, while at the same time holding on to the hope that in the end, even the flag bearer will desert the army that desires to make war against the Lamb.[82]

---

81. In powerful passages about the restitution of all things, Jürgen Moltmann proposed to consider God's judgment at the end of history an exercise in rectifying justice, parallel to the justification of the sinner in the middle of history (*The Coming of God: Christian Eschatology*, transl. Margaret Kohl [Minneapolis: Fortress, 1996], 235–55). The result of God's judgment thus conceived fits well with our desire for the final triumph of God's love, but we should keep in mind that nothing could guarantee the achievement of this result without divine "violence." There is no need to postulate the existence of full self-immunized incarnations of evil to make plausible that, from the perspective of such a person, his or her transformation into a cheerful doer of what from God's perspective is good will involve violence. It suffices to point to a thinker such as Gilles Deleuze to see that, within the framework of a particular set of values and a given reading of the human condition, being a citizen of the New Jerusalem can easily appear as troubling as finding oneself in the lake of sulfur (Deleuze, *Kleine Schriften*, 114). Consequently, the divine transformation of a person into a holy citizen of the New Jerusalem, which would not take place in accordance with his or her will, must appear from the perspective of that person to be an act of violence. We find this act of transformation tolerable and tend not to call it "violent" only because, as Christians, we share the perspective of the divine transformer and identify with the desired result. The only way to avoid divine violence toward those who refuse to be changed nonviolently is to stipulate in advance that no one will refuse to be changed by the lure of God's love. Though those who have been touched by God's love ought to hope for a universal nonrefusal, if they are not blind to the human condition they will be hesitant to count on it. Hence the possibility of the final condemnation.

82. Jürgen Moltmann sums up the eschatological position presupposed in my reflection on divine anger with his characteristic precision and grace: "There is no particularism in principle, and there is no automatic universalism" (*The Coming of God*, 249). A different way of putting the same point would be to say, as I have heard said, that "I am not a universalist, but God may be."

Should not a loving God be patient and keep luring the perpetrator into goodness? This is exactly what God does: God suffers the evildoers through history as God has suffered them on the cross. But how patient should God be? The day of reckoning must come, not because God is too eager to pull the trigger but because every day of patience in a world of violence means more violence and every postponement of vindication means letting insult accompany injury. "How long will it be before you judge and avenge our blood," cry out the souls under the altar to the Sovereign Lord (Rev 6:10). We are uncomfortable with the response that calls the souls "to rest a little longer, until the number would be complete both of their fellow servants and of their brothers and sisters, who were soon to be killed as they themselves had been killed" (6:11). But the response underlines that God's patience is costly, not so much for God, but above all for the innocent sufferers. Waiting for the evildoers to reform means letting suffering continue.

The creation of the world involved no violence. As René Girard observed, "In the story of the creation of the world, the founding moment comes at the beginning, and no victimage is involved."[83] No chaotic powers need to be overcome; the world emerges through an act of pure positing.[84] The chaos sets in as a distortion of the peaceful creation. Redemption cannot, therefore, be an act of pure positing but entails negation and struggle, even violence. First God suffers violence on the cross for the salvation of the world. Then, after God's patience with chaotic powers who refuse to be redeemed by the cross has come to an end, God inflicts violence against the stubbornly violent to restore creation's original peace. Hence in the Apocalypse, the creative word at the dawn of creation becomes the double-edged sword at the sunset before creation's new and unending day (Rev 19:15).[85]

Does violence then have the last word in human history? Is overpowering the last act of God in the original creation? No, the judgment against the beast and the false prophet is the obverse of the salvation of those who suffer at their hands. God can create the world of justice, truth, and peace only by making an end to deception, injustice, and violence. The

83. René Girard, *Things Hidden Since the Foundation of the World,* transl. S. Bann and M. Metteer (Stanford: Stanford University Press, 1987), 143.

84. Milbank, *Theology and Social Theory.*

85. Catherine Keller objected that the "sharp sword" of the Apocalypse is like "a melodramatic phallic parody of the creative word of the first creation" ("Why Apocalypse, Now?" *Theology Today* 49 [1992]: 191). Yet she is unwilling to give up the "warrior" motif completely because she, rightly, wants to cling to the project of liberation. She retains the sword but blunts its edges. Phallic?

purpose of the judgment is not the deadly calm of the final closure, but an eternal dance of differences that give themselves to each other in peaceful embrace. *The end of the world is not violence, but a nonviolent embrace without end.*

Does not the Apocalypse paint a different picture of the end, the one more congruent with its violent imagery of the Rider's conquest? Is not its last vision dominated by "the throne" (Rev 22:1) from which earlier "flashes of lightning" and "peals of thunder" were coming (4:5)? Is not the nameless "one seated on the throne" (4:9; 5:1) a perfect projection of the ultimate and incontestable warrior-potentate? If this were so, the Apocalypse would simply mirror the violence of the imperial Rome it had set out to subvert. The most surprising thing about this book is that at the *center* of the throne, holding together both the throne and the whole cosmos that is ruled by the throne, we find the sacrificed *Lamb* (cf. 5:6; 7:17; 22:1). At the very heart of "the One who sits on the throne" is the cross. The world to come is ruled by the one who on the cross took violence upon himself in order to conquer the enmity and embrace the enemy. The Lamb's rule is legitimized not by the "sword" but by its "wounds"; the goal of its rule is not to subject but to make people "reign for ever and ever" (22:5). With the Lamb at the center of the throne, the distance between the "throne" and the "subjects" has collapsed in the embrace of the triune God.

The Cross or the Sword?

The key question is *who* should be engaged in separating the darkness from the light? Who should exercise violence against the "beast" and the "false prophet"? Echoing the whole New Testament, the Apocalypse mentions only God. But what does its silence about human agency in the apocalyptic violence mean? Is this silence a censure of historical violence or a silence of implicit approval, even complicity?

There is an important chorus of theologians who would dismiss these questions as naive. They claim a straightforward correspondence between divine action and human behavior. Since the primary religious motivation is to "imitate deity," whatever God does, God's worshippers are mandated to do too. If your God engages in warfare, you will become a warrior too.[86] The thesis about the correspondence between divine and human action

---

86. David Ray Griffin, "The War-System and Religion: Toward a Post-Anarchist Hermeneutic," unpublished paper, 1993, 3ff.

rightly underlines that the fundamental theological question in relation to violence is the question about God: "What is God like?"—the God who "loves enemies and is the original peace maker"[87] or the God of vengeance, out to punish the insubordinate? The thesis has, however, one small but fatal flaw: humans are not God. There is a duty prior to the duty of imitating God, and that is the duty *of not wanting to be God*, of letting God be God and humans be humans. Without such a duty guarding the divinity of God the duty to imitate God would be empty because our concept of God would be nothing more than the mirror image of ourselves—as we are or as we desire to be.

Preserving the fundamental difference between God and non-God, the biblical tradition insists that there are things that only God may do. One of them is to use violence. Unlike many ancient cultures, Israel's political theology did not operate with the "model of representation" according to which all the attributes of God were also the attributes of the king. The anger of the king, to take as an example that eminently political emotion, was in this model but the outworking of the anger of God; and inversely, the anger of God served as legitimation for the anger of the king. As Jan Assmann has argued, instead of secularizing the anger of God by transferring it to the king, Israel has "theologized" the anger of the king, "transferred it from earth to heaven." As a consequence, history and destiny were subjected to the immediate judgment of *God's* justice rather than the execution of God's justice being placed into the hands of the king.[88]

The New Testament radicalized this process of the theologization of divine anger and boldly proclaimed *God's* monopoly on violence, at least as far as Christians are concerned. Whatever relation may exist between God's and the state's monopoly on violence—Romans 13 and Revelation 13 give radically different answers to this question—Christians are not to take up their swords and gather under the banner of the Rider on the white horse, but to take up their crosses and follow the crucified Messiah. In 1 Peter we read: "Christ also suffered for you, leaving you an example, so that you should follow in his steps.... When he was abused, he did not return abuse; when he suffered, he did not threaten; but he entrusted himself to the one who judges justly" (1 Pet 2:21, 23; cf. Rom 12:18-21).

---

87. John Howard Yoder, *He Came Preaching Peace* (Scottdale: Herald, 1985), 104.
88. Assmann, *Politische Theologie zwischen Ägypten und Israel*, 98, 105.

The close association between human nonviolence and the affirmation of God's vengeance in the New Testament is telling. The suffering Messiah and the Rider on the white horse do indeed belong together, but not in the way Deleuze maintained. They are not accomplices in spilling blood, but partners in promoting nonviolence. Without entrusting oneself to the God who judges justly, it will hardly be possible to follow the crucified Messiah and refuse to retaliate when abused. The certainty of God's just judgment at the end of history is the presupposition for the renunciation of violence in the middle of it. The divine system of judgment is not the flip side of the human reign of terror, but a necessary correlate of human nonviolence. Since the search for truth and the practice of justice cannot be given up, the only way in which nonviolence and forgiveness will be possible in a world of violence is through *displacement* or *transference* of violence, not through its complete relinquishment.

On the basis of similar reasoning, Jewish scholar Henri Atlan has quite rightly argued for the radical thesis that insofar as one is going to refer to God in the struggle against violence at all, "it is perhaps more economical—more effective and less dangerous—to refer to the God of violence rather than the God of love."[89] The stark contrast between "the God of violence" and "the God of love" in this formulation notwithstanding, Atlan does not oppose the two but uses the phrase "the God of violence" to refer to "a God who takes upon Himself the founding violence" and is therefore not "entirely love" in relation to the world.[90] For a Christian theologian even the description of God as "not entirely love" will be unacceptable; a Christian theologian will insist that God's violence, if it is to be worthy of God who "*is* love" (1 John 4:8), must be an aspect of God's love. But Atlan's point about the relation between divine violence and human nonviolence is well taken. Since violence is sometimes both necessary and justified in a world of violence, he argued, "the best way to rid the world of the violent sacred is to reject it onto a transcendence. The transcendence of violence...culminates in its being expelled from the normal horizon of things."[91] "The only means of prohibiting all recourse to violence by *ourselves*" is to insist that violence is legitimate "only when it comes from

89. Atlan, "Founding Violence and Divine Referent," 206.
90. Ibid.
91. Ibid., 207.

298

God."[92] The "theologization" of violence is a precondition for the politics of nonviolence.

One could object that it is not worthy of God to wield the sword. Is God not love, long-suffering, and all-powerful love? A counter-question could go something like this: Is it not a bit too arrogant to presume that our contemporary sensibilities about what is compatible with God's love are so much healthier than those of the people of God throughout the whole history of Judaism and Christianity? Recalling my arguments about the self-immunization of the evildoers, one could further argue that in a world of violence it would not be worthy of God *not to wield* the sword; if God were *not angry* at injustice and deception and *did not* make the final end to violence God would not be worthy of our worship. Here, however, I am less interested in arguing that God's violence is not unworthy of God than in showing that it is beneficial to us. Atlan has rightly drawn our attention to the fact that in a world of violence we are faced with an inescapable alternative: either God's violence or human violence. Most people who insist on God's "nonviolence" cannot resist using violence themselves (or tacitly sanctioning its use by others). They deem the talk of God's judgment irreverent, but think nothing of entrusting judgment into human hands, persuaded presumably that this is less dangerous and more humane—and perhaps more reliable—than to trust in a God who judges! That *we* should bring "down the powerful from their thrones" (Luke 1:51-52) seems responsible; that *God* should do the same, as the song of that revolutionary Virgin explicitly states, seems crude. And so violence thrives, secretly nourished by belief in a God who refuses to wield the sword.

My thesis that the practice of nonviolence requires a belief in divine vengeance will be unpopular with many Christians, especially theologians in the West. To the person who is inclined to dismiss it, I suggest imagining that you are delivering a lecture in a war zone (which is where a paper that underlies this chapter was originally delivered). Among your listeners are people whose cities and villages have been first plundered,

---

92. Ibid., 206. Following partly D. H. Lawrence's suggestion that Revelation is an expression of anger, hatred, and envy, Adela Yarbro Collins argued that Revelation "limits vengeance and envy to imagination and clearly rules out violent deeds" ("Persecution and Vengeance in the Book of Revelation," *Apocalypticism in the Mediterranean World and the Near East*, ed. David Hellholm [Tübingen: J. C. B. Mohr (Paul Siebeck), 1983], 747). Her distinction between the violence of imagination and of deeds is too simple and misleading, however. Leaving aside the question of whether Revelation in fact does express envy rather than the search for truth and justice, it is crucial to underline that Revelation does not simply limit violence to imagination but that in "imagination" it further clearly limits violence to God.

then burned and leveled to the ground, whose daughters and sisters have been raped, whose fathers and brothers have had their throats slit. The topic of the lecture: a Christian attitude toward violence. The thesis: we should not retaliate since God is perfect noncoercive love. Soon you would discover that it takes the quiet of a suburban home—protected by police and military force!—for the birth of the thesis that human non-violence corresponds to God's refusal to judge. In a scorched land, soaked in the blood of the innocent, it will invariably die. And as one watches it die, one will do well to reflect about many other pleasant captivities of the liberal mind.

Prospects for War, Prospects for Peace

In his book *Aussichten auf den Bürgerkrieg*, Hans M. Enzensberger reminds his readers of Sisyphus, that tragic figure from Greek mythology who was condemned to push a heavy stone up a hill, again and again. "This stone is peace," reads the last sentence of Enzensberger's pessimistic book.[93] The very first sentences explain why the prospects for war are so much better than the prospects for peace:

> Animals fight but they do not wage wars. Humans are the only primates who pursue enthusiastically mass killing of their own kind in a planned way. War belongs to the most important human inventions; the ability to make peace is probably a later achievement. The oldest traditions of humanity, its myths and epic poetry, speak primarily of killings.[94]

According to Enzensberger, the nasty human habit of destroying and killing inscribed into their very nature leaves room only for a negative utopia—the "Hobbesian myth of the struggle of everybody against everybody."[95] Peace can be nothing more than a short and precarious interruption of ever present and inescapable war. Violence had the first word in history; it will have the last word—and most of the words in-between too.

Contrast the image of the sisyphal struggle against war with the vision of peace we find in the Bible. In the prophet Isaiah we read (11:1-9 CEB):

---

93. Enzensberger, *Aussichten auf den Bürgerkrieg*, 93.
94. Ibid., 9.
95. Ibid., 36.

A shoot will grow up from the stump of Jesse;
> a branch will sprout from his roots.
The Lord's spirit will rest upon him,
>> a spirit of wisdom and understanding,
>> a spirit of planning and strength,
>> a spirit of knowledge and fear of the Lord.
He will delight in fearing the Lord.
He won't judge by appearances,
>> nor decide by hearsay.
He will judge the needy with righteousness,
>> and decide with equity for those who suffer in the land.
He will strike the violent with the rod of his mouth;
>> by the breath of his lips he will kill the wicked.
Righteousness will be the belt around his hips,
>> and faithfulness the belt around his waist.
The wolf will live with the lamb,
>> and the leopard will lie down with the young goat;
>> the calf and the young lion will feed together,
>> and a little child will lead them.
The cow and the bear will graze.
>> Their young will lie down together,
>> and a lion will eat straw like an ox.
A nursing child will play over the snake's hole;
>> toddlers will reach right over the serpent's den.
They won't harm or destroy anywhere on my holy mountain.
The earth will surely be filled with the knowledge of the Lord,
>> just as the water covers the sea.

If the text had not referred to wolves and lambs, to the needy and the wicked, little children and cobras, we would have been tempted to think that it is about a world that has nothing to do with our own. But it is a vision of our world—our world freed from injustice and destruction, our world in which peace rather than terror has the last word.

The biblical vision—shall we call it utopia—is more hopeful than Enzensberger's. Violence is not human destiny because the God of peace is the beginning and the end of human history. The biblical vision of peace invites, however, us to a task more difficult than Sisyphus's. Granted, pushing the stone of peace up the steep hill of violence—doing those small neighborly acts of help even though one knows that the killer might return the next day, the next week, or year[96]—is hard. It is easier, however, than carrying one's own cross in the footsteps of the crucified Messiah. This is what Jesus Christ asks Christians to do. Assured of God's justice and undergirded by God's presence, they are to break the cycle of violence by refusing to be caught in the automatism of revenge. It cannot be denied that the prospects are good that by trying to love their enemies they may end up hanging on a cross. Yet often enough, the costly acts of nonretaliation become a seed from which the fragile fruit of Pentecostal peace grows—a peace between people from different cultural spaces gathered in one place who understand each other's languages and share in each others' goods.

It may be that consistent nonretaliation and nonviolence will prove impossible to sustain in the world of violence. Tyrants may need to be taken down from their thrones and the madmen stopped from sowing desolation. Dietrich Bonhoeffer's decision to take part in an attempt to assassinate Hitler is a well-known and persuasive example of such thinking. It may also be that measures that involve preparation for the use of violent means will have to be taken to prevent tyrants and madmen from ascending to power in the first place or to keep the plethora of ordinary kinds of perpetrators that walk our streets from doing their violent work. It may be that in a world suffused with violence the issue is not simply "violence versus peace" but rather "what forms of violence could be tolerated to overcome a social 'peace' that coercively maintained itself through the condoned violence of injustice."[97] But if one decides to put on soldier's gear instead of carrying one's cross, one should not seek legitimation in the religion that worships the crucified Messiah. For there, the blessing is given not to the violent but to the meek (Matt 5:5).

There are Christians who have a hard time resisting the temptation to seek religious legitimation for their (understandable) need to take up the sword. If they give in to this temptation, they should forego all attempts to exonerate their version of Christian faith from complicity in fomenting violence. Of course, they can specify that religious symbols should be used to legitimate and inspire only *just* wars. But show me one warring party that does not think its war is just! Simple logic tells us that at least

96. Ibid., 92.
97. Marjorie Hewitt Suchocki, *The Fall to Violence: Original Sin in Relational Theology* (New York: Continuum, 1995), 117.

half of them *must* be wrong. It could be, however, that simple logic does not apply to the chaotic world of wars. Then all would be right, which is to say that all would be wrong, which is to say that terror would reign— in the name of the gods who can no longer be distinguished from the devils.

EPILOGUE
Two and a Half Decades Later

This epilogue is not a "how-I-changed-my-mind" kind of text, for, on the whole, I haven't changed my mind about the subject of the book. I consider now the thrust of its argument to be as plausible as it was when I originally wrote it. But this is also not simply a "reply-to-my-critics" kind of text, for that could suggest either that I haven't gotten things wrong—say, aspects of the thought of major figures I discuss—or that I haven't learned much in the intervening years, neither of which is true. Instead of either simply retracting or defending my positions, I will here (1) sketch the theological frame for the main argument of the book, (2) explain some of the book's misunderstood claims, (3) push against some criticisms I consider misplaced (like the one leveled against my account of the doctrine of the Trinity and how it bears on social issues), (4) correct some partly-wrong turns I have taken (as in my discussion of justice), and (5) make up for some missing pieces in the argument (for instance, an account of "the final reconciliation" as an aspect of the eschatological transition or "restitution" as a crucial dimension of reconciliation).

Basic Convictions

My official title is Professor of Systematic Theology, suggesting that my primary interest is exploration of the systematic arrangement and interlinkages of theological convictions. Like much of my theological writing, *Exclusion and Embrace* is an "occasional" text. I wrote it in response to a burning existential question that arose in the process of the breakup of Yugoslavia at the end of the twentieth century: What does it mean to live as a Christian—to think and act as a Christian—in the context of a

305

violent struggle among people sharing a political space but divided along ethnic and religious lines? More abstractly: What does the Christian faith have to say about negotiating identities, both personal and communal, under the conditions of struggle for power? Clearly, *Exclusion and Embrace* is not an exercise in classically-understood systematic theology. It is nothing like *Christian Faith*, the famous text of the greatest modern systematic theologian, Friedrich Schleiermacher, or, for an example from the twentieth century, Wolfhart Pannenberg's *Systematic Theology*.[1]

In one sense, I am a self-consciously and intentionally "unsystematic" theologian.[2] Friedrich Nietzsche exaggerated when, in *Twilight of the Idols*, he wrote that "the will to a system is a lack of integrity,"[3] but he was making an important point. I believe that human finitude, temporality, and fallibility, as well as God's incomprehensibility, stand in tension with theology's aspiration to comprehensive systematicity. If I were to name a model from the past for my style of theologizing, Martin Luther would come to mind, though, going further back—in fact, as far back as the origins of Christian theology—I could point to the Apostle Paul as well. Luther was an occasional thinker, but he was not an inconsistent, let alone arbitrary, thinker. Within a given phase of his development, a set of fundamental and interrelated theological convictions informed rather consistently the positions he took. Similarly, a set of interrelated basic theological commitments frames my theological writings, all the way from *Work in the Spirit* (1991), through *After our Likeness* (1998), *Free of Charge* (2005), and *The End of Memory* (2006), and up to *A Public Faith* (2011), *Allah* (2011), *Flourishing* (2017), and *For the Life of the World* (2019).

Exclusion and Embrace was conceived and born at the interface of the concrete situation, exemplifying as it did a more general feature of our world, and a set of basic theological commitments. What are they? In the introduction to a collection of essays in my honor, *Envisioning the Good Life*, Matthew Croasmun and Ryan McAnnally-Linz have articulated them well. I reproduce below their formulation with some clarifying emendations and additions:[4]

---

1. Friedrich Schleiermacher, *Christian Faith*, vol. 1–2, transl. Terrence N. Tice, Catherine L. Kelsey, and Edwina Lawler (Louisville: Westminster John Knox, 2016); Wolfhart Pannenberg, *Systematic Theology*, vol. 1–3, transl. Geoffrey W. Bromiley (Grand Rapids: Eerdmans, 1991).

2. For an argument for being a "systematically unsystematic" theologian see David Kelsey, *Eccentric Existence: A Theological Anthropology* (Louisville: Westminster John Knox, 2009), 1:44–45.

3. Friedrich Nietzsche, *Twilight of the Idols and The Anti-Christ*, transl. R. J. Hollingdale (London: Penguin, 1990), 35.

4. See Matthew Croasmun and Ryan McAnnally-Linz, "Introduction: Miroslav Volf and Theology

Two basic sets of convictions underlie this theological vision. The first flows from among the most central claims of the Christian faith: "God is love" (1 John 4:16). This is not to say merely that God loves, but rather that God *is* love, which is why God's loving is original and originary, situation-independent and unconditional. This basic biblical claim takes in Christian theology a fundamentally trinitarian form. God is the Holy Trinity, and therefore the love that the One God is always already includes love of "the other"; only *via the other*, only in the modes of such self-differentiation, is it possible to talk about self-love in God. Such love is *who* God is.

This God, the God who is love, *creates*. God creates *out of love* and *for love*. The reality of creation is a display of God's non-self-seeking love—that is, creation is a *gift*. As the gift of a good giver, creation itself is good; and even fallen creation, bearing marks of "futility" and "sin," is good. Its goodness is contingent and dependent (since creation is not God), but it is creation's own. Moreover, God's creatures are genuinely good for each other. Not, of course, to the exclusion of God, the source of all goodness. But God does not demand to be creatures' sole good.

This same God who is love *redeems*. God in Christ and through the Spirit redeems wayward creation *out of love*. On the cross, God "dies" for God's beloved creatures who have become God's enemies; Christ justifies the ungodly. This is God's love of the unlovely—God's embrace of what is other than God even in face of its denial and enmity to God.

The God who loves *indwells* the human being, not as an extraneous and intruding presence but as the fulfillment of the human being's created character. By faith, human beings receive Christ, who dwells in them through the Spirit. As a consequence, God's kind of love, situation-independent and unconditional, is the hallmark of the Christian life. So the love of enemy, no less than the love of neighbor, is essential to Christian life. Though completely rooted in God—all things are from God, through God, and to God—the Christian life is not exlusively oriented toward God. Instead, having God behind, underneath, and in them, Christians are oriented toward the world, participating in God's mission to suffuse the world with God's love and make it God's and creatures' home. (Jesus says in John: "As I have loved you, you should also love one another" [13:34 NRSV], *not* the reciprocal "As I have loved you, you should love me.") We love God when we

---

of the Good Life," *Envisioning the Good Life: Essays on God, Christ, and Human Flourishing in Honor of Miroslav Volf*, ed. Matthew Croasmun, Zoran Grozdanov, and Ryan McAnnally-Linz (Eugene: Cascade Books, 2017), 3–5. Compare the text below with the pages in Croasmun and McAnnally-Linz's essay for my changes.

open ourselves in faith to receive Christ, the embodiment of God's love, and become "Christs" to one another and the world.[5]

The God who is love draws all creation to *consummation*. The world to come is the world *of love*, especially the eschatological "love that dances,"[6] love as it can be in the world of peace and joy. In this world, both the realities that make up our contexts and features of our interiority—human perceptions, emotions, values, etc.—are transformed. Gone are the enmity and sorrow caused by sin, replaced by peaceful and joyful communion.

In the present world, not yet so transformed, love—Christ's and our own—often needs to suffer; but love's suffering is a *means*, love's dance is the *goal*. That goal is a *world* of love, a community of creatures rightly related to God and one another ("peace"). This world, and not God alone, is our final end.

Such is the first set of convictions, all of which flow from the central conviction that *God is love*. The second set is, in a sense, a formal or "structural" obverse of the more substantive and "personal" lineup of convictions just described. These deal with the kinds of identities associated in the above account of God's love and God's mission in the world.

First, the one God who is love lives in perichoretic unity of three divine persons. The One God is neither an undifferentiated divine being nor a tight community of individual divine persons. A divine person is a person only in a uniquely divine and humanly unreplicable relation of "being-in" (rather than just "being-with") other divine persons; just that mutual "being-in" of the three persons is the One God who is love.

The perichoretic unity of divine persons has an anthropological and cosmological analogy (not mirror image!). Human beings, along with the entire creation, are created to be indwelled by God, to be God's "temple" or "home." That is, they are created for God to be in them and work through them. To be human is to be created for this divine indwelling. Openness to God is not an optional add-on to human life, the human equivalent to a car's power sunroof. It is simply what it means to be human.

This anthropology sets the stage for Christology, soteriology, and ecclesiology. God's indwelling of humans is realized in a unique way in Christ.

---

5. The idea of "becoming Christs" is the culmination of Martin Luther's summary of the Christian faith in *Freedom of the Christian* (*Luther's Works*, vol. 31, ed. Harold Grimm [Philadelphia: Fortress, 1957], 368).

6. For the idea of "love that dances," see the appendix.

As evident from his baptism, his identity is a trinitarian reality: Christ *is* the Son, sent by the Father, and indwelled by the Spirit. It follows that Christian life is not merely one religious choice among many but the unique fulfillment of what it is to be a human being, a life in which a person is "in Christ" and Christ is in that person by the power of the Spirit—a perichoretic relation of God and humans analogous to the perichoretic relations among divine persons.

Given the original trinitarian *perichoresis* and its soteriological analogue, the relations among humans are also analogously perichoretic, though in a weaker sense. They are perichoretic in a way appropriate to them as finite, embodied, and (for a while at least) fallible creatures.[7] Within the church, our identities are—or at least ought to be—porous, which is to say bounded and yet permeable. This porousness does not compromise our individuality, but rather expands and enriches it. We are richer precisely as *individuals* the more *others* (all and any created good, in fact) across times and spaces "indwell" us. We can describe this sort of personal identity as "catholic personality,"[8] an identity enriched by otherness—"a microcosm of the eschatological new creation."[9]

This same catholicity applies to relations to other ecclesial communities and to cultural goods: individual Christians and their ecclesial communities are enriched by living their own identities with porousness to all other churches across time and place, and they are better when enriched by all cultural goods—including other religions. At the same time, to quote from *Exclusion and Embrace*, "a truly catholic personality must be an *evangelical* personality—a personality transformed by the Spirit of the new creation and engaged in the transformation of the world."[10] This engagement is energized and guided by hope that God will make the entire world into a dwelling place, a "home," of God (Rev 21:3).

Note the movement in each of these sequences. The core commitments, the ones that organize and propel the whole, are theological in the strict sense. They are claims about God. They drive persistently, however, toward implications for human life in the world in relation to God and others. One cannot just say, "God is love," and leave it at that. To say,

---

7. See the appendix for an attempt to carefully delineate proper limits of anthropological, ecclesiological, and political analogies to the trinitarian nature of God.

8. See Miroslav Volf, *After Our Likeness: The Church as the Image of the Trinity* (Grand Rapids: Eerdmans, 1998), 278–82.

9. See Suzanne McDonald about my account of "catholic personality" (*Re-Imagining Election: Divine Election as Representing God to Others and Others to God* [Grand Rapids: Eerdmans, 2010], 128).

10. Miroslav Volf, *Exclusion and Embrace*, 52.

"God is love," is to imply a whole vision of human and creaturely flourishing, and a way of life aiming to exemplify and promote it.

These three pages are not a miniature systematic theology, though they could be developed into one; they are my "credo" of sorts. I intend that these convictions shape all of my theological work. If one were to think in musical analogy, these convictions are my way of integrating and rendering multiple themes that make up a complex composition that is the Christian faith.[11] In a given situation, I pick up one or the other theme and play it up, all the while keeping in mind that there has to be a "goodness of fit" between what I played up and the rest of the integrated whole—and, more importantly, a "goodness of fit" with the revelation of God in Jesus Christ contained in the scriptures.

Practicing Embrace

Some criticisms leveled against *Exclusion and Embrace* rest, unsurprisingly, on misunderstandings. More specifically, they rest on the kinds of misunderstandings that arise when readers forget that an author can neither say everything in one book nor write all books that would need to be written so that all that needs to be said on a topic could be said. Here are a few examples.

Vision, Spirituality, and Conflict-Resolution

Some have complained that the book isn't sufficiently practical. I write about what we ought to aspire to do and who we ought to aspire to be, but not about *how to do* what we ought to do and *how to become* who we ought to be. Encountering this objection in person, I often respond, in jest, that I am an "impractical" theologian and that answering these "how to" questions is "beyond my paygrade." But I take "how to" questions very seriously. Though it was crucial for me to articulate the vision of embrace and to bolster it with theological reasons, I knew that having a compelling vision of life isn't enough. For it is possible to fully embrace a vision and have good reasons for doing so, but find oneself incapable of living it out.

---

11. The analogy comes from sociologist David Martin (*Does Christianity Cause War?* [Oxford: Oxford University Press, 1997], 32).

During a lecture I gave in Zagreb at the launch of the Croatian translation of *Exclusion and Embrace*, I noticed in the audience a man growing restless in a slightly troubled, searching sort of way. I was certain he would come to talk to me after the lecture. He waited for a while in the back and then placed himself at the end of the queue. When his turn came and after all others were gone, he looked me intently in the eyes and asked: "But how do I get it?" The breathlessness of the question took me aback. "How do you get what?" I asked. "How do I get the will to embrace the enemy?" he clarified. His was a "how to" version of the pointed "can you" question Jürgen Moltmann asked me in Berlin when I first presented publicly a sketch of my theology of embrace: "But can you embrace a četnik?" he asked. I begin the book with that question, and proceed to answer why I ought to be able to embrace a četnik, but the book contains no concrete help with regard to how to do what I ought to do, no spirituality of embrace, except for a few scattered gestures toward it.[12]

Exclusion and Embrace needs two practical companion volumes. One should be about the *spirituality of embrace*: a guidebook for the formation of a self capable of practicing embrace. The other should be about *conflict resolution*: a guidebook for acquiring skill in resolving protracted conflicts, personal as well as communal. Writing such books is beyond my area of expertise. The best I can do is give occasional pastoral advice, as I briefly did to my questioner in Zagreb.

Will to Embrace

There is a theoretical aspect to the objection that the book is insufficiently practical. Whereas the first objection concerns the book's scope—the complaint being that I failed to write the book some of my readers (also) wanted to read—this objection concerns one of my main claims. I make much of the "will" to embrace. In a sense, everything in the book revolves around that will: if you have it, embrace can happen; if not, it can't. The objectors, mostly "church" theologians who espouse communitarian virtue ethics, argue that the will to embrace presupposes "sovereign subjects," morally self-standing individuals, who decide to embrace or not to

---

12. For a text that recognizes the main intention behind *Exclusion and Embrace* but still notes the need to address more practical questions of transformation of agents and resolution of conflicts, see Corneliu Constantineanu, "Exclusion and Embrace: Reconciliation in the Works of Miroslav Volf," *Kairos: Evangelical Journal of Theology* 7, no. 1 (2013): 35–54.

embrace others, to obey or not to obey the "law of (unconditional) love."[13] Such elevation of the will is anthropologically and morally implausible, they argue. I should have therefore written more about the Christian community and practices, about the kinds of communal settings and habits that make doing what is right under adverse circumstance not a matter of mere exertion of the will but the outflow of the character we have acquired.[14]

The objection projects into my text the anthropology that has come to dominate important strands of modern moral theory. But I disagree with that anthropology in important ways. First, I believe that God's relation to human beings is not extrinsic to who we are. We don't first come into relation with God—or to one another—as established, let alone sovereign, individuals. God's creative, sustaining, and redeeming relation to us is abidingly constitutive of us and therefore intrinsic to who we are. Second, as Martin Luther put it, "[God] does not work in us without us,"[15] (though, of course, God mostly works in us without us being aware of the divine work in us). We are no mere inanimate tools in God's hands. (With these two convictions in place, Luther could claim both that faith is God's gift and that the nature of faith is will.)[16] The will to embrace of which I write is always God's work, and when we as individuals or as communities claim it as "our work," we misconstrue the nature both of our humanity and of God's work in human lives.[17]

But it is not just that humans are in their constitutions and activity "open" to God in the way I just described. We are also "porous" to one another, becoming who we are through many and variegated inter-human relations, from before our birth to the moment of our death (and for those

13. It is, perhaps, helpful to note that even in Kant's moral philosophy, for which both a sovereign subject and individual's will are fundamental, the good will does not stand in contrast to character (see Immanuel Kant, *Groundwork of the Metaphysics of Morals*, ed. Mary Gregor [Cambridge: Cambridge University Press, 1997], 7).

14. See L. Gregory Jones, "Finding the Will to Embrace the Enemy," *Christianity Today* 41, no. 5 (1997): 29. Similarly William Cavanaugh, review of *Exclusion and Embrace: A Theological Exploration of Identity, Otherness, and Reconciliation* by Miroslav Volf, *Modern Theology* 15, no. 1 (1999): 98.

15. Martin Luther, "The Bondage of the Will," *Luther's Works*, vol. 33, ed. Philip S. Watson (Philadelphia: Fortress, 1972), 243.

16. Ibid., 64–65.

17. Let this serve as a response to Ellen Charry, who thinks that "at the end of the day" in my account of the embrace "there remains an aura of Pelagianism." Why? For me, she claims, "embracing the other appears to be an act of will," whereas "in truth such an ability is really a miracle that happens only by the grace of God. Reconciliation is the supreme work of God" (Review of *Exclusion and Embrace: A Theological Exploration of Identity, Otherness, and Reconciliation* by Miroslav Volf, *Theology Today* 56, no. 2 [July 1999]: 249). As I see it, following one of the most anti-Pelagian Christian theologians, human will and God's agency should not be played against each other.

who believe in the "communion of the saints," beyond death as well). That's where communities of practice fit in as shapers of character. They are crucial in my account, as is evident from the place of baptism and eucharist in Chapter IV on "Embrace." In terms of the genesis of the book as well, I trace a good deal of its vision to a Christian micro-community of practice—the family in which I was raised, and not just my parents, extraordinary as they were in their striving, suffering, many failures and even more successes, but also my seemingly effortlessly saintly nanny, teta Milica.

All this I assume, but do not stress. Part of the reason is the occasion of the book. It was a conflict in which two *Christian* communities stood on opposite sides as implacable enemies, each seeing itself as engaged in the war of liberation, each claiming for itself the "right practice." Important leaders of these Christian communities championed enthusiastically "the spirit of exclusion" that ruled over many influential intellectuals and institutions and had burrowed itself into the souls of some of the best people I knew on both sides. (The same was true of the Muslim community, the third group in the conflict, but that is not the issue here.) More importantly, *I wrote the book above all for myself*, a person who was shaped by and who identified with communities of radical discipleship. I needed both clarity about what it is that a good will ought to will in the situation, and compelling reasons to will and to do what I sensed I ought to. That was the purpose of the book: to argue against my own proclivities and against the sensibilities of many Christians.

Those advocating virtue ethics are fond of telling stories of people who act in morally exemplary ways under extraordinarily adverse circumstances, and yet who insist with modest matter-of-factness that there's nothing special about what they did, that in fact "anybody would have done the same" (as some leading Huguenots from Le Chambon-sur-Lignon have said of their heroic work to save Jews facing extermination during World War II).[18] But I had no such practiced "natural" moral virtuosity, and most of those I thought had it were faltering. For me, and for most people I knew, a battle was raging to know what I ought to know and to do what I knew I ought to do, as well as a struggle not to let the incapacity in doing undermine the truth of knowing.[19]

---

18. For their story, see Philip P. Halle, *Lest Innocent Blood Be Shed: The Story of the Village of Le Chambon and How Goodness Happened There* (New York: Harper Perennial, 1984).

19. On the dynamic of truthful knowing and right doing, see Miroslav Volf and Matthew Croasmun, *For the Life of the World: Theology That Makes a Difference* (Grand Rapids: Brazos, 2019), Chapter 5 (written with Justin Crisp).

This kind of inadequacy in knowing and impotence in doing is not simply an experience of people living on their own, outside of the salutary discipline of communities of virtue. It is an experience of self-aware people *in such communities*. That's because communities of virtue are also communities of vice, and members of even the best communities of virtue are themselves internally morally divided. We all are morally divided, and not just because we embrace the undisciplined freedom of sovereign subjects, but above all because sin is both the rot deep in our souls and a prowling beast of exclusion that holds captive entire societies, cultures, and communities.[20]

That's where the importance of the *will* to embrace comes in, not as a simple switch to turn the practice of embrace on, but as a site of struggle for the truth of our humanity. Membership in the community of virtue is important, but it is hardly ever a substitute for the struggle for moral excellence. Inversely, finding oneself caught in a community that marches to the drumbeat of the power of evil is not an excuse for moral failure. For even in such cases I am responsible. Whether I live on a sun-bated and wildflower-bejeweled meadow or in a filthy swamp, the Apostle Paul's injunction applies: "whatever is true, whatever is honorable, whatever is just, whatever is pure, whatever is pleasing, whatever is commendable, if there is any excellence and if there is anything worthy of praise, think about these things" (Phil 4:8)—or keep them in the forefront of our attention and orient your life toward them. That seems an impossible task, yet there are many human equivalents to water lilies, and we rightly admire their startlingly unfitting beauty.

The Spirit "helps us in our weakness," wrote the Apostle Paul (Rom 8:26)—through communities and apart from any community, when we meditate and pray, and often when we don't even believe.

Social Agents, Social Arrangements

As noted, "church" theologians, especially those under the influence of Alasdair MacIntyre, missed communities of practice in *Exclusion and Embrace*. "Political" theologians, especially those under the long shadow of Karl Marx (but not my own doctoral supervisor, Jürgen Moltmann!), missed the discussion of social arrangements. As I wrote early in the book,

---

20. On the power of sin acting through trans-personal structures of sin see Matthew Croasmun, *The Emergence of Sin: The Cosmic Tyrant in Romans* (New York: Oxford University Press, 2017).

I consider "attending to social arrangements essential."[21] After all, part of the reason for the breakup of the former Yugoslavia and for the identity-driven war that ensued was the authoritarian character of the Tito regime and, after 1974, a weak and illiberal state. Similarly, without some form of pluralistic political arrangements, in a world marked by ease of communication and increasing interdependence, conflicts along religious and ethnic lines of difference will perdure. It is a myth that to solve all social ills all you need is sufficiently moral individuals, whether those ills are economic exploitation, political oppression, or conflicts around communal identities.

In *Exclusion and Embrace* I claim that theologians *qua* theologians can make only a limited contribution to political philosophy and therefore also to the shape of social arrangements in any given setting, much like theologians *qua* theologians can make only a limited contribution to many other domains of life, such as economics, medicine, or law. To bring a Christian perspective to bear on these domains, we need not so much theology as theologically informed "Christian learning."[22] Leaning on philosophers like Nicholas Wolterstorff and Charles Taylor, in *A Public Faith* (2011) and in *Flourishing* (2015), I have offered an account of political arrangements that rests on deep Christian moral convictions—above all, freedom of conscience and the equal dignity of every human being—and is designed to make possible the common life of individuals and communities with distinct religious, ethnic, or more broadly cultural identities.[23] This was in part an exercise in "political" theology. In contrast, *Exclusion and Embrace* was more an exercise in "personal" theology, or, more precisely, theology of socially situated persons. Such theology is important for persons and their relations, but it is also indispensable if we are to address adequately the political side of the identity-driven struggle among groups.

But why so much stress on persons? In the book I note that the main contribution Christian faith and Christian theologians have to make is to articulate a social vision and to foster the kinds of social agents capable of living it out, including creating just, truthful, and peaceful societies. But,

---

21. See doc 1, p. 15; 1st ed., p. 21.

22. See Nicholas Wolterstorff, "Public Theology or Christian Learning?" *A Passion for God's Reign: Theology, Christian Learning, and the Christian Self*, ed. Miroslav Volf (Grand Rapids: Eerdmans, 1998).

23. Miroslav Volf, *A Public Faith: How Followers of Christ Should Serve the Common Good* (Grand Rapids: Brazos, 2011), 77–145; Miroslav Volf, *Flourishing: Why We Need Religion in a Globalized World* (New Haven: Yale University Press, 2015), 97–194.

for theology, the stress on persons is not just a matter of niche-specific concentration. It is no less of a myth to believe that all you need is properly designed social arrangements to solve most social ills than it is to believe that all you need are morally responsible persons. From the first pages of the Bible we know that a person can feel oppressed and stymied in what by all accounts is a paradise. Inversely, we can live in circumstances of "cozy slavery," to use a phrase of Karl Marx, blissfully unaware of the actual evil to which we are both subjected and contributing. Marx had in mind participation in a dehumanizing economic system. In the book, I sketch a scenario of enthusiastic participation in grand political projects, which from within seemed to many like an unquestionable good of a national renaissance but were either deeply evil (as were those represented by slogans like "Deutschland über alles!" or "Hakko ichiu!") or morally highly questionable (as are those represented by slogans like "Hungary Belongs to Hungarians!" or "Make America Great Again!"). To resist various forms of a cultural and political slide into barbarity, we need social agents with rich interior lives who are invested in the nobility of their own spirit.

Personal theology, church theology, and public theology (including in this last category not just political but also economic and ecological theologies) are not mutually exclusive alternatives. To the contrary, they belong integrally together. Such a multifaceted theology is implied in the universality of the Christian faith. By "universality" I mean that a Christian vision of flourishing life concerns every person and the entire world. The universality of this vision implies more than that everyone, each in his or her own way, ought to live it out. For all humans and all life on the planet are interdependent. For one person truly to flourish, the entire world must flourish; for the entire world truly to flourish, every person in it must flourish; and for every person and the entire world truly to flourish, each in his or her own way and all together must live in a world become God's home.[24]

The universality of a Christian vision of flourishing life is not just a matter of scope but also of depth. The most common image in the New Testament for a Christian vision of the true life is the "kingdom of God." In Romans 14:17, the Apostle Paul states that the kingdom of God consists in "righteousness, peace, and joy in the Holy Spirit." Together with Ryan McAnnally-Linz and Matthew Croasmun, I have tied righteousness,

---

24. See Volf and Croasmun, *For the Life of the World*, 69–80.

peace, and joy to three mutually interpenetrating dimensions of life: righteousness, summed up in the command to love God and neighbor, which is about *life being led well*; peace, understood as a set of appropriate physical, social, economic, political, and ecological circumstances, which is about *life going well*; and joy, which gathers in itself all positive emotions, which is about *life feeling as it should*.[25]

For theology to discern, articulate, and commend a Christian vision of flourishing life in this comprehensive sense, it must concern itself with the entire range of human life, from the most intimate stirrings of the human heart to terrestrial interdependencies of all created life, and everything in between. And it must concern itself with all of that in the light of God's self-revelation in Jesus Christ. Since everything cannot be said at once, theologians might shift from one aspect of flourishing life to another while preferably keeping the entire range in mind. In *Exclusion and Embrace* I zeroed in on "social agents."

Religious Violence and Political Power

The main goal of *Exclusion and Embrace* is to sketch a theological vision guiding the practice of embrace. Such theological vision implicitly contains a critique of theological visions that legitimize the practice of exclusion. One disadvantage of concentrating on social agents (their beliefs and practices) is that I only briefly mention reasons why the Christian faith is often configured such that it provides legitimation for the practice of exclusion. Reading only *Exclusion and Embrace* one could think that the practice of exclusion is simply a moral failure of individual Christians, a result of the pressure of sinfulness within and the power of sin from without. But that's not the case. Without wanting to exculpate individuals entirely, it is important also to note that individuals often find themselves inheriting exclusionary versions of Christian faith. I have explored the reasons for the formulation of exclusionary versions of faith in subsequent publications, above all in *A Public Faith* and *Flourishing*.[26]

Many critics think that Christian faith is exclusionary by nature. I obviously disagree; *Exclusion and Embrace* is one cumulative argument

---

25. See Miroslav Volf, *Flourishing*, 75; Miroslav Volf and Ryan McAnnally-Linz, *Public Faith in Action: How to Think Carefully, Engage Wisely, and Vote with Integrity* (Grand Rapids: Brazos, 2016), 13ff.; Miroslav Volf and Matthew Croasmun, *For the Life of the World*, 16–17; and Miroslav Volf, Matthew Croasmun, and Ryan McAnnally-Linz, "Meaning and Dimensions of Flourishing" (forthcoming).

26. Volf, *A Public Faith*, 56–62; Volf, *Flourishing*, 161–94.

against this view. Exclusionary forms of Christian faith are distortions. To answer the question why such distortions arise so that Christian faith comes to legitimize exclusion and violence, I draw on the work of David Martin, a sociologist and "accidental theologian."[27] In *Does Christianity Cause War?* he suggested that we think of the Christian faith as a repertoire of "linked motifs internally articulated in a distinctive manner, and giving rise to characteristic extrapolations" about a way of life in the world, a repertoire that is tied back to the original revelation but not identical with it. Depending on the setting and guiding interests, the character of the faith changes: some motifs from its repertoire are foregrounded, others are backgrounded, and most are "played" with various types and degrees of consonance or dissonance with the situation. Though changing depending on circumstances, Christian faith is not infinitely malleable, however. The original revelation provides subsequent articulations of the faith with "a flexible but distinctive logic and a grammar of transformations."[28]

If we follow Martin's suggestion about how faith gets configured and reconfigured, then the crucial question becomes: Under what conditions is a faith likely to come to legitimize exclusion and violence? Martin's response is, "when religion becomes virtually coextensive with society and thus with the dynamics of power, violence, control, cohesion, and marking out of boundaries."[29] When Christian faith becomes a mere marker of group identity (according to Immanuel Kant, the main public function of religions),[30] it tends to harden the boundaries by providing groups with the aura of the sacred, thus energizing and legitimizing their struggles; inversely, conflicts between groups associated predominantly with a single religion push those religions to function as markers of that group's identity. Similarly, entanglement of the Christian faith with political power pushes toward the kind of configuration of a religion's motifs that will provide the political power with legitimacy (and in some cases rulers themselves, with the help of religious elites, engage in "nourishing, dressing, and forming" native religious inclinations to shore up their legitimacy, as Thomas Hobbes noted).[31] In situ-

---

27. For the category of "accidental theologians," see Miroslav Volf and Matthew Croasmun, *For the Life of the World*, 12n3.

28. David Martin, *Does Christianity Cause War?* (Oxford: Oxford University Press, 1997), 32, 120.

29. Ibid., 134.

30. Immanuel Kant, "Toward Perpetual Peace," *Practical Philosophy*, transl. and ed. Mary J. Gregor (Cambridge: Cambridge University Press, 1996), 336.

31. Thomas Hobbes, *Leviathan*, ed. C. B. MacPherson (New York: Penguin, 1968), 168.

ations of conflict, a religion thus configured ends up justifying the group's practice of exclusion and its deployment of violence.

A certain kind of distance from one's primary social group—refusal to identify fully with it or any of its political projects—is essential if the Christian faith is not to be given an exclusionary form. I implied this in Chapter II on distance and belonging, but did not develop the idea.

Humans, Christ, and Trinity

Trinity and a Social Vision

In her important book, *Christ the Key*, my Yale colleague Kathryn Tanner writes:

> When contemporary theologians want to form judgments about social and political matters they often turn immediately to the trinity for guidance. Rather than Christology, a theology of the trinity is enlisted to support particular kinds of human community—say, egalitarian, inclusive, communities, in which differences are respected—or to counter modern individualism by greater regard for the way personal character is shaped in community.[32]

Tanner considers the procedure of said contemporary theologians "very easy and clear-cut"—and completely mistaken. To make her point, she discusses extensively Jürgen Moltmann's *The Trinity and the Kingdom* and my own texts in which I take up the relation between the Trinity and human community, including *Exclusion and Embrace*.[33] Though aware of significant differences between us, Tanner treats the two of us—and the other three advocates of the position she rejects: Leonardo Boff, Catherine LaCugna, and John Zizioulas—as representing, roughly, a single position. At least in my case, that's a problem, for I often find myself on her side of the debate. I am with her, for instance, when she chastises Moltmann for rejecting monotheism in favor of trinitarianism as if trinitarianism were

---

32.   Kathryn Tanner, *Christ the Key* (Cambridge: Cambridge University Press, 2010), 207.

33.   For Jürgen Moltmann, see especially *The Trinity and the Kingdom: The Doctrine of God*, transl. Margaret Kohl (San Francisco: HarperCollins, 1981). In my case, *After Our Likeness*, 191–214; *Exclusion and Embrace*, 1st ed. 22–31, 125–31; and "'The Trinity is Our Social Program': The Doctrine of the Trinity and the Shape of Social Engagement," *Modern Theology* 14, no. 3 (July 1998): 403–23.

not a form of monotheism,[34] when she objects to associating monotheism only with authoritarianism or totalitarianism ("one God, one ruler") while forgetting its egalitarian impetus ("no ruler but God"),[35] or when she wonders whether Moltmann's position, in which the Trinity, according to critics, appears as "a group of friends," does not come too close to sliding into tritheism.[36]

Tanner thinks that we should keep the nature of and the relations among trinitarian persons out of consideration when reflecting theologically about human identities and relations. What the Trinity is like is not "the best indicator of the proper relationship between individual and community" and does not "establish how human societies should be organized." Theologians should therefore not seek "to base conclusions about human relationships on the trinity."[37] The attempt to do so is both mistaken and vacuous, she maintains. It is mistaken because the Trinity is radically different from human community and therefore one cannot serve as the pattern for the other. The attempt is vacuous for the same reason: to the extent that the Trinity is said to provide the pattern, it has to be pulled down from heaven to earth, which means that it "fails to do any work; it does not tell one anything one did not already know."[38]

I'll respond only to what Tanner writes about the two pillars of *Exclusion and Embrace*: the unconditional will to embrace and the dynamic character of personal and group identities. Ultimately, at issue are partly diverging accounts of the Trinity and of the nature of salvation, but this epilogue is not the place to discuss our differences on these two matters. I will interweave into my response to Tanner a response to Karen Kilby's article,[39] in which she offers appreciative but firm critique of the two trinitarian pillars of the argument in *Exclusion and Embrace* as I articulated them in my subsequent article titled "'The Trinity is Our Social Program'"[40] (reprinted here with slight editing as an appendix). Tanner's and Kilby's critiques are not fully identical, but they build on each other's work in critiquing mine.

34. Tanner, *Christ the Key*, 217. See Miroslav Volf, *Allah: A Christian Response* (New York: HarperOne, 2011), 127–48.
35. Tanner, *Christ the Key*, 208–9.
36. Ibid., 244.
37. Ibid., 207, 221.
38. Ibid., 230.
39. Karen Kilby, "The Trinity and Politics. An Apophatic Approach," *Advancing Trinitarian Theology: Explorations in Constructive Dogmatics*, ed. Oliver Crisp and Fred Sanders (Grand Rapids: Zondervan, 2014), 75–93.
40. Volf, "'The Trinity is Our Social Program.'"

On Correspondences between Trinity and Human Community

Let me start by noting the biblical basis for affirming such correspondences, which Tanner explicitly denies. While not widespread in the New Testament, the idea of humans aligning their lives with God's is clearly present. "Be perfect…as your heavenly Father is perfect," we read in the Sermon on the Mount (Matt 5:48). I take it that "Father" here stands for "God" and not for one person of the Trinity to the exclusion of others. Given the later trinitarian understanding of God, I take it also that Christians ought to read the text as an injunction to be perfect as God, who is the Trinity, is.[41] More to the point, the idea that relations among humans should in some sense correspond to relations among divine agents (later recognized as comprising the Trinity) is clearly present in one significant and historically influential New Testament text, the last prayer of Jesus in John 17. Jesus addresses the Father asking that his disciples, "may be one, as we are one" (17:11; also 20-22). Commenting on the passages, Tanner claims that the point of the adverb "as" in the passages "is not to highlight the similarity between our unity with the Father and Jesus's unity with him but the difference."[42] That's because she believes that the adverb "as" ties the unity between Jesus and the Father to the unity between believers and the Father. The relevant passages in John 17 are then about "the centrality of Christ, and of his relation with the Father, for our relation with the Father" and not about "the unity of human persons on the analogy with unity among persons of the trinity."[43] For the interpretation to work, however, we would have to read 17:11 with the brackets added: "Holy Father, protect them in your name that you have given to me, so that they may be one [with you], as we are one." If the unity with the Father were in view, a more natural way to formulate the last clause would be "as I am one with you."[44] Notwithstanding her appeal to Athanasius, the point of "as" in John 17:11, 20-23 is clearly to underscore similarity in the kind of oneness that exists between the Father and Jesus and the unity among

41. Kilby objects to this way of reading the text, though without giving reasons why ("The Trinity and Politics," 82n19).

42. Tanner, *Christ the Key*, 239.

43. Ibid., 238.

44. Similarly she would have to read John 17:21-23 with implied brackets insertions: "that they may all be one [with you, Father], as you, Father, are in me and I am in you, may they also be in us, so that the world may believe [observing believers' being in Jesus and the Father] that you have sent me. The glory that you have given me I have given them, so that they may be one, as we are one [i.e., as I am one with you], I in them and you in me, that they may become completely one [with you]." To me this reading of the text is highly implausible.

disciples. All major modern commentaries are agreed on this.[45] Now, the unity among believers is here not merely modeled on the unity between Jesus and the Father. Rather, it is rooted in the believers' unity with Jesus, and through Jesus in their unity not so much with the Father as with the Trinity, in their being "in us" (17:2), which is to say in Jesus and the Father who are united by being in one another (John 10:31). The unity of believers comes about through indwelling and being indwelled and is modelled and lived out as the visible image of the Trinity ("so that the world may believe," 17:21).[46] I will return to the relation between indwelling and imitating.

Tanner's second argument against the biblical basis for some kind of correspondence between God's unity and human community concerns the practice of Jesus in the Gospels. Had he thought of the unity among disciples in analogy to his unity with the Father, why is it, inquires Tanner, that "Jesus' relations with Father and Spirit do not appear in any obvious way to be the model for his relation with other human beings in the story"?[47] After all, Jesus is supposed to exemplify proper human relation to God and to one another. The response is surely that he cannot relate to humans the way he relates to the Father and the Spirit because he relates to humans not simply as a fellow human but primarily as the incarnate Word. Correspondingly, human beings ought to relate to him not simply as one among them but as "the Lord."

The correspondence between the two notwithstanding, the nature and unity of divine persons and the nature and unity of human beings cannot be anything close to identical, which is what Tanner suggests that those of us imply who think that the nature of the unity of divine persons is relevant for the nature of the unity among human beings. In my view, the position Tanner criticizes, namely that what "the trinity is like . . . establish(es) how human societies should be organized,"[48] is false as it stands, unless

---

45. Charles Kingsley Barrett, *The Gospel According to St. John: An Introduction with Commentary and Notes on the Greek Text*, 2nd ed. (Philadelphia: Westminster, 1978), 512; Rudolph Bultmann, *The Gospel of John: A Commentary*, transl. G. R. Beasley-Murray et al. (Philadelphia: Westminster, 1971), 512–13; Jean Zumstein, *L'Évangile selon Saint Jean (13–21)*, Commentaire du Nouveau Testament (Genève: Labor et Fides, 2007), 183; Rudolph Schnackenburg, *The Gospel According to St John*, Herder's Theological Commentary on the New Testament, transl. David Smith and G. A. Kon (Tunbridge Wells: Burns and Oates, 1982), 3:191; Udo Schnelle, *Das Evangelium nach Johannes*, Theologische Handkommentar zum Neuen Testament (Leipzig: Evangelische Verlagsanstalt, 1998), 258–59.

46. Commenting on "as" (kathos) in John 17:21 Raymond E. Brown writes: "heavenly unity is both the model and source of the unity of believers" (*The Gospel According to John [XIII–XXI]*, Anchor Bible [Garden City: Doubleday, 1970], 3:769).

47. Tanner, *Christ the Key*, 237.

48. Ibid., 207.

we *extensively* qualify it. I myself make that very point, and I do so for a simple and incontrovertible reason: in fundamental and unalterable ways, human beings are unlike divine persons, and their respective unities must differ. Human beings are fragile and limited creatures, whereas the divine persons, in the unique mode of their unity, are the eternal and limitless Creator. Human beings are also sinful, bent in on themselves, whereas the divine persons are the primordial Love and therefore always unconditionally loving.[49] We cannot derive normative visions of human persons and relations by transposing on them the character of divine persons and relations. We must construe the significance of divine persons and relations for the normative vision of human persons and relations by taking into account the character of human beings as creatures and sinners. If we don't, we end up either divinizing human beings or "secularizing" the Trinity. If we do, we end up with something like a weak analogy between the Trinity and human communities as they should be, but nothing like identity between them. I advocate for such analogy. In fact, I advocate analogy in which difference is always greater than similarity and which, precisely as such, funds an affirmation of similarity.

On Deriving the Shape of Human Community from the Trinity

As I see it, the purpose of identifying such an analogy is not mainly to derive the shape of human persons and relations, not accessible to us in any other way, from divine persons and relations, so we can "mimic" or "reproduce" these. In the original version of "'The Trinity is Our Social Program,'" I use the language of derivation and copying, sparingly but still perhaps too unguardedly.[50] But I state very clearly that the conceptualization work cannot proceed simply from above (Trinity) to below (church and society).[51] It must also proceed the other way around: from the kind of beings humans are, as creatures and sinners, to the nature of possible correspondence with the Trinity. Instead of aiming simply to "derive and replicate," I am first of all seeking to show something like the goodness of analogical fit. Given that God creates humans in God's image, this kind of a God fittingly creates these kinds of human beings with these kinds of communal and personal identities and relations. This is in part what I

---

49. See Volf, *After Our Likeness*, 198–200.
50. Volf, "'The Trinity is Our Social Program,'" 403–5. See appendix.
51. Volf, *After Our Likeness*, 194.

meant when, in *After Our Likeness,* I stated that "conceiving the church in correspondence to the Trinity does not mean much more than thinking with theological consistency."[52]

More than any of my critics, Kilby clearly affirms my methodological proposal to proceed in the constructive work both from above and from below. Still, she believes that I inconsistently set out "to develop an understanding of identity from the concept of *perichoresis.*"[53] She considers my account of human identity "appealing and to a large extent plausible," but insists that "what is not so plausible is that it is supposed to be derived from an understanding of the immanent Trinity."[54] Two things are wrong with that claim. First, as I explicitly state (as Kilby also notes early in her article), I build "mainly on the narrative of the Triune God's engagement with the world,"[55] rather than on the immanent Trinity. When it comes to the question of identity as distinct from self-giving, this means that I mainly rely on the account of the relation between the Father and Jesus Christ in the Gospel of John. Second, Kilby thinks that as I proceed in giving an account of identity I forget the methodological principle that I have proposed: I proceed straight from divine *perichoresis* to human forms of identity. Why does she think so? Because I give "no hint" that I am "beginning to introduce considerations drawn from finitude and sin into" my discussion of the meaning for identity of *perichoresis.*[56] I don't explicitly state this in the original version of the article, but it should have been obvious that I am in fact introducing "considerations drawn from finitude and sin" because I write about negotiation of identity in a finite and sinful world. The argument is that there is an analogy—a weak analogy on account of human finitude and sinfulness—between divine "non-self-enclosed" and "non-reducible" identities visible in *perichoresis,* and the kind of human personal and group identities marked by "porous and shifting" boundaries that nonetheless need to be maintained and negotiated in conflictual settings in which finite and sinful beings live.

"Derivation" is not an adequate designation for this complex constructive endeavor. But Tanner and Kilby seem to read my texts through the lens of the "requirement of exclusive derivation," which I explicitly reject. They believe that the fact that we can derive the kinds of personhood and

---

52. Ibid.
53. Kilby, "The Trinity and Politics," 79.
54. Ibid., 81.
55. See appendix.
56. Kilby, "The Trinity and Politics," 81.

social relations I advocate from other sources—other theological topics (for instance, incarnation, as Tanner suggests)[57] or other nontheological and secular ones as well—undermines my position. It does not. Integral to my position is the claim that it is impossible to derive human personhood and social relations from the Trinity alone and that it is therefore necessary to derive it from other sources as well.[58]

Does it follow that in appealing to the Trinity for social vision we in fact end up emptyhanded, that the Trinity "fails to do any work" because it does not "tell one anything one did not already know"?[59] So what is accomplished through the appeal to the analogy between divine and human persons and relations, understood as a goodness of fit? It informs and legitimizes a particular vision of human personhood and human unity—for instance, how boundaries are negotiated—as well as motivates people to strive after them. Consider once again Jesus's prayer that his disciples be one as Jesus and the Father are one. It indicates, by way of analogy, that the disciples' unity ought to correspond to the kind of unity Jesus and the Father enacted in the story of their interactions as portrayed in the Gospel. It also states that it is ultimately God who brings about such unity among humans, while at the same time providing motivation for humans to aspire and work toward such unity.

On Being a "Social Trinitarian"

An analogy between the unity of the triune God and human unity is possible because we have to posit an analogy—again, a weak analogy, but an analogy nonetheless—between divine and human persons. This conviction lies at the heart of my "social trinitarianism." I am not fond of the term because it is prone to serious misunderstanding. It conjures up three independent divine beings, a kind of divine team or family, and therefore risks implicitly denying the most basic Christian affirmation that there is "no god but one" (1 Cor 8:4). The content of my "social trinitarianism" is the conviction that social analogies are indispensable when thinking about the triunity of the one God, that without social analogies we could not express something essential about God. Psychological analogies are appropriate and indispensable as well; they stress the singularity of God while

---

57. Tanner, *Christ the Key*, 241.
58. See Volf, *After Our Likeness*, 191–200, and appendix.
59. Tanner, *Christ the Key*, 230.

seeking to articulate distinctness of persons. I also believe that describing Eastern accounts of the Trinity as "social" and Western as "psychological" is mistaken, though it is true that Eastern church fathers are, rightly, more comfortable with social analogies than Western church fathers.[60]

Kilby recognizes that I am a "social trinitarian" who "proceeds—on the whole—with such an alertness to the dangers and possible difficulties of the project."[61] Just for that reason she is puzzled as to why I feel comfortable theologically mining the implications of social analogies for the Trinity. She toys with the idea that the source of my "social trinitarianism" is two accidents of my biography: I am a student of a social trinitarian, Jürgen Moltmann, and I have written a book on communion ecclesiology. She quickly discards biographical explanation in favor of a "justification-of-existence" explanation: social trinitarianism helps theologians like me to justify our work and "our salaries," because it seems to give our discipline "its own unique trove of ideas to source social and political theory," ideas unique with respect to secular thinkers and ordinary Christians alike. And then she adds a "need-for-excitement" explanation: it is alluring to have "such an elusive, even paradoxical concept to work with" like trinitarian *perichoresis*.[62]

Kilby never considers the explanation of my "social trinitarianism" that I have given above, namely that I believe social analogies are indispensable because only with their help can we say something that is true about the Trinity—true in the sense in which any of our statements about God can be said to be true. I believe that alluring and useful but untrue ideas about God are idolatrous. I am committed to the position that only true ideas about God can be put to good use. The non-manipulability of God is fundamental to God's divinity.

So what's true about social analogies for the Trinity? I believe that it is mistaken to think that "person" is "a rather ill-defined placeholder for whatever there might be three of in the trinity."[63] I am not suggesting that "person" is adequate to refer to the Father, the Son, and the Spirit. Noting that in John 10:30 Jesus speaks of his oneness with the Father in plural ("the Father and I are one"), Augustine rightly states that we use "person" to express that of what there are three in the Trinity "not in order to say that precisely, but in order that we might not be obliged to remain

---

60. See Miroslav Volf, "Being as God Is: Trinity and Generosity," *God's Life in Trinity*, ed. Miroslav Volf and Michael Welker (Minneapolis: Fortress, 2006), 5–6.

61. Kilby, "The Trinity and Politics," 81.

62. Ibid., 82–83.

63. Tanner, *Christ the Key*, 220.

326

silent."[64] For "human speech labors under a great dearth of words" when speaking about God.[65] "Person" is inadequate, but so are all other terms we use for God as well. Its inadequacy notwithstanding, it does express correctly the fact that in the New Testament we encounter the Father, the Son, and the Spirit as three actors and speakers, and crucially, actors and speakers who not only act toward the world and address humans but also who act and converse among themselves. As is evident throughout the Gospels and the Epistles, the Father sends the Son and speaks to the Son, and the Son obeys the Father and speaks to the Father; and both the Father and the Son send the Spirit and the Spirit intercedes with the Father on behalf of humans (cf. Rom 8:26).

It is largely this "dialogue" of the Father, the Son, and the Spirit among themselves and with humans in the economy of salvation that the doctrine of the Trinity was articulated to "explain," namely how such a dialogue can happen among characters deemed divine given the uncompromisable oneness of God. I find implausible attempts to root the doctrine of the Trinity either in the character of God's self-revelation (Karl Barth)[66] or in God's self-communication (Karl Rahner).[67] As I see it, the root is the history of engagement of the divine three that are uniquely one in the economy of salvation (Jürgen Moltmann).[68] For the divine three to speak to each other and to humans as well as to act with respect to each other and humans in the "economy," there must be something in them before the creation of the world that allows such dialogue and interaction, even if we stutter when we try to express what that something might be.[69] If an account of "person" at the level of the immanent Trinity makes the dialogue and interactions among divine persons in the economy unintelligible, the gap between economic and immanent Trinity becomes such that the unity between the two cannot be maintained, a sure sign that this construal of the doctrine of the Trinity has failed. The conceptualized doctrine of the Trinity should not make impossible what it was designed to make plausible in the first place.

---

64. Augustine, *De Trinitate*, V.10

65. Ibid.

66. See Karl Barth, *Church Dogmatics*, I/1, transl. G. W. Bromiley and T. F. Torrence (Edinburgh: T & T Clark, 1975), 296–98.

67. See Karl Rahner, *The Trinity*, transl. Joseph Donceel (New York: Crossroad, 1999), 34–37.

68. See Jürgen Moltmann, *The Trinity and the Kingdom: The Doctrine of God*, trans. Margaret Kohl (New York: Harper & Row, 1980), 64. See also Miroslav Volf, "Being as God Is: Trinity and Generosity," in *God's Life in Trinity*, ed. Miroslav Volf and Michael Welker (Minneapolis: Fortress Press, 2006), 6.

69. This is in contrast to Karl Rahner, for whom there is no reciprocity among divine persons; according to him, they cannot be said, for instance, to love one another (see *Trinity*, 106).

Christology versus Trinity

Tanner writes critically of the procedure followed by "social trinitarians": "rather than Christology, a theology of trinity is enlisted to support particular kinds of human community."[70] For her, and perhaps for some theologians she criticizes, this is an exclusive alternative: either Christology or a theology of Trinity. For me it is not. Both the relations among divine persons and their work in the world, especially in the life of Christ, are relevant. Indeed, my main emphasis is on Christ and his life. For reflection on the dynamic nature of personal and communal identities and relations—for what both Tanner and I refer to as "formal" questions[71]—I utilize primarily the trinitarian relations in both economic and immanent domains. For reflection on the "will to embrace," and more broadly on human self-giving for the good of the world—for what both Tanner and I refer to as "substantive" questions—I utilize primarily, though by no means exclusively, Christ's life, especially his way to the cross and his death on the cross. As I see it, the Trinity informs, legitimizes, and motivates our social vision in these two interconnected ways; there is no "isolated attention to what is narrated about the relationships among the trinitarian persons" in my case.[72]

Behind my approach is the claim that the following three convictions are interdependent: (1) God is love, (2) God is the Holy Trinity, and (3) God was in Christ reconciling the world. As is clear from the nature of his baptism, in which the Father speaks about the Son and the Spirit descends upon him, the life of Christ was a "trinitarian" story. In his mission, Christ is intimately related to the Father whose will he is doing and the Spirit who energizes him. God in Christ living human life and taking on the sin and the pain of the world and thus enacting unconditional divine embrace of humanity is the Trinity at work. The kind of dynamic divine unity and divine persons' identities enacted in the story of Christ along with the presuppositions of that unity and these identities in the immanent Trinity, are the formal side of the substantive divine love, which is what the triune God is and which is what Christ enacted in a world of suffering and sin.

Tanner objects that in addition to diverting their attention from Christ, theologians who bring trinitarian reflection to bear on social and

---

70. Tanner, *Christ the Key*, 207.
71. Ibid., 230.
72. Ibid., 237.

political matters stress the formal side of the matter (the structure of identities and relations) and marginalize the substantive side of the matter (the loving nature of the relations). Not I. In the life of God *a se* and in God's dealings with the world, the two are closely intertwined. Correspondingly, I stress both, though highlighting in some writings one and in others the other. In *After Our Likeness*, for instance, I am concerned primarily (not exclusively!) with the formal side of the matter because there I am pursuing the limited goal of developing a nonindividualistic congregationalist ecclesiology.[73] In *Exclusion and Embrace* I am concerned primarily with the substantive side of the matter, though, as is evident from my interpretation of the story of the Prodigal, a certain account of the dynamic of identity negotiation is in fact a necessary dimension of the substantive side of the relationship. In "The Trinity is Our Social Program" (in this volume: the appendix "Trinity, Identity, and Self-Giving") I bring the two together.

Imitation, Incorporation, Indwelling

Much of Tanner's objection to my rendering of how the Trinity relates to social vision concerns what she describes as human endeavors of "imitating" or more derisively "mimicking" the Trinity, of seeking to attain "the heights of trinitarian relations by reproducing them in and of themselves."[74] Though I am very much in favor of imitation properly understood—of the imitation of Christ as well as of the triune God—together with Tanner I very much oppose mere "mimicking" God and even more "reproducing" divine relations.[75] As noted earlier, humans are manifestly not God, and therefore mere mimicking and reproducing of

---

73. Volf, *After Our Likeness*, 191.

74. Tanner, *Christ the Key*, 236.

75. Mark Husbands, similarly, states that "Volf offers us a doctrine of the triune God for which the immediate significance of the Trinity lies principally in being a model for us to imitate rather than the constitutive ground of our reconciliation and promise of life" ("The Trinity Is *Not* Our Social Program," *Trinitarian Theology for the Church: Scripture, Community, Worship*, ed. Daniel J. Treier and David Lauber [Downers Grove: IVP Academic, 2009], 126). But this interpretation of my texts on the Trinity is just plain wrong because it simply disregards what I write about the "indwelling" of Christ and the Spirit in the believer and in the church. It also fails to consider what anybody who writes about such indwelling must assume about the relation between God and creation. Inexplicable to me is his suspicion that the project "risks a nominalist reduction of the doctrine of God to ecclesiology and, in turn, of ecclesiology to social practices" (122). What could my embrace of the distinction between the immanent and economic Trinity and my embrace of Yves Congar's pushback (*I Believe in the Holy Spirit*, transl. David Smith [New York: Seabury, 1983], 3:13–15) against Karl Rahner's axiom—"The economic Trinity is the immanant Trinity and vice versa" (*Trinity*, 22)—mean if not that I *energetically reject* seeing the world as a necessary dimension of God's life, let alone reducing God to a dimension of the world (social practice)?

divine relations are futile and misguided endeavors. The same applies, in a qualified sense, to mimicking or reproducing Christ's life. There are things Christ does for us that we cannot do for others, for Christ is the creative Word incarnate, and we humans are creatures of that Word. So mere "mimicking" is out because it mistakenly presupposes near identity of kind between humans and God.

But even when we reject "identity" in favor of "analogy"—a "weak analogy" with regard to the Trinity and "strong analogy" with regard to Christ—as I have argued we should, the primary relation of humans to the Trinity and the incarnate Word should not be that of imitation. I reject the position Tanner imputes to me, namely that the Trinity shows us "a form of itself that we can hope to approach" thereby "providing us an external model to which we might more easily conform."[76] Creation and preservation of the entire non-divine reality, Christ's dwelling by the Spirit in the believer and the church, and, ultimately, God's indwelling the world are the primary ways in which the Trinity and creatures are related. Still, I maintain that the practice of "imitation" is important. How?

Tanner's alternative to "mimicking" is to affirm that the Trinity enters into our world in Christ and closes the gap between itself and humanity "by actually incorporating the humans into its own very life through the incarnation." She continues, "We are therefore not called to imitate the trinity by way of the incarnation but are brought to participate in it."[77] But the opposition between imitation and participation is false. If we reject the account of Christ or the Trinity as mere external models (which I do), we can affirm what Tanner affirms and still insist on imitation as an important, even indispensable, way humans ought to relate to the Trinity. There is no reason Tanner could not affirm that God is both external and internal to human beings, and therefore can be plausibly construed as both a model and presence. After all, one of her key convictions is that the relation between God and the world and between divine immanence and transcendence is not competitive.[78]

---

76. Tanner, *Christ the Key*, 234.

77. Ibid., 234.

78. I owe this last point to Ryan McAnnally-Linz. See Kathryn Tanner, *Jesus, Humanity, and the Trinity* (Minneapolis: Fortress, 2001), 1–34.

It is not hard to find examples of Christian thinkers who think along the lines I do. Following the evangelist John and the Apostle Paul,[79] Martin Luther, for instance, thought that Christ is in us without being "ours" and therefore remains, in the technical sense, *extra nos*. As such, he is an internal model, or rather, a model that in its externality is also internal. In *The Freedom of the Christian*, he affirmed both the union with Christ and the imitation of Christ, and he insisted emphatically that the union precedes and makes possible imitation, with the result that Christians are to be "Christs" to one another and to the world.[80] The same can be said of the imitation of the Trinity. On my reading of John 17, the Father and the Son in their mutual interiority are both an internal presence in believers and an external "object" of imitation. The unity of the divine persons is a model in that what Jesus prays for ("that they may be one, as we are one" [17:11]) the disciples need to live out: they are to seek to embody in their mutual relations important elements of what they see displayed in the story of mutual relation between Jesus and the Father. But the model to be lived out is also, and more basically, an internal presence. Jesus prays "that they all may be one, as you, Father, are in me and I am in you, may they also be in us...I in them and you in me" (17:21, 23; see also 17:26).

Building on patristic sources, Tanner prefers the language of human "participation" in the divine life and sees this taking place by all humans becoming "members of the one Son" and moving "as a whole, as one body."[81] Building on the Reformers, I prefer the language of Christ's and the Spirit's "indwelling" the believer and the church (in analogy to the Word's coming and taking a dwelling in the flesh): by the Spirit, Christ lives in individuals and in ecclesial bodies—two modes of indwelling that are related but not reducible to one another—and, eventually, in the whole world. The life Christians now live is Christ's life in them, a life lived by faith in the Son of God who loved them and gave himself for them (see Gal 2:20). The creature's participation in God and God's indwelling the creature should not be played-off against each other. Both are in fact present in Pauline and Johannine texts; in Paul: the believer is "in Christ" (Gal 2:17) and "Christ in" the believer (Gal 2:20), and in John: disciples are

---

79. In the writings of the Apostle Paul, Christ is internal to the believer ("it is no longer I who live, but it is Christ who lives in me" [Gal 2:20]) and Christ is an external model to be imitated [Gal 2:3; Luther interprets Paul as modeling Christ in this verse]. In the Gospel of John: Christ is internal to the believer (John 17:26) and Christ is an external model to be imitated (John 13:15).

80. Luther, *Luther's Works*, vol. 31, 368.

81. Tanner, *Christ the Key*, 238.

"in us [the Father and Jesus]" and "I [Jesus] in them" (John 17:21, 23). Indeed, it is by God indwelling creatures—through God's coming into the world and being received by the world (John 1:10-18)—that creatures come to participate in God as distinct from just living through God and in God's ambiance. But whatever the theological, anthropological, christological, soteriological, ecclesiological, and eschatological merits and demerits of either conceptuality or its primacy may be, they both affirm a deep union of God with humans. There is no need to think of this union as an alternative to imitation.

Hope and Memory

Provisionality and Hope

In the long central Chapter IV on "embrace," at the end of the critique of grand narratives and before the explication of the elements of embrace, I wrote that the pursuit of embrace is a struggle "for a nonfinal reconciliation based on a vision of reconciliation that cannot be undone."[82] In the book, I have written some about the imperfectability of all historical reconciliations. Elaborating a bit, I could note that every memory presupposed in embrace is partly cloudy and twisted, that every judgment about wrongdoing is partly mistaken and injurious to the other, that every forgiveness is not just a gift but also partly a prideful self-assertion and sometimes an insult, that every embrace includes in itself elements of exclusion. Relating imperfection to repentance and reparation (see below), I could note that every repentance is partly untrue and every reparation inadequate. The insistence on perfect reconciliation and embrace will result in no embrace at all. As I see it, the practice of embrace requires "courage to imperfection"—and hope for the final embrace (in the dynamic sense sketched in the section "The Drama of Embrace") in the coming world of love.

In the book I don't distinguish clearly between reconciliation and embrace, but the two are not identical. The first is a movement from conflict to a dynamic peace; the second is that dynamic peace itself. Historically, each is imperfect; eschatologically both are final. In the traditional theological account of the Last Things, the final embrace is a particular instance of the interpersonal life in the world to come, which is a world of love,

---

82. See p. 114.

peace, and joy. But what about the *final reconciliation*? Where does it fit in the theological account of the Last Things? It belongs to the transition from the world as it is to the world to come. Generally, this transition is taken to consist of two major events: the resurrection of the dead and the last judgment. But though the final reconciliation presupposes both, it is part of neither. The resurrection is about giving an everlasting life to the dead, freeing them from corruptibility; the last judgment is about each receiving not just a part in the world to come but also acquiring clarity about the character of their already-lived life and undergoing moral transformation.

One might think that the final reconciliation is part of the last judgment. At the last judgment each person stands facing Christ, the judge (2 Cor 5:10), and given that the last judgment is not just a judgment based on works but also a judgment based on grace, the last judgment is also the site of the *final reconciliation with God*, the fulfillment of the act of God "who reconciled us to himself through Christ" (2 Cor 5:18). To usher in the world of love, eschatological transition cannot be only an event between God and human beings, but also must be "a social event between human beings, more precisely, a divine act toward human beings, which is also a social event between them." So in addition to each human standing before the judgment seat of Christ, each will stand face to face with other human beings to be fully reconciled with them in cases where there is a history of wrongdoing. This was the main argument of my essay "The Final Reconciliation."[83]

Along with the argument that the world to come is marked by temporality—that its denizens have an everlasting rather than eternal life[84]—the vision of social reconciliation is the eschatological presupposition for my controversial reflection in *Exclusion and Embrace* on the memory of wrongdoing committed and suffering endured.

On Not Coming to Mind

No part of the book has prompted more discussion than the section "Paradise and the Affliction of Memory," both "approbation and

---

83. Miroslav Volf, "The Final Reconciliation: Reflections on a Social Dimension of the Eschatological Transition," *Modern Theology* 16, no. 1 (2000): 93.

84. Miroslav Volf, "Time, Eternity, and the Prospects for Care: An Essay in Honor of Jürgen Moltmann's 90th Birthday," *Evangelische Theologie* 76, no. 5 (2016): 345–54; see also "Enter into Joy! Sin, Death, and the Life of the World to Come," *The End of the World and the Ends of God: Science and Theology on Eschatology*, ed. John Polkinghorne and Michael Welker (Harrisburg: Trinity Press International, 2000), 256–78.

pushback," as Linn Marie Tonstad noted in her engagement with my "imaginative proposal" about "the weight of the past in the world of love."[85] I have written an entire book in response to critics, *The End of Memory*,[86] which did little to settle the matter, of course, though much, I hope, to clarify the issues. The pushback is due partly to cultural sensibilities around remembering wrongs that gradually emerged after the middle of the last century ("Never forget!") and partly to substantive theological concerns. I will limit my comments here to theological concerns, but will not repeat all the arguments from *The End of Memory*.

Let me state here clearly what might not have been entirely clear in *Exclusion and Embrace* (but is clear in *The End of Memory*): I advocate the idea that the wrongs committed and suffering endured *will not come to mind* for the citizens of the world to come, and that this will happen *after* the wrongs have been named, forgiven, and repented of, *after* the perpetrators and the victims have reconciled, and *after* the world has been made safe from all evil. I am not advocating "forgetting" instead of remembering and forgiving (which was Nietzsche's position, for instance). Nor do I advocate "forgetting" instead of reconciling and instead of transforming the world.[87] I am advocating "forgetting" *after* these have been done. In an important sense, in my account "forgetting" is not something we do, but something that happens to us, something we receive as a gift. That idea is best expressed by using not "forgetting," but the biblical phrase "not...come to mind" (Isa 65:17).[88]

My sense is that there is something deficient in forgiveness and reconciliation that do not result in the wrong committed "not coming to mind" of the victim and the perpetrator alike. If I forgive, and add "But I will never forget," I drape around the gift of forgiveness a gray shroud of warning, even a cloak of threat. I also place on the perpetrator and the victim

---

85. Linn Marie Tonstad, "The Weight of the Past in the World of Love," *Envisioning the Good Life: Essays on God, Christ, and Human Flourishing in Honor of Miroslav Volf*, ed. Matthew Croasmun, Zoran Grozdanov, and Ryan McAnnally-Linz (Eugene: Cascade Books, 2017), 225.

86. Miroslav Volf, *The End of Memory: Remembering Rightly in a Violent World* (Grand Rapids: Eerdmans, 2006).

87. My main interest was not the nature and the uses of "forgetting" more generally but the role of "forgetting" in the process of reconciliation and the vision of wholeness. For a recent and very rich work on the importance of forgetting more generally, see Lewis Hyde's fascinating and generative book of "citations, aphorisms, anecdotes, stories, and reflections," *A Primer for Forgetting: Getting Past the Past* (New York: Farrar, Strauss and Giroux, 2019).

88. For the importance of a certain kind of forgetting for our ability to live well in situations of conflict, see Yehuda Elkana's seminal brief article, "The Need to Forget," published in *Ha'aretz* (March 2, 1988).

an indelible mark of offense; the memory of the forgiven offense nails perpetrators' identities unalterably to their misdeeds and victims' identities to their victimization: once an offender, always an offender; once a victim, always a victim—even if offender and victim past.[89] Identities are thus permanently defined in part by sin. And as I have argued in *The End of Memory*, since justice would require complete memory of all the sins of all the citizens of the world of love, it is not clear that such memory wouldn't completely undo the reality of the world of love.[90]

Some have suggested that there are more benign and necessary uses of the memory of wrongs committed and sufferings endured. It helps us, the argument goes, truly and properly to enjoy the goodness of life in the world to come. Joys require memory of sorrows past as their condition. Clearly, joys of deliverance are particularly powerful in our ordinary experience. Think of Miriam, the sister of the great liberator Moses: rhythmic movements of tambourine over her head, heavy necklaces, the spoils of the Egyptians, bouncing over her breasts, hair and clothes flying as she leads the dance of celebration for the destruction of the oppressor's armies (Exod 15:19-21). But these very joys are a tribute to the primacy of the good and therefore also to its being a sufficient cause of joy. We rejoice in deliverance as a good because freedom is a good and deliverance is an instrument for achieving it; we normally don't rejoice over getting delivered from a frying pan into the fire—or for that matter even in getting delivered from the fire into the frying pan. The possession of the good itself is—and in the world to come will be—reason enough for rejoicing. If goodness is original, as the Christian faith claims, then it must be attractive and joy-generating as goodness without the need for the memory of negativity overcome to accompany it.

Would not non-remembrance of wrongs committed and of sufferings endured not just diminish but eventually extinguish our gratitude to God for deliverance? It would, which is exactly my point. As I see it, it would not be worthy of God and of God's unconditional love to require or accept *everlastingly abiding* gratitude for rescuing humanity from perdition. If a daughter of mine I saved from a fatal accident were to thank me, or feel grateful to me, every time she saw me, I would consider her gratitude an insult to my goodness. I would want her to thank me sincerely

---

89. For a brief account of a forgiver's memory, see Miroslav Volf, *Free of Charge: Giving and Forgiving in a Culture Stripped of Grace* (Grand Rapids: Zondervan, 2005), 173-77.

90. See Volf, *The End of Memory*, 193ff. See also Tonstad, "The Weight of the Past in the World of Love," 228-34.

once, express her gratitude perhaps once or twice if we reminisce about the event, and then go on delighting in life and in my presence in it. I am not suggesting that there be no gratitude to God, for there are more immediate reasons for gratitude: the entirety of our individual lives and of the world in that world to come are and will be abidingly the result of God's generosity.

But what about Jesus Christ, the scars of crucifixion marking his resurrection body, as we read in the Gospels? Do they not mark his ascended body as well? Does not John the Seer have a vision of the Lamb on the throne with God? In *Icons of Hope*, John Thiel makes much of the wounded, resurrected body of Christ in the world to come, even of "the abiding presence of the cross in heaven."[91] Correspondingly, as the cost of redemption in pain and blood is commemorated in heaven, it is inescapable that, as he puts it, "a kind of sadness...prompted by the guilty burden of the effects of sin" mark eternally life in the world to come.[92] A vision of the world to come covered with mists of sadness is tied to his conception of heaven as a purgatory with no foreseeable end in sight. The alternative Thiel's position sets before us is this: you either have a sad heaven, or you don't have in it the cross and memory of wrongs committed and suffering endured. I opt for heavenly joy, which is what God promises (see Matt 25:20-22).

But will we remember the cross? By building on the story of Joseph and his brothers in Genesis, in *Exclusion and Embrace*, I suggested that the cross may be "a paradoxical memorial to forgetting," as was the name of Joseph's son Manasseh, "one who causes to be forgotten."[93] That is one possible way to go for those who opt for everlasting joy. But perhaps it is more compelling to suggest that the cross will not be remembered. We are, of course, speculating. But I don't see why speculating in favor of remembering is better than speculating against it, and can see why the opposite might be the case. Some find the reference to the Lamb on the throne in the book of Revelation as an indication of the presence of the crucified in the world to come. It is not easy to parse out how the imagery of the Lamb functions in the book of Revelation. Clearly it is a literary metaphor invoking the Passover lamb of the exodus (Exod 12:21); no one expects that an actual lamb—let alone a slaughtered lamb (Rev

91. John Thiel, *Icons of Hope: The "Last Things" in Catholic Imagination* (Notre Dame, IN: University of Notre Dame Press, 2013), 42, 184.
92. Ibid., 186.
93. See final text.

13:8)—is sitting on the heavenly throne with God. Most don't expect even that God is sitting on an actual throne either; God on the throne is an earthly image of the rule of God who cannot be encompassed by the universe let alone fit to a throne. Invoking the images of crucifixion makes sense while history lasts and the cross is continuing to do the saving work. But when the history ends and the work of saving is done, the cross will have accomplished its purpose and its memory will not need to come to mind.[94]

Whatever we decide about Jesus Christ, the nature of his resurrection body, including the question of whether Jesus Christ will everlastingly have a discrete physical body, *if* Jesus Christ everlastingly bears the healed scars of crucifixion, what Tonstad writes about the cross—about scars as reminders of the cross—in the world to come, seems exactly right:

> In a world in which God and human beings love each other face to face, however, it does not seem necessary to assume that the cross has a place. We will be in the presence of the one who loves us as much as we were loved "then" (i.e. on the cross). But we will know that one much better when we see face to face and are changed in that beholding.[95]

When it comes to memory of wrongs committed and sufferings endured in the world to come, the most fundamental issue concerns the "redemption of the past." In *Exclusion and Embrace* I quote in the text Friedrich Nietzsche's exclamation from *Thus Spoke Zarathustra*, "to redeem the past that alone do I call redemption."[96] Strictly speaking, the *past* cannot be redeemed; only *people* who lived and endured the affliction of having committed or suffered wrongdoing and pain can be redeemed. For Nietzsche, the redemption of the past occurs through the transformation of the attitude toward the past: a person boldly embraces the past by saying with regard to the entirety of what was: "I willed it thus."[97] Redemption of the past is here an act of self-assertive will identifying with what happened: I affirm and celebrate the reality as it was, is, and will be.

"I willed it thus" is a "God-is-dead" version of the way many theologians have advised us to relate to the past that cries for redemption: "God

94. See Volf, *The End of Memory*, 145–47.
95. Tonstad, "The Weight of the Past in the World of Love," 236.
96. Friedrich Nietzsche, *Thus Spoke Zarathustra*, 161.
97. Ibid., 163.

willed it thus—or at least infinite divine wisdom permitted it!" This theo-centric way of "redeeming" the past presupposes a successful theodicy; it requires being able to say with confidence that the wreckages of history, its horrendous and not-so-horrendous evils, are compatible with divine goodness and have a purpose in divine providence.

My own proposal about non-remembrance of evil committed and suffered stems partly from doubt that any theodicy can succeed and from suspicion that if it did succeed it would justify what from my vantage point seems unjustifiable. Now, *I don't claim* that a theodicy is impossible and that if it were possible it would necessarily be morally reprehensible. When history runs its course and "the kingdom of this world has become the kingdom of our Lord and of his Messiah" (Rev 11:15), *perhaps* we will have a theory that will show that the horrendous evils of history were all part of the plan, even that the world of which they were part was the best of all possible worlds. But we don't have that theory now, and I believe that, in principle, we are not able to have it before history has run its course and the meaning of events within it can be at least in principle settled. I don't mean to disparage philosophers and theologians who work on theodicy, but I worry that the likely theoretical overreach of these projects could have terrible practical consequences for the most vulnerable.

Unless we come up with—or can hope to come up with—a theodicy that will celebrate all evils suffered as arduous goods, the proposal I made about such evils not coming to the minds of the citizens of the world to come deserves to be considered. This, too, does not amount to redemption of the past, but is a way of keeping the evils of the past consigned to the past, of preventing them from entering the lives of the redeemed in a transfigured world through the gate of memory and undoing their joy in what is and will remain.

Justice and Justification of Violence

Justice and Embrace

In the book I write: "Embrace is part and parcel of the very definition of justice." I still believe that this is correct, if by justice we mean what in the older translations of the Bible was termed as "righteousness." In the New Testament, right living is summed up in the commandment to love God and neighbor, for which the term in both Hebrew and Greek is simply *justice.* Since the writing of the book and under the influence of Nicholas Wolterstorff,[98] I have come to believe that we must distinguish "justice" and "righteousness," or, if we want to stick to the single word "justice," that we must distinguish between "justice 1" (justice) and "justice 2" (righteousness). In his fine book *Just and Unjust Peace: An Ethic of Political Reconciliation,* Daniel Philpott pushes against this distinction of mine, and states, similarly as I do in *Exclusion and Embrace,* that "reconciliation *is* justice."[99] The best way to explain why I disagree both with Philpott and with my former self is by examining the place of justice in forgiveness, a critical element of reconciliation and the resulting embrace, and the element most contested by the critics of reconciliation.[100]

If embrace as a result and reconciliation as a process is doing what is just, then forgiving, too, must be justice, a process of doing what is just. But is it? To forgive is no longer to count the perpetrators' misdeeds against them. Defined in this way, forgiveness has two components, one implicit and one explicit, and both essential. The *implicit* component is identification and condemnation of an act as a wrongdoing and of the person who had committed it as a perpetrator. That identification requires an account of how a perpetrator ought to have acted or how the victim had the right to have been treated. A person should have acted justly and not violated the right of another, but he or she acted unjustly and therefore the act is rightfully called a wrongdoing and he or she a perpetrator. At work here is "justice 1." The *explicit* component of forgiveness consists in no longer counting the perpetrator's misdeed against him or her and viewing the prepetrator as a person in good standing; that's what one explicitly and primarily does when one forgives. If "the grace of embrace" is "part and parcel of the idea of justice," this explicit component of forgiveness should also be called justice; when one forgives one acts justly ("justice 2"). But to name "justice" both (1) "respecting a person's rights and not wronging him or her" ("justice 1") and (2) "not counting the wrong against the person who committed it" ("justice 2") is not only confusing, but mistaken. For if "justice 2" is in fact nothing more or less than acting

---

98. See Nicholas Wolterstorff, *Justice: Rights and Wrongs* (Princeton: Princeton University Press, 2008).

99. Daniel Philpott, *Just and Unjust Peace: An Ethic of Reconciliation* (New York: Oxford University Press, 2012), 53.

100. In the following I reproduce, with some minor changes, a portion of my review of Philpott's *Just and Unjust Peace,* "Reconciliation, Justice, and Mercy," *Books & Culture* (September/October 2013): 24–25.

justly, then a victim would *owe forgiveness* to a (contrite) perpetrator; *not to forgive* would be *to wrong* the perpetrator. But when a person forgives, he or she is giving a free gift; and when a person refuses to forgive he or she is withholding generosity rather than incurring guilt by *wronging* the perpetrator. When the perpetrator receives forgiveness, the perpetrator receives something to which he or she has no claim; the perpetrator must always receive it as an undeserved gift. In the Christian tradition, the victim has a duty to forgive; though a gift, forgiveness is *not* a supererogatory gift but an obligatory one. But from the victim's duty to forgive it doesn't follow that he or she owes forgiveness to the perpetrator and that the perpetrator can claim forgiveness as rightfully his or hers.

On my current account, "justice 1" is *justice*, "justice 2" is *mercy*, and the two together are key components of the right relationship among people and are best termed *righteousness* (which is equivalent to love). On my account in *Exclusion and Embrace*, "justice 1" and "justice 2" together make "justice" defined as right relationship. This way of putting things would have the advantage of letting us organize reflection about political reconciliation around the key political virtue of justice. On my current way of thinking, on the other hand, precisely because justice as a political virtue names what we *owe* other people, it would be misleading to talk of reconciliation and embrace as justice, for there are elements of reconciliation we don't owe others and to which others have no claim.

Repentance and Reparation

The central part of the book is Chapter IV on embrace, and the central part of that chapter contains a sketch of the key elements of embrace. I analyzed them concentrating on the hard—and unfair—work the wronged person needs to do. That was in part the consequence of the conviction that being wronged does not exempt one from the obligation to follow Christ and that the unconditionality of God's love enacted in Christ implies the unconditionality of the will to embrace. The main thesis of the book is that the will to embrace is

> prior to any judgment about others, except that of identifying them in their humanity. The will to embrace precedes any "truth" about others and any construction of their "justice." This will is absolutely indiscrimi-

nate and strictly immutable; it transcends the moral mapping of the social world into "good" and "evil."[101]

This is all as it should be; none of it do I want to retract. But this is not all that needs to be said about embrace. The *will* to embrace is unconditional; the *embrace itself* is not, as I stated clearly as well, for instance, in the last chapter when insisting that "dirty shoes" need to be left at the gate of the eschatological world of love.[102] I have not written much in the book, however, about conditions wrongdoers need to satisfy before the actual embrace can take place. In addition to the transformation of the wrongdoer from a source of danger to a trustworthy, aspiring agent of love—in traditional theological vocabulary: a degree of sanctification—the two necessary conditions for the movement of embrace to end in an actual embrace are *repentance* and *restitution*.

In *Free of Charge* I argued that forgiveness is an interpersonal event and that it has the formal structure of gift-giving: somebody gives something to somebody else.[103] The first somebody is the wronged person; the second somebody is the wrongdoer; the "something" that the wronged gives to the wrongdoer is not counting his or her wrongdoing against the wrongdoer, which is to say, that after identifying and naming the wrongdoer as the person who has wronged him or her, the wronged gives the wrongdoer the gift of treating the wrongdoer as if he or she had not wronged him or her. When one person gives a gift, the other has to receive it, otherwise the gift gets stuck between the one who gives and the other who won't receive it. The way we receive forgiveness is by repenting. To repent means to (1) *say that we are sorry*—and sorry, as I have put it in *Flourishing*, "not that we have been caught, sorry not merely that the other person has been wronged, but sorry that we have committed the wrongdoing"[104]—to (2) actually *be* sorry, and to (3) *commit ourselves to act otherwise* in the future. These three things together—confession, contrition, and commitment to change—signal that the forgiver's gift has been received, that the forgiver's not counting my wrongdoing against me corresponds to who I in fact am or at least aspire to be.

---

101. See page 20.
102. See page 151.
103. Miroslav Volf, *Free of Charge: Giving and Forgiving in a Culture Stripped of Grace* (Grand Rapids: Zondervan, 2005), 157–92.
104. Volf, *Flourishing*, 179.

Repentance alone does not suffice, however; *reparation* is necessary as well. For I would not be who in repenting I claim to be and who in forgiving the wronged person treats me to be if I failed to want to repair the damage my wrongdoing has caused. Time does not run backward, and the done deed cannot be undone; reparation cannot make the wrongdoing not to have happened. So what is the ideal case of possible reparation? My colleague from Yale, John Hare, has put it this way: the best possible reparation is designed to bring it about that you as a victim

> are roughly equally content with two states of the world: the first contains the offence together with my repentance, apology, and reparation; the second contains neither. If you, because of my actions, are indifferent between these two states of the world, or have a preference for the first, then my tasks have been accomplished on my side.[105]

Reparation is both necessary and, understood in the way Hare rightly suggests, very costly. But if it weren't, the gift of forgiveness would be treated as a very cheap grace.

---

105. John Hare, *The Moral Gap: Kantian Ethics, Human Limits, and God's Assistance* (Oxford: Clarendon, 1996), 231.

Trinity, Identity, and Self-Giving

Imaging the Trinity[1]

It was Nicholas Fedorov, an erudite friend of such great Russian intellectuals as Leo Tolstoy, Vladimir Solovyov, and Fyodor Dostoyevsky, who first formulated the startling phrase, "The dogma of the Trinity is our social program." What he had in mind is daring to think, but not difficult to formulate. Through his incarnation, the Son of God became consubstantial with humanity and hence his resurrection was the resurrection of the whole of humanity into a new ontological state marked by participation in the divine life. Paul Evdokimov, on whose account of Fedorov's thought in *Le Christ dans la pensée Russe* I lean, puts it this way: through Christ the whole of humanity "enters into God as its ontological place."[2]

Though bold, the thought of "entering into God" is not unusual; it is but a variation on a familiar Orthodox soteriological theme of divinization. What was novel were the social implications Fedorov drew from it. Inscribed in the new ontology of resurrection with Christ is an ethical "must," he believed. More than just the good news of what God has done, the Gospel is a social project humanity needs to accomplish. Because the resurrection of Christ is immanent to all human beings, the participation

---

1. This text was written shortly after the completion of *Exclusion and Embrace* and was originally published as "THE TRINITY IS OUR SOCIAL PROGRAM: THE DOCTRINE OF THE TRINITY AND THE SHAPE OF SOCIAL ENGAGEMENT," *Modern Theology* 14:3 (July 1998): 403–23. © Blackwell Publishers Ltd 1998 Published by Blackwell Publishers Ltd, 108 Cowley Road, Oxford OX4 1JF, UK and 350 Main Street, Malden, MA 02148, USA.

2. Paul Evdokimov, *Le Christ dans la pensée Russe* (Paris: Cerf, 1970), 84.

in the triune life of God is not just an eschatological promise, but a present reality and therefore also a historical program.[3]

No arguments need to be wasted on showing that Fedorov's proposal is specious and his vision chimerical. It is one thing to espouse the belief that in the resurrection of Christ power is at work "capable of transfiguring nature."[4] But the claim that "God has placed in our hands all the means for regulating cosmic disorders"[5] because we participate in the divine life, is the stuff of which dreams are made. Do Fedorov's airy and potentially dangerous musings invalidate his basic idea, however?

Judging from what Ted Peters has to say in *God as Trinity* about the attempts to see the Trinity as a model for human society, he would argue that Fedorov's proposal is mistaken at its core. The basic flaw of all attempts like Fedorov's is that they "operate conjunctively rather than disjunctively," Peters maintains. By insisting that social relations should reflect trinitarian relations, such proposals disregard the simple fact that "God alone is God" and that "we as creatures cannot copy God in all respects."[6] From this perspective Fedorov's fairyland social program would seem a case in point of a strange malady that afflicts theologians seeking to model society on the Trinity: amnesia regarding the most basic theological insight that it is impossible to model society on God because oneness is etched into the very notion of God,[7] and a shroud of mystery rooted in God's categorical difference from the world, envelops the Holy Trinity.

If one cannot "copy" God in all respects, as Peters rightly underscores, does it follow that in relating God to social realities we must operate only disjunctively rather than conjunctively, as he argues? Should we follow the early Karl Barth and his students who insisted that there are no earthly analogues to God, but who nevertheless felt compelled to ascribe to God attributes with strong political overtones, such as might, majesty,

---

3. Proposals about a correspondence between the Trinity and society, and less eschatologically intoxicated ones for that matter, can be traced back further than the nineteenth century, for instance in the thought of John Donne in the seventeenth century, and are to be found in other nineteenth-century thinkers, such as F. D. Maurice. See David Nicholls, "Divinity Analogy: The Theological Politics of John Donne," *Political Studies* 32, no. 4 (1984): 570–80; David Nicholls, "The Political Theology of John Donne," *Theological Studies* 49, no. 1 (1988): 45–66; Torben Christenson, *The Divine Order: A Study in F. D. Maurice's Theology* (Leiden: Brill, 1973); Guy H. Ranson, "The Trinity and Society: A Unique Dimension of F. D. Maurice's Theology," *Religion in Life* 29, no. 1 (1959): 64–74.

4. Evdokimov, *Le Christ dans la pensée Russe*, 83.

5. Ibid., 84.

6. Ted Peters, *God as Trinity: Relationality and Temporality in Divine Life* (Louisville: Westminster John Knox, 1993), 186.

7. As Tertullian puts it in *Adverse Marcionem*, "Deus si non unus est, non est" ("If God is not one only, he does not exist") (I,3).

dominion, and power?[8] In seeking strictly theological sources of social theology, should we leave behind the inclusive Trinity as a model and concentrate instead on the demands of the inimitable and exclusive "kingship of God," as Peters would have it? I do not think so.

Quite apart from the fact that we know what divine "kingship" means only from the narrative of the triune God's engagement with the world,[9] would it not be odd to claim that there are no *analogues* to God in creation and yet to maintain, as Christian theologians must, that human beings are made in the image of God? And would it not be anomalous to insist that human beings, created for communion with the triune of God and renewed through faith and baptism into the triune name "according to the likeness of God" (Eph 4:24), should not seek to be like God in their mutual relations? If the idea of an image that is not supposed to reflect the reality of which it is an image does not strike us as odd, Jesus's injunction in the Sermon on the Mount should set us straight: "Be perfect," he commands his disciples, "as your heavenly Father is perfect" (Matt 5:48; cf. 1 Pet 1:16). The earthly children should be like their heavenly parent, he states (5:45); the character of God should shape the character and behavior of those who worship, he implies.

Where does this brief face-off between Fedorov's proposal and Peters' critique of all proposals like Fedorov's leave us? With two equally unacceptable options, the one consisting of seeking to imitate the triune God in a blatant disregard of the fact that we are not God and the other consisting of respecting our creaturely difference from God but failing to pursue our most proper human calling to be like God? We do not have to choose, however, between Fedorov's divinization of humanity and Peters' total alterity of God, God's being "shrouded in eternal mystery apart from the time in which we live."[10] In fact, the alternative is false. Between "imaging God in all respects" (so seemingly Fedorov) and "not imaging God at all" (so seemingly Peters) lies the widely open space of human responsibility, which consists in "imaging God in some respects." As I see it, the question is not whether the Trinity should serve as a model for

---

8. David Nicholls, *Deity and Domination: Images of God and the State in the Nineteenth and Twentieth Centuries* (London: Routledge, 1994), 113–15, 233–34.

9. Jürgen Moltmann, *The Trinity and the Kingdom: The Doctrine of God*, transl. Margaret Kohl (Minneapolis: Fortress, 1981).

10. Peters, *God as Trinity*, 114.

human community; the question is rather in which respects and to what extent it should do so.[11]

In *After Our Likeness* I argued not only that human community (in the book, the ecclesial community) should be modeled on the Trinity, but also that there are two basic and in principle unsurmountable limits on all such modeling.[12] First, since ontologically humans are manifestly not divine and since noetically human notions of the triune God cannot correspond exactly to who the triune God is, trinitarian concepts such as "person," "relation," or "*perichoresis*," which are themselves analogies, can be applied back to human community only in an analogous rather than a univocal sense. As creatures, human beings can correspond to the uncreated God only in a creaturely way; any other correspondences than creaturely ones would be wholly inappropriate, not because God is governed by "petty and passionate" jealousy, as Thomas Mann puts it in his rendering of the story of Joseph and his brothers,[13] but because human beings should not succumb to the pathetic and self-destructive temptation to jump over their own shadows.

Second, since the lives of human beings are inescapably marred by sin and saddled with transitoriness, in history human beings cannot be made into the perfect creaturely images of the triune God, which they are eschatologically destined to become. Sinful and "fleshly" as we are (Isa 40:6ff.; 1 Pet 1:24), human beings can correspond to the triune God only in historically appropriate ways; any other correspondences than historically appropriate ones would be misplaced, not because human beings should put up with evil, but because the struggle against it will be effective only if we recognize the depth of its entrenchment in persons, communities, and structures.

The two limits to the correspondences between the Trinity and human communities have one significant methodological consequence. The conceptual construction of the correspondences cannot proceed on a one-way street starting from above—from the doctrine of the Trinity down to a vision of social realities. Since the mode and the extent of the correspondences are not only determined by the character of the Trinity but

---

11. The doctrine of the Trinity is, of course, not *all* we have to take into account when reflecting theologically on human communities. Other doctrines are significant, too. So also are biblical texts.

12. Miroslav Volf, *After Our Likeness: The Church as the Image of the Trinity* (Grand Rapids: Eerdmans, 1998), 198–200.

13. Thomas Mann, *Joseph and His Brothers*, vol. 1, transl. H. T. Lowe-Porter (New York: Knopf, 1946), 347.

also shaped in the very fabric of social realities themselves, the conceptual construction of the correspondences must go back and forth on a two-way street, both from above and from below. By describing God in whose image human beings are created and redeemed, the doctrine of the Trinity names the reality that human communities should image. By describing human beings as different from God, the doctrines of creation and of sin inform the way in which human communities *can* image the triune God, now in history and then in eternity.[14]

Fedorov's proposal is flawed not because he builds his social thought on the doctrine of the Trinity but because he proceeds exclusively from above and disregards the two inherent limits on the correspondences between the Trinity and social realities. In his case, the belief that Christ's incarnation and resurrection initiated a new ontology issues in an eschatological intoxication, in which the boundaries between God and creation set by human creatureliness, transitoriness, and sinfulness acquire an air of unreality. Fedorov's bad habits should not detain us, however, from embracing his basic insight that in an important sense the doctrine of the Trinity does entail a "social program" or, as I prefer to put it, that it ought to shape our "social vision."

Before I go on to suggest positively how the doctrine of the Trinity should shape our social vision, allow me to comment briefly on why I prefer the phrase "social vision" to Fedorov's "social program" and make a preliminary remark on the aspects of the doctrine of the Trinity on which I want to draw. The choice of the term "program" owes much to Fedorov's eschatological intoxication. When it refers to social issues, "program" usually means "a plan or system under which action may be taken toward a goal." Unless we advocate something close to a merger between humanity and divinity, however, the doctrine of the Trinity manifestly does not constitute such a plan or system of action. What it does contain, provided we respect the differences between God and creation I just sketched, are the

---

14. There is a discrepancy between the vast amount of reflection devoted to the possibility of positive correspondence between the triune God and human community and the virtual absence of reflection on the inherent limits of all such correspondences. Most proposals about the relation of the Trinity and human community do not explicitly thematize the idea that the doctrines of creation and sin have to shape the way we think of the correspondences between the Trinity and human community and instead proceed *as if* the construction were moving simply from above. In fact, however, most take into account fundamental dissimilarities between God and humanity and adjust correspondences accordingly. For instance, though Moltmann parallels divine and creaturely *perichoresis* (*God and Creation: A New Theology of Creation and the Spirit of God*, transl. Margaret Kohl [Minneapolis: Fortress, 1991], 17), the way he actually develops the idea makes it plain that he does not intend to assert their identity.

contours of the ultimate normative end toward which all social programs should strive.[15] Hence I speak of "vision."

The term *social* is often used to designate social arrangements, a way of structuring societies and networks of societies. Correspondingly, the doctrine of the Trinity is employed to pursue primarily the project of re-arranging (worldwide) socio-economic structures.[16] While such projects are by no means misplaced, the road from the doctrine of the Trinity to proposals about global or national social arrangements is long, torturous, and fraught with danger.[17] Since I am ill equipped to make such a journey and unwilling to take shortcuts, instead of concentrating on the structure of social arrangements I will concentrate on the character of social agents and their relations, an issue no less *political* than the issue of social structures. Here *social* primarily refers to the way in which the self, by its very nature, is inserted into small and large networks of relations, both as their unique sediment and as their creative shaper. I will explore the implications of the doctrine of the Trinity for the shape of the social self and of the relations that constitute the self and that the self in turn shapes.

But on what in the doctrine of the Trinity should we concentrate? The question arises when one recalls the classical distinction between the immanent and the economic Trinity. In his essay *The Trinity*, Karl Rahner has formulated the now famous rule about the identity of the economic and immanent Trinity: "The 'economic' Trinity is the 'immanent' Trinity, and vice versa."[18] On the one hand, the rule makes sense. Clearly, if the immanent and the economic Trinity were not one and the same Trinity, we would have two gods in six persons rather than one God in three persons. And yet, a strict identity between the economic and immanent Trinity is untenable because it would entail the belief that the world is necessarily an integral part of God's life. On the basis of this argument, Yves Congar

---

15. As the best representatives of "political theology" have argued, "theology is political simply by responding to the dynamics of its own proper themes. Christ, salvation, the church, the Trinity: to speak about these has involved theologians in speaking of society, and has led them to formulate normative political ends.... It is not a question of adapting to alien requirements or subscribing to external agenda...but of letting theology be true to its task." (Oliver O'Donovan, *The Desire of Nations: Rediscovering the Roots of Political Theology* [Cambridge: Cambridge University Press, 1996], 3).

16. Leonardo Boff, *Trinity and Society*, transl. Paul Burns (Maryknoll, NY: Orbis, 1988).

17. That the road from the Trinity to general proposals about social arrangements, let alone to concrete social programs, is fraught with danger can be illustrated by the fact that people who take it end up walking in opposite directions. Michael Novak is as enthusiastic about grounding democratic *capitalism* in the doctrine of the Trinity as is Leonardo Boff about grounding democratic *socialism* in the doctrine of the Trinity. See Boff, *Trinity and Society;* Novak, *The Spirit of Democratic Capitalism* (New York: American Enterprise Institute, 1982).

18. Karl Rahner, *The Trinity*, transl. Joseph Donceel (New York: Herder and Herder, 1970), 24.

suggested in *I Believe in the Holy Spirit* that the rule "the economic Trinity is the immanent Trinity" applies only if it is not reversible—only if it does not imply the rule "the immanent Trinity is the economic Trinity."[19] There is always a surplus in the immanent Trinity that the economic Trinity does not express. And it is also the other way around: something new is introduced into the life of the Trinity with creation and redemption— the encounter of the self-giving love of God with the world of enmity, injustice, and deception. In what follows I presuppose both the unity of and the distinction between the immanent and the economic Trinity;[20] and though the immanent Trinity serves as the ultimate horizon, I build mainly on the narrative of the triune God's engagement with the world.

Identity

In recent years theologians have devoted a great deal of attention to the debate about hierarchical versus egalitarian understandings of the Trinity. During most of the doctrine's history, hierarchy was uncontested in the Trinity—as uncontested as it was in human communities. The primacy of the one person seemed a necessary precondition both of the unity of the three and of their distinctions.[21] Egalitarian constructions of the Trinity appear from this perspective as projections onto God of the democratic sentiments that emerged when modern, functionally-differentiated societies replaced traditional, hierarchically-segmented societies. The denials of hierarchy in the Trinity, so the argument goes, seem to be fueled more by the falsely egalitarian spirit of the age than shaped by the revelation of the character of God.

---

19. Yves Congar, *I Believe in the Holy Spirit*, vol. 3, transl. David Smith (New York: Seabury, 1983), 13–15.

20. In *The Spirit of Life: A Universal Affirmation*, Jürgen Moltmann has rightly objected that the distinction between the immanent and the economic Trinity proves "to be too wide-meshed a grid" (transl. Margaret Kohl [Minneapolis: Fortress, 1992], 290). Though in and of itself insufficient because it provides only an inadequate framework for narrating the history of God with the world, as the most basic distinction the duality of "immanent and economic Trinity" still stands.

21. On the primacy of one for the unity of the three, see Wolfhart Pannenberg, *Systematic Theology*, vol. 1, transl. G. W. Bromiley (Grand Rapids: Eerdmans, 1991), 325; John Zizioulas, "The Teaching of the 2nd Ecumenical Council on the Holy Spirit in Historical and Ecumenical Perspective," in *Credo in Spiritum Sanctum Atti del congresso theologico internationale di pneumatologia* (Vatican: Libreria Editrice Vaticana, 1983), 29–54, esp. 45. On the primacy of one for their distinctions, see John Zizioulas, *Being as Communion: Studies in Personhood and the Church* (Crestwood, NY: St. Vladimir's Seminary Press, 1985), 45n40.

Voices have emerged contesting hierarchical constructions of the doctrine of the Trinity and advocating trinitarian egalitarianism.[22] Joining this growing group of theologians, I have suggested elsewhere that hierarchy is not necessary to guard either the divine unity or the distinctions between divine persons.[23] Here I want to add that in a community of perfect love among persons who share all divine attributes a notion of hierarchy is unintelligible. Hierarchical constructions of the trinitarian relations appear from this perspective as projections of the fascination with earthly hierarchies onto the heavenly community. They seem to be less inspired by a vision of the triune God than driven either by a nostalgia for a "world on the wane" or by fears of chaos that may invade human communities if hierarchies are levelled, their surface biblical justification notwithstanding.

Though the debate between the advocates of hierarchy and equality in the Trinity is of great significance for how the doctrine of the Trinity should shape social vision, I will not pursue it here further. Having sided with the egalitarians, I will instead explore two issues on which I hope that even those who disagree profoundly on hierarchy versus equality in the Trinity may find significant common ground. The one issue is "identity," a relative newcomer in trinitarian thinking,[24] and the other is "self-donation," a topic on which a great deal has been written throughout history but which never ceases to surprise us with new depths.

In recent decades the issue of identity has risen to the forefront of discussions in social philosophy. If the liberation movements of the 1960s were all about equality—above all gender equality and racial equality—major concerns of the 1990s seem to be about identity—about the recognition of distinct identities of persons who differ in gender, skin color, or

---

22. Moltmann, *The Trinity and the Kingdom*.

23. See Volf, *After Our Likeness*, 216n106. Wolfhart Pannenberg distinguishes between "ontological equality" and "moral subordination"—the fact that the Son, though not ontologically inferior, subordinates himself to the Father—and argues that the "moral subordination" of the Son is the precondition of his unity and "ontological equality" with the Father (*Systematic Theology*, vol. 1, 324–25). Apart from the difficulty of conceptualizing "moral" subordination of a person with all the attributes of the divinity to another person with the same attributes, it is not at all clear how "ontological equality" could be, as Pannenberg suggests, a consequence of "moral subordination."

24. In *The Triune Identity: God According to the Gospel*, Robert W. Jenson has elevated the notion of "identity" into a primary trinitarian term (Philadelphia: Fortress, 1982). He suggests that it replace the ancient *hypostasis* (105–11). As will be apparent below, in the present section I am more interested in what may be described as the "Trinitarian construction of identity"—in the formal features of the identity of a divine person in relation to other persons—than in offering a contemporary alternative to the traditional notion of *hypostasis*.

culture.[25] Does the doctrine of the Trinity have anything to say to these debates? What notion of identity is inscribed in the character and relation of divine persons and what analogues might it have in the human realm? What does the doctrine of the Trinity suggest about how to go about negotiating identities under conditions of enmity and conflict?

A proposal that the beliefs about God should shape our social vision needs to consider these questions and that not simply in their own right but also in the light of a severe attack on monotheism in recent decades for its alleged deleterious effects on the processes of identity formation. Regina M. Schwartz's discussion of the relation between monotheism and identity in *The Curse of Cain*, subtitled *The Violent Legacy of Monotheism*, is a good example. "Whether as singleness (this God against the others) or totality (this is all the God there is), monotheism abhors, reviles, rejects, and ejects whatever it defines as outside its compass," she argues.[26] Since the belief in one God "forges identity antithetically,"[27] it issues not only in a truncated notion of identity in which "we are 'us' because we are not 'them'"[28] but also in violent practices that stem from such a conception of identity.[29] She proposes that we free ourselves from "the tentacles of the injunction 'you shall have no other gods before me'"[30] and embrace the prophet Micah's vision (4:5) of a world in which everyone walks "in the name of his god."[31] Though I doubt the adequacy of her analysis and believe that her proposal, if implemented, would do more harm than good, she rightly claims that any understanding of divinity centering on the singleness of an omnipotent subject will tend to forge "hard" identities and foster violence. I want to argue here that a viable alternative to such an understanding of monotheism is available. It is enshrined in the doctrine of the Trinity.[32]

Notice first how persons and community are related in the doctrine of the Trinity. No "unencumbered self" of modern liberalism, so ably analyzed

---

25. Charles Taylor, "The Politics of Recognition," *Multiculturalism: Examining the Politics of Recognition*, ed. Amy Gutmann (Princeton: Princeton University Press, 1994), 25–73; Louis Menand, "The Culture Wars," *The New York Review of Books* 41 (1994): 18.

26. Regina M. Schwartz, *The Curse of Cain: The Violent Legacy of Monotheism* (Chicago: University of Chicago Press, 1997), 63.

27. Ibid., 16.

28. Ibid., x.

29. Ibid., 88.

30. Ibid., 69.

31. Ibid., 38.

32. For a critical discussion of Schwartz's book, see Miroslav Volf, "Jehova on Trial," *Christianity Today* 42, no. 5 (1998): 32–35.

by Michael Sandel, is to be found there.[33] As Colin Gunton points out in *The One, the Three and the Many*, "the persons [of the Trinity] do not simply enter into relations with one another, but are constituted by one another in the relations."[34] Community is not simply a collection of independent and self-standing persons; inversely, persons are not merely so many discrete individual parts and functions of a social aggregate. Persons and community are equiprimal in the Trinity. Although this observation is significant in its own right because it suggests, as Anne Carr puts it in *Transforming Grace*, that "perfect sociality embodies...qualities of mutuality, reciprocity, cooperation, unity, peace in genuine diversity,"[35] I want to explore here the significance of this observation for the understanding of identity. It is immense and is best studied by delving into the notion of the "mutual indwelling" of divine persons, technically, *perichoresis* (meaning "making room,"[36] not "dancing round").

Traditionally, *perichoresis* has been used mainly to reflect on divine unity.[37] In *De Fide*, John of Damascus, who popularized the term that Pseudo-Cyril first extended from christological into trinitarian language,[38] writes, "For...they are made one not so as to commingle, but so as to

33. For Michael Sandel's analysis, see *Liberalism and the Limits of Justice* (Cambridge: Cambridge University Press, 1982). For important parallels between the "unencumbered self" of modern liberalism and what Catherine Keller calls the "separative self," which she argues is a typically *male* self, see *From a Broken Web: Separation, Sexism, and Self* (Boston: Beacon, 1986), 7–9. As a consequence of its absence from the doctrine of the Trinity, the "unencumbered self" can find no proper legitimation in the belief in the God of Jesus Christ. Historically, of course, such legitimation has been offered. As Michael Walzer has noted, the "unencumbered self" bears in its "original form the encumbrances of divinity. The individual is bound to his God—the singular possessive pronoun is very important—and unencumbered only with reference to his fellow men...It is because of his close and personal relation to God that someone like that is capable of 'Protestantism' in every other relation" (*What It Means to be an American: Essays on the American Experience* [New York: Marsilio, 1996], 109–10). Walzer is right to draw attention to the singular possessive pronoun. For it is precisely here that the position which seeks to underwrite the "unencumbered self" by its possession of a solitary God errs. Such a thing as "'his' [or 'her'] God" is manifestly not the God of Jesus Christ but an idol. The God of Jesus Christ is either the God of all people or no God at all. Moreover, this God is a community of divine persons that seeks to create a community of people.
34. Colin Gunton, *The One, the Three and the Many: God, Creation and the Culture of Modernity* (Cambridge: Cambridge University Press, 1993), 214.
35. Anne E. Carr, *Transforming Grace: Christian Tradition and Women's Experience* (San Francisco: Harper, 1988), 156–57.
36. The understanding of *perichoresis* as "making room" is independent of whether one thinks of divine *perichoresis* in analogously spatial terms or not (Gunton, *The One, the Three and the Many*, 163–66).
37. Eberhard Jüngel, *The Doctrine of the Trinity: God's Being is in Becoming* (Grand Rapids: Eerdmans, 1976), 31–33. More precisely, *perichoresis* has been conceived as "the exact reverse of the identity of *ousia*" (G. L. Prestige, *God in Patristic Thought* [London: S. P. C. K., 1956], 298) understood as the ground of unity among divine persons. Elsewhere I have argued that in fact the postulate of the numerical identity of divine *ousia* must be, properly speaking, seen as an *alternative* to *perichoresis* as a way of conceiving trinitarian unity (Volf, *After Our Likeness*, 210n87).
38. Michael G. Lawler, "Perichoresis: New Theological Wine in an Old Theological Wineskin," *Horizons* 22, no 1 (1995): 49–51.

cleave to each other, and they have their being in each other without any coalescence or commingling."[39] Here *perichoresis* describes the kind of unity in which the plurality is preserved rather than erased. But the resources of *perichoresis* for thinking about identity are as rich as for thinking about unity. For it suggests that divine persons are not simply interdependent and influence one another from outside but are personally interior to one another. The Johannine Jesus speaks repeatedly of such personal interiority: "the Father is in me and I am in the Father" (John 10:38; see John 14:10ff.; 17:21). Every divine person is indwelled by other divine persons; all the persons interpenetrate each other. They do not cease to be distinct, however. Rather, their interpenetration presupposes their distinctions; persons who have been dissolved in some third thing cannot be said to be interior to each other. The distinctions of the persons notwithstanding, their identities partly overlap. Every divine person is and acts as itself and yet the two other persons are present and act in that person.

The identity of the Son—in the context of the economic Trinity, the identity of Jesus Christ—is shaped through his twofold relationship to the Father and the Spirit (which I will explore here as portrayed in John's Gospel but which could equally well be studied in the synoptic Gospels). Take first the Father's relation to Jesus Christ. In a passage that fascinated Augustine, the Johannine Jesus states: "My teaching is not mine but his who sent me" (John 7:16). In his commentary on the Gospel of John, Augustine elaborates on the paradox of

"my, not mine" by suggesting that "Christ Himself is the doctrine of the Father, if He is the Word of the Father. But since the Word cannot be of none, but of some one, He said both 'His doctrine,' namely, Himself, and also, 'not His own,' because He is the Word of the Father."[40]

Mutual personal interiority makes "my" (Jesus's) to be simultaneously "not-mine" (the Father's) without ceasing to be "mine," just as "not-mine" is simultaneously "mine" without ceasing to be "not-mine." Similarly, Jesus

39. John of Damascus, *De Fide*, I, vii.
40. Augustine, *Tractates on the Gospel According to St John*, vol. 10, The Works of Aurelius Augustine, ed. Marcus Dods (Edinburgh: T. & T. Clark, 1873), 404; cf. Joseph Ratzinger, *Introduction to Christianity*, transl. J. R. Foster (New York: Herder and Herder, 1970), 136–37. In his treatise on the Trinity, Augustine interprets the statement to refer to Christ's divine and human natures. "According to the form of God, [the teaching is] His own, according to the form of a servant, not His own" (I, xii, 27). But the reason the text gives that the teaching is not of Jesus Christ is that the teaching is of the one who sent Jesus Christ, that is, of the Father. The text implies *perichoresis* of the divine persons, not *perichoresis* of Christ's natures. And as we have seen, this is in fact what Augustine asserts in his commentary of the Gospel of John.

Christ is the one upon whom "the Spirit" descended from heaven and re-mained (John 1:32). The mission of Jesus Christ, including the death on the cross, is carried out in the Spirit, and hence his identity is shaped by the Spirit. If, as Dumitru Stăniloae puts it, "All that Christ achieves, he achieves through the Spirit,"[41] then the same dialectic of "mine" and "not-mine" pertains in relation to the Spirit just as in relation to the Father.

What does the play of "mine" and "not-mine" implied in the paradox-ical claim "my teaching is not mine"—a claim whose paradoxes are those of the trinitarian identity itself[42]—suggest about the construction of hu-man identities, fallible and fallen creatures marked by finitude and fragil-ity? First, *identity is non-reducible.* Persons cannot be translated fully into relations. A person is always already outside of the relations in which he or she is immersed and through which she is co-constituted. If this were not the case, "not-mine" could never become "mine" because it would have no place outside of itself to land, so to speak. Hence the need for boundary maintenance—which at least at the human level always implies a certain kind of assertion of the self in the presence of the other and a certain kind of deference of the other before the self. Since negotiation of human iden-tities is always conflictual, nonassertiveness of the self in the presence of the other puts the self in danger either of dissolving into the other or being smothered by the other.[43] Similarly, non-deference of the other before the self puts weak selves who struggle to assert themselves in danger of being either manipulated or violated. The combination of nonassertiveness of the self in the presence of the other and non-deference of the other before the self presents the greatest danger: it threatens to obliterate the weaker self. To ward off these dangers, we must attend to the boundaries of iden-tities by enforcing rules that protect identities and by providing environ-ments that nurture them.

Second, *identity is not self-enclosed.* The other is always already in the self and therefore the identity of the self cannot be defined simply oppo-sitionally. To build on the play of "mine" and "not-mine" by using a triple

41. Dumitru Stăniloae, *Theology and the Church,* transl. Robert Barringer (Crestwood, NY: St. Vladi-mir's Seminary Press, 1980), 39. See also Ralph Del Colle, *Christ and the Spirit: Spirit-Christology in Trinitarian Perspective* (New York: Oxford University Press, 1994).

42. Commenting on Paul's statement in Galatians "Become as I am, for I have become as you are" (Gal 4:12), Daniel Boyarin rightly notes in *A Radical Jew: Paul and the Politics of Identity* ([Berkeley: University of California Press, 1994), 3), that "the paradoxes and oxymorons of that sentence are those of identity itself." This is an example of human identity analogous—not identical!—to the divine identities expressed in the notion of *perichoresis.*

43. Carr, *Transforming Grace,* 58.

negative: "mine" is not that which is not "not-mine"; to the contrary, "not-mine" is in an important sense also mine. The boundaries of the self are porous and shifting. The self is itself only by being in a state of flux stemming from the self constitutive "incursions" of the other into the self and of the self into the other. The self is shaped by making space for the other and by giving space to the other, by being enriched when it inhabits the other and by sharing of its plenitude when it is inhabited by the other, by reexamining itself when the other closes his or her doors and challenging the other by knocking at the doors.

The notion of identity, which the trinitarian *perichoresis* suggests is, I propose, a viable alternative to what Luce Irigaray in *This Sex Which Is Not One* calls "oppositional logic of the same"—a "logic" that drives all remnants of nonidentity out of the conceptual space occupied by a given identity, the same logic, in other words, that Regina Schwartz argued was underwritten by biblical monotheism.[44]

The complex and dynamic notion of identity that the doctrine of the Trinity both instantiates and whose anthropological analogue it nudges us to construct seems to speak directly to the contemporary debates about identity.[45] And yet, it is by no means new, at least not in its rough contours. In fact, there is a long theological tradition that implicitly operates with a similar notion of identity. It is at home in ecclesiological thought and hides behind terms such as *anima ecclesiastica*[46] or "catholicity of person."[47] Its most sophisticated proponent is John Zizioulas. *In Being as Communion* he argues that

> in and through his communion a person affirms his own identity and his particularity ... The person is the horizon within which the truth of existence is revealed, not as simple nature subject to individualization and recombination but as a unique image of the whole and the "catholicity" of being.[48]

44. See Luce Irigaray, *This Sex Which Is Not One*, transl. Catherine Porter with Carolyn Burke (Ithaca, NY: Cornell University Press, 1985); Schwartz, *The Curse of Cain*.

45. Allison Weir, *Sacrificial Logics: Feminist Theory and the Critique of Identity* (New York: Routledge, 1996).

46. Joseph Ratzinger, *Das Fest des Glaubens: Versuche zur Theologie des Gottesdienstes* (Einsiedeln: Johannes, 1981), 28.

47. Vladimir Lossky, *In the Image and Likeness of God* (Crestwood: St. Vladimir's Seminary Press, 1985), 175.

48. Zizioulas, *Being as Communion*, 106.

A person can be a unique image of the whole, argues Zizioulas, only by being located in Christ and partaking of Christ's identity. On the divine side, Christ is constituted through the Father's filial relationship to him; on the human side, he is a corporate personality constituted by the many who are "in him." Zizioulas connects the anthropological notion of identity via ecclesiology and Christology to the Trinity in which it finds its most proper foundation.

Though in many respects significant, the argument of Zizioulas is not fully persuasive. I find problematic the suggestion that a person images "the whole" and misguided the postulate that the same eternal relation with which the Father relates to the Son is the constitutive element of every person. The combination of these two moves, I suggest, prevents Zizioulas from being able to conceptualize adequately the particularity of a person.[49] The obverse of this significant weakness, however, is an important strength. He is able both to affirm the presence of multiple others in the self and not lose the self in its own fluidity. What Zizioulas does well is specify the character of a person: each is determined by Christ in the double relation that Christ stands with the Father and with humanity. By contrast, my account, which stresses both the need to maintain boundaries and keep them fluid, though able to ground the particularity of a person, seems to leave the person's identity underdetermined. How does one know when to close the boundaries of the self in order to stabilize one's identity and when to open them in order to enrich it? Moreover, on what grounds should one decide what may come in and what must stay out?

No answer can be given to the first question in advance of concrete situations. Whether the borders will be opened or closed will depend on the specific character of both the self and the other at a given juncture in their relation. The only advice possible is to seek supple wisdom rather than stable rules. The answer to the second question—the question about the grounds for negotiating fluid identities—is contained in the narrative of the divine self-donation on the cross with its dual and interrelated messages about "indiscriminate welcome" and about the importance of "truth and justice."

Self-Donation

It is essential to situate reflection on the construction of identity in the narrative of divine self-donation. Otherwise, talk about fluid identities

---

49. Volf, *After Our Likeness*, 85–88.

is in danger of becoming not only underdetermined but also too formal and, in the end, theologically empty, its putative derivation from the doctrine of the Trinity notwithstanding. If what I say about the construction of identity were not inserted into the framework of reflection on self-donation, it would parallel a plethora of proposals about the relation between the Trinity and human communities, which, though significant, are of limited value because they remain at the level of overly diffuse generalities, say about "plurality-in-unity," the dialectic of "one and many," or the balance between "relationality and otherness."[50] In such proposals the doctrine of the Trinity serves more or less as the ore from which the presumed gold of abstract principles should be extracted and then used to construct images of human community or even of the whole reality. But this makes a misjudgment about what is in fact gold. Abstract principles are not pure gold; the narrative of the life of the Trinity, at whose heart lays the history of self-donation, is pure gold. The talk about fluid identities, no less than the generalities about "plurality-in-unity" and "one-and-many" will be helpful only if they are "gilded" by being dipped into the narrative of divine self-donation.

In a sense, we can "dip" the proposal about the trinitarian identities into the gold of self-donation because it is out of this gold that the proposal has emerged in the first place. The proposal was built on the central trinitarian notion of *perichoresis*, which itself rests on the innertrinitarian activity of self-donation. But how should we think of trinitarian self-donation? How is it related to the world we inhabit, a world of deceit, oppression, and violence? What does it mean for human beings to image the self-giving God? It is to these questions that I now turn. And it is the answer to these questions that contains the wisdom necessary for making the right decisions about when to close and open the boundaries of our identities and about what to let in and what to keep out.

---

50. In *Revelation and Reconciliation: A Window on Modernity* ([Cambridge: Cambridge University Press, 1995], 171), Stephen N. Williams has rightly objected that Colin Gunton's reflection on the relation between one and many and between relationality and otherness in *The One, the Three and the Many* is "excessively abstract." From my perspective, the problem with Gunton's approach is, however, not that he is engaged in the task of getting "*concepts*... right" (ibid.), but that in his otherwise significant reflections on the interrelations of one and many he pays too little attention to the concrete trinitarian narrative of the historical self-donation of God (but see Colin Gunton, "The Church on Earth: The Roots of Community," *On Being the Church, Essays on the Christian Community*, ed. Colin E. Gunton and Daniel W. Hardy [Edinburgh: T. & T. Clark, 1989], 48–80, 78–79), an approach which partly explains why the interrelated and socially central notions of "power," "conflict," "violence," "justice," and "love" play such a surprisingly marginal role in a book on "God, Creation, and the Culture of Modernity." Williams is, of course, right that getting concepts right is not yet getting people to act rightly, but, in a sense, that goes without saying and applies equally well to those who *argue* against "intellectualism."

The self gives something of itself, of its own space, so to speak, in a movement in which it contracts itself in order to be expanded by the other and in which it at the same time enters the contracted other in order to increase the other's plenitude. This giving of the self that coalesces with receiving the other is nothing but the circular movement of the eternal divine love—a form of exchange of gifts in which the other does not emerge as a debtor because he or she has already given by having joyfully received and because even before the gift has reached him or her, the other was already engaged in a movement of advance reciprocation.[51] If we adjusted the famous statement of John, "We love because God first loved us" (1 John 4:19) to fit the cycle of exchange between perfect lovers, we would have to say that each always both loves first and loves because he or she is loved. Put less paradoxically, the perfect cycle of self-donations must start moving simultaneously at all points.[52] This is why only God is love properly speaking (1 John 4:8)—God conceived as a communion of perfect lovers.[53]

When Jesus commanded his disciples to "be perfect" as their "heavenly Father is perfect" (Matt 5:48), it could seem that he was demanding that they emulate, in a humanly appropriate way, the perfection of the eternal divine love. Yet this is not the case. Perhaps, the most profound reason for the absence of such a command is that the perfect cycle of self-donation—again, perfect as humanly possible—cannot be commanded

---

51. In "Can a Gift be Given? Prolegomena to a Future Trinitarian Metaphysics," John Milbank has argued for "delay" and "non-identical repetition" between a gift and counter-gift as necessary structural elements of giving (*Modern Theology* 11, no. 1 [January, 1995]: 125). The idea of "advance reciprocation" can be seen as *inverted* delay in non-identical repetition and is suggested by the need to conceive of the receiver as always already a giver.

52. My primary interest here is the reciprocity in love conceived as self-donation, and hence I only name but do not explore the all-important *circularity* of such love. Without circularity love would die either because it would freeze, so to speak, or because it would turn into its opposite, possession. Hence when I offered a "phenomenology of embrace" in *Exclusion and Embrace: A Theological Exploration of Identity, Otherness, and Reconciliation*, I argued that in addition to (1) "the open arms" of desire and (2) "the closed arms" of mutual holding, a properly understood embrace must also contain (3) "waiting" as a postponement of desire until response has occurred and (4) "the open arms of letting go" as an expression of respect for the alterity of the other ([Nashville: Abingdon Press, 1996], 140–47). In *Eros for the Other: Retaining Truth in a Pluralistic World* ([University Park, PA: Pennsylvania State University Press, 1996], 72), Wendy Farley has expressed a similar thought by stressing the importance of "absence" in relation between the lover and the beloved:

Eros swims in the water of absence, when this water dries up, Eros dies. Possessed by Eros, one thinks one wants nothing more intensely than to possess the beloved. The beloved is present to the lover as that which is desired. It is not sheer absence or nonbeing. But the beloved is present as absent, so to speak. It is related to the lover not by sheer immediacy but by the echo left by its absence.

53. Richard Swinburne, *The Christian God* (Oxford: Clarendon, 1994), 170–91.

but must be given to all that engage in it, and it must be given to all at the same time. As the preceding verses indicate, Jesus demanded of his disciples something much less sublime but, in a sense, much more difficult precisely because what he demanded was not a pure fruit of grace but a result of labor. The disciples will be the children of God, not so much when they, echoing in their own human way a divine kind of reciprocity, love those who love them (5:46), but when they imitate an equally divine kind of love's one-sidedness of the God who makes "the sun rise on the evil and on the good, and sends rain on the righteous and on the unrighteous" (5:45) by loving "their enemies" and praying "for those who persecute" them (5:44). This is not so much a kind of giving that feeds on and delights in love's reciprocities that the disciples are called to emulate; that kind of giving will eventually, in the coming world of love, take care of itself if the other kind of giving is practiced, the kind that seeks to elicit the nonexistent response of love even in those who practice the very opposite of love. Jesus demanded not so much that we imitate the divine dance of love's freedom and unthematized trust but the divine labor of love's risk and suffering. The love that dances is the internal love among the persons of the Trinity; the love that suffers is that same love turned toward a world suffused with enmity. In their human analogues, the first is the perfect love of the world to come and its echo in the unstable and incomplete mutualities of the best of our loves;[54] the second is that same love engaged in the transformation of the deeply flawed world that is.

How are the two loves related? One could imagine a relation of simple identity: the love of God on the cross reiterates the eternal love in God, and, analogously, human love, engaged in the transformation of the present world simply repeats the love of the world to come. Divine engagement in the world takes here the form of a repetition of divine "dance" in heaven; human engagement with the world repeats in the world the love of the world to come. But is the postulate of identity plausible? Though I called both loves "the same," I nevertheless described them as "first" and "second." Why? Because, unlike the internal love of the immanent Trinity and human love of the world to come, the love engaged in the transformation of the world is not simply positive; in an important sense it is also

---

54. In *The Gifting God: A Trinitarian Ethics of Excess*, Stephen H. Webb has rightly underscored that the "embodiment of God's excesses within a completely reciprocal community, where giving begets itself in mutuality, integrity, and harmony" is "the meaning of Christian eschatology" ([New York: Oxford University Press, 1996], 150).

reactive.[55] By this I do not mean that the shape of this "second" love is governed by the pragmatics of the engagement's efficacy. Rather, this love is reactive in the sense in which love's engagement cannot be an *engagement* if it proceeds as if that to which love stands in opposition were not there and were not to be opposed. The trinitarian cycle of perfect self-donations *cannot* be simply repeated in the world of sin; the engagement with that world entails a process of complex and difficult *translation*. Sent by God in the power of the Spirit, the Word became "the Lamb of God who takes away the sin of the world" (John 1:29). In the labor of "taking away the sin," the delight of love is transmuted into the agony of love—the agony of opposition to non-love, the agony of suffering as the hand of non-love, and the agony of sympathy with non-love's victims. Hence the cross of Christ. And hence taking up of the cross for the followers of Christ as well.

Consider the greatest gifts of the Crucified: "grace" and "forgiveness." They are the forms that the spontaneously creative cycle of love takes in encounter with prior evil to be overcome. Though the affirmation of grace entails a denial that God's acceptance must be brokered "by an intermediary or a system of administered conditions,"[56] grace, unlike the innertrinitarian love, is not beyond "law"; grace is grace only because it keeps affirming the law by suspending it. Similarly, though forgiveness releases the offender from debt, it does so not by treating the offense as if it were not there;[57] forgiveness is forgiveness only because it keeps affirming justice by transcending it.[58] Such affirmation of "law" and "justice" is one important thing that distinguishes the positive act of redeeming self-donation from the passive act of self-sacrifice. In the first, the self reaffirms its own creation in the image of the triune God and seeks to draw the other into communion with God and neighbor; in the second, the self simply lets itself be obliterated by the evil other.

55. John Milbank, *The Word Made Strange* (Oxford: Blackwell, 1997) and Rowan D. Williams, "Interiority and Epiphany: A Reading in New Testament Ethics," *Modern Theology* 13, no. 1 (January, 1997): 29–51.

56. Williams, "Interiority and Epiphany," 38.

57. John Milbank, *Theology and Social Theory: Beyond Secular Reason* (Oxford: Blackwell, 1990), 411; Milbank, "Can a Gift be Given?" 148. Treating the offense as if it were not there is Nietzsche's alternative to forgiveness (see Friedrich Nietzsche, *Thus Spoke Zarathustra: A Book for Everyone and No One*, transl. R. J. Hollingdale [London: Penguin, 1969], 161).

58. See Miroslav Volf, *Free of Charge* (Grand Rapids: Zondervan, 2005), 140–44. See also L. Gregory Jones, *Embodying Forgiveness: A Theological Analysis* (Grand Rapids: Eerdmans, 1995), 135–62; Lewis B. Smedes, *The Art of Forgiving: When You Need to Forgive and Don't Know How* (Nashville: Moorings, 1996), 77–85.

In Romans 13:8-14, Paul subtly but clearly makes the same point about love's struggle against non-love. "The night is far gone," he writes, "the day is near. Let us then lay aside the works of darkness and put on the armor of light; let us live honorably *as in the day*" (13:12-13; emphasis added). The "day" is the light of the new creation and the "night" is the darkness of the sinful world. Behind the injunction "Let us live honorably as in the day" lies, therefore, the very question I am pursuing here: What shape ought the love of the perfect world to come take in the present world of sin? Ought Christians to practice love "as if evil were not there"? It could seem that to live "as in the day" is simply a different way of saying that we ought to live "as if it were not night" or behave in a sovereign disregard of the still pervasive night. Yet this is not so. The crucial difference between living "as in the day" and living "as if it were not night" is signaled in the distinction between "the works of darkness" and "the armor of light." "Works" are something that can simply be done—and in the case of the works of darkness they are done, as Paul puts it, in "sleep" (13:11), that is, with a kind of automatism with which one indulges in "debauchery and licentiousness" and participates in "quarreling and jealousy" (8:13). "Armor," however, suggests struggle since it designates both defensive and offensive weapons.[59] As long as it is "night," one can live "as in the day" only by putting on the armor to fight the night. Love is a weapon. And it is a weapon in the precise sense in which the self-giving of Jesus Christ was a weapon against evil. As Origen already noted in his commentary on Romans, putting on "the armor of light" (8:12) parallels putting on "the Lord Jesus Christ" (8:14).[60] Hence when Paul turns to

59. See C. E. B. Cranfield, *The Epistle to the Romans*, ICC (Edinburgh: T. & T. Clark, 1979), 686. In 1 Thessalonians 5:1-11, Paul brings together in a similar fashion "the day" and armor: "But since we belong to the day, let us be sober, and put on the breastplate of faith and love, and for a helmet the hope of salvation" (5:8). Since breastplate and helmet are primarily defensive weapons (F. F. Bruce, *First and Second Thessalonians*, WBC 45 [Waco: Word Books, 1982], 112; Richard B. Hays, *The Moral Vision of the New Testament: Community, Cross, New Creation. A Contemporary Introduction to New Testament Ethics* [San Francisco: Harper, 1996], 23), one could argue that active struggle against "the night" is not implied in the injunction to live as in the day. Elsewhere, however, these two are mentioned as part of "the whole armor" (cf. Eph 6:13ff.), and in general armor is to be used in the battle against evil both offensively and defensively (D. G. Reid, "Triumph," in *Dictionary of Paul and His Letters*, ed. G. F. Hawthorne and R. P. Martin [Downers Grove, IL: InterVarsity, 1993], 950–53). Moreover, Paul is "not consistent in the significance he attaches to the various pieces of armor" (Leon Morris, *The First and Second Epistles to the Thessalonians*, NICNT [Grand Rapids: Eerdmans, 1991], 158). So, though in 1 Thessalonians 5:8 he mentions only the breastplate and helmet, it may well be that they stand for the whole, especially since they are the most important pieces in the entire battle regalia and are thus analogous to the crowning virtues of faith, hope, and love, with which they are here associated (see ibid.).

60. Origen, *PG*, Vol 14, col. 659.

address the relationship between "the 'strong' and the 'weak'" (Rom 14:1–
15:13), he repeatedly appeals to the self-giving of Christ as the model to
emulate.

If the trinitarian love is not practiced as "weapon," if it is not translated into grace and forgiveness, which both transcend and affirm law and
justice, its proclamation will, in the end, amount to false "glad tidings"
that eternal life is "not promised" but fully given, that faith is "its own
'kingdom of God,'" that sin is not overcome but "abolished," that there
are "no opposites," and that denial of anything is "totally impossible"—an
exact summary of Nietzsche's "psychology of redemption" in *The Anti-
Christ* conceived of as an explication of "how one would have to live in
order to feel oneself 'in Heaven,' to feel oneself 'eternal.' "[61] "Heaven" is
here re-narrated; "heaven" is even practiced—in theory, that is—but the
movement of its transformative engagement with the world whose earth
soaked with Abel's blood is halted.[62]

If my argument is cogent, then to propose a social knowledge based
on the doctrine of the Trinity is not so much to "project" and "represent"
"the triune God, who is transcendental peace through differential relation," as John Milbank argues in his justly acclaimed *Theology and Social
Theory*.[63] Rather, to propose a social knowledge based on the doctrine of
the Trinity is above all to re-narrate the history of the cross, the cross understood not as a simple repetition of heavenly love in the world, but as
the triune God's engagement with the world in order to transform the unjust, deceitful, and violent kingdoms of this world into the just, truthful,
and peaceful "kingdom of our Lord and of his Messiah" (Rev 11:16). The
same *imitatio crucis* holds true not only for "social knowledge" but also for
"social practices." No doubt, we are often given a foretaste of the perfect
love of the Trinity, say in the delights of friendship and of erotic embrace,
or in the joy of celebrating communion. But we are called above all to
imitate the earthly love of that same Trinity that led to the passion of the
cross because it was from the start a passion for those caught in the snares
of non-love and overcome by power of injustice, deceit, and violence.

61. Friedrich Nietzsche, *Twilight of the Idols and The Anti-Christ*, transl. R. J. Hollingdale (London: Penguin, 1990), 153–58.
62. Richard H. Roberts has rightly pointed out that Milbank's constructive proposal in *Theology and Social Theory* in its final analysis may "encourage a form of 'hibernation' that sanctions the masquerade of eschatological-political impossibilism in the guise of 'praxis.'" See "Transcendental Sociology? A Critique of John Milbank's *Theology and Social Theory: Beyond Secular Reason*," *Scottish Journal of Theology* 46, no. 4 (1993): 534.
63. Milbank, *Theology and Social Theory*, 6.

What, then, does the trinitarian self-donation translated into the world and therefore enacted on the cross by the power of the Spirit mean for the life of human communities? Summarizing a good deal of his argument in the letter to the Romans, the Apostle Paul writes, "Welcome one another, therefore, just as Christ has welcomed you" (15:7). In earlier chapters of this book, I argued that this divine welcome in Christ, which in the New Testament is consistently and almost universally portrayed as the model for Christians to emulate,[64] translates into the claim that the will to give ourselves to others and welcome them, to readjust our identities to make space for them, is prior to any judgment about others, except that of identifying them in their humanity. The will to embrace precedes any "truth" about others and any construction of their "justice." This will is absolutely indiscriminate and strictly immutable; it transcends the moral mapping of the social world into "good" and "evil."

With the endorsement of such indiscriminate will to embrace, have I reached the point beyond "truth" and "justice" and so transgressed the limits set by the logic of grace and the need for boundary maintenance that I stressed earlier? Notice that I describe the *will* to embrace as indiscriminate, not the embrace itself. Though in the proclamation of God's welcome Jesus "makes...no appropriate distinctions and discriminations," as Dominic Crossan rightly maintains in *The Historical Jesus*,[65] it is manifestly not true to the Gospels that Jesus made no "appropriate distinctions and discriminations" *after* the divine welcome was issued. An indiscriminate welcome of everyone by no means entails an indiscriminate affirmation of everything. Correspondingly, Jesus welcomed (see Mark 2:13-17) *and* he sent away (see Mark 10:17-31), he renamed falsely labeled sins (see Mark 7:1-23), and he re-made actual sinners by forgiving their sins (see Mark 2:1-12). Similarly, because the cross is not a negation of "law" and "justice," the wisdom of the cross tells us that embrace cannot take place until the truth has been said and justice done. Hence, even if the *will* to embrace is indiscriminate, the *full embrace* itself must discriminate. For perfect embrace is unthinkable outside the world set aright—a world in which matters of truth and justice have been attended to and a world in which the resurrection of the dead has undone what Oliver

---

64. See Hays, *Moral Vision of the New Testament*, 197; Luke Timothy Johnson, *The Real Jesus: The Misguided Quest for the Historical Jesus and the Truth of the Traditional Gospels* (San Francisco: Harper SanFrancisco, 1996), 151–66.

65. John Dominic Crossan, *The Historical Jesus: The Life of a Mediterranean Jewish Peasant* (San Francisco: Harper SanFrancisco, 1991), 262.

O'Donovan in *Desire of Nations* calls "the monstrous inequality of generational succession" in which all our possessions become "a kind of robbery, something we have taken from those who shared it with us but with whom we cannot share in return."[66] The full participation in the perfect cycle of self-donations depends on the creation of all things new.

Has my unwillingness to reach in this still unredeemed world the point beyond "truth" and "justice" led me back to the struggle for "truth" and "justice" as a necessary precursor of self-donation? Has the wisdom of the cross led me to the point where that very wisdom appears as foolishness, not just to those "who are perishing" but also to us "who are being saved" (1 Cor 1:18)? Has the self-giving love of the Trinity been translated into the world of sin only to be swallowed up by the conditions that such translation imposes on it? Not quite. For "truth" and "justice" themselves need to be redeemed by self-giving love. Nietzsche underscored rightly, I believe, that there is far too much dishonesty in the single-minded search for truth and too much injustice in the uncompromising struggle for justice.[67] Yet no follower of the Crucified will endorse Nietzsche's self-contradictory "nothing is true" and "everything is permitted" rhetoric.[68] The negative claim about truth and justice is but the obverse of the positive claim that rests squarely on the "wisdom of the cross": truth and justice in social settings are unavailable outside the *will to give ourselves to others and embrace them.*

And so grace triumphs again: the same grace that disregarded the untruthfulness and injustice of the other when it initiated the movement of embrace also guides the re-construction of "truth" and "justice" in order to complete the embrace. This primacy of grace in the establishment of truth and justice, I propose, inscribed in the inner dynamic of divine justification, which is the inner dynamic of the cross, which is the inner dynamic of trinitarian love translated into the world of sin. That's why the love of enemy is essential to Christian faith.

God's Reflection, God's Glory

Appended to the passage from Romans, on which my argument about self-donation leans, is a short phrase about God's glory. "Welcome one

---

66. O'Donovan, *Desire of Nations*, 287–88.

67. Nietzsche, *Thus Spoke Zarathustra*, 229.

68. Friedrich Nietzsche, *The Birth of Tragedy and The Genealogy of Morals*, transl. Francis Golffing (Garden City: Doubleday, 1956), 287.

another, therefore, just as Christ has welcomed you," writes Paul, and then continues, "for the glory of God" (Rom 15:7). Commenting on the verse, Rowan Williams points out that

> generosity, mercy and welcome are imperatives for the Christian because they are a participation in the divine activity; but they are also imperative because they show God's glory and invite or attract human beings to "give glory" to God—that is, to reflect back to God what God is.[69]

What aspect of God's being ought to be reflected back to God? According to Paul, it is not so much the circular movement of the divine love, though that's not excluded, of course; it is the linear movement of that same love—downward toward sinful and suffering humanity in order to take it up into divine community. The reason is simple: the one-sidedness of the linear movement—a one-sidedness that aims at reciprocity but does not presuppose it—is the shape the self-giving love of the divine Trinity takes in the world of sin and suffering, which is the world we inhabit.

Nicholas Fedorov, it will be remembered, proposed the doctrinal renarration of the triune God as the social program. His proposal rests on the upward movement by which God placed humanity into the very life of God. An ontology based on the participation in the resurrection life grounds a social practice modeled on the eternal life of the Trinity. In contrast, I have argued that the social vision based on the doctrine of the Trinity should rest primarily on the downward movement in which God, in a sense, comes out of the circularity of divine love in order to take humanity into the divine embrace. A soteriology based on the indwelling of the Crucified by the Spirit (Gal 2:19-20) grounds a social practice modeled on God's passion for the salvation of the world.

In my proposal, where is the social import of the "empty tomb" and of the translucent body of Christ ascending into heaven? Am I keeping social practices, so to say, "nailed to the cross"? Where is the eschatological new creation? Has it evaporated into an impossibility that fascinates the thought in order to seduce the practices into disloyalty to flesh and blood human beings on a fragile earth? No. As I see it, the new creation has not disappeared; it is situated in the midst of history because it is hanging crucified for the sins of the world. The Crucified One is the new

---

69. Williams, "Interiority and Epiphany," 42.

creation—the perfect enactment of the eternal love of the triune God in the godless world (cf. Rom 5:6-11). More precisely, the Crucified One is the new creation as it enters into the present creation become old through the practice of injustice, deception, and violence in order to transform humanity into the image of the triune God. Hence the body nailed to the cross is the body, which the clutches of death cannot hold; the tortured flesh is the translucent and ascending body of glory. The passion of self-donation has the promise of glory because it already participates in that glory; the hell of crucifixion has its heavenly obverse in the glory of the life of the resurrection.

Is there nothing in between the hidden glory of earthly suffering and the open glory of heavenly bliss? Will the glory of love only shine forth in suffering until evil is fully conquered? Will the new creation be present only in pain and never in joy? Clearly not. After the resurrection of Christ and the sending of the Spirit, the new creation is *coming* into the sinful world ever anew in the movement from the cross to the empty tomb, in the labor of love and its many and repeated transformations into the dance of love.

Following a similar train of thought, John the Evangelist surprisingly narrates the story of the crucifixion as a story of the glorification of the Crucified[70]—in the hour of the Son's passion, the Father will glorify the Son with the same glory that the Son had before the foundation of the world (John 17:5; cf. 1:14), so that through the passion the Son may glorify the Father (John 17:1). The historical reflection of God's character in the labor of self-donation gives glory to God and receives back God's glory because it *is* that very glory. The downward linear movement already participates in the circular movement in which the glory of God, which is nothing else but the purity of God's self-giving love, is eternally exchanged.

And it is in this downward movement of divine love that the Johannine Jesus Christ empowers his followers to participate. The resurrected Christ appeared to his disciples, breathed on them, and said, "Receive the Holy Spirit" (John 20:22). The Spirit whom the disciples received was the same Spirit whom John the Baptist saw descending upon Jesus when he identified Jesus as "the Lamb of God who takes away the sin of the world" (John 1:29-34). The one who went to the cross in the power of the Spirit, now dispenses the same Spirit to empower his followers to

---

70. C. K. Barrett, *The Gospel According to St. John* (Philadelphia: Westminster, 1978), 422–23, 501.

participate in the downward movement of God's love, which forgives sins and creates a community of joy in the midst of suffering (John 20:19-23). The "Breath" of Christ risen from the dead gives birth to the "body of Christ" offered to the world.[71] It forms a people whose social vision and social practices image the triune God's coming down in self-emptying passion in order to take human beings into the perfect cycle of exchanges, in which they give themselves to each other and receive themselves back ever anew in love.[72]

---

71. This brief reference to the church as a "community of embrace," which complements my discussion of "the cross" and the love of the "world to come," serves to indicate that what I am after in this essay is consonant with the thrust of Richard Hays's *Moral Vision of the New Testament*, which develops the New Testament ethical themes around the three focal images of "community," "cross," and "new creation." One way of putting my project here is to say that I seek to connect all three by rooting them in the doctrine of the Trinity understood as the doctrinal expression of the narrative of the triune God's engagement with humanity.

72. This essay was delivered as Waldenstroem lectures at Stockholm School of Theology, May 6, 1998. An earlier and shorter version was presented at the conference "The Doctrine of God and Theological Ethics" at King's College, London, April 28–30, 1997. Eugene Matei provided valuable research help in initial stages, Medi Sorterup continued where Matei left off, and also helped keep feminist concerns before my eyes. Maurice Lee, my teaching assistant, and my doctoral students read critically a previous version of the text. The discussion at the conference at King's College and with my colleagues, members of the Restaurant Theology Group, helped shape its final version.

Acknowledgments

It is a pleasure to thank here many people and institutions that made my work possible, even delightful. When I was writing the first edition, Fuller Theological Seminary, Pasadena, California, afforded me two sabbaticals and a partial leave of absence during which most of the material was researched and written. The Alexander von Humboldt Foundation supported me during one of those sabbaticals. My students at Fuller Theological Seminary, the Evangelical Theological Faculty of the University of Tübingen, Germany, and the Evangelical Theological Seminary in Osijek, Croatia, engaged the arguments presented in the book (especially the upper division and graduate students in Osijek in the spring of 1996, whose passion for the subject was matched by the sharpness of their arguments). I presented earlier versions of various chapters and received important feedback at conferences in Croatia, Germany, Holland, Hungary, India, New Zealand, Sri Lanka, and the United States, including the Theology Lectureship at the Mennonite Brethren Biblical Seminary, Fresno, California (April 21–22, 1996). Portions of the chapters were published in *Evangelische Theologie, Ecumenical Review, Journal of Ecumenical Studies,* and *Synthesis Philosophica* (though they appear here in substantially revised form). Many friends and acquaintances have commented on earlier versions of individual chapters, including Ellen Charry, Jayakumar Christian, Clifford Christians, Philip Clayton, Robert Gundry, Bruce Hamill, Thomas Heilke, Stanley Hauerwas, George Hillery, David Hoekema, Serene Jones, Robert Johnston, Hans Kvalbein, Maurice Lee, Dale Martin, Marianne Maye Thompson, Jürgen Moltmann, Nancey Murphy, Linda Peacore, Amy Plantinga-Pauw, Claudia Rehberger, Juan Sepúlveda, Marguerite Shuster, Medi Sorterup, James Taylor, Michael Welker, and Tammy Williams.

Matthew Colwell and Richard Heyduck served as research assistants for some of the work. Janice Seifrid helped with indexing. I received secretarial help from Peter Smith, Todd Nightingale, and especially Michael Beetley, who went beyond the call of duty in numerous ways. John Wilson of *Books & Culture* read a good deal of the manuscript and offered invaluable advice, above all about what to read and what *not* to say.

Many have contributed to this second edition as well; I suspect that without them it would have taken me twice as long to write texts that were only half as good. The larger community that makes much of my work possible are people associated with the Yale Center for Faith and Culture, above all its generous Advisory Board members: Denise Adams, Roger and Lynne Bolton, Marjorie Calvert, William Cross, Warner Depuy, Jeppe Hedaa, Edward "Peb" Jackson, Julie Johnson, Philip and Patty Love, Harold Masback, Fred Sievert, Beth and Scott Stephenson, and Gregory Sterling. Some of the Center staff has directly contributed to this second edition. Ryan Ramsey did the patient work of reformatting the entire text and gathering into one document the voices of my detractors and champions. Dr. Karin Fransen saved me, a non-native speaker and mild dyslexic, major embarrassment and did the patient work of proofreading the entire manuscript, for which I am immensely grateful. My friend and close collaborator, Dr. Ryan MacAnnally-Linz, along with Dr. Dane Andrew Collins, has helped sharpen the argument in the new introduction and the epilogue. Marietta D. C. van der Tol, too, offered valuable comments from Dutch and European perspectives. Professor Willie Jennings, a friend and a colleague, was my guide through the complexities of recent scholarship on "black identity" in the United States. Dr. Caroline Sommerfeld, who was kind to read and comment on the whole book, also introduced me to the thinkers of European identarian movements. Professor Peter Kuzmič, my brother-in-law to whom I originally dedicated the book and who is intimately familiar with identity-centered struggles in Central Europe both twenty-five years ago and today, offered insightful comments about the new introduction. Paul Franklyn is an amazingly efficient editor and a joy to work with.

I am grateful to my two sons, Nathanael and Aaron, as well as to my wife, Jessica, and my toddler daughter, Mira, for reminding me daily of things that matter more than those which I am fortunate to have been called to do: being a theologian who teaches, writes books, and lectures.

Index of Names and Topics

Biblical Index